The Upstart Spring

The Big Sur coastline. (STEVE BECK)

THE UPSTART SPRING

Esalen and the American Awakening

by Walter Truett Anderson

Addison-Wesley Publishing Company
Reading, Massachusetts ● Menlo Park, California
London ● Amsterdam ● Don Mills, Ontario ● Sydney

Excerpt from "Human Potentialities" lecture (page 11) delivered by Aldous Huxley at the University Medical Center, San Francisco Medical Center (1960), reprinted by permission of Laura Huxley.

Excerpt from "Big Sur: The Tropic of Henry Miller" (page 53), *Rogue,* July 1961; Copyright © 1961 by Hunter S. Thompson. Reprinted by permission of ICM.

Excerpts from *This Is It and Other Essays on Zen and Spiritual Experience* by Alan Watts (pages 57, 58), copyright © 1958, 1960 by Alan Watts. Reprinted by permission of Pantheon Books, a Division of Random House, Inc.

"The Times They Are a-Changin' " by Bob Dylan (page 102), © 1963 Warner Bros., Inc. All Rights Reserved. Used by Permission.

Excerpt from *A Sleep of Prisoners* by Christopher Fry (page 118), Copyright 1951, 1979 by Christopher Fry. Reprinted by permission of Oxford University Press, Inc.

Excerpt from "Where the California Game Is Taking Us" by George B. Leonard (pages 143–144), © 1966 by Cowles Broadcasting, Inc. (from *Look* magazine, June 28, 1966, issue).

"My Back Pages" by Bob Dylan (page 146), © 1964 Warner Bros., Inc. All Rights Reserved. Used by Permission.

Excerpt from Richard Claiborne, "This Year at Marienbad" (page 282), *The Nation,* June 24, 1968. Reprinted by permission of The Nation Magazine, Nation Associates, Inc.

Library of Congress Cataloging in Publication Data

Anderson, Walter Truett.
  The upstart spring.

  1. Anderson, Walter Truett. 2. Group relations
training—Biography. 3. Esalen Institute. 4. Humanistic psychology. I. Title.
HM134.A52 1983   158'.2   83-9231
ISBN 0–201–11034–2
ISBN 0–201–11035–0 (pbk.)

Cover design by Glenna Lang Graphics
Set in 11-point Compano by Datapage Division, Western Publishing Co.

ISBN 0–201–11034–2
0–201–11035–0 (pbk.)

ABCDEFGHIJ-DO-86543

First printing, August 1983

For Bill and Lois Wilcoxen

The Upstart Spring

Preface: Looking In, Looking Out

I first visited Esalen in the mid-1960s, stopping over there for a night on one of my frequent drives up and down the California highways between Los Angeles, where I lived then, and San Francisco. My recollections of that brief visit have to do mainly with breakfast in the lodge. Fritz Perls was there; I knew who he was, because I had recently read *Gestalt Therapy* and been profoundly impressed by it, and I observed him closely—old man drinking coffee—for signs of abnormal mental health. Michael Murphy and his brother Dennis were standing in line at the serving table, laughing between themselves in great animation about something not apparent to anybody else. I am not sure I knew exactly who they were—I definitely did not know which was which—but I had the impression that one of them more or less owned the place.

An overnight stay, breakfast, a few images of people seen . . . my memoirs do not add up to much. Yet although that event is not, as they say, etched in my memory, I do recall precisely why I was there, and recall also that I counted it a successful visit. I had done what I intended to do, which was to check it out, touch base. I thought it was a place where some of whatever it was that was happening, was happening, and in stopping by there I had made a kind of ritualistic contact with the events of the times.

We are talking about the 1960s, a decade that gets so much attention you begin to think it must have hired a press agent. I have some misgivings about our national penchant for decade watching: we treat decades like supermarket commodities, to be labeled and packaged and put in their proper places on the shelf, and in so doing render ourselves insensitive to processes that develop over long periods of time, to continuities and repetitions and variations on themes. We overstate the differences. Still, it cannot be denied that certain spaces

1

of time do have their own personalities, quirks that we remember them by.

In the mid-1960s there was a general feeling in circulation that something exciting and important was happening, and that it was happening in California. This was a new and stunning idea. California was a fine place, the weather was good, it had Hollywood and all that; but we never believed anything really happened there. The sound of history always echoed from other places, other times. Then suddenly that changed, and there blossomed in our midst a delirious consensus that the world was turning before our very eyes, here, now. "It's happening right now, baby," a phrase in currency for a while, pretty well summed it up.

This feeling was real. It may not have been justified. I am not here to argue that California circa 1965 was a Hegelian world-historical state, a banner carrier for the march of time. Yet the feeling, justified or not, was part of the common experience. Not that anybody knew what it was that was happening, or where it would lead. People rarely do have clearly defined ideas about such things anyway, and when they do, it usually turns out that they were wrong. The feeling was sort of a collective hunch, amorphous and not altogether rational.

It manifested itself in individual lives chiefly in the form of a heightened sense of possibilities, a belief that you could rather easily change yourself, or society, or both. Hadn't the students at Berkeley gotten themselves organized and forced the administration to change its rules about political activity on the campus? Hadn't the blacks in Watts, in a spontaneous outburst of rage, made the world pay attention to their community and its pain? Couldn't you similarly grab your own life and create for yourself a new appearance, a new occupation, a new (1960s term) *life style*? Couldn't you ingest this or that chemical and change your very consciousness?

This ebullience came with its share of fear and doubt. I knew many people—more as time went on—who foresaw catastrophes, backlash, breakdown, revolution from the left or from the right. But even the doubters participated in that exhilarating sense of motion and opportunity, that feeling of ground shifting beneath the feet.

My own life was, appropriately, much in motion. I had entered my thirties, had recently cut loose from my last full-time salaried job to start free-lancing, and was a part-time graduate student taking seminars in political science and social psychology. Free-lancing was what I had always expected to do; the graduate work was one of the decade's many surprises. In the places where I had grown up even a B.A. was regarded as an excessive amount of schooling, and I had supposed it would be all I needed. But then when I tried part-time graduate work I found it a bracing change of milieu from the television industry, which had recently been my employer. It was also a signal to myself that I was setting the course of my life in some other direction.

One summer I took a seminar in psychodrama, grandfather of the group psychotherapies. This decision, which hardly seemed of great moment to me at the time (I didn't even know what psychodrama was), had a major effect on my life over the next decade or so, and incidentally put me on a path that had many points of contact with Esalen. I had already been reading the works of the humanistic psychologists, and the psychodrama seminar—which turned out to be a rousing series of real group sessions, right there in the classroom at San Fernando Valley State College—rapidly took this line of inquiry from theory to practice. As it happened, I started attending psychodrama groups at about the same time that Esalen, unknown to me, was shifting its emphasis from intellectual seminars to group experiences. I went into a training group for psychodrama directors (something else I had never expected to do) in the summer of 1967, a time when Esalen entered a new phase as a center of encounter groups.

My involvement with psychodrama was an avocation (one of two—I also started teaching American government part time), and it was a splendid place from which to observe the amazing proliferation of group therapies that was then taking place in Southern California. That scene is briefly described in this book, because it is one of the sources that fed into Esalen. I saw it partly as an outsider, having only recently wandered into marginal status as a group psychotherapist; partly as an insider working in the field, getting to know others who were also in it, becoming familiar with its lore and language and ancient feuds.

I heard of Esalen often, knew people who went there to lead groups and people who went there to be in them. I went there for an Alan Watts seminar in 1967, and I went again a year or so later to an encounter weekend led by Steve Stroud and John Heider, two young graduates of Esalen's second residential program. Most of my exposure to what was then going on at Esalen, however, came about in a less direct way. There were a couple of Esalen-style "growth centers" in the Los Angeles area, as there were in other parts of the country, and these had become links in a kind of Chatauqua circuit, along which traveled the likes of Watts, Perls, Bernie Gunther, and Will Schutz. Watts did more or less conventional lectures, although he liked to dress up in a Japanese kimono and bang on an Oriental chime from time to time to emphasize a point; the others were not so much lectures as demonstrations: Gunther did sensory awakening exercises, Schutz did encounter exercises, Perls did gestalt therapy on a stage. I attended many of these events and sometimes had occasion to meet the visiting dignitaries. Doing some volunteer publicity work for the local growth center, I arranged to have Watts appear on a television talk show hosted by Maureen Reagan, our governor's daughter. I interviewed Fritz and wrote an article about him.

Thus, with my life sorting itself out into several occupations, I stalked about the edges of what later became known as the human potential movement and observed it from several perspectives: as a student, learning about the origins of group therapy; as a journalist, writing occasional pieces about it; as a political scientist, trying to figure out how it connected with the other events of the time; and increasingly as a practitioner—leading psychodrama groups and encounter groups, teaching group process to college students, doing group work with churches, schools, businesses, and hospitals.

In 1969 I started leading groups for Esalen. I probably would have gotten around to this sooner or later, but the way it happened is typical of how such things came about at Esalen. I visited Murphy at his San Francisco office in 1968 and, during a lull in the conversation, suggested that somebody lead a hike in the mountains and graft some of Esalen's techniques onto the experience of being in the High Sierra. Murphy agreed that it was a good idea and asked me if I wanted to do it. I said I was only suggesting that he get somebody to do it. Murphy said that since it was my idea I should do it. I said I would think about it and flew back to Los Angeles, amazed by what I had just seen of Esalen's way of doing business. Finally I did lead a mountain encounter and it was a success, but it could easily have been a disaster and I often marveled that the portals had swung open so readily, allowing me to stumble through with a group process that was accepted before it was invented. People have assured me that when Murphy made such decisions it was out of intuition, not carelessness. I would like to believe that, but I'm not sure; Abraham Maslow is reported to have said that if Satan himself came to Esalen, Mike Murphy would have invited him to lead a seminar.

I continued to lead occasional programs at Big Sur (and, after we moved north, at Esalen's San Francisco branch), but I was never central to Esalen's existence, nor was it to mine. I do not mean to imply by this that I am neutral or objective toward Esalen, only to identify with some precision my own role in relation to it. I visited Big Sur two or three times a year and had grown to love it. The place will do that to you; it creeps into your affections and makes you want to organize your life in such a way that you can return there from time to time. I had some contact with Michael Murphy and Richard Price, but not much sense of Esalen as an organization and no particular opinions about it except a general charge of approval. I knew about such things as the rivalry between Perls and Schutz (Perls had talked about that when I interviewed him in 1969); but I had no idea of what went on in the inner circles of Esalen's management, nor did I know about the suicides that were such shattering events for those who were living at Big Sur.

But although I was only distantly connected to the Esalen Institute, I was deeply involved in the wider sweep of things of which Esalen was a part. Humanistic psychology—by which I mean the intellectual movement identified with such people as Abraham Maslow, Perls, Carl Rogers, and Rollo May—seemed to me then (and does still) to contain an important part of the answer to what is tragically wrong with American life. I remain equally partisan about that much-lampooned pastime, group therapy. I know its shortcomings well, but I have seen too many good things come out of it to be able to dismiss it all with the facile disdain that comes so readily to many who have written about it. I have seen, in fact, more manifestations of the major human virtues, such as courage and compassion and commitment and honesty, in groups than in any other realm of human interaction. And they have touched my own life in many ways. I don't think my wife and I would ever have made it to the altar in 1968 without the aid of a couple of psychodrama sessions that got us through turmoils that could otherwise have scuttled the relationship, and an ongoing group for couples that we joined later was a major support for us in the early years of marriage. Such personal experiences left me strongly skeptical toward the view of group therapy as the great wrecking yard of relationships.

It was easy for me to see humanistic psychology and group therapy as a cause; and when they began to take on a recognizable identity as a movement, I was in it. This meant that I was resistant toward criticisms of it and inclined to think well of whoever or whatever was also a part of it. That is still my general bias, and the one that pervades these pages—but it is one that has been buffeted by twenty years of experience, during which time I have come reluctantly to the conclusion that many of the criticisms are pretty well on target. My involvement with this movement has given me a more sympathetic understanding than I ever had before of people—George Orwell comes to mind—who were committed to socialism but less than enthusiastic about some of the directions it took. I have watched the humanistic psychology movement become the human potential movement, seen that give way in turn to the various Aquarian, estian, and transformational faiths of the 1970s and 1980s, and there have been times when it has seemed to me that the tendency has been steadily in the direction of promising more and delivering less. I fear that if the movement perishes, it will be because it has strangled on its own rhetoric and not because it has been done in by its enemies. In this respect and in others, I am a troubled and critical follower of the cause.

The cause itself is a complex affair, not at all the simple hot-tub binge it is taken to be. For some reason the general practice has been to view as a single unit all the things that Esalen and the human potential movement have embraced, and to vote them up or down accordingly. This might be excusable in a hasty newspaper article, but it has also been done in books that purport to be informed and thoughtful critiques. Esalen and the movement—or movements—linked with it constitute a large and varied field of activity, some of its wings and ideas much at odds with others, and anybody who does not have mixed feelings about it cannot have been paying attention.

The story of Esalen could have been written as an exercise in trashing the human potential movement, or as a hymn to Esalen, the fountainhead of transformation. But, for reasons I have tried to indicate with these biographical fragments, I could not have done either. It is not a matter of being objective or neutral, but of being true to my own very subjective point of view. I think Esalen is important, a subject whose history is worth being recorded; it is, as I suspected when I first looked in there, a place where a part of "it" was happening. It is a subject that I approach with respect, but not with reverence. You would miss an important part of American life if you failed to take Esalen seriously, and you would be making an equally great mistake if you took it too seriously.

This book is primarily a chronicle, a story of Esalen and the people and ideas that became associated with it. In that regard I am, like any other historian, a retailer of other people's experiences. The analysis that weaves through the narrative is, of course, mine. I am grateful to the many people who told me their stories; I want to acknowledge, especially, the generosity of Michael Murphy and Richard Price, who gave many hours of their time for interviews and spoke frankly about their lives with no guarantee as to how I would use the material and no right of final approval over the book. I am grateful also to those who read the manuscript in various drafts (Tom Greening, Gerry Haigh, Abe Levitsky, Stuart Miller, Ted and Betty Roszak); to Cheryl Brandt for some valuable editing and typing assistance; to Barbara Lowenstein for setting the project in motion and then reminding me about once a week that I was taking too long to finish it; to Cyrisse Jaffee for editorial work at the final stages; to Frances Apt for copyediting; to my dear wife, Mauriça, for many things, including going with me to that funny place up the coast to hear Alan Watts in 1967 and providing a vast amount of help and encouragement and hard work on this book; and to my son Dan, who was no help at all but nice to have around.

My title is taken from some lines by Christopher Fry. The reader will encounter them farther along, at the point where they are quoted from an Esalen brochure. It seemed to me preferable to let them appear in their own due time rather than to use the traditional quotation in the front of the book. The subtitle, *Esalen and the American Awakening,* is the result of a search for some phrase to describe the context of the times, the whatever-it-was that was happening of which Esalen was a part. The word *awakening* feels right, even though it does invoke other, more specifically religious, upheavals—especially that curious period in colonial history called the Great Awakening, when a spontaneous wave of spiritual fervor, a stampede in pursuit of direct religious experience, swept the land.[1] It seems far-out to suggest a parallel between the 1960s and the 1740s, but when I return occasionally to the history books I am struck by the similarities. The Great Awakening of colonial times had its Timothy Learys, its itinerant preachers traveling the lecture circuit, its excesses, and its charlatans. It was also strongly individualistic, personalistic; the psychological concept of narcissism had not been invented yet, and its detractors settled for dismissing it as an outburst of—supreme word of Puritan contempt—*enthusiasm.*

The Great Awakening was characterized not only by a hankering for personal participation in the mysteries, but also by a sense of an agenda; some believed it was the prelude to the Millennium, the beginning of Christ's rule on earth. Years later, when the Awakening had been eclipsed by the American Revolution, there were those who believed its business was not yet done. David Austin wrote in 1794: "It seems no unnatural conclusion from ancient prophecy, . . . that in order to usher in . . . the latter-day glory, two great revolutions are to take place; the first outward and political, the second inward and spiritual."[2] That suggests another point of contact with the awakening of the 1960s: an uncertainty about the connection between the political and the personal.

The Sufis say that ordinary life is a kind of slumber from which only a few extraordinary human beings have ever truly awakened. They also say that there are occasions in the lives of the rest of us when we awaken for a moment and catch a fuller glimpse of the true vastness of our being before we fall asleep again. I find that a cogent and unusually scrutable piece of Oriental wisdom, and I think a good case could be made that it is true for societies as well as for individuals—that there are periods in the history of any civilization when its rest is disturbed, and that in such periods the inner life runs near the surface, ordinary people crave mystical experience, there is much odd behavior, and many things seem possible.

1

Summer 1961. It was hot and smoggy in Santa Monica, a day the two young men, just getting out of a battered red pickup, would remember well. The day was not a turning point, exactly; they were already embarked on a certain course of action, and their conversation with the older man that afternoon did not divert them from it. They remembered it, rather, as a day when the gears shifted, when they took on a new momentum.

They were each thirty years old and had been living in San Francisco on the periphery of the subculture that the press called the Beat Generation. You would not mistake either one of them for a Beat poet. They were trim, clean-shaven, neatly dressed in casual clothes. One of them, Michael Murphy, was dark-haired and dark-eyed, with a flashing smile; the other, Richard Price, had light brown hair, blue eyes, and a slim, handsome face. They were products of prosperous upper-middle-class families. Stanford graduates. So far, neither Murphy nor Price had done anything the world would notice or record, but they had hopes. They had a project that was part business venture and part crusade. They were just getting ready to take over the management of a little hot-springs resort on the Big Sur coast, and they wanted to put on some lecture programs there—make the place a kind of forum for the exploration of religion and philosophy and psychology, for new ideas about the meaning and possibilities of life.

The decade was young and full of hope. A youthful president of the United States, who had campaigned on a promise to get America moving again—a vague yet stirring aspiration—was in office. New energy, new idealism, seemed to be emerging in the land. Brisk intellectuals were going to Washington to give the nation's government the benefit of their brilliance and boundless self-confidence. A new agency called the Peace Corps was being started up, and many Americans were thinking about going abroad to help people in other countries. Freedom riders in Atlanta, blacks and whites struggling together against discrimination, signaled to the world that there still survived in America, even after the numbing decade of Joseph McCarthy and the witch hunts, some of the old spirit of Thoreau and the abolitionists and the Underground Railroad. There was plenty of trouble, much to fear, yet the mood was definitely one of exuberance and optimism. The world watched the exploits of astronauts and cosmonauts; someday soon, it was expected, a man would walk on the moon. After that there would be expeditions to the planets and the stars, great adventures out in the cosmos.

In San Francisco, a different and more local kind of awakening had been going on. The Beat writers, Jack Kerouac and Allen Ginsberg and the rest of the North Beach crowd, were more than just another literary movement; they had somehow caught the public fancy with their attack on middle-American morality and rejection of the work-and-get-ahead ethic. The national attention had turned not only toward them, but toward San Francisco; some spoke about a "San Francisco Renaissance," of which the Beat movement was only a part. Suddenly, California was not a distant cultural outpost, its eyes fixed on the East Coast, but a place where ideas were stirring, a place where things began.

About a year earlier, Richard Price had gone over to Berkeley to hear a lecture by Aldous Huxley, English novelist turned California visionary, who was going about the college campuses talking on a subject he called "human potentialities." It was Huxley's view of where civilization stood in 1960, and where it needed to go from there:

> Let us begin [said Huxley, in his kindly Oxonian accents] by asking a question: What would have happened to a child of 170 I.Q. born into a Paleolithic family at the time of, say, the cave paintings of Lascaux? Well, quite obviously, he could have been nothing except a hunter and a food gatherer. There was no other opportunity for him to be anything else.
>
> The biologists have shown us that, physiologically and anatomically, we are pretty much the same as we were twenty thousand years ago and that we are using fundamentally the same equipment as the Aurignacean man to produce incredibly different results. We have in the course of these twenty thousand years actualized an immense number of things which at that time and

for many, many centuries thereafter were wholly potential and latent in man.

This, I think, gives us reason for tempered optimism that there are still a great many potentialities—for rationality, for affection and kindliness, for creativity—still lying latent in man; and, since everything has speeded up so enormously in recent years, that we shall find methods for going almost as far beyond the point we have reached now within a few hundred years as we have succeeded in going beyond our Aurignacean ancestors in twenty thousand years. I think this is not an entirely fantastic belief. The neurologists have shown us that no human being has ever made use of as much as ten percent of all the neurons in his brain. And perhaps, if we set about it in the right way, we might be able to produce extraordinary things out of this strange piece of work that a man is.[1]

Huxley had several ideas about how these latent human potentialities might be actualized. He was a man of immense curiosity, forever exploring. He had been following recent research in pharmacology, and thought it possible that science might develop chemicals that would increase people's ability to think, feel, and create. He was also fascinated by new trends in education and psychotherapy. He had read about an obscure form of psychotherapy called gestalt, which proposed to treat neurosis by turning the patient's attention to events in the here-and-now instead of having him or her search through the past for causes. Huxley thought this kind of therapy, developed by a man named Frederick Perls, offered a practical way of following the ancient precept "Know thyself."

There were also paths of physical development that fascinated him. An Australian, F. Matthias Alexander, had developed a technique of physical re-education, a way of discovering more about the self by developing greater awareness of how the body moves and feels. Other people, most of them influenced by the writings of Wilhelm Reich, were working with the problem of anger and finding effective ways to express it in intense physical activity.

Huxley thought it would be good if some institution, perhaps one of the great foundations, would launch a program of research into all the methods for actualizing human potentialities that had been discovered so far. The methods would be studied, evaluated, and then put to use by society in a program of lifelong education. Such an undertaking, he thought, might be "quite revolutionary."

11

Huxley's proposal was not quite the same as the project Murphy and Price were now trying to put together, but it was close, and they liked the sound of "human potentialities." They had written Huxley, telling him what they hoped to do and asking for his advice. He had replied that he was going to be away from his Hollywood Hills home the month they were going south, but suggested they look over Rancho La Puerta, a place in Mexico that he and his wife often visited, and that he thought might give them some ideas. It was a resort that featured health foods, yoga classes, and evening self-improvement lectures—a precursor, in its way, of what would later be called a growth center, although most of Rancho La Puerto's clients were interested mainly in growing thin. And Huxley suggested that they really ought to stop off in Santa Monica and visit his friend Gerald Heard.

Heard, an energetic red-bearded Irishman, had been a close friend of Aldous Huxley's since 1929 and had immigrated to the United States with the Huxley family in 1937. The two had gone on lecture tours together, the shortish Heard and the willowy Huxley making a rather oddly matched pair. Huxley's wife, Maria, called them Mutt and Jeff, and noted the difference not only in their heights, but also in their speaking styles: "Aldous so slow and calm and passive, Gerald vehement and busy and coercive."

That difference was strikingly apparent when Murphy and Price went to see Heard in his Santa Monica cottage. Huxley had so diffidently advocated a research project, had so hesitantly suggested its revolutionary possibilities. He thought something of that sort *might* happen. Heard thought it *had* to happen. Mankind, he believed, was at the turning point and could be saved from destruction only by a great leap, a new vision. There would have to be a psychological revolution, and, yes, there would have to be institutions to serve it. He had written of the need for "gymnasia for the mind" and in the 1940s had launched his own version in Southern California, a spiritual / educational center called Trabuco College. It had failed, but Heard remained irrepressibly optimistic about the prospects for new undertakings, new horizons, vast evolutionary transformations. He was a man of limitless energies, a brilliant and tireless talker. He welcomed the two young visitors, and they had a long conversation, a stunning four-hour exploration of evolutionary theory, biology, theology, philosophy. They spoke of many things, all connected to Heard's vision of a huge transformation of the human species that was, he was sure, trying to take place.

Murphy and Price came away from the meeting feeling—as people who entered into conversation with Gerald Heard often felt—a slight buzzing in the head, a certain overloading of the mental circuits. Yet it had been an invigorating and positive experience. Until then their project had been tinged with uncertainty, with a maybe-it-will-work-out-and-maybe-it-won't sort of doubtfulness that naturally accompanies thoughts of risky new ventures into the unknown. But Heard's enthusiasm, his sense of a cosmic mandate, changed all that. Murphy and Price were now both filled with a new sense of urgent conviction about their project: it *would* happen. It seemed to them, that day, that it had to happen.

2

If you drive down from San Francisco, taking Highway 1 along the coast, you pass through the outskirts of Monterey and Carmel and then come to a junction of roads. One road heads eastward toward Salinas, through the Carmel Valley's sprawl of housing developments and shopping centers. The other road continues south. If you stay on it, you are soon plunged into a different kind of terrain, a stretch of wild and sometimes desolate country that seems strangely out of place along the central coast of America's most populous state. The houses thin out below Carmel, and the environment begins to change. You see a sign warning you that there is dangerously curving road ahead for the next seventy-four miles. After that there are no more suburban developments, no more supermarkets. You do not see many houses at all, except a few of the newer ones, angular creations that hang above the Pacific in lonely and expensive splendor.

Highway 1 is now a curving strip of pavement, two lanes wide, that winds along the mountainside a few hundred feet above the water. Now and then, when the winter rains are heavy, a segment of the highway breaks loose from the hillside and slides down the slope into the ocean. There are a few restaurants and resorts and stores and gas stations along the highway, but nothing that quite adds up to a town. The place that is officially marked on the map as Big Sur seems not much more than a post office and a ranger station. Actually, Big Sur, which gets its name, half-anglicized, from a river the Spanish named El Rio Grande del Sur, is the whole stretch of coastline, fifty miles or so of it.

The chief features of the Big Sur country are mountains and ocean, side by side. There are a few beaches, but this is not beach country like the Southern California shoreline. Here, the Santa Lucia range heaves abruptly from the water, and the shore is mostly a long rocky precipice, which the waves beat against day and night, filling the air with deep sound and the smell of salt water. The hillsides are covered in some places with a sparse growth of heather, and other parts of it are thickly forested with pine and cedar and redwood trees. There are deer and raccoons and rattlesnakes in the hills, and every few miles there is a stream, running through shady canyons where ferns grow.

About ten miles south of the post office is the Esalen Institute, Big Sur's unique contribution to American culture and counterculture. From the highway, all you can see of it is a sign that says ESALEN INSTITUTE BY RESERVATION ONLY and a road that angles steeply down toward the shore.

Millions of people have heard of this place and have been indirectly touched by things that have happened here; thousands have come here to sample its intangible products. Some seekers have been disappointed in their quest; they found Esalen's programs silly, false, painful, or just not what they were looking for. Others have found it superficial— a few days of euphoria and newborn high hopes, followed by the depressing discovery, when they returned home, that their lives were about what they had been before. But there are those who came away with at least a part of what they had sought, and who count the time there well spent. Many marriages, new careers, and religious awakenings have been inspired by Esalen experiences . . . and so have a lot of divorces and dropouts, and a few deaths.

Esalen occupies a shelf of land above the Pacific, its back snuggled against the hillside below Highway 1. It is a strikingly beautiful place, with its trees and green lawns and flowers and warm-toned redwood buildings and broad expanses of water and sky. If a place can have charisma, then surely this one has it.

It is a small place: it covers a few hundred acres of flat land, hillside, shoreline, and cliffs. Its social center is the low board-and-batten structure called the lodge, which houses the office and the dining room and a large meeting room named Huxley. For many years, before the Huxley room was added, the dining room doubled as a meeting room and was witness to a sparkling array of great minds. Arnold Toynbee and Paul Tillich lectured here, Alan Watts dazzled audiences with his verbal bridge-building between Eastern religion and Western psychology, Fritz Perls demonstrated his skills in the art of gestalt therapy. Now the room is just a dining room, and on any given day, at mealtime, it fills with an oddly assembled collection of people—some young, some old, some hip, some square, mostly white, mostly prosperous, some American, some foreign.

The dining room is a center of conviviality for a while, and then most people go off to their workshops and it becomes a quiet place to sit by the windows with a cup of tea and a book. The windows look out over a profusion of flowers and cacti and a lush, springy lawn that slopes downward toward the swimming pool. Next to the swimming pool is a wooden sun deck, perched on the edge of the cliff above the ocean.

South of the lodge is a cliffside trail that descends to the celebrated baths. Here a bathhouse has been constructed over the place where the hot mineral waters issue from the rocky slope. The building is divided into two sections. Once there was a men's section and a women's section; now there are just two, both androgynous. Each has two large concrete-block tubs, some regular bathtubs, and a number of massage tables. The west wall is completely open, giving the bathers a view of the ocean.

The bathhouse, extensively remodeled, with redwood, new tiled floors, and some new tubs, was originally a humble concrete-block structure built by a group of Christian fundamentalists from Fresno, who would have thrown down their trowels in disgust if they had known that they were erecting what would one day become America's best-known center of public and coeducational nudity. You would be embarrassed to wear a swimsuit here. The bathhouse is a California landmark of sorts; some of Western civilization's leading philosophers, theologians, educators, scientists, therapists, and artists have come to this place, have eased their eminent rears down into the hot water to sit and consider the surging sea.

Uphill from the lodge, set like the tiers of an amphitheater, are the various buildings that house the guests and staff. They are mostly of redwood, and the feel of them is part motel, part monastery: the rooms have walls of unfinished wood and are austerely decorated with woven wall hangings or Oriental prints.

To the north of the lodge is a field given over to organic gardening, where fresh vegetables are grown for the kitchen. Beyond this is a deep canyon, where one of the coast streams, Hot Springs Creek, comes down out of the forest. More or less in the middle of the creek, built cleverly onto the rocks, are two one-room structures, the Round House and the Waterfall House. North of the creek is another shelf of land, with another deep lawn, and a couple of white buildings called the Big House and the Little House.

Once, the land along the Big Sur coast was occupied by an Indian tribe called the Esalen. They were part of the history of another California, almost lost and forgotten now; a civilization that survived for thousands of years and then disappeared in less than a century. The Esalen were remnants of an ancient California people who had been displaced from the fertile valleys by gradual migrations of tribes from the north, from what is now Oregon and Washington; they became an enclave of mountain dwellers, surrounded by the newcomers.

When the Spanish came to California, they found the Esalen—five hundred or so of them altogether—living in small villages along the coast. The Esalen were herded into the missions at Monterey and Carmel, and they perished in a few generations. They were the first California Indians to become totally extinct. Nothing is left of them except the name, which is transcribed in many forms (Eslen, Ecclemach, Excelen, Ensen), and whose meaning nobody knows. The scholars who came along later in search of information about them had to settle for gossip from not altogether friendly neighbors, people of different linguistic groups and different ancestries. From these unreliable sources they heard stories that the Esalen were an odd bunch who worshiped the hot springs, ate unusual foods, and often went naked.

In the 1800s, American settlers moved into the Big Sur country. They cut down a lot of the trees, raised beef cattle and sheep, and killed off the grizzly bears. Once in a while visitors would come to the Big Sur—Jack London rode down that way a time or two—but it was not an easy place to get to. There was no highway connecting Big Sur with the cities to the north and south; the modern road was carved slowly out of the hillsides by convict labor in the 1930s and was not finished until 1937.

In the 1940s, people began to hear about Big Sur. The man who first nudged it into the national consciousness was Henry Miller, the free-thinking author of *Tropic of Cancer* and *Tropic of Capricorn*. When the war chased Miller out of Paris, he returned to the United States, where his books were banned, looking for a suitable place to live. He stayed for a while in Beverly Glen Canyon in Los Angeles, then went to Monterey in 1944 to visit his friend Jean Varda, the artist. During that trip he drifted down the coast to have a look at Big Sur. He liked the place, an uncrowded and silent refuge on the outer edge of the country he had called an air-conditioned nightmare, and lived in the area for over twenty years.

Miller lived first in a log house near where the restaurant called Nepenthe now stands; the house was later sold to Orson Welles. Later he lived by Anderson Creek, in one of the cabins that had been built to house the convicts who were building the highway. Most of the time he spent high up on Partington Ridge, in tame domesticity, with a wife and children.

Gradually some of Miller's friends came to Big Sur. Not long after he settled there, Miller wrote to his old friend from Chicago, Emil White, who had gone to Alaska to hide out from the draft board. He told White to come to Big Sur: nobody would bother him, and the weather was better. White came to Big Sur and became an artist. He had never especially wanted to become an artist, but Miller, who had known plenty of artists in Paris, advised him that it was not all that hard. So White began to paint, in a style that vaguely resembled that of Grandma Moses. Soon he was selling some of his paintings to tourists and earning a living by doing so. It didn't cost much to live in Big Sur in the 1940s. You could rent one of the convict shacks at Anderson Creek for $5 or $10 a month, and all you needed above that was enough money for food and some California wine. You could hitchhike when you wanted to go somewhere. There were no telephones or electricity to raise your cost of living and complicate your life.

Although Miller's *Tropic* books could not be sold in the United States, they were widely read anyway. Travelers to Europe would buy copies of them at the bookstalls along the Seine and smuggle them in. Those fat paperbacks, full of Miller's pungent ramblings about the expatriate life (and with even more explicit sex in them than *Lady Chatterley's Lover*), circulated around college campuses and wherever people followed the kind of life style that was then called Bohemian. For many Americans, especially those who read and wrote for the little literary magazines, Miller was a special hero, a Rabelaisian rebel against American prudery. And the people who talked about Miller usually knew where he lived: Big Sur. Now and then young admirers would make a pilgrimage to Big Sur to visit him, and a few who found the place congenial stayed on there to try to write or paint. The area became known as an artists' colony, a rural West Coast Greenwich Village.

19

This reputation was helped along by a woman named Mildred Edie Brady, who in 1947 wrote an article for *Harper's* entitled "The New Cult of Sex and Anarchy." The mecca for postwar Bohemians, she reported, was the Big Sur country. She told about the shacks they lived in, their beards and sandals and tattered clothes, the abstract paintings on their walls, their parties and poetry-reading sessions. Their philosophy, she wrote, was based on opposition to the traditional institutions of Western civilization—church, state, and family—and it expressed itself in an erotic, sentimental mysticism. The new Bohemia, she reported with surprise, was religious. Its religion, however, was nothing like the standard American fare. It was a belief in something that went by such names as "the life force" or "the great oneness." Miller's books, of course, were standard reading, as were the novels of D. H. Lawrence, the poetry of William Blake, the philosophy of Henri Bergson, the mysticism of G. I. Gurdjieff and P. D. Ouspensky, the astrology of Dane Rudhyar. The Bohemian philosophy combined mysticism with a profound distrust of government and an equally profound reverence for sex. The person they admired most of all, Mildred Brady reported, was Wilhelm Reich, the renegade psychiatrist who called the state a conspiracy against the healthy needs of the natural human body and the orgasm the supreme human experience.

At the time the Brady article appeared, Wilhelm Reich was living in Maine, experimenting with a device called the orgone accumulator, which was supposed to intensify, for healing purposes, the basic force of the universe. He had never been to Big Sur, but his popularity in the Bohemian community there brought about, oddly enough, his eventual demise. Mildred Brady, who became rather obsessed with Reich in the course of her research on Big Sur, wrote another article about him. Entitled "The Strange Case of Wilhelm Reich," it denounced his subversive sexual and political ideas and demanded that somebody do something about him. Somebody did. After the article appeared in the *New Republic* in 1948, officials of the Food and Drug Administration began an investigation of Reich and the orgone accumulator—an investigation that led ultimately to that tormented man's death in a federal prison.

Mildred Brady's articles mark the first turning of national attention toward what became known as the alternative life styles of the West Coast. Her reporting began a series of media spasms that would recur with mounting intensity in subsequent decades; next came the excitement about Jack Kerouac, Allen Ginsberg, and the Beat Scene of the 1950s, and then the obsession with hippies, the Haight-Ashbury, and all the California dreaming of the 1960s.

Henry Miller claimed, as so many would claim after him, that the publicity Ms. Brady generated was overblown and inaccurate. He granted that there was a certain amount of sex and anarchy around, sure, but there was no cult. Something you might call a community, perhaps, a few dozen people, scattered up and down the coast, who knew each other, visited around, got together to eat and drink and talk. But the social life around Big Sur was never intense. It was a quiet place; the great majority of the people who came there expecting to stay found it boring and moved on to livelier Bohemias in Carmel or San Francisco or Berkeley. The people who stayed on had to adjust themselves to spending time alone. They read, walked in the woods, and meditated. They practiced their art or craft, if they had one, and they busied themselves with the routine chores of rural life—chopping wood, preparing food, gardening. The ones who made the adjustment best were those who were working on themselves, struggling to find their own way of being. "It is here, and nowhere else," Miller wrote, "that I have witnessed people re-cast their lives and live them out."[1] Whatever stimuli you may have been searching for when you came to live at Big Sur, you found, sooner or later, that the conditions of life there turned you toward contact with the physical environment and with yourself.

Big Sur never had a true center to it, a natural congregating place such as you might find in Paris or Greenwich Village. There was a cluster of houses around Nepenthe, another bunch strung out along Partington Ridge, and the convict shacks by Anderson Creek, but these were far apart from one another. Going out to visit somebody might involve several miles of hiking along a lonely road. The Grange Hall was the social center for the old-timers, the country people. For the artists and writers, the only public hangouts were the restaurant at Nepenthe and the hot springs. People driving up and down the coast generally stopped at the springs; you could usually find somebody to talk to there and—no less important—get a bath. The plumbing in most of the houses around Big Sur did not amount to much, so the springs served many homely purposes. Henry Miller, when his daughter was young, used to make the six-mile round-trip hike from Partington Ridge to the hot springs every night with a bucket full of diapers.

21

*   *   *

The hot springs property, which eventually became the Esalen Institute, was called Slate's Hot Springs. It got its name from Tom Slate, who had homesteaded there in 1882. The property changed hands once, and then was purchased in 1910 by Henry Murphy, a doctor from Salinas. Dr. Murphy and his wife, Vinnie, had recently been to Europe, where they visited Baden-Baden and some of the other spas, and he got the idea of turning the springs into a Continental-style resort, where people would come to bathe and drink the mineral waters. That was a much-postponed project. Nothing could be done until the highway was completed, of course, but then the war came along. So for thirty or forty years the property served as a family vacation place. In 1914 Dr. Murphy hired a fishing boat from Monterey and with the help of its owner, an elderly Chinese, brought two huge claw-footed Victorian bathtubs down the coast and hauled them up the rocks to the springs. Those were the first bathing installations: two big tubs sitting there elegantly on a wooden platform on the edge of the cliff. In 1937 the Murphys built the Little House, and from time to time they put up other structures to accommodate the various friends and relatives who came to stay there.

There were plenty of Murphys to use the place. Dr. Murphy and his wife had four children, three girls and a boy. The boy was named John, after an ancestor who had been an officer in the American navy during the Revolution. Young John Murphy thought of becoming a naval officer himself and did get as far as Annapolis, where he distinguished himself by becoming the academy's welterweight boxing champion in his first year. But on the whole he didn't like it much. When the year was over he dropped out and went back to California. He enrolled at Stanford University and, while a student, fought a few bouts as a professional boxer. Later he turned amateur again and fought for the San Francisco Olympic Club. He went to Hastings Law School in San Francisco, and married a beautiful young French Basque woman named Marie Bedecarré. He took Marie back to live in Salinas, where he set up his own law practice and took over the legal side of his family's growing business interests.

Old Dr. Murphy had built the first hospital in Salinas, but he wasn't really much of a businessman. It turned out, though, that his wife, Vinnie—Bunny, the family called her—had a knack for making money. She managed the hospital and then started buying up and developing real estate. The doctor, somewhat to his surprise, became a millionaire.

John was an intelligent, energetic man; if anything, a little too intelligent and energetic for Salinas. He was probably better suited to a more expansive life than that of a small-town attorney, but he performed his role reasonably well. He helped manage Bunny's ever-growing empire and made a local reputation as a criminal defense lawyer, gaining seven acquittals at seven murder trials. He and Marie lived in a big house on Santa Lucia Street, entertained often, and raised two sons: Michael, born in 1930, and Dennis, born in 1932.

Both the boys turned out to be lively and precocious. Physically, Michael resembled his mother, with dark eyes and a Mediterranean look. Dennis was more like his father, with lighter skin, blue eyes, and a slightly hooked nose. Both of them inherited something of their mother's capacity for joy, a wild buoyancy that people who knew them later would mistakenly identify as Irish charm.

Their father took his parenting seriously. He passed on to them his love of literature by reading to his sons when they were small. Both Michael and Dennis grew up to be lovers of books and writers of them. The Murphys were a rather literary bunch. Bunny was mad for culture of any kind, and the boys' Aunt Beth was a writer who had had pieces published in *Smart Set*, one of the most prestigious magazines of the time. Among the family's close friends was John Steinbeck, who, like most Salinas kids, had been brought into the world by Dr. Murphy. He was around Salinas from time to time, and when he was away he wrote letters to the Murphys about his adventures in the literary world.

Another thing John Murphy gave his sons was a love of sports. He used to talk about the "glow of health," the physical and emotional high that came after a good strenuous workout. He often went running, and he had a well-equipped gymnasium in the basement, with weights and punching bags. He taught the boys to box, and frequently worked out on the bags himself. In the fall, he would take them up to Stanford to football games.

Both of the boys had athletic talent. Dennis also had musical talent. He studied piano for years, and his teacher thought he could be a great concert pianist. But one day Dennis said he didn't want to play the piano anymore—he was tired of it. His teacher, who had dreamed of bringing forth a genius out of this unpromising little farm town, was crushed. He came to the Murphy house, sat in the living room, and actually wept as he pleaded with Marie to make Dennis come back. But Dennis refused to take any more music lessons.

Dennis and Michael got along well with each other, but they were turning out to have vastly different personalities. Dennis had a tough and rebellious streak. Michael was less given to conflict and opposition, more adroit at getting along with people. Dennis got into more than his share of scrapes, fistfights, troubles with teachers. Michael rarely had such problems. Sometimes people called them the Devil and the Saint.

In 1952, when the Murphy boys were in their early twenties, John Steinbeck's *East of Eden* was published. The novel, set in the Salinas Valley and echoing the mythic themes of the Old Testament, was about a man named Adam Trask and his two sons, Cal and Aaron. The boys were twins, but quite unlike one another. Cal was a brooding, devious, and unloved outsider; Aaron was an eager, open, beautiful youth who easily inspired affection in others. The characters were obviously suggested by Cain and Abel, but some of the people in Salinas who read the novel thought they recognized the Murphy boys, the Devil and the Saint. There sprang up a persistent legend that Steinbeck had taken the two sons of his old friend John Murphy as the models for Cal and Aaron.

While the boys were growing up, they frequently spent weekends and summer vacations down at Big Sur, at their grandparents' place. They first visited it in 1935, the year the highway reached the hot springs. Michael was five then and Dennis was three, and it was an exciting event for them to drive down that precarious and still-unfinished road, past work gangs of convicts in striped uniforms. There was a big family camp-out there that year, around an all-night bonfire.

Dennis took to the Big Sur country more enthusiastically than Michael did. He loved to hunt, fish, climb trees, and go hiking in the woods. Michael appreciated the beauty of the place and thought it was fun to sit in the bathtubs by the hot springs, but he didn't care for shooting deer or pulling steelhead trout out of the creek. He usually got carsick during the drive there, and in the long summers at Big Sur, without much to do, he often longed to be back home in Salinas, where he could be with his friends and play baseball.

When Michael was in the eighth grade he became an altar boy in St. Paul's, the Episcopalian church in Salinas. Throughout his high school years, church service was an important part of his life. It gave him a way to express his religious feelings and expanded his social horizons. He would play chess with the minister or make a special trip to serve at Grace Cathedral in San Francisco. Undoubtedly, the church's leaders had their eye on Michael as a likely candidate for the ministry, and he once thought seriously of following such a career. Many years later, when Esalen was co-sponsoring programs with churches and even, for a while, holding encounter groups in the meeting rooms of Grace Cathedral, it seemed to Michael that he was, in a way, picking up his early vocation.

During his high school years, he read some of Jung's books and Will Durant's *Story of Philosophy,* and he worked out a philosophy of his own. It was a package of psychological-religious ideas that he devoutly thought about every morning while he was walking to school—a kind of ritual—and would discuss freely with anyone who would listen. One of his ideas was that people's personality quirks—neuroses or whatever you wanted to call them—were either a form of stunted growth or were attempts to express new strengths and capacities that the person did not yet fully understand. And he had a theory about what we would now call altered states of consciousness. Sometimes in moments of prayer or during sports activities, he would catch a glimpse of what seemed to be another level of reality; he took these experiences seriously and thought hard about what might lie behind them. He believed that there was another way of being, a higher consciousness that was natural and available to people if they could only figure out how to get into it. He was sure his life work would have something to do with these ideas, but he wasn't always certain how. Sometimes he thought he might become a priest, and sometimes he thought he would go to medical school and become a psychiatrist.

Being an altar boy and having a lot of odd philosophical ideas can easily make someone an outcast in a place like Salinas, but Michael was not one of those wan lads who pass invisibly through the school years, whose names you can never remember when you see their pictures in an old yearbook. He was handsome, gregarious, and athletic—student body president, class valedictorian, basketball player, and star of the golf team. Golf was his favorite of all sports; he was captain of the high school team and played in tournaments against some of the state's best golfers.

During these years, while Michael was busy being the shining light of Salinas High School, Dennis was turning into one of its leading troublemakers. His teachers suspected that Dennis' rebelliousness was in part a reaction to being compared unfavorably with Michael. One day the assistant principal called Michael into his office to talk to him about his brother's problems. "You know, Mike," he said, "the best thing for Denny will be when you get out of town." Michael, who loved his brother, was terribly depressed by the idea that his own success was somehow making it harder for Dennis to get through the travails of early adolescence.

The odd thing about it was that there was no reason at all for Dennis to feel inferior. He was good-looking and intelligent and probably a better athlete than his brother. Michael had given up sparring with Dennis when Dennis' punches became too fast for him to see, and Dennis was a brilliant competitor at Michael's favorite sport, golf. Dennis was playing with a two handicap when he was fifteen, and probably could have been a professional golfer. But that didn't appeal to him any more than did the promise of Carnegie Hall.

Michael went on to Stanford University to play out his promising-young-man role on a bigger stage. He was elected freshman class representative to the student executive committee; other class representatives on the committee at that time were Derek Bok, future president of Harvard, and Mark Hatfield, future senator from Oregon. He got on the Stanford golf team. He joined Phi Gamma Delta, one of the most prestigious fraternities, and some of his fraternity brothers saw him as a likely prospect for student body president. He did the things that fraternity boys at Stanford did around 1950: went to football games and sat in the rooting section wearing a red cap, went to costume parties and formal dances, took dates up to San Francisco to drink at the Top of the Mark and neck in the back seats of convertibles.

He was in the premedical course, which was heavily scientific. In studying evolutionary theory, he embarked on a phase of undergraduate atheism, discarding the idea of becoming a priest. He planned to go on to medical school, following his grandfather's profession, and then probably become a psychiatrist. The social forces around him were guiding him gently toward becoming a conventional, successful, and wealthy man.

Yet Stanford, even though it had given the world Herbert Hoover and seemed to want desperately to give the world many more, had its undercurrents of strange and subversive thinking. Most of the exotic ideas that seethed on the campus failed to interest the average member of Phi Gamma Delta, but they affected Michael Murphy. Much of the credit (or blame) for the birth of Esalen goes to Stanford.

26

Every university has its academic stars, spellbinders who can dazzle a lecture hall full of students and lure their minds for an hour or so away from sex and football. One of the spellbinders at Stanford was Frederic Spiegelberg, of the Asian studies department. Spiegelberg, a refugee from Hitler's Germany, was a product of the great burst of intellectual activity that had flowered in Germany in the 1920s and 1930s.

He was a colleague and friend of two of the leading existentialists, Martin Heidegger and Paul Tillich. He himself was one of Europe's leading scholars of Oriental religion and, unlike many such scholars, had the ability to communicate his knowledge; his courses at Stanford were immensely popular.

Murphy didn't get around to hearing one of Spiegelberg's lectures until his sophomore year, when he stumbled into it by chance. The administration had switched lecture halls for Spiegelberg's course on the third day of the quarter, because the enrollment had outgrown the space originally assigned to it. Murphy came into the lecture hall for a social psychology course he was taking, and found that it had been moved elsewhere. He decided to stay around and hear Spiegelberg. Spiegelberg had just returned from a sabbatical year in India, where he had visited Sri Aurobindo, religious mystic, social activist, and head of the great ashram at Pondicherry, and the religious leader Ramana Maharshi.

Spiegelberg lectured that day on the Vedic hymns, and he talked about the Brahman, rolling out the name of THE BRAHMAN in a sonorous voice that seemed to carry within its own resonance all the grandeur of the Hindi concept of the great spirit of the universe. Murphy had never been exposed to these concepts before, nor had he ever read any of the Eastern religious texts. But when he walked back to the fraternity house for lunch that day, he knew that his world had changed.

The only immediate outward change was in his class schedule; he dropped the social psychology course and stayed with Spiegelberg that quarter as the professor unfolded his vision of the perennial philosophy contained in Eastern religion. He still lived in the fraternity house, although he had begun to dislike it even before his encounter with Spiegelberg. He also began to meditate, and discovered that the mental state he entered in meditation—the inner silence, the steady concentration—could be reached even while he was playing golf. That summer when he went home, he played golf and read Sri Aurobindo's best-known philosophical work, *The Life Divine.* Nobody noticed anything different about him except Dennis, who had just graduated from high school. Dennis had a sharp eye for what went on with people (later Michael would say he could have been a great gestalt therapist), and he knew his brother well. He observed Michael's choice of reading material, his golf game, and said, "My God, we've got a golfing yogi here."

Murphy went back to Stanford in the fall. He was still living at the fraternity house and still enrolled in the premedical program, but his way of living was beginning to feel more and more like a thin outer shell, ready to crack. The thing that finally cracked it, and sent him flying away from Phi Gamma Delta and medicine, was a discussion group led by a graduate student named Walt Page.

It was more than a discussion group, however; it was nine or so disciples, who came to hear Walt Page interpret Hegel, Nietzsche, Carlyle, Aurobindo. It was a tight little group of bright young men and women, clustered around a brilliant and unstable center. Page was in his late twenties, older than most of them. He was a demanding and inspiring leader. Murphy was duly impressed by his knowledge of philosophy, but at the same time he detected a subtle sickness in the group, and kept some distance from it. On the whole, for people with such high hopes for what they could accomplish with so much wisdom, they did not turn out well. One member of the core group did become a professor of philosophy, but several disappeared into obscurity, and a few spent their lives in and out of mental hospitals. Walt Page shot himself in 1965.

Although Murphy was not of the group's inner circle, he came to its meetings and absorbed much of Page's heady synthesis of Eastern and Western thought. At the same time, he was still struggling with his premedical studies. It was hard going. His mind would leap out to embrace the thoughts of Hegel or Aurobindo, but it would have nothing to do with organic chemistry. One night, before an organic chemistry examination, Murphy spread his notes out before him and tried to decide what to do. He felt totally out of touch with the material and was beset by an unfamiliar feeling: he hadn't the vaguest idea of what it meant. He was so desperate, he was ready to cheat on the exam, but he couldn't figure out how to do even that. Finally, he realized that the time had come to do what he really wanted to do—forget about medicine and set out on the path of spiritual exploration.

So, in mid-January of his junior year at Stanford, Murphy moved out of the fraternity house and took a room in an old building in Palo

Alto called the Frenchman's Tower, where he spent eight hours a day meditating—four hours early in the morning, four hours later in the afternoon. He notified his parents that he did not intend to go on to medical school, and took a job hashing in the fraternity house, because he felt guilty about accepting their money. His plan was to drop out for the spring quarter and take some classes in San Francisco at the American Academy of Asian Studies, an institution Spiegelberg had started, and then to go back to Stanford to study religion and philosophy.

The hardest part about his decision was telling his parents. They had enough trouble with Dennis. Dennis had gone off for a riotous sojourn in Europe and then had drifted to North Africa, where it was rumored that he was earning his money by boxing Arabs in nightclubs. When John Murphy heard Michael's news, he told Michael to forget about coming home.

Despite his father's reaction, Murphy proceeded with his plan. He dropped out for the spring quarter to study in San Francisco, then went back to Stanford. He had to take a few psychology courses to complete the requirements for his B.A., and he used the remainder of this time on directed-reading courses on the subjects that interested him now. He read the American transcendentalists, the German idealists, and the Christian mystics; studied the works of the Buddhists and the Hindus; and investigated the literature of theosophy.

Michael Murphy graduated in 1952, was drafted not long afterward, sent off to Puerto Rico, and put to work interviewing draftees. The army assumed that a psychology degree from Stanford would enable him to determine whether the Puerto Ricans who couldn't pass the examinations were faking it or not. This demanded little of his time, and in his spare hours he meditated, read, and became a winning pitcher on the company baseball team.

Less than two years later, Michael completed his army service and returned to Stanford to go to graduate school. He was trying to map out some reasonably respectable way to pursue his interests, a career that would relate to his own needs and still look good in Salinas. He thought he would get a Ph.D. in philosophy and become a professor so he could pass on to future generations of students the teachings that inspired him.

The trouble with this idea was that Stanford's philosophy department was, like departments in philosophy and the social sciences all over the country, going through an intellectual revolution. In the social

29

sciences, a new generation of hard-nosed postwar scholars was pushing for more emphasis on science: more rigor, more measurement of behavior instead of abstract speculation about its inner meaning, more quantifiable data that could be fed into computers. In philosophy there was a comparable shift toward analytical thinking: forget about those dusty volumes of medieval mysticism, and get on with analysis and rationality. Such was the climate in which Murphy, a meditator and student of Aurobindo, had to survive as a graduate student.

Murphy began to feel tense and unhappy. His spiritual/intellectual search had already begun to go through a subtle change; had become less joyous and more intense. He was reading history almost compulsively, trying to take in everything, from the earliest beginnings of human civilization up to the present, so that he could fully comprehend the evolutionary ideas of Aurobindo and the majestic scientific/theological thinking of Teilhard de Chardin. He hadn't really wanted to return to Stanford; he would have preferred to go to Aurobindo's ashram in India. Now he found himself in an atmosphere that was hostile to the things he most wanted to study. He felt constant pressure, and found his mind playing host to strange ideas that he clearly recognized as neurotic symptoms. One was a fear that he was going to have an epileptic fit, an uncontrollable release of the pent-up pressure within him. Another was an intense discomfort associated with getting a haircut—he couldn't stand having anyone mess around with his head. He did not, during this time, resort to the usual releases that are practiced by graduate students; he was living a strictly religious life—celibate, vegetarian, given to long hours of meditation. It was the closest he ever came in his life to a real emotional breakdown.

Finally, after two years of struggling, in April of 1956 he left graduate school and took off for India, intending to apply for admission to Aurobindo's ashram in Pondicherry. On the way he took a tour through Europe and made a pilgrimage to Scotland to play on the legendary links at St. Andrews. Other Americans have gone to India in search of wisdom, but Michael Murphy was one of the very few who went there by way of a golf course. It was a splendid journey, and when Michael presented himself at Pondicherry he was admitted to the ashram.

Sri Aurobindo is one of the great figures in Indian history, and also one of the most important contributors to Michael Murphy's philosophy of life. Born in 1872, Aurobindo synthesized, in his life and writings, the polarities of body and mind, of inner growth and species evolution, of mysticism and political action. Educated in England, Aurobindo spent several years at Baroda College in southern India, where he was an administrator and professor of English. He later became a political revolutionary, trying to organize an armed insurrection against the British rulers of India. Like that of his contemporary, Gandhi, Aurobindo's political thinking was on a cosmic scale, in which ideas of social change mingled with ideas of spiritual transformation. He was profoundly influenced by India's religious traditions, including the teachings of the Bhagavad Gita, the Upanishads, and the disciplines of yoga and meditation. While imprisoned for his revolutionary activities and put in solitary confinement, he had a profound religious experience that turned him toward a more contemplative life. In 1910, about a year after he was released from prison, he retired to the old French colonial city of Pondicherry. A group of followers and students gathered around him, and the group evolved into a formal ashram that became, in time, the largest in India.

Aurobindo had died in 1950, and his work was being carried on by a Frenchwoman named Mira Richard, known to Aurobindo's followers as the Mother. When Michael arrived at the ashram in 1956, it had about fifteen hundred residents. Although life centered on Aurobindo's teachings, the place had no fixed daily routine, and residents were free to arrange their own programs of work and study. Murphy resumed his eight-hours-a-day meditation and took part in the ashram's sports activities. Aurobindo's philosophy was favorable to organized games as part of the religious life (a novel idea among Indian holy men, who traditionally favored noncompetitive disciplines such as hatha yoga), and the ashram was a hotbed of spiritual sports. Murphy, strongly attracted to this part of Aurobindo's thinking, coached the basketball team and introduced the ashram to softball. By the time he left, almost a year and a half later, it had four softball teams.

Michael liked the ashram's emphasis on sports and its liberal policies on how residents could organize their time. However, he disliked the cult aspects of it—the almost idolatrous reverence for the works of Aurobindo and the daily pronouncements of the Mother. Murphy thought Aurobindo was one of the great philosophers of all time, but he was disturbed by the way Aurobindo's followers seemed to want to surrender their ability to think for themselves. Aurobindo's works were an eloquent statement of the need for being open to all dimensions of human experience, and yet they were being petrified into another gospel.

Without any sense of what he would do next, Michael left Pondicherry after sixteen months. He went back to California and took a room in the same house in Palo Alto where he had stayed while a graduate student. He got a part-time job as a bellhop at a nearby hotel. It paid for his room and meals, and left him time to read and meditate. He also began to write, and outlined the book that would much later become his first novel, *Golf in the Kingdom,* a fantasy about a magical golf course in Scotland and a golfer-guru named Shivas Irons. He lived this way—reading and writing and meditating and lugging suitcases—for over two years.

John Murphy, after recovering from his angry outburst when Michael announced his plans to abandon the premedical course, no longer passed judgment on his son's life style. Marie remained serenely confident that both her boys would turn out all right.

Nevertheless, Michael was fully aware of the disparity between his life style and the prevailing values of his time and place. Once, on a visit home, he went out to play golf with his father and the mayor of Salinas. The mayor, in a painful attempt at golf course bonhomie, kept asking Michael questions about what he was doing. What he found out, of course, was that the son of one of Salinas' most prominent families worked part time as a bellhop and meditated a lot. John Murphy did not take part in this awkward conversation or try to apologize for his son. He had made his own peace with what Michael was doing; he just kept his eye on the ball.

It may have made things easier for John Murphy that Michael's wild brother Dennis was turning out rather well. Dennis had gone to Stanford for a year, dropped out to go into the army, then returned to Stanford and plunged into its creative writing program. Things came together for him with amazing ease: one of his short stories won several prizes, and then his first novel, *The Sergeant,* was accepted for publication and won the first Joseph Henry Jackson Prize, an award established in memory of the *San Francisco Chronicle*'s late literary critic. *The Sergeant* was a brilliant first novel, a taut and disciplined story about a macho career soldier who finds himself caught up by a homosexual passion for a young draftee. It appeared that Dennis was going to be a success, and a writer, no less, something the family admired. He might even become, in time, a novelist equal in stature to Steinbeck. Steinbeck thought so; he befriended Dennis and wrote to John Murphy, warning that their son was a writer, and a very good one.

I hasten to offer Marie and you my sympathy but I must also warn you that you are helpless. Your function as a father from now on will be to get him out of jail, to nurture him just short of starvation, to watch in despair while he seems to be irrational—and your reward for all this will be to be ignored at best and insulted and vilified at worst. Don't expect to understand him, because he doesn't understand himself. Don't, for God's sake, judge him by ordinary rules of human virtue or vice or failings. Every man has his price but the price of a writer, a real one, is very hard to find and almost impossible to implement. My advice to you is to stand aside, to roll with the punch and particularly to protect your belly. If you are contemplating killing him, you had better do it soon or it will be too late. I can see no peace for him and little for you. You can deny relationship. There are lots of Murphys.[2]

They built a house for Dennis on the Big Sur property—the Round House, on the rocks in the middle of Hot Springs Creek—and he settled there with his wife, a Big Sur girl named Pokey.

Now it was Michael, oddly enough, who seemed to be the social misfit. He was encouraged by J. D. Salinger's tales about young people who seemed a bit crazy to everybody else but who had a certain inner strength and honesty, who ransacked the world's religions for insights into the difficult business of being alive and human. He was not particularly touched by the Beat Generation writers, although he did enjoy going up to San Francisco now and then to observe the action in North Beach.

In 1960 he moved to San Francisco and took a room in a pleasant old brick mansion on the fringes of Golden Gate Park that had been converted—by a man named Haridas Chaudhuri, an Aurobindo follower—into a living and meditation center, a low-keyed urban ashram. Here he felt less isolated than he had in Palo Alto, and had the opportunity to be around a rapidly growing number of people who were interested in the same things as he was.

One day a young man named Richard Price came by the house. Price said a friend of his had suggested he look up Murphy. They exchanged some information and discovered they had been classmates at Stanford—not only classmates, but psychology majors as well. Probably they had sat in some of the same overcrowded postwar classes together. It was not surprising that they had not become acquainted in those days, but it seemed almost providential that now, after all these years, two 1952 Stanford psychology graduates should both be drop-outs in San Francisco, meditating and studying Oriental religion.

Although the two had much in common, there were vast differences between their social backgrounds. Murphy came from a secure and fairly tolerant small-town California aristocracy; Price was the son of a striving-and-succeeding Midwestern couple who had been determined to create a better life for their children . . . whether the children liked it or not.

His father had come to this country from Lithuania as Herman Preis, a Jewish immigrant. Preis changed his name to Price and discarded his Jewish identity. He became a top-level executive with Sears, Roebuck and Company, and married a woman whose family were Methodists, and they bought a large house in the very Gentile Chicago suburb of Kenilworth, on the North Shore. In this atmosphere, Herman Price's Jewishness was, like other difficult subjects, simply not spoken of. Richard, growing up, did not even know for a long time that his father was Jewish or understand what that meant. He knew only that there was something within the family that was not to be discussed. His father, meanwhile, came and went, busy with business and rarely seen. Price went to New Trier High School and dreamed, as all his friends did, that he might someday become president of a major corporation. When it was time for college, he chose Stanford, which had the dual advantages of being socially prestigious and a long way from home.

At Stanford he pledged Chi Psi fraternity and went through the same social rituals as his classmate Michael Murphy had—football games and fraternity-house dances. He was interested in sports, and made the wrestling team. He had expected to major in business, but discovered that, although Stanford had a graduate business school, there was no corresponding undergraduate department. Casting about for something to major in, he tried economics for a while and finally settled on psychology. Although he had no great interest in the subject when he made the choice, he soon found himself strongly drawn into it. He de-emphasized his fraternity-house social life and concentrated on being a student instead of a college boy.

Price also formed a new career plan: he would become a psychologist, perhaps a professor of psychology. He was especially taken with the notion of doing some kind of psychological-anthropological research, studying the ways different societies dealt with mental health and illness. He thought he eventually might become a psychoanalyst.

He got his B.A. in psychology from Stanford in 1952 and went on to do his graduate work at Harvard, which had recently created a new department of social relations. He hoped it would be more oriented toward human beings and less preoccupied with rats and question-naires than the psychology department at Stanford was. He even entertained the naïve hope that in the department of social relations at America's most eminent university there would be pleasant social relationships among the people who were working together.

But the department, like all good psychology departments of the era, was rigorously scientific, totally authoritarian, and racked by aca-demic backbiting. Toward the end of his first year at Harvard, Price wrote an examination paper in which he criticized the psychology of the program itself. This was the first psychology course in which he did not receive an A; he got a C. For a graduate student, it was almost as bad as a failing grade, and after that he was no longer in good favor in the department.

Price found that his mental and physical condition was deteriorat-ing. He had little social life and no time for the physical exercise that had been so important to him as an undergraduate. The only thing in his life was academic psychology, and it was beginning to seem strangely unnourishing.

That summer he spent some time at home, which seemed to him even more emotionally sterile than Harvard, and then proceeded west. He stayed for a few months at Stanford, had a summer romance that didn't work out too well—nothing was working out too well—and in the fall registered at the University of California in Berkeley. But he was no longer securely connected to the intellectual ambitions that had seemed so clear and worthwhile to him a few years earlier. He had applied for an army commission and was waiting for the military to come along and impose some temporary order on his life and give him space to work things out. When the commission did not come through, he enlisted in the air force. He had heard from a friend at Berkeley that the air force had a good place for psychologists, the Human Relations Research Institute, where you could get some experience while doing your time in the military. Price succeeded in getting assigned to duty with the institute, in Colorado, but it turned out that most of its human relations research had to do with gunnery. His job was running an adding machine. It was worse than Harvard.

He put in for a transfer and got reassigned to a teaching job at Parks Air Force Base in California, about forty miles east of San Francisco.

35

This was no great intellectual challenge either, but it was good duty. The work was light, and there were people around who shared some of his intellectual interests. In the long and easygoing days of training-camp routine, there was plenty of time for unstructured philosophical bull sessions without the sense of pressure and competitiveness that had always lurked about the edges of such conversations at Harvard. After a while he got into a schedule of night duty that was flexible enough to allow him time to take some courses at Berkeley or Stanford. He decided to see what was going on at Stanford, and in the spring quarter of 1955 he enrolled in classes there. One of them was taught by Frederic Spiegelberg.

The contact with Spiegelberg was not quite the instant epiphany it had been for Michael Murphy a few years earlier, but it produced, over time, an equally profound change in the course of Price's life. He had never been interested in religion, which seemed to him to be nothing more than a system of deceit that existed mainly to enforce social rules of behavior. Yet he found himself oddly moved by the content of Spiegelberg's presentation. It was the first time he had experienced religion as something that might relate to his own life.

In one of his lectures Spiegelberg mentioned a yogi who was giving a talk at the Vedanta Society, and Price went to hear him. Again he found himself, somewhat to his surprise, quite impressed. Later he went to hear another lecturer Spiegelberg recommended, an Englishman named Alan Watts, a former Episcopalian minister who had become a student of Zen Buddhism. Watts was not just *studying* Zen; he was making something new out of it, synthesizing it with ideas from some of the more adventurous realms of Western psychology. At Watts's lecture Price heard, for the first time, of a man named Frederick Perls, who had developed a system of therapy based on awareness of one's own mind and body. Watts also spoke of Wilhelm Reich's ideas about how the human organism is damaged by the socially enforced repression of its instinctual drives. Price had heard Reich mentioned in the psychology departments, of course, but only as a crazy man with a weird invention, not as somebody whose ideas were of any value.

Price began taking courses at the Academy of Asian Studies, where Watts was the star attraction. Watts was rapidly becoming a leading popularizer of Zen Buddhist ideas, and in San Francisco he was the intellectual mentor of a group of young writers and artists who were trying to make Zen—or something that sounded like Zen—a part of a new Zeitgeist. *Time* declared, in the summer of 1958, that "Zen Buddhism is growing more chic by the minute,"[3] and took note of Watts as its leading American interpreter; a similar article in the *Nation* a few months later called him "the brains and the Buddha of American Zen."[4] These were the people who became known as the Beat Generation, whose moment in time was called the Beat Scene.

The Beat Scene was part literary movement, part tourist attraction. On the literary front it was represented by such writers as Lawrence Ferlinghetti, Allen Ginsberg, Jack Kerouac, and Gary Snyder, all of whom came to Watts's lectures and wove Zen themes into their writings. Kerouac's novel *The Dharma Bums* was the best known of these efforts. It was a novelized paean to Zen and the free-flowing West Coast Bohemian life style. *The Dharma Bums* was an easily decoded roman à clef: its chief character, Japhy Ryder, was based on Gary Snyder, and also visible in its pages are Allen Ginsberg as the poet Alvah Goldbook (author of a poem entitled *Wail*), and Alan Watts as Arthur Whane. Snyder was the most serious scholar of the lot; he had studied Zen in Japan and had translated some Chinese Zen poems into English.

The tourist aspect of the scene centered on San Francisco's old Italian district of North Beach, which now suddenly blossomed with art galleries and hip hangouts, like The Place and the Co-Existence Bagel Shop, where young people and not-so-young people came to live out the 1950s version of *la vie bohème.* The clientele there was a mélange of artists, writers, neighborhood hangers-on, tourists, and San Francisco businessmen who hurried home to shed their button-down shirts for black turtlenecks, and hurried back to where the action was.

Price took a room at the academy and began spending more time in San Francisco, studying Buddhism and watching the Beat Scene unfold around him. He did not particularly consider himself a part of it, did not participate in such rites of passage as writing poetry or smoking marijuana, but he relished the sense of excitement and change. He knew he was changing inwardly, and all the activity around him seemed to echo and affirm that. When he first moved into the academy, he started going to The Place, which was still an unknown and uncrowded joint where you could buy a pitcher of beer and find somebody to talk to, and within six months' time he saw it turn into a frantic hub of San Francisco nightlife.

He was meditating at the Soto Zen temple now, and had even begun to think seriously about becoming a Buddhist monk. That prospect was both attractive and frightening. It would be a very long step from the career visions he had formed in New Trier High School, and it brought up the issue of marriage. Sometimes he felt that he wanted to get married, but he also knew that he hadn't seen much to give him great confidence in the institution.

One day a friend of his, Gia-fu Feng, came by the academy to have lunch and introduce a new girl friend. Born and raised in China, Gia-fu had come to the United States to learn high finance, had studied at the Wharton School of Finance, and worked for a while on Wall Street, until—passing through San Francisco on his way back to the Orient— he had been captivated by all the excitement about Eastern religion and decided to stay on and learn about it. Alan Watts's San Francisco was a considerably better place to explore Buddhism than Mao Tse-tung's China.

The girl Gia-fu brought to lunch was named Bonnie; she came from Chicago originally and had studied at the Royal Academy of Dramatic Art in London. She was small, brown-haired, bright-eyed, and theatrical, and Price felt strongly drawn to her. Then something very strange happened: he heard an inner voice, the experience that psychologists call an auditory hallucination. It said to him, "This is your wife." He sensed that the voice came from within himself, and yet it was so loud and clear that he looked around the room to see if anybody else had heard it. Everything seemed to be the way it had been before, and he went back to eating his rice.

The voice was a disturbing yet exciting experience. It fit with a new concept of self that was developing within him, an intuition that his old self—the compact knot of rational ideas and conflicted needs he had heretofore identified as Richard Price—was only a fragment of a much larger being, who was stronger and smarter and not entirely trustworthy.

He married Bonnie a few months later. His parents came out for the wedding, and it was like nothing they had ever seen in Kenilworth. It was held in the Soto Zen temple; the rites were performed in Japanese by the Reverend Tobasi, with the help of a translator. The wedding guests were a mixture of whites and blacks and Orientals; the bridesmaid was black, the best man Japanese. Price knew that a part of him had deliberately arranged all this to shock his parents, but at the same time he was deeply moved by the ceremony, the exotic sounds and music that went with it, the interracial group of friends who had come there to be with him.

Although Richard continued to go through the motions of rational living—marriage, a honeymoon, studying—he was, in fact, going crazy. He experienced wild ideas, a sense of vast possibilities, and a constant stream of almost uncontainable energy. He knew he was acting strangely, but a little strangeness was okay around the Academy of Asian Studies, and nobody bothered him there. At other times, when he went into a store, he would wonder if anybody noticed anything odd about him. He was spending hardly any time at all at the air base now—his friends there were covering for him, so he had to show up only every couple of weeks to get his paycheck—but when he went there to fill out the necessary forms to get married, he felt he could barely hold on to himself.

He had the same sense of barely being able to contain his energy during the wedding, and it was with him as he and Bonnie took off on a frenetic honeymoon trip, in which they drove hundreds of miles down the coast to Ensenada and then hundreds of miles north again into the Sierra Nevada range. They came back to San Francisco and moved into an apartment. Price divided his time between being married, going once in a while to the air base, studying at the academy, and hanging out in North Beach. He had time for all of that, since he was now getting by on about two hours of sleep a night.

Finally, one night in a bar in North Beach, all the energy came to a head. He felt a tremendous opening-up inside himself, like a glorious dawn. The place he was in had a fireplace, and he thought it would be appropriate for them to light a fire there, in celebration of this great and mysterious event. "Light the fire," he kept saying; "light the fire."

The bartender, of course, was not about to build a fire that spring night to signal the occasion of another North Beach regular going round the bend, and in due time six large policemen appeared and wrestled Price into a paddy wagon. In captivity, he felt the euphoria turn into anxiety and pain.

They put him in an army hospital in San Francisco for a couple of days, then transferred him to a hospital on the base. On the way there, when he realized where he was being taken, he thought that it was all over and they were now going to let him go. But it was a long way from being over.

He spent about three months in the hospital, being crazy. He was given a few electroshock treatments and some Thorazine, but not enough of either to prevent him from processing all the material that welled up out of his unconscious. He went through, among other things, a vivid experience of seeing his own past lives. Reincarnation had seemed a superstitious notion when he encountered it in classes at the academy; but for a while in the hospital it was a powerfully present reality as he swept back through history, flashing in and out of thousands of previous existences, pausing, for a long while, in a life where he had been some kind of a monk or hermit who spent many hours in meditation.

He ran through all his visions, acted out all his fantasies, burned up the strange energy that had been coursing through him—and then he was finished. He felt himself fully alive, clear, balanced, and touched with gratitude for what had happened to him; his religion was not one that included a personal God, but he was deeply indebted to whatever it was in the nature of things that had enabled him to open up to all the parts of himself that had been so long closed off.

He wanted to go back to San Francisco and try to put his life together again, and the air force was ready to release him from the hospital and give him an honorable discharge. He looked for somebody he could go into therapy with. While he was still in the hospital, he talked with Gregory Bateson, his anthropology professor at Stanford, who referred him to a young psychiatrist named Stephen Schoen. Price had known Schoen around North Beach; Schoen worked at the Langley-Porter Neuropsychiatric Clinic in San Francisco and was Allen Ginsberg's therapist.

Waiting to be discharged, Price was suddenly notified that he instead was being transferred to another hospital. His father, exerting influence through a high-level contact in Washington, had managed to get him transferred to an air force hospital in Illinois, about fifteen miles from Kenilworth.

It was a tolerable, if not pleasant, time. He got put into the open ward at the hospital. He was able to get books from the library, go jogging around the grounds, and sign out on weekends to be with Bonnie, who had come to live with her mother in Chicago. Things began to get difficult when Bonnie moved into the Prices' house in Kenilworth. It had seemed a logical idea—the house was much larger and closer to the hospital—but Bonnie and Mrs. Price did not get along. One day when Price came home, his mother told him she had read some of Bonnie's letters and that Bonnie was not a fit wife for him. He blew up—it was the first time in his life he had ever openly expressed anger to his mother—and moved Bonnie out of the house and back to Chicago. He reported to the hospital and began making inquiries about his discharge. He wanted to leave for California, and it would have been easy enough to get out of the hospital, but he knew that if he left while he was still in the air force, he would be AWOL and subject to arrest. He didn't know that he had already been discharged and was free to leave for California.

One day his father came to see him at the hospital, took him out for an expensive lunch, and started telling him about a private clinic on the East Coast. He wanted Price to go there for a few months. As he talked about what a good place it was supposed to be, the words wrapped around Price like a net. He was ready to get out, to take Bonnie back to California, and now his father wanted to ship him off to some hospital he had never even heard of. "What if I don't want to go?" he asked. The question was a challenge, an expression of barely contained anger, and his father knew it. The conflict was out in the open, and the older man was ready for it. "If you don't want to go," he said harshly, "then I'll commit you." It was kind of ironic, in a way: Price's father had never taken that much interest in him, never showed much emotion, even anger. Price had always regretted that and wished he had a real father. Now, at last, he had one.

He got out of the argument with what seemed to be a fairly good compromise. He agreed to go to the clinic, voluntarily, for three months. It was a place in Connecticut called the Institute of Living. He entered there on December 7, 1956.

The Institute of Living was a high-priced establishment; among its inmates were film star Gene Tierney, a member of the Du Pont family, a man who owned one of the largest shoe stores in Kentucky but could no longer remember any shoe sizes, and a man from Massachusetts whose wife had had him committed after he went to a neighboring town one day and purchased a pink Cadillac.

Price was put in a locked ward and spent about a month trying to get permission to use the exercise room. Although he was nominally under the care of a psychiatrist, he was getting no treatment of any kind—no groups, no individual therapy, no counseling—only occasional drugs to keep him quiet. He spent his days hanging around in closed rooms full of people who smoked too much, wondering what was going to become of him. He no longer felt wild, energetic, elated, or, indeed, much of anything except bored.

His status as a voluntary patient meant that he could sign himself out and, after a ten-day waiting period, be released. He decided to do that. As soon as he signed himself out, the hospital notified his father, who promptly had him legally committed.

He was forced to remain in the institute, where his doctor informed him that he was to undergo a series of sixty insulin-shock treatments. Price did not want them, but he was now an involuntarily committed patient, diagnosed as paranoid schizophrenic, and had no legal right to refuse any treatments. He had fifty-nine insulin treatments and about ten electroshock treatments.

They were, as far as he could tell, merely different kinds of punishment for having been crazy. The electroshock treatments were like being smashed really hard in football or boxing, knocked out cold, and then getting over it. The insulin injections were deeper assaults on the body and mind; they left him feeling as if he had been filled with cement. They also made him unconscious, and when he came to he was given sugared orange juice. He began to gain weight. He had always been lean and wiry, usually around 145 pounds, and in the next few months he went up to 175. He was not permitted to use the exercise room.

While he was in the clinic his parents had his marriage to Bonnie annulled. He responded to this—to the treatments, to everything—with passive acceptance. He had decided that he was going to be a very good boy, take whatever they handed him, and hope that sooner or later they would let him out. He spent nearly a year at the Institute of Living.

He came home broken and defeated, understanding very clearly that a person can be made to pay a very high price for violating society's rules of how a human being should think and behave.

He lived at home and took a job working as an assistant purchasing agent for one of his uncles, who owned a company in Chicago that manufactured illuminated beer signs for bars. He went woodenly through the motions of that life for nearly three years, until he heard that a group of his old friends in San Francisco, Gia-fu Feng and some others, had started a cooperative called East-West House. He had saved up his money and had lived a very sane and dull life for a long time now; his parents did not try to stop him from leaving. In May of 1960 he got on a plane and went back to California, the part of the world that felt the most like home.

* * *

Price and Murphy were both trying to keep their expenses down. Price had some stock and the money he had saved while working for the beer-sign business in Chicago; Murphy had a two-day-a-week job as a copyreader for a trade magazine called the *Pacific Shipper.* The publisher at the *Shipper* decided he needed a full-time copyreader, and asked Murphy to work full time or quit. He quit.

Murphy had been playing around with the idea of going down to live at Big Sur. The Big House, the house his grandparents had built for themselves, was standing empty. Dr. Murphy was dead, and Bunny, now in her eighties, rarely went there anymore. Dennis was living in his own house, carousing around and working on a second novel. The property south of the creek was now a resort motel, Slate's Hot Springs. He could live in the Big House for nothing and probably find a part-time job.

This seemed to be the time to try it, since he was out of work anyway. He talked it over with Price and invited him to come along. There was plenty of room. They would just go down there and see how it felt; if they didn't like it, they could always go back to San Francisco. If they did like it, they could stay on indefinitely, meditate, and read.

3

One day in the spring of 1961 Murphy and Price loaded their possessions into the back of an old red Jeep pickup that Price had obtained on a long-term loan from a woman he knew, and they started out on the 150-mile trip from San Francisco to Big Sur. It was a happy trip as the pickup slowly navigated the twists and turns of Highway 1. But it took a long time, and it was already dark when they got to Slate's Hot Springs. They found their way to the Big House, went in, and wandered about, looking at rooms. Price decided to move into one of the guest rooms on the main floor, and Murphy took the master bedroom upstairs.

In the middle of the night somebody came into Murphy's room, shining a flashlight at him. He awoke to see a shadowy figure standing over him, holding a flashlight in one hand and a billy club in the other.

"Who the hell are you guys?" the man wanted to know. "What are you doing here?"

The young man's name was Hunter Thompson. Bunny Murphy had hired him to guard the property, but she neglected to notify him that her grandson was coming down to stay there. He took his job seriously. He was twenty-two years old and wanted to become a writer. He was working on a novel about Puerto Rican baseball players.

Slate's Hot Springs, 1961. The ocean fogs rolled in and rolled out, keeping the hillsides green. Sea otters floated happily on their backs in the surf below, munching on abalones. A few people lived on the Murphy property, in the various houses and cabins; not a community, only a random assembly of people, an ill-assorted collection of cultures and life styles.

After Dr. Murphy's death, Bunny had developed the property into a modest tourist establishment, the sort of mom-and-pop place you saw in the pre-freeway days, with a restaurant and a bar and a huddle of boxlike cabins. The motel was being managed by Mrs. Webb, a woman from Fresno who rented that part of the property from Bunny on a month-to-month basis. Mrs. Webb had hired several members of her church, the First Church of God of Prophecy, to help her run the place. They were sober, hard-working types who used the lodge for their Saturday night services when they gathered together to sing hymns and speak in tongues.

The old Big Sur Bohemia was represented by Emil White, who rented one of the cabins. White was publishing a tourists' guide to the Big Sur country; it was a glossy magazine-size booklet, with dramatic photographs of the surf and hills, and articles by the local writers. It was typical of its genre, not much different from the productions sold in other scenic areas, except that the others did not have copy written by Henry Miller.

Miller and his friends still frequented the baths during the daytime, and it was a favorite hangout for old-timers up and down the coast. Italians, fishing people from Monterey, would often come to spend the day and go back home with jars full of mineral water. The Italians were the only people at Slate's who "took the waters" in the old European style, drinking it as a tonic. The rest of the visitors just soaked in the tubs and did their drinking at the little wine-and-beer bar in the lodge.

Most of the steady customers were homosexuals from San Francisco, who came down on weekends. They had some wild parties in the baths at night, but generally Mrs. Webb and the members of the First Church of God of Prophecy got on well with all these nice young men and were—or affected to be—ignorant of the afterdark festivities at the bathhouse.

The young men from San Francisco had been coming to Slate's for some time, but in the early 1960s that part of the scene was beginning to turn ugly. There was a lot of fighting going on around the place—sometimes in the bar, sometimes in the baths, sometimes in the parking lot. The bar was frequented by a vague, roughhewn, and ever-changing group that Murphy and Price called the Big Sur Heavies. Some of them sculpted or painted or wrote; some roared up and down Highway 1 on motorcycles; some of them lived back in the hills, where they grew marijuana for sale to, among others, the customers at Slate's.

Murphy and Price lived in the Big House across the Hot Springs

Creek. Michael was back into his marathon meditation regimen; Price, still suffering from the aftereffects of his insulin treatments, relaxed and read and helped out with odd jobs around the property. Hunter Thompson occupied a wing of the Big House, where he spent his spare time working on his writing. He fully expected to become a famous writer. One day when Emil White went out to the mailbox to pick up his mail, Thompson, who was waiting there, asked him if Henry Miller had much trouble with uninvited people coming to see him. Thompson added that when he became famous, he wouldn't want to put up with a lot of disturbance of that sort. Emil was too shocked to answer; it was unthinkable to him that this skinny gun-collecting kid would ever be the equal of Henry Miller.

There were a few other more or less permanent residents. A man named Henry Maynard, a carpenter, lived in the Little House with his wife. Two of the cabins by the lodge were occupied by young couples who were building a boat, a trimaran on which they planned to sail to Tahiti. One of the members of this foursome was Joan Baez, nineteen years old then, and just becoming known to the world. She would sit in the sun in front of her cabin, playing her guitar and singing in her clear voice for anybody who had the time to stop and listen.

And so it went through the spring and summer of 1961: sodomy in the baths, glossolalia in the lodge, fistfights in the parking lot, folk music in the cabins, meditation in the Big House. Hunter Thompson marched amid all this with his billy club, representing the forces of law and order. Unlike Mrs. Webb and her associates, who always managed to be elsewhere when there was trouble, Thompson kept trying to enforce straight morality at the baths and break up fights; this raised the level of violence considerably.

One night Thompson got into a serious battle. He had been somewhere up the coast with his girl friend, and on the way back they picked up a couple of soldiers from Fort Ord who were hitchhiking south. With these reinforcements Thompson felt it would be safe to brave the baths, a place where he had few friends and rarely ventured after dark. The young men were ready for him and jumped him as soon as he got to the bathhouse. The soldiers disappeared into the night, the girl also got away, and Hunter slugged it out until he was severely beaten. He finally found his way back to the Big House, nearly unconscious, his clothes soaked with blood. All the next day he sat moodily in his room, firing random gunshots through the window; he did not bother to open it first.

Michael Murphy was naturally distressed by what had become of his old family vacation spot, the place he and Price had come to in search of a haven for meditation and study. Sometimes he thought about taking it over and running the business himself.

This was an idea that he had toyed with before, from time to time. Once, when he was living in Palo Alto, he drove down to Salinas with a friend from the old Walt Page Stanford group to talk to Bunny about it. He thought he would run the motel and also hold some lectures and educational programs there as a side line. Bunny refused to let Michael take over the property. She said he would just give it away to the Hindus. But he never quite gave up that idea, and believed that someday Bunny might change her mind. He went to visit her, from time to time, and would soften her up by telling her about what was going on around the place.

He and Price talked about the possibility of such a venture with a growing sense of enthusiasm. It made sense to them. Alan Watts was already holding occasional weekend seminars in the area, sometimes at the Big Sur Gallery and sometimes at the house of the architect Nathaniel Owings. Probably Watts could be persuaded to use the lodge for his lectures; other programs of that sort might be put on there as well. This would augment the motel and restaurant operation, and also serve to change the tone of the place—bring in people who were more interested in religion and philosophy, less given to knocking each other down.

Murphy and Price agreed that their programs would be open and flexible, not wedded to any particular school or discipline. They would establish a center for the exploration of new ideas. The guiding principle would be synthesis: the flowing-together of East and West, the ancient and the modern, science and religion, scholarship and art.

Some time during the spring and summer of 1961, the project became more concrete. Murphy's family supported the undertaking. John Murphy came around—no doubt moved partly by a desire to see his older son finally take on an occupation—and persuaded Bunny to let them have a long-term lease on the property. Until then, she had maintained a certain tenuous control over the place by refusing to give anybody a lease on it. Everybody who lived there, including Mrs. Webb and her motel business, was subject to dismissal on short notice if he or she did anything to offend Bunny.

Bunny had a reputation for being capricious about those things. Once, Frieda Lawrence, D. H. Lawrence's widow, came to Big Sur and was taken with the idea of renting the Big House and living there. Emil White showed her the place and arranged for her to see Bunny. She went up to Salinas—carrying, as she always did, the urn containing her late husband's ashes—and presented herself at Bunny's house. Bunny, for all her love of culture and literature, was rather taken aback by this lady with the jar of ashes, and refused to let Frieda Lawrence rent the Big House. She told Emil that she did not want an unmarried couple (Frieda was now living with another man) staying in the house that she and Dr. Murphy had occupied. Emil thought Bunny was crazy.

Moral considerations were also involved in her decision to let Murphy and Price take over the business: Bunny had finally heard from enough sources that the situation at the bathhouse was—at least after dark—completely out of control.

As the plans for taking over the hot springs became a reality, Murphy and Price went seeking advice and support. They talked to Frederic Spiegelberg, and the courtly old professor, who knew all kinds of people, was most helpful. They talked with Alan Watts, whom they had first met through Spiegelberg. They talked with Gregory Bateson, whom Price had known at Stanford. They wrote to Aldous Huxley and went to see Gerald Heard. Such contacts as these were the beginning of what was to become a formidable cadre of philosophers, psychologists, artists, writers, theologians, and wise souls who took an interest in their project, gave them suggestions, and agreed to come to Big Sur to lead seminars. It helped, each time they approached some new luminary, to be able to mention the other people of stature who were involved already. And so the circle widened.

Murphy and Price were equal partners in the venture, but Murphy tended to take the lead. It had, after all, been his idea to begin with, and it was his family's property. And he had an affable personality, plus a certain social knack, even boldness, that served him well in the hunt for potential seminar leaders. This was the same youthful sociability that had impressed high school teachers, Episcopalian priests, and fraternity brothers earlier. Now that he was on a track of his own choosing, his genuine enthusiasm reinforced it. Price recognized Murphy's special qualities and accepted his own role, even though it meant that he was sometimes seen by others as the junior partner.

Price made his own contribution to getting the project in motion. He took charge of working expenses, utility bills, monthly lease payments. They would have to put out some sort of announcements or brochures, and that would mean printing and mailing costs. Murphy, with the help of his family, had provided the site. Now Price provided the capital. There was about $17,000 in stock registered in his name but owned jointly with his father; these were assets that conceivably could serve as collateral for a business loan. Price, with some trepidation, wrote his father and asked him to release his share of the stock. Herman Price agreed, and the two young men went to a bank in Monterey and borrowed $10,000. Although they both came from wealthy families, it was the largest amount of cash either of them had ever owned.

Bunny gave notice to Mrs. Webb that summer, and October was agreed upon as the month when Murphy and Price would take over management of the business. Taking over, however, involved considerably more than just acquiring a lease on the property. It also called for convincing the carousing legions of the bathhouse that the place was truly under new management.

The baths were part of the property and one of the chief assets of the business, but at night it was not easy to tell who, if anybody, owned them. Mrs. Webb—a living embodiment of clean-living, overweight, small-town, fundamentalist American morality—had established détente with her customers. The only employee who ever ventured into the baths was a handyman named Charlie—Wednesday Charlie, the regulars called him—who went there once a week to clean out the tubs. Mrs. Webb herself never went to the baths and assumed a pose of monumental naïveté about the whole scene. One night, not long after he had come to stay at Big Sur, Murphy noticed that the lights down at the bathhouse were blinking. On, off, on, off, on, off. He pointed this out to Mrs. Webb and asked her if she knew what could be causing it. "Loose wire someplace," she said. "I'll have to tell Charlie about that tomorrow and have him fix it." Later, Murphy found that there was no loose connection. The connection, in fact, was extremely good. The blinking light was a signal commonly used down at the bathhouse to warn its occupants when straight strangers were on the way down the path. Everybody who lived at Slate's had seen it many times before.

That summer Murphy and Price had a high metal fence, with a gate in it, erected across the pathway leading down to the baths, and instituted a policy of closing the baths down at 8:00 P.M. They tried to do this as gently as possible, merely announcing to whoever happened to be at the baths that the place was under new management. As often as not, the occupants moved on, with nothing more than a mild grumble or two, and all was secured for the night. At other times, there was some fairly heated resistance, and once there was an outright rebellion that led to a showdown of sorts, the ludicrous Armageddon that is remembered in old Esalen lore as the Night of the Dobermans.

On that night Murphy and Price went down to the baths, as usual, before closing the gate, and were confronted by a group of young men who flatly refused to leave. Well outnumbered and having no urge to repeat Hunter Thompson's earlier debacle, Murphy and Price retreated and walked up to the cabins, looking for reinforcements. They rounded up five people, including Hunter Thompson and Joan Baez, and three dogs. The dogs were Doberman pinschers, two males and a female. This was all the help they could get. Mrs. Webb was away at a church convention; her temporary replacement was a Mrs. Moon, a portly lady whom Michael saw only once that night, from the rear, her ample body disappearing around the corner of the lodge at the first sign of trouble.

They didn't really know how large the opposition was; there were a few gays from San Francisco staying at Slate's, and untold numbers of other young men floating about in the hills. Murphy and Price had the feeling that they were far outnumbered, that they were a little band of citizens uniting against a huge and malevolent group of usurpers. Actually, the usurpers they saw close up were not a particularly threatening lot. They all looked like college students, and many of them probably were: young men of twenty or so, full of energy on a warm summer night, defending the turf, looking for excitement.

Murphy and Price, allies and dogs, gathered themselves together and started out toward the baths. "I think you ought to know," one of the allies told Michael apologetically, "that none of these dogs has ever bitten anybody."

The dogs, it turned out, were primarily interested in fighting with each other. They commenced doing this along the narrow pathway, setting up a horrendous noise in the darkness. They were all on leashes, and their owners pulled them apart without too much difficulty, but they continued to bark at each other—Dobermans have excellent voices—as the little procession straggled down toward the baths. When they got to the baths, there was nobody there.

After a few minutes of looking around the dark and deserted bathhouse, they started back up the path toward the lodge. Along the way, the Dobermans began their antics again. And again it took a while to get them separated while they set up a chorus of mind-bending screeches and snarls that echoed about the hills. Hearing it from a distance in the darkness, you could have imagined the most terrible of scenes: vicious animals running wild, bodies being ripped apart in the brush.

As they approached the lodge, it was clear that something was going on, some new surge of activity. A few people were leaving their cabins, headlights were flickering against the hillsides as cars pulled out of the parking lot, climbed the road toward Highway 1, and then headed south. Gradually they realized what it was: a retreat, an utter rout. Everybody was leaving. The parking lot emptied; the dogs stopped barking. A deep hush descended over the place. The allies went back to their cabins; Murphy and Price walked about the property, still not quite sure what had happened. They strolled up the road toward Highway 1, and near the top they saw a man and woman standing in the middle of the road, embracing in the bright moonlight. The young couple explained that they had been driving by, had been struck by the beauty of the place, and had decided to stop and walk down the road. For Murphy, the image of the young couple embracing in the moonlight stood as an auspicious omen, a symbol of the hot springs' turn toward a more peaceful future.

That summer Hunter Thompson made a modest step toward his goal of becoming a professional writer; he sold an article entitled "Big Sur: The Tropic of Henry Miller" to a men's magazine called *Rogue.* The article, which gave some hint of Thompson's future as a gonzo journalist, was a loosely assembled batch of impressions of the scenic wonders and shifting population of Big Sur. The scenery came off well ("so vast and so varied and so beautiful that the imagination of the visitor is tempted to run wild at the sight of it"), but his description of the local residents was less lyrical. He identified four main groups in the population: expatriates, ranchers, out-and-out bastards, and genuine deviates. The expatriates, he explained, "have come from all over the world to make a stab at The Good Life." The ranchers are those "whose families have lived here for generations." The bastards "live in isolation because they can't live anywhere else," and the deviates "live here because nobody cares what they do as long as they keep to themselves." As sociology, the classifications were a bit shaky, but then the Big Sur population has never been easy to define. Thompson's generic descriptions might never have gotten him in much trouble, but he also described a few of the better-known individuals:

> People are always taking Emil White, publisher of the Big Sur Guide, for a hermit or a sex fiend; and Helmuth Deetjen, owner of the Big Sur Inn, looks more like a junkie than a lot of real hopheads. If you saw Nicholas Roosevelt, of the Oyster Bay Roosevelts, walking along the highway you might expect him to flag you down, wipe your windshield with an old handkerchief, and ask for a quarter . . .

Everybody in Big Sur read the article, nobody liked it much, and it led to Thompson's dismissal from his caretaking post at the hot springs. Mrs. Webb had got a copy of the magazine and sent it to Bunny Murphy. Bunny noted that Thompson's article also described life at the hot springs:

> This place is a real menagerie, flavored with everything from bestiality to touch football . . . The list of tenants reads something like this: one photographer, one bartender, one publisher, one carpenter, one writer, one fugitive, one metal sculptor, one Zen Buddhist, one physical culturist, one lawyer, and three people who simply defy description—sexually, socially, or any other way. There are two legitimate wives on the property; the other females are either mistresses, "companions," or hopeless losers. Until recently the shining light of this community was Dennis Murphy, the novelist, whose grandmother owns the whole shebang. But when his book, *The Sergeant,* became a best-seller, he was hounded by people who would drive hundreds of miles to jabber at him and drink his liquor. After a few months of this, he moved up the coast to Monterey.
>
> Old Mrs. Murphy lives across the mountains in Salinas, and luckily, gets to Big Sur only two or three times a year. Her husband, the late Dr. Murphy, conceived of this place as a great health spa, a virtual bastion of decency and clean living.[1]

Bunny was deeply upset by the article. It was bad enough that the hot springs property had become what it had become; it was intolerable that one of her own employees should write about it. She made one of her rare trips down to Big Sur, in her black Cadillac with her Filipino chauffeur, for the specific purpose of firing Thompson.

She was a somewhat bizarre-looking person at this point: tall, aged, gaunt. She had lost the sight of one eye. She fixed the other one balefully upon Thompson, told him he was no longer working for her and was to get off the property.

"What if I won't go?" he asked her.

"In that case," she replied, "I will call the sheriff and have him throw you off."

Thompson went back to the Big House and packed up his belongings and moved on, leaving behind a few friends and a number of enemies and a room with a window full of bullet holes.

Slate's Hot Springs was now officially under new management. Price moved over to the lodge, into a room that became a combination bedroom and office. Michael stayed in the Big House. They had agreed that Price would be in charge of the resort and that Murphy would go to work lining up the seminar programs. But it would not be a complete division of responsibilities; they would work together on all parts of the operation.

In January of 1962 Alan Watts gave a seminar at the lodge. This was one of his own programs, attended by his own private clientele and not organized by Murphy and Price, but it was an opportunity to give the place a test run, to get a little philosophy vibrating through its rooms. Watts, then in his mid-forties, had a considerable, if hard-to-categorize, reputation as a philosopher, theologian, writer, and lecturer. He liked to describe himself as a philosophical entertainer. He had taken a strong interest in Oriental religions while still an English schoolboy and had converted to Buddhism at the age of fifteen. Soon after that, he had discontinued formal education and had worked for his father while spending all of his spare time reading philosophy and socializing with the colorful array of characters who populated London's spiritual underground.

London of the 1930s was teeming with Oriental scholars, eclectic students of world religions, charlatans, seekers, yogis, gurus. One major organizational focus to this spiritual energy was the Theosophical Society, founded in America by a Russian-born woman named Helena Petrovna Blavatsky. Madame Blavatsky claimed that the basic principles of theosophy were based on esoteric Buddhist teachings that she had learned in Tibet from two high priests named Koot Hoomi and Maurya. Many scholars over the years have pointed out that Koot Hoomi and Maurya are unlikely Tibetan names and that theosophy does not quite fit in with other works of Tibetan Buddhism. Nevertheless, the theosophical movement was important both in Europe and the United States; it was responsible for introducing many people—including a sizable segment of the British aristocracy—to the great works of Buddhist and Hindu philosophy, and it was a major force behind the spiritual ferment that Watts discovered in London.

Watts's major teacher during this period was Christmas Humphreys, a judge who was also one of England's leading Buddhist scholars. Humphreys had been a member of the Theosophical Society while a student at Cambridge and later founded the Buddhist Lodge of London, which became the center of Watts's philosophical explorations. Watts, under Humphreys' supervision, established himself as a serious scholar of Buddhism while he was still in his teens; his first book, *The Spirit of Zen,* was published when he was just twenty years old.

Another of Watts's spiritual guides during these years was a mysterious Yugoslavian named Dmitrije Mitrinovic, a student of occult lore and an admirer of whiskey, good food, and fast cars. Mitrinovic was also interested in psychological works, like those of the British psychoanalyst Trigant Burrow. One of the books that Watts studied under his guidance was Burrow's *The Social Basis of Consciousness,* which argued that the ego, the sense of the individual self separate from its environment, was a fictitious concept, created and maintained by social pressure. Watts was most intrigued by this notion, which he found compatible with some of his own ideas about Buddhism and with the then-novel idea that there were connections between psychology and Oriental philosophy. Watts liked Mitrinovic's style; the persona of the rascal-mystic appealed to him, and its influence was evident in his own approach to life.

Another acquaintance that Watts made during these years—more as a colleague than a teacher—was Frederic Spiegelberg. In his autobiography, Watts recalled that Spiegelberg "wore a hat with an exceedingly wide brim, spoke English with a delicate German accent which always suggests a sense of authority and high culture, and was propagating the theory that the highest form of religion was to transcend religion." The religion of nonreligion, Spiegelberg called it. It was another notion that became a basic part of Watts's message to the world. Religion is fine, he would tell his listeners, but you should never take it too seriously; that leads only to holy wars and inquisitions, not to an enhanced understanding of life.

During his London years, Watts met J. K. Krishnamurti, the remarkable Indian teacher who had a similarly iconoclastic view of the spiritual life. Krishnamurti had been groomed from boyhood by the leaders of the Theosophical Society to assume a messiah-like role within it, and then had stunned the society by announcing that its whole apparatus of hierarchy and dogma was an obstacle to spiritual growth, and one that he wanted no further part of. He dissolved the Order of the Star, of which he was the head, and told his disciples that to become a follower of any person is to cease to be a follower of the truth. This very nearly destroyed the entire theosophical movement and remained a subject of passionate controversy in spiritual circles for years. Watts agreed strongly with Krishnamurti; he admired his stand and his decision to live a life as a free-floating teacher without formal ties to any organization or spiritual heritage.

Watts, having married an American woman, immigrated to the United States in 1939. He lived for a while in New York, writing and lecturing sporadically, and then, searching hard for a stable occupation, came up with the idea that he should become a priest of some sort. He told his astounded friends that it was, after all, a logical way for a theologian to make a living. One denomination would have suited this purpose as well as another; he chose the Episcopalian, knowing that its Old World equivalent, the Church of England, found room within its generous bosom for both communists and theosophists, as long as they observed a few rules of proper behavior and used the Book of Common Prayer in their services. With a bit of pull from his wife's family, and on the basis of his having already published numerous writings on theological subjects, Watts was admitted to a graduate theological seminary in Illinois and in 1945, at the age of thirty, was ordained. He passed five lively years as the Episcopalian chaplain at Northwestern University, in Evanston, during which time he staged colorful church services emblazoned with the best in music and ritual, offered sermons based on his personal theology, and wrote his most Christian book, *Behold the Spirit*.

Even during this relatively conventional period in his life, Watts continued to hold avant garde views on many subjects. One of these— his open support of free love in theory and practice—led to the end of his first marriage and, after an extensive debate on the subject with his superiors in the church, to the end of his career as a clergyman. He resigned from the priesthood and spent some time in New York, where he wrote another book, *The Wisdom of Insecurity*, and then accepted an invitation from Spiegelberg to come to San Francisco and join the faculty of the American Academy of Asian Studies. His route west took him through Los Angeles—where he visited Huxley, Heard, Christopher Isherwood, and other members of the sizable circle of Southern California students of Buddhist and Hindu philosophy.[2]

In San Francisco in the 1950s, Watts became a kind of guru to the West Coast artists and writers, a role that began to bring him national attention. Watts had some personal reservations about the Beats and their brand of Buddhism. He thought Gary Snyder had caught the true essence of Zen in his poetry, and he also admired Ginsberg's work, but he was less sure about Kerouac. In "Beat Zen, Square Zen, and Zen," an article that appeared in the San Francisco literary magazine *Contact* in 1958, he wrote that Kerouac "is always a shade too self-conscious, too subjective, and too strident to have the flavor of Zen."[3]

Watts also had some reservations about the Beat writers' enthusiasm for marijuana, peyote, and other mind-altering substances—not because he disapproved on moral grounds (he was one of the least moralistic theologians in the business), but because he doubted that drug-induced highs were, as Kerouac believed, portals to religious experience. (Later, not long after he gave his first lecture at Slate's Hot Springs, Watts was persuaded by Aldous Huxley to try LSD for the first time. After a series of experiments with it, he concluded that a drug could, in certain cases, produce a mystical state of consciousness.)

Watts was living an appropriately Bohemian life style in the early 1960s, sharing a Sausalito houseboat with the artist Jean Varda, Henry Miller's old friend; yet he was at the time an extraordinarily straight-looking individual who had a crew cut and wore neat suits and ties when he went off across the country on speaking tours. He had written ten books, and his articles had appeared in religious journals, literary magazines, and even the *American Journal of Psychoanalysis.* He smoked, drank, and had open liaisons with miscellaneous women, and loved it when his audiences asked him, as they often did, how a theologian could behave that way. He would tell them that what he was trying to communicate was not really a theology, certainly not a system of morality, but a state of consciousness.

> I am neither a preacher nor a reformer [Watts wrote in 1960], for
> I like to write and talk about this way of seeing things as one sings
> in the bathtub or splashes in the sea. There is no mission, no intent
> to convert, and yet I believe that if this state of consciousness

could become more universal, the pretentious nonsense which passes for the serious business of the world would dissolve in laughter. We should see at once that the high ideals for which we are killing and regimenting each other are empty and abstract substitutes for the unheeded miracles that surround us—not only in the obvious wonders of nature but also in the overwhelmingly uncanny fact of mere existence. Not for one moment do I believe that such an awakening would deprive us of energy or social concern. On the contrary, half the delight of it—though infinity has no halves—is to share it with others, and because the spiritual and the material are inseparable this means the sharing of life and things as well as insight. But the possibility of this depends entirely upon the presence of the vision which could transform us into the kind of people who can do it, not upon exhortation or appeals to our persistent, but consistently uncreative, sense of guilt.[4]

Although he did not choose to offer himself to the world as a preacher, he had a speaking gift that any preacher would have envied. He was a brilliant and lucid talker who could go on for hours, in perfectly constructed sentences, without notes or prepared text. He had a good speaking voice, and knew it, and used it well. At his chosen craft—philosophical entertainment—he was a talented and polished professional.

He had visited Carl Jung and had lectured at the Jung Institute in Zürich in 1958, and he had been impressed by Jung's abandonment of formal lectures in favor of seminars that lasted for a weekend or some comparable period of time. In these seminars an instructor and a group of students would work together more or less continuously, with plenty of time for questions and discussion. On his return to California, Watts (who had left the Academy of Asian Studies) began to hold private seminars based on this model. He gradually built up a clientele for such events, a loose aggregation of followers who would be notified by mail in advance of the next seminar. The sessions were held here and there, mostly in the San Francisco Bay Area, sometimes in Los Angeles, usually in the homes of friends or students, for people interested in the subjects he liked to call "these things." Watts had many friends in the Big Sur area, a place he had been attracted to ever since he first drove up that coast on his way to San Francisco, and often gave seminars there, too. So the precedent had been set, and when Watts gave his first seminar at Slate's Hot Springs, sitting in front of the old stone fireplace, drinking an occasional beer, and conversing with a couple of dozen people about these things, it was not a leap into the unknown, only a continuation of a kind of activity that had been going on at Big Sur for some time.

Over the next few months, as they were preparing their first formal series of programs, Murphy and Price put together various events intended to keep the business afloat during the transition period, and give them some practical experience at running the place. Among these was a series of weekend gatherings of Stanford students. Youth hostels, they were called. Murphy had arranged them with the help of a former classmate who was now a dean at Stanford.

The first was a leaderless weekend, pleasant enough but unstructured. The next one resembled the kind of bold content of future seminars. It had a topic for discussion—psychic phenomena, always one of Murphy's favorites—and a couple of leaders. For that role, Murphy looked around and found Dell Carlson, a high school teacher, and Joe K. Adams, a psychologist. Carlson was a member of Sequoia Seminars, a nonsectarian religious group then going strong in the San Francisco Bay Area; Adams had done research on psychic phenomena at Stanford and was a friend of Gregory Bateson's.

Adams was one of the first psychologists to become interested in the new venture at Big Sur, and the first psychologist to lead a program there. He was also one of the first Americans to land in a mental institution as a result of a psychotic episode directly linked to LSD.

For most of his life, up until the early 1960s, Adams had been the very model of a conventional American psychologist. A thin, mild-mannered man, a courteous Texan, he had his doctorate from Princeton, had been chairman of the psychology department at Bryn Mawr, and was best known in his field for a book on statistics. Even his period of research on psychic phenomena at Stanford was a badge of membership in the psychological middle-of-the-road establishment. Thomas Welton Stanford, a member of the university's founding family, had endowed a fellowship for research in psychic phenomena, but the psychology department, which was trying hard to become more scientific, found it a bit of an embarrassment. The department dealt with the problem by deliberately subverting the benefactor's intent and awarding the fellowship periodically to some distinguished, right-thinking experimental psychologist who could be trusted to spend a year messing about at Stanford on something or other that would not unduly advance the cause of psychic research. Adams, who had always been skeptical about such things, performed admirably in this role. When the year was over, he decided to stay in California and become a clinical, rather than an experimental, psychologist. In his clinical training he worked with the Mental Research Institute in Palo Alto, where some of the early research in LSD was being conducted under grants from the National Institute of Mental Health, and was also employed at the Veterans Administration hospital where Gregory Bateson was anthropologist-in-residence, studying the causes of schizophrenia.

The LSD research had started out within the framework of the current scientific notion that it created a chemically induced "model psychosis," and thus provided the sane an opportunity to perceive the world of the insane. It started out that way, but it veered speedily into another dimension entirely: the researchers began to regard LSD as something much more valuable, a tool for studying states above or beyond everyday consciousness. LSD sessions became sophisticated experiments in self-exploration, with seasoned "guides" helping the research subjects wander through heretofore unexplored territories of the mind.

In January of 1961, not long after one of his LSD sessions, Adams went through an episode of acute psychosis, with vivid hallucinations. This lasted about sixty hours. A year later he had a second episode. During the first he managed to keep his external behavior reasonably well under control, even though he knew that he was losing his mind. The second was much more powerful: at one point he attempted to run naked through the streets, in the manner of Archimedes, to announce that the millennium had arrived. He was then hospitalized.

The experience of being a patient in a mental hospital was not, for Adams, a painful or embittering one. He was in a small and well-run hospital under the care of a psychiatrist who was a personal friend. His wife refused to consent to electroshock therapy, and after the most intense phase of the episode had passed, he was permitted to discontinue taking medication so that he could think more clearly and try to assimilate what had happened to him.

He did not believe that he had been persecuted, but nevertheless he came away from his period of hospitalization with a radically altered view of the mental health establishment. He had been around and seen it from the other side, and he was not impressed by what he had seen.

He no longer believed that its collective wisdom contained any particularly helpful insights into what madness was about.

He did not doubt that he had been psychotic. There is a deep strain of Texas conservatism in Adams (in his madness he had experienced paranoid fears of communists and had fancied himself at one point to be a reincarnation of John Calvin), and he never adopted the notion, chic in some circles, that psychosis is a higher form of sanity. Psychosis, as far as he was concerned, is mostly craziness. Yet he had come to believe that the craziness signaled the awakening of something, a rough attempt of the human organism to grow, and that in among the fantasies and hallucinations there were crystal-clear moments of insight into the truth, glimpses of reality that the sane mind never quite permits itself to see. He also came to believe that most of the procedures for dealing with psychosis were elaborate structures of deceit and intrigue, which were no help at all to patients in regaining sanity and, if anything, served only to drive them farther into madness.

Adams was certainly not the only psychotherapist who ever had an experience of being a mental patient. But he was unique in choosing to be quite open about the experience and in regarding it as a valuable part of his professional development. He thought the experience would make him a better psychologist, and he was naïve enough to believe that his colleagues would think so, too. They did not, of course. He applied for a low-paying hospital job and was turned down. He tried to launch a research program to study the effects of teaching psychology to mental patients; he had found his knowledge of psychology (especially Jung's work) to be most helpful in understanding his own psychosis and thought such information might help others as well. The director of research at one hospital liked the project, but the application was turned down by the hospital administrators. Adams was never told precisely why, but he reasonably assumed that the authorities thought it would be a bit far-out to have a former mental patient—even though he was also a distinguished psychologist—lecturing to the inmates about Jung and Reich and Harry Stack Sullivan, encouraging them to read sociologist Erving Goffman's analysis of mental asylums and the works of the renegade psychiatrist Thomas Szasz, who thought modern psychiatry was roughly equivalent to medieval witch hunting.

Having failed to find any path open to the new role of therapist and patients' rights advocate that he vaguely envisioned, Adams was living in semiseclusion and trying his hand at writing. He was also involved

61

in the early efforts of a small group of psychologists to band together various dissident schools—Jungians, Reichians, existentialists, neo-Freudians, and others—into a new organization that would be called the American Association for Humanistic Psychology. The new organization, its founders hoped, would provide a forum and a source of strength to those whose psychological views tended to be treated with contempt by the Freudian-dominated psychiatric profession and the behaviorist-dominated college departments of psychology. But these activities were only minor fillers of time. When Adams got an invitation to come down to Big Sur and join in leading a weekend youth hostel, he found it easy to accept. He had never been to Big Sur, and he did not have much of anything else to do.

In accepting the invitation, Adams made it clear that he was personally very skeptical about psychic phenomena. LSD trips and two bouts with psychosis had shaken some aspects of his world view, but he remained a hardheaded rationalist, strongly suspicious of all hankerings after the occult and the supernatural. This was fine with Murphy and Price; openness and free inquiry were what they were after. So Carlson and Adams came down and ran a program that was in some respects a debate on psychic phenomena, with Carlson pro, Adams con. Adams talked about the history of psychic research and told of some of the great hoaxes that had been perpetrated in its name. It was a weekend of spirited discussion and debate, with time out for the participants to take long walks, sit in the baths, drink coffee, and talk in the beam-ceilinged dining room at the lodge. The group of twenty-odd students filled up most of the guest rooms. Things seemed to be off to a good start. Adams liked Murphy and Price and was interested in their plans; a couple of months later he drove down to Big Sur again and was there for the next program, a four-day seminar led by the poet Kenneth Rexroth.

This seminar, an extended workshop that ran from a Wednesday afternoon through Sunday morning, was another step in the direction of converting Slate's Hot Springs into a fully operating seminar center. This time Murphy and Price put together the whole package and even printed up a brochure announcing the event, and sent it out to a mailing list of Sequoia Seminars members, Alan Watts followers, and all their personal acquaintances. The seminar leader, Rexroth, was a durable figure of the San Francisco literary scene who had emerged to new prominence with the rise of the Beat Generation writers. Like Alan Watts, he was an elder and mentor to that group, and, like Watts, he occasionally chose to distance himself from it. Generally he preferred to talk about what he called the San Francisco Renaissance, a larger movement whose luminaries included not only the Beats but other writers, like the novelist Herbert Gold and young Dennis Murphy, as well as painters, sculptors, and musicians. He had written about the movement in articles and essays and books. He was also a great student of Oriental art and philosophy, which enabled him to fit comfortably into the Zen-bent San Francisco of the 1950s and gave him an easy connection to the Murphy-Price aspiration of synthesizing the best of Eastern and Western cultures. So he came down to Big Sur to discourse at length on religion, art, literature, cultural change, and other topics, and a capacity crowd of customers came down to hear him and talk with him.

People from up and down the California coast were already discovering, in the spring of 1962, that a trip to Big Sur was a very pleasant way to pass a few days—a beautiful, albeit harrowing, drive along Highway 1, a chance to spend some time in the presence of a prominent thinker, an opportunity for good meals and conviviality in the bar, walks among the pines, and restful soaks in the hot tubs overlooking the Pacific.

Murphy and Price began to assemble a staff. One of the first to sign on was Gia-fu Feng, Price's old friend from the San Francisco Zen Center. Gia-fu, a diminutive, smiling man, occupied several different roles: accountant (he brought his own abacus), keeper of the baths, resident Oriental mystic. Another all-around hand was Bill Quinn, a man in his mid-thirties who had been a follower of Krishnamurti and a student at the Academy of Asian Studies. For a while Murphy's mother came down to Big Sur to cook for the guests. This did not work out too well. Marie was an excellent cook who gave magnificent dinner parties at home, but she had never before taken on the challenge of serving up three meals a day to a shifting population of motel guests. The clientele at the time consisted of seminar and hostel participants, passing tourists, and laborers working on the new bridge that the state highway department was building across Hot Springs Creek.

Through the summer of 1962 Murphy and Price were busy composing a brochure that would formally announce their seminar center. It would include a series of programs, all grouped together under some general thematic heading. The choice of a theme, a basic title or slogan to announce what they were about, was a hard one. They sifted through the writings of various philosophers of evolutionary transformation, such as Sri Aurobindo and Teilhard de Chardin, considered and discarded several concepts and phrases. Finally they turned to Huxley. He had spoken of "human potentialities"; they offered their first series of programs under the heading "The Human Potentiality."

The Big Sur coastline. (JOYCE ROGERS)

John and Marie Murphy, late 1930s. (COURTESY OF DULCE MURPHY)

Michael and Dennis Murphy, ages fourteen and twelve, at Big Sur. (COURTESY OF DULCE MURPHY)

The baths, late 1930s. (COURTESY DULCE MURPHY)

Late 1950s gathering of Henry Miller and friends at Emil White's cabin, at what was then Slate's Hot Springs. (White is standing, wearing a white shirt; Miller is seated, far right.)
(F. FLORIAN)

Henry Miller at the baths, mid-1950s. This bathhouse was later destroyed by a landslide and a new one was constructed in the same spot. (COURTESY EMIL WHITE)

Richard Price and Michael Murphy breaking ground for their new project, 1962. The main lodge and buildings of the hot springs resort are in the background. (RICHARD ROWAN)

Entrance to the Esalen property, mid-1960s. (PAUL HERBERT)

Human potentiality. It had a down-to-earth sound to it, yet allowed room for great expectations. It was clear in its meaning, yet ambiguous enough to accommodate psychologists and mystics, scientists and artists, professors and poets.

So began the era that Murphy and Price would later talk about as the Apollonian age, the time of lofty thoughts and intellectual discourse. Its common project was what they generally described as the Vision. This was a vision of what was happening in the world, or what could perhaps be made to happen: a major cultural change, an evolutionary leap, a psychological revolution. The Vision was forming, it was powerful, and yet it was elusive. It needed to be thought about and talked about, approached from many directions. And it needed concepts, terminology—such as "human potentiality"—to give it concreteness and a core of ideas on which people of divergent views could agree. It also needed to be made respectable, and in this regard it was helpful to be able to link it to someone of Huxley's stature.

Huxley himself took an interest in the doings at Big Sur. He corresponded with Murphy and Price and came to visit them in January of 1962, the same month that Alan Watts gave his first lecture there. Huxley's first wife, Maria, had died and he had remarried. Laura, his second wife, was a musician, a lay psychotherapist, and an avid student of the things Huxley talked about in his Human Potentialities lectures. Aldous Huxley had less than two years to live at the time of that visit and did not return to Big Sur again, but Laura Huxley returned many times, first as a seminar participant and later as a leader, and remained one of the most faithful friends of Esalen, as the community came to be known in 1964.

Another important contributor to the Vision was Abraham Maslow. Maslow, then teaching at Brandeis University, was a psychologist with a national reputation, and an activist who, during the 1960s, spoke with sympathy and unpretentious eloquence to the needs of that restless decade. He thought that both of the dominant schools of psychology, the Freudian and the behaviorist, had become so preoccupied with mental illness that they had lost sight of mental health. "It becomes more and more clear," he had written in 1954, "that the study of crippled, stunted, immature, and unhealthy specimens can yield only a cripple psychology and a cripple philosophy."[1] To counter this, he embarked on a study of healthy, fully functioning human beings—self-actualizers, he called them, adopting a phrase of the Frankfurt psychologist Kurt Goldstein—and hoped to convince his fellow psychologists that optimum human development was a proper subject for scientific study. He also thought he might interest them in taking a thoughtful look at the phenomena he called peak experiences, those powerful moments of clarity, joy, or religious ecstasy which occur in the lives of so many people, but which most psychologists since William James had been inclined to dismiss as mere aberrations. A newfound respect for the higher reaches of human health was needed, Maslow thought, not only in academic circles but in American society generally. In his 1962 book *Toward a Psychology of Being,* he wrote:

> Every age but ours has had its model, its hero. All these have been given us by our culture; the hero, the gentleman, the knight, the mystic. About all we have left is the well-adjusted man without problems, a very pale and doubtful substitute. Perhaps we shall soon be able to use as our guide and model the fully growing and self-fulfilling human being, the one in whom all his potentialities are coming to full development, the one whose inner nature expresses itself freely, rather than being warped, repressed, or denied.[2]

Toward a Psychology of Being was one of those books that goes around changing people's lives. Like Frederick Perls's *Gestalt Therapy,* the book that Aldous Huxley and Alan Watts often recommended in their lectures, it was talked about, passed along from person to person, cherished, read, and remembered. People would get into conversations about significant events in their lives, ask each other if they could remember turning points, and often, after thinking about it for a while, would answer, "Well, I read this book . . ." Its message was so simple, yet so different from most psychology. It affirmed that life was, and could be for everybody, something deeper and richer.

Maslow used to say that he had started out on his particular line of inquiry (after having been a conventional behaviorist) by trying to figure out what it was in the people he admired that was most admirable. Gradually this had evolved into a systematic search for principles of health, and to research into self-actualization. Most of the people whom Maslow took as his models of health were scholars, intellectuals of one sort or another. It was always part of his own vision (a point that was often missed as the growth and self-fulfillment ethic spread) that health involved making use of one's mental abilities, and doing so with some social purpose in mind.

To many people, Maslow was as good a model of self-actualization as they could find anywhere. With a graying crew cut and a round and homely face, he was a hard-working theorist and researcher who had reached the top ranks of his discipline, but was still an unpretentious, available person. Although a proponent of freedom, he was a solid family man, inseparable from his wife, Bertha. People who knew him and loved him—and there were many—always recalled his warmth and generosity. The only thing anybody had against him was that sometimes he seemed *too* nice, *too* warm and generous, suspiciously lacking in rough edges. Gregory Bateson, who didn't much care for Maslow, would sniff and say, "He was always so *good.*"

In the summer of 1962, in one of those events that made it easy to believe some higher power had a personal interest in the Vision, Abe and Bertha Maslow came driving down the road to Slate's Hot Springs. They had never met Murphy or Price, did not know about them or the project that was then being cooked up at the little resort. They merely happened to be vacationing in California that summer, driving along Highway 1 and looking for a place to spend the night. They came into the office—Gia-fu was on desk duty at the time—asked for a room, and signed the register. Gia-fu looked at the name and recognized it. He ran off and got the copy of *Toward a Psychology of Being* that Murphy had given him and asked Maslow if he was the same Abraham Maslow who had written the book. Maslow said yes, he was. Gia-fu began bowing repeatedly, saying, "Maslow! Maslow! Maslow!" Price came and introduced himself (Murphy was away from the springs that day) and told the Maslows something about what they were hoping to do there. Maslow was interested. He corresponded with them afterward, carefully read the brochures they sent him, and thought the work at

Big Sur might be of great value. He became one of the institute's strongest boosters through the Apollonian period, and once called Esalen one of the country's most important educational institutions. The statement became what was probably the institute's best-known testimonial.

The series of workshops that Murphy and Price had put together in the first Human Potentiality brochure in that summer of 1962—the real beginning of their institute as an ongoing operation—was made up mostly of people who lived in the Stanford area and had some connections, close or remote, with the university.

The first seminar was a survey of the Vision. It was entitled "The Expanding Vision" and was led by Willis Harman, a Stanford professor of engineering who had branched out into multidisciplinary explorations far beyond the dry subject matter of his own department. The seminar was described in the brochure as "a review of the current conceptual revolution in psychology." Like the descriptions of many other seminars that appeared in the brochures in the institute's early years, this one came complete with a list of recommended readings: John Langton-Davies' *On the Nature of Man,* Maslow's *Toward a Psychology of Being,* Kenneth Walker's *Diagnosis of Man,* Franz Winkler's *Man: The Bridge Between Two Worlds.*

As the titles suggest, the books were ambitious speculations about the human species. They were mostly works of psychology, but they were psychology mixed with philosophy, evolutionary theory, religions Eastern and Western. Franz Winkler, for example, was an Austrian-born New York psychiatrist who also happened to be a follower of Rudolf Steiner, probably the best-known popularizer of the esoteric doctrines of Buddhist and Hindu philosophy in late-nineteenth-century and early-twentieth-century Europe.

Winkler's book argued for a rediscovery of the capacity for intuitive thought to balance and inform rational/cognitive thinking. Winkler believed that Western society needed new techniques of education to develop intuitive thinking and should pay more attention to the wisdom available from religion, art, and nature. The book ended with a call for a new and different kind of space program, completely different from the one that gripped the public's imagination in those astronaut-happy years:

The new frontier of our age does not lie in outer space, but in the human soul. All the bewildering events of this era are mere portents. They give warning that the torch of individual consciousness can no longer shed sufficient light and meaning on the vast expanse of man's material domains. New resources must be opened in the human soul, if man is not to lose himself in the conquest of outer space or turn his heart to stone while building a civilization of robots.

We are living in a stage of history as much in need of inner exploits as the fifteenth century was of geographical exploration.[3]

Such were the ideas that circulated at Big Sur Hot Springs, as it was then called, in the summer and fall of 1962. Bear in mind that it was all purely intellectual discussion: a couple of dozen people seated in wooden chairs, listening to a professor from Stanford talking about opening up new resources in the human soul. It was thrilling, in a cerebral way, and it was safe.

The age of risk-taking had not yet dawned at Big Sur. Neither Murphy nor Price had any strongly developed notions about an experiential component to the Vision, any idea that people who came to programs at Big Sur would do anything other than talk or listen. They did, it is true, give a fair amount of attention to the arts as one method for exploring other dimensions of human consciousness. They held poetry readings and concerts of folk and chamber music and theatrical presentations in the lodge from time to time, sometimes as scheduled events and sometimes as additions to the formal program. But most of these readings, recitals, and performances were still in the realm of culture, not counterculture.

But the Apollonian era was short-lived. Almost from the time the first programs were held, there was an expressed yearning for something else, some way of turning those lofty concepts into lived reality. You cannot, it turned out, tell people that human life can be immeasurably better without their wanting to get some taste of the better living as soon as possible. You cannot discuss the Zen concept of satori, instantaneous spiritual awakening, as Watts did, or study peak experiences, as Maslow did, or sound calls for inner exploits, as Winkler wrote in the closing passage of his book, without some of those in hearing range saying, All right, lead me to them.

And the criticisms of the rational mind were bound to take their toll. It was inevitable that sooner or later somebody would start doing something irrational. Murphy and Price, enamored of the positive, creative side of change, were rather naïve about the possibility that they or the seminars might be mounting any kind of serious challenge, or, if they were, that anyone might care.

But gauntlets were being flung down on all sides. Willis Harman, the soft-spoken Stanford professor, celebrated intuition in his workshop of October 1962, proclaiming that the dimensions of the human mind were immensely greater than contemporary psychology believed. Alan Watts had always insisted that there was something essentially subversive about genuine religious experiences, because in the process of revealing the grandeur of the cosmos they tended to reveal also the silliness and inadequacy of society's official version of reality.

> Such experiences [he said] imply that . . . our normal perception and valuation of the world is a subjective but collective nightmare. They suggest that our ordinary sense of practical reality—of the world as seen on Monday morning—is a construct of socialized conditioning and repression, a system of selective inattention whereby we are taught to screen out aspects and relations within nature which do not accord with the rules of the game of civilized life.[4]

Stronger challenges were forthcoming. In the fall of 1962 there was a seminar called "Individual and Cultural Definitions of Reality," led jointly by Joe K. Adams and Gregory Bateson. It was a well-reasoned and intelligently argued attack on some of the basic ideas and institutions of Western civilization.

Watts had talked about the politics of spiritual experiences; Adams and Bateson talked about how the experiences called psychosis or schizophrenia also bring the individual into conflict with a social reality, one that happens to be supported by a great deal of power. They warned that the belief systems of a society are also power structures, capable of defending themselves in malevolent and devious ways. They talked about definitions of reality. The society, they said, defines reality in a certain way, and labels that definition sanity. A person who sees things differently is called insane and is subject to certain kinds of social disapproval and punishment. Adams knew about this. "Once a patient is admitted to a mental hospital," he said, "he is likely to be treated . . . as though his conscious processes, the ways in which he sees the world, have no validity." This absolutely ruled out the possibility that the patient might have any valid insights at all, that there might be any area in which the society was wrong and the patient right—or, to put the matter in a slightly different way, any area in which the society (or those who represented it) were lying and the patient was telling the truth. "Mental hospitals," he said, "like our present society in general, tend to be cesspools of intended deception and intrigue."

Bateson had the unusual position of resident anthropologist in the Veterans Administration hospital in Palo Alto, where he was investigating the social context of mental illness, much as he and his former wife, Margaret Mead, had studied the social interactions of natives of Bali and New Guinea. His studies had led him to form an ingenious and novel theory of the cause of schizophrenia, the "double-bind" theory, which held that schizophrenia begins when people are repeatedly given sets of conflicting messages that make it impossible for them to do the right thing. Typically, the giver of such messages is a mother who becomes hostile and withdrawn when approached by her child. When the child responds to the hostile and withdrawn behavior by withdrawing also, the mother suddenly changes and begins to treat the child with feigned loving behavior. The child knows that the loving behavior and words are specious but has to accept them as real. In order to survive, the child must systematically learn to deny his or her own perceptions of reality.

Adams and Bateson were both interested in the same subject—the conflict between individual and cultural definitions of reality—but they were after slightly different game. Bateson was trying to explain the causes of mental illness; Adams was trying to expose the deficiencies in the institutional treatment of it. They did not simply say that society is crazy and mental patients are sane, or that one version of reality is about as good as another—ideas that were to gain some popularity before the decade was out—but they were nevertheless toying with one of the most explosive ideas of the twentieth century: the idea that social belief systems, definitions of reality itself, are relative truths, open to challenge, subject to change.

If you had attended the next weekend workshop in the series, you would have gathered one very good clue as to how the institute's Apollonian phase might end, how the visitors to Big Sur might make the transition from merely talking about the unexplored territories of the mind to embarking on some do-it-yourself travels through inner space. The seminar was entitled "Drug-Induced Mysticism" and was led by Paul Kurtz, a psychologist, and Myron Stolaroff, an inventor and industrialist. Stolaroff was a small, odd-looking man, a Russian-born inventor who had made a fortune in the electronics business. The legend about him was that he had obtained, during World War II, a German recording device that used magnetic tape. After the war he had developed a similar device and, with the help of a few investors, launched Ampex, the first manufacturer of tape-recording equipment. Ampex prospered, and Stolaroff retired from the business and took an interest in LSD research. He and Kurtz had founded an organization called the International Foundation for Advanced Studies, which was actively engaged in research with LSD.

This was about a year before LSD was discovered by the national mass media, but it was already well known to most of the people involved in leading seminars at Big Sur. Every one of the program leaders listed in the first Human Potentiality brochure—Harman, Adams, Bateson, Heard, Kurtz, Stolaroff—had participated in LSD experiments.

The psychedelic movement predated the human potential movement by a good eight years, yet the origins of both are closely connected to the same person: Aldous Huxley. Psychopharmacology was making rapid strides in the late 1950s, with whole new classes of substances coming into use—the tranquilizers—and others being studied by researchers. LSD, one of the most powerful of the new substances, was being tried as a cure for schizophrenia, alcoholism, and various other problems. In the early 1950s Huxley had befriended a young English psychiatrist, Humphrey Osmond, who was then working at a mental hospital in Saskatchewan, doing research on mescalin as a treatment agent in cases of schizophrenia. He invented a new word, psychedelic, meaning mind-manifesting, to describe such drugs as mescalin and LSD. When Osmond visited Huxley in Los Angeles in 1953, he found the author not only knowledgeable about his research, but eager to find out personally what mescalin was like. "Thus it came about," Huxley wrote, "that, one bright May morning, I swallowed four-tenths of a gram of mescalin dissolved in a half a glass of water and sat down to wait for the results." Osmond and

Maria, Huxley's wife, both stayed with him throughout the eight-hour session.

The experience was, for Huxley, a profoundly positive and meaningful one. He had no hallucinations, but he discovered an amazing beauty and significance in ordinary objects:

> The books, for example, with which my study walls were lined. Like the flowers, they glowed, when I looked at them, with brighter colors, a profounder significance. Red books, like rubies; emerald books; books bound in white jade; books of agate; of aquamarine, of yellow topaz; lapis lazuli books whose color was so intense, so intrinsically meaningful, that they seemed to be on the point of leaving the shelves to thrust themselves more insistently on my attention.[5]

He wrote a book about this, a straightforward account of what had happened to him, the title taken from William Blake's poem *The Marriage of Heaven and Hell*: "If the doors of perception were cleansed every thing would appear to man as it is, infinite. / For man has closed himself up, till he sees all things thro' narrow chinks of his cavern."

The Doors of Perception was a small book, but in its way one of the most important of the decade. It was a disturber of the peace, a troublesome challenge to the prevailing ideas about drugs. The social consensus held at that time by the vast majority of civilized people in the Western world was made up of certain generally accepted axioms about drug use:

To use drugs is to escape from reality.

Drug users are misfits and deviants.

Drug use leads to addiction.

Drug use produces short-range pleasures and long-range suffering.

Now here was a world-famous author, most unlike the archetypal Dope Fiend, proclaiming that drug use brought him a heightened ability to perceive and appreciate reality, apparently unaccompanied by any compulsive need to repeat the experience. Without making any attempt to *argue* about anything, Huxley shook the foundations of all these stereotypical beliefs. The book was controversial, and it was influential. Many people who read it developed a new interest in the subject and became willing to consider that there might be a positive side to drug-induced experiences.

In the early 1960s, those on the West Coast who were involved in

LSD research at such places as the Mental Research Institute in Palo Alto were hearing about work that was being done at Harvard's Center for Research in Personality by two young psychologists, Timothy Leary and Richard Alpert. Leary and Alpert had begun by giving psilocybin, a synthetic form of mescalin, to maximum-security inmates at a Massachusetts prison, and had then moved into a freewheeling program that, over the next couple of years, administered some thirty-five-hundred doses of psilocybin to volunteers, many of them Harvard students. This was not the kind of research the authorities at Harvard had had in mind, and they ordered Leary and Alpert to separate their psilocybin activities from the university. The two then formed a new organization of their own, the International Foundation for Internal Freedom. IFIF was launched in November 1962, the same month that Kurtz and Stolaroff were lecturing about drug-induced mysticism at Esalen. The psychedelic movement was proceeding rapidly, and Leary was becoming its chief spokesman, a role for which Huxley thought he was ill suited.

> Yes, what about Tim Leary [Huxley wrote to Osmond in December 1962]? I spent an evening with him here a few weeks ago—and he talked such nonsense (about the conscious mind being merely a robot, about true intelligence residing only in the DNA molecule, about some kind of Providence looking after the population problem, which therefore wasn't any problem at all) that I became quite concerned. Not about his sanity—because he is perfectly sane—but about his prospects in the world; for this nonsense-talking is just another device for annoying people in authority, flouting convention, cocking snooks at the academic world. It is the reaction of a mischievous Irish boy to the headmaster of his school. One of these days the headmaster will lose patience—and then good-bye to Tim's psilocybin research. I am very fond of Tim—but why, oh why, does he *have* to be such an ass? I have told him repeatedly that the only attitude for a researcher in this ticklish field is that of an anthropologist living in the midst of a tribe of potentially dangerous savages. Go about your business quietly, don't break the taboos or criticize the locally accepted dogmas. Be polite and friendly—and get on with the job.[6]

Apparently Huxley did not know at the time he wrote the letter how accurate his predictions were. Harvard, having said good-bye to Leary's psilocybin research, was preparing to say good-bye to Leary, who was fired in the spring of 1963. Leary and Alpert (who had been dismissed also) went forth into the world with the message that the psychological revolution was about to take place, and that it would be a *psychedelic* revolution, brought about by chemicals. The psychedelic drugs would bring the transcendent religious experience within reach of everybody, overthrow the old consciousness that is the source of all oppression, and swiftly change the world.

If there was any rival to Leary as a spokesman for psychedelia (other than Huxley himself), it was Alan Watts. Watts described his own experience with various drugs in a book entitled *The Joyous Cosmology*, which was published in 1962. Watts was much more reserved in his pronouncements. He did not prophesy imminent cultural transformations as a result of drug-induced revelation, nor did he (as Leary did) speak of chemically induced enlightenment. He merely suggested that the psychedelics had the potential, if they were used in the proper context—perhaps in conjunction with psychotherapy, a spiritual discipline, or changes in one's pattern of life—to bring about a genuine change of consciousness. Watts and Leary were good friends and considered themselves allies, but their personal styles were different. Leary liked to blow people's minds, but Watts was more inclined to discuss the matter in a literate (in fact, highly intellectual) way, while chuckling over the foolishness of the conscious intellect that thought itself sane and in control. In the end he probably blew more minds than Leary did, and he never went to jail.

The psychedelics rapidly became a matter of social controversy, reflecting a larger polarization that was beginning to take place. On the one hand were those who saw the need for new values, new ethics, new consciousness; on the other were those who strove to protect those bastions against the strange new assaults that were being mounted against them. It was a new *kind* of conflict, and it took the mass media and the public a while to make the connection between consciousness and political power. Leary and Alpert, in their speeches and writings, frequently drew attention to the connection, as in their 1963 *Harvard Review* article, "The Politics of Consciousness Expansion," which described the university as "the Establishment's apparatus for training consciousness-contractors. The intellectual ministry of defense."[7] The mind was the Bastille in this new version of oppression; mescalin, psilocybin and LSD were the weapons of the revolutionaries.

The immediate and specific issue involved was who should be allowed to use the psychedelic drugs. The legal situation was murky.

Drugs could be obtained for use by "qualified" researchers, but the qualifications were not always clearly defined. Those who were then legally experimenting with LSD and other psychedelics feared an offical crackdown. The first hint of this came in 1962, during the first series of Human Potentiality programs at Big Sur. Murphy, sleeping in his room at the Big House, awoke one Sunday morning to find Myron Stolaroff sitting on the foot of his bed, patiently waiting for Murphy to wake up. Then he said, "Mike, the audience here this weekend is full of agents, and I have to leave immediately."

"How do you know there are agents? I didn't see any agents," Murphy replied.

"You wouldn't know them," Stolaroff said mysteriously. He did not say what kinds of agents they were, but insisted that he could not safely continue with the program. His work at the institute was too delicate, as he put it, and might be contaminated. Murphy did not really believe there were agents in the audience that particular weekend, but still it was a strange and disturbing incident. It raised the possibility that some people not only might disapprove of the Apollonian discussions at the hot springs, but might even consider them illegal.

Murphy had already had his own experience with a psychedelic drug a few months earlier, not long before the first Human Potentiality series. A young man named Jack Leffler came to Big Sur and got a job working in the lodge. He was a loner and a mystic. Among his many adventures had been an experience with the peyote rites of the Southwestern Indians. He still had some of this peyote, a bunch of little dry mushroomlike buttons. They were old, and he wasn't sure they still worked, but he told Michael he was welcome to try them. So Murphy chewed a bunch of peyote buttons and waited for something to happen. An hour or two went by and nothing happened, so Leffler went off to the lodge to do his chores, and Murphy went to his room upstairs in the Big House.

As he lay on his bed, he became aware that, sure enough, something was happening. It didn't seem to be anything like what had happened to Aldous Huxley, according to *The Doors of Perception.* Murphy kept getting the sensation of something like a camera shutter at work in his mind. It would pop open, quickly, and he would catch a glimpse of something different, almost as though there were some other world being revealed to him in teasing instants. He played with that for a while, and then his attention drifted to the curve of the roof that he could see through his window. It came curving upward at the end, like the smile of the Mona Lisa, and he began to think of all the wry things in life, all the things that had that bitter, humorous, little upward twist to them. He was tripping along on that when the door flew open and Gia-fu entered.

Gia-fu, for all his sly go-with-the-flow suppleness, had an explosive side to him that surprised people sometimes; he would burst upon them like a small firecracker, usually with some piece of news to be announced in breathless urgency. This time the news was that a group of women connected with some church had arrived, and he was showing them around the property. That was all. But Gia-fu delivered the message with great intensity. What he said was "Michael! I have many heavy Christian ladies, led by Mrs. Lightfoot!"

Murphy started laughing and, once started, couldn't stop.

Gia-fu didn't know that Murphy was stoned out of his mind on peyote, nor apparently did he pay any heed to the fact that Murphy was unable to stand up. All he knew was that he had said something about heavy ladies led by Mrs. Lightfoot and that Murphy seemed to think it was exceedingly funny. He decided it *was* funny, and started laughing also. The two of them whooped and hollered until Gia-fu staggered out of the room, holding his sides, to rejoin his guests. Through the open window, Murphy could hear his Oriental cackle echoing among the hills as Gia-fu led the bewildered Christian ladies back across Hot Springs Creek.

The peyote trip lasted, in all, about six hours. During the afternoon and evening the word spread among the small population of Big Sur that Murphy was up there in his room, doing his solo version of the peyote rites, and one by one they went up to visit him. Richard Price came in for a while and sat silently. Dennis looked in, and Michael saw his brother as an Indian warrior, fierce and battle-scarred. Erica Weston—a granddaughter of the photographer Edward Weston—who had come to work at Big Sur, entered just as it was growing dark and lit a candle.

Murphy was thirty-one years old and still a virgin. Back in Salinas, in the pubescent high school years, there had been two distinct sexual groups: the boys from the farms and the working-class families who moved quickly into sexual activity, got their girl friends pregnant, and married soon after graduation; and the nice guys, the clean-cut kids headed for college, who seemed to take longer getting started. Murphy was definitely in the second category. Probably that would have changed in his college years, if he had not taken his detour into mysticism and philosophy. For eleven years, his life had consisted mainly of meditation and reading. And chastity.

In the first few minutes the young woman was in the room, he saw her many different ways. She was at first terribly repulsive, then an Earth Mother, a toothless old woman, a gigantic Indian squaw (the Indian motif kept repeating itself), and then she became incredibly beautiful. She took on a rich, sensuous, Rubens-like beauty, appealing and erotic.

Nothing much happened in the room that evening, outwardly. But at some deeper level, Murphy had changed. After that, it would be only a matter of time, and not very much time at that, before he moved into full sexual activity.

5

It was hardly surprising that Murphy, who was primarily responsible for what went into programming, heeded those who thought Big Sur's programs needed something in the way of *activity*. He felt a similar urge. So much was happening to him, such a kaleidoscopic onrush of new experiences: all the contact with great and famous people, all these seekers, customers, friends, and strange characters continually pouring through Big Sur, the exhilarating work of running the business, not to mention his personal sally into the realms of psychedelia and sexuality.

The second Human Potentiality series, which ran through the winter and spring of 1963, showed a distinct shift toward more variety in the programming. There were still weekends devoted to verbal explorations of Great Ideas ("The Vision of Sri Aurobindo," "The Evolution of Human Experience"), but there was also a weekend prayer and meditation retreat; two weekend seminars on the psychedelics (intended as intellectual discussions, although those who attended were frequently inspired by the subject matter to bring their own supplies and use them on the premises during the weekend); more activities involving art, music, and poetry; and programs that presented the first tentative samplings of what would become the three basic components of the Esalen inventory: encounter, gestalt therapy, and body work.

All three of these personal-development commodities soon became so strongly identified in the public mind with the Esalen Institute, California, and with the 1960s that many people seemed to have the impression they had been cooked up overnight by a group of suntanned West Coast entrepreneurs. But all of the methods that became popular at Esalen were anchored firmly in Europe in the early decades of the twentieth century. It is quite possible that some Continental version of the human potential movement would have emerged in

Austria or German thirty years earlier, perhaps in one of those spas which Dr. Murphy and his wife visited, if Hitler and the war had not come along to break everything apart. Instead, those seeds of thought dispersed and drifted for a few decades before landing in the fertile soil of California.

The *idea* of encounter abounds in the works of European sociologists and philosophers. The early-twentieth-century existentialists worried about the increasing alienation in modern society and hoped some way would be found to remedy the absence of authentic interaction between people. In *I and Thou,* which was published in 1923 and became a kind of manifesto of existentialism, Martin Buber charged that "modern developments have expunged almost every trace of a life in which human beings confront each other and have meaningful relationships." Buber saw this as a severe social malaise that could be cured only through a rediscovery of human closeness.

Many agreed with Buber's diagnosis, but few knew what to do about it. The changes that had created the problem—industrialization, urbanization—were not reversible, and if the old sense of community were to be regained, apparently it could be done only through the invention of new social forms, perhaps new rituals. One person who had ideas about this—lots of them—was an excitable young Austrian psychiatrist named Jacob Levy Moreno.

Moreno believed that alienation, the separation that prevented people from interacting deeply with one another, was not only a social problem but a spiritual crisis. As early as 1908, when he was scarcely out of his adolescence, he tried to start a "religion of encounter." Later, as a practicing psychiatrist, he experimented with therapy done in groups instead of on a one-to-one basis between patient and therapist. Moreno also edited a literary magazine called *Daimon* (whose most famous contributor was Martin Buber) and for some years was involved with an avant-garde drama group called the Stegreiftheatre (Spontaneity Theater). Moreno believed that all written plays were rigid artifacts of past culture that inhibited genuine self-expression and were therefore on the side of the forces of alienation. Spontaneity was what the world needed.

In the 1920s and 1930s Moreno drew together all his theological, philosophical, psychiatric, and artistic interests for the creation of an entirely new form of therapy, which he called psychodrama, a group

80

process in which the therapist was like a director and the members of the group took part in spontaneous enactments of real or imagined life scenes. People would play themselves, and sometimes they would reverse roles and play other people. They would re-enact dreams and past experiences, or they would create entirely new scenes to express their feelings. Acting out, the psychodramatists called it.

To Freudian psychoanalysts the term was familiar, but it carried an entirely different value connotation. Acting out meant to express the emotions—to shout or weep. The desire to act out should, they thought, be restrained during the course of therapy while the patient sought to become better adjusted to society's ideas of proper behavior. Moreno had created the psychodramatic setting, although a relatively safe one, for the precise purpose of *letting* people lose their inhibitions and act out. It was one of the first forms of therapy (Wilhelm Reich would later move in a similar direction) in which the goal was not only insight, but catharsis.

Moreno talked a lot about spontaneity. For him it had a truly religious importance. It was the life force, the creative spirit of the cosmos. Spontaneity, he said, was being wrung out of people by the numbing experiences of regimented modern life, and it was spontaneity that he hoped to have people rediscover in psychodrama therapy, which he also referred to as spontaneity training. The psychodrama session was, for Moreno, therapy, social ritual, and religious ceremony all in one. He offered it as his personal antidote to dehumanization, and he immodestly offered himself as a model of the spontaneous, unadjusted, acting-out human being in the flesh.

> I wanted to show [he said of himself] that here is a man who has all the signs of paranoia and megalomania, exhibitionism and social maladjustment, and who can still be fairly well controlled and healthy, and indeed, of apparently greater productivity by acting them out than if he would have tried to constrain and resolve his symptoms—the living antithesis of psychoanalysis.[1]

Moreno transferred his operations from Vienna to New York in 1925 and went to work promoting psychodrama. He was an ambitious man who dreamed of an intellectual empire that would be at least the equal of Freud's. And he was, without doubt, productive. He wrote books and articles, founded a professional society and a journal, held public psychodrama sessions for years in New York City, gave lecture-demonstrations at colleges and professional meetings, and opened a training center in upstate New York. He also developed a research method, called sociometry, for measuring the hidden substructure of interpersonal relationships in groups. He attracted followers, but many people who were interested in his ideas were not charmed by his megalomania. Sociometry slipped away from his control and was absorbed into the growing academic discipline of social psychology; psychodrama found its way into new experiential methods, such as sensitivity training.

The origins of sensitivity training can be found in a human relations workshop that was held at a state teachers' college in New Britain, Connecticut, in 1946. The purpose of the workshop was to train a group of people, most of them teachers and social workers, to work in their communities on behalf of fair employment practices. One of the sponsoring organizations, the Research Center for Group Dynamics at the Massachusetts Institute of Technology, was also interested in observing the workshop and gathering some data about it. Most of the people running the program were connected with the center, and many of them, including the head researcher, Kurt Lewin, had training in psychodrama and sociometry.

The workshop was pretty much the same as a lot of human relations programs that were current in those days. What people did was discuss, in great detail, the situations they had to deal with in their communities, take in information spooned out to them by the leaders, and occasionally participate in sessions of a mild-mannered adaptation of psychodrama called role-playing. It was extremely businesslike and quite dull. During each session a research observer was present, a remote, inscrutable character who made notes to himself about the behavior of the group and its individual members.

What made this workshop different was a decision, which seemed inconsequential at the time, to let some of the participants attend the meetings at which the trainers and researchers got together to pool their data and evaluate the progress of the workshop. No one guessed the far-reaching implications of that decision. The few participants who attended the first of these evening sessions soon tired of sitting quietly and listening to a bunch of professors and graduate students talk about what had happened. Some of them challenged the reports, said that wasn't the way it had happened at all, and offered their own versions. There were some tense, heated confrontations, yet there was also a growing sense of exhilaration. The evaluation process was out in the open at last, with people working together to analyze the workshop. Some of the participants were getting, directly from the observers, feedback on how their behavior had been perceived.

The word spread quickly, and soon all of the participants in the workshop were coming to the evening meetings to hear the researchers' reports and offer their own perceptions in an open, honest exchange—an encounter. The leaders of the workshop began to think that they had accidentally stumbled on a powerful method of human relations training.

They did not quite realize at the time—although they became more explicit about it later—that what they had done was to shift the focus from the "there and then," the situations that people dealt with back in their communities and then talked about in the group, to the group itself. The group became the mirror in which each person caught the reflection of his or her personal style of interaction; it became the laboratory for working out interpersonal conflicts and communications breakdowns. It was a living replica of all the other groups—the departments, committees, boards of directors, and management teams —that the participants dealt with in their working lives. In the same way that psychodrama, or spontaneity training, created a relatively secure environment in which people, by acting out, gained insight into their personal behaviors, the group created a safe place that allowed people to let off steam, tell each other the truth, and develop new communication skills. The people who took part in the invention of this new group process called it sensitivity training.

After the New Britain workshop things moved along quickly. The following summer, at a three-week workshop at Bethel, Maine, the kind of group meeting that had evolved accidentally at New Britain was made the core of the whole program. This workshop led to the establishment of a new organization, National Training Laboratories, whose stock-in-trade was workshops based on the new group model.

The first NTL workshop leaders used most of the methods adapted from psychodrama that they had used before they discovered the group-interaction process. Role-playing was still one of their favorite tools. Trainers would lead the participants through rehearsals of the situations they confronted back in their jobs and communities, and give them the opportunity to act out different ways of dealing with the problems, to reverse roles with bosses and co-workers. But soon these older methods were discarded by most NTL leaders, and the

feedback meetings—T-groups, they were being called; short for training groups—took over the whole process.

Sensitivity training became popular with many businesses and gov-
ernmental organizations in the 1950s. It was the great psychological
assembly line that helped produce people who were adept at perceiv-
ing the emotional undercurrents of a situation and smoothing off the
rough corners of interpersonal communications. The group process
was stripped of its philosophical heritage, the traces of rebellion
against large organizations that had been present in Buber's work, the
linkage with avant-garde art and spiritual overtones that had been
present in Moreno's. It was given a crew cut and a white shirt and
transformed into boot camp for legions of Eisenhower-era organization men and organization women. True, there were always a few for
whom sensitivity training did not lead onward and upward to new
triumphs in the committee meetings and the board rooms. Some found
that the group process, by permitting them to get in touch with their
feelings, got them in touch with feelings of not wanting to be organizational people after all. There were enough of these T-group drop-
outs, as they were called, to give a few company presidents second
thoughts about sending their bright young executives off to sensitivity-training workshops, but for every one who became disenchanted
with it there were a dozen others discovering it for the first time, and
sensitivity training rode high in corporate America through the 1950s
and early 1960s.

Encounter arrived at Big Sur quietly. In February 1963 Paul Kurtz,
the psychologist who had helped lead the earlier seminar on LSD, led
a workshop entitled "Leadership Training in Group Dynamics." The
workshop was offered more as a training session for professionals than
as a self-discovery event in its own right, and it was a mild and
cerebral gathering, combining some discussion of group-dynamics
theory with a bit of cautious talking about personal feelings in the
group. Michael Murphy, who attended the seminar, found it not much
different from various church retreats he had attended over the years.

Then, a month or so later, Murphy was invited to attend an event
that was being put on by the American Management Association up
at the Highlands Inn at Carmel. It was a five-day T-group for junior
executives, a real *encounter* session in which people talked about their
feelings, confronted each other, worked through their problems right
there in front of everybody. Murphy found the workshop as much of
a mind-blower as psychedelic drugs. In fact, he wrote an essay about

the similarities between the group experience and the drug experience, and concluded that, of the two, groups were more powerful and effective. Groups, he decided, would be one of the New American Yogas—a path of union between the individual and the cosmos. Straight out of the world of the corporations and the bureaucracies came a process that was showing people how to heighten their awareness of one another, to grow and change and communicate. The spiritual view of encounter, the part of it that had gone underground when the sensitivity trainers moved away from Moreno and his philosophy, was suddenly born again.

The other two components, gestalt therapy and body work, both arrived at Big Sur in 1963 and were each connected, directly or indirectly, to Frederick Perls, the founder of gestalt.

Gestalt therapy was introduced as part of another weekend seminar. You would not have guessed from the seminar's title ("The Psychology of Ultimates") or from the descriptive paragraph in the brochure (which made some murky pronouncements about the union of theology with psychology) that it was another leap into the technology of heightened consciousness.

Willis Harman, the Stanford professor of engineering, was scheduled to lead the seminar with Wilson Van Dusen, chief clinical psychologist at Mendocino State Hospital, north of San Francisco, but he changed his mind after the brochures were printed. Harman, like his friend Stolaroff, had developed fears that appearing at Big Sur might jeopardize his research activities. Van Dusen invited another psychologist, Eugene Sagan, to join him in leading the seminar. As a result, it turned out to be entirely different from what had originally been planned; instead of a philosophical discussion, it was a practical demonstration of gestalt therapy.

Several of the people who came to that workshop had heard of gestalt therapy from Aldous Huxley or from Alan Watts, who often mentioned, in his lectures, how closely it paralled the awareness practices in Oriental religions. But few people had actually experienced it, not even Huxley or Watts; they had only read about it in *Gestalt Therapy*. Michael Murphy and Richard Price hadn't even read that much-cited book. They, like the others who gathered in the lodge that weekend, had heard of gestalt therapy only secondhand, from people who said it was good stuff.

Van Dusen and Sagan were precisely one half of all the gestalt therapists then practicing in California. Both had gained their practical training the way future gestalt therapists would soon find themselves doing: by spending as much time as possible in the presence of gestalt therapy's irascible founder, Frederick Perls. (Perls and James Simkin, a former student of his who had moved to Los Angeles, made up the other half of all the California gestalt therapists at this time.)

Van Dusen had discovered Perls at the American Psychological Association meeting in San Francisco in 1958. Perls, then in his mid-sixties, was participating in a panel on psychodrama. A young psychiatrist who spoke just before Perls had gone off on a tangent about world peace, a subject with which he was deeply and passionately involved. Perls, in responding, had called attention to the peculiar wailing quality in the young man's voice.

Well, you didn't *do* that at professional conventions, certainly not in 1958. You stayed with the content, and if you noticed anything about the personal behavior of the speaker, you kept it to yourself. Perls's action was rude and audacious—and electrifying in its effect. The young psychiatrist responded that he was in the middle of a divorce, that he felt as though his world was falling apart, and, yes, he had been wailing. Perls made several impressive interruptions of this sort and eventually took over the meeting. That, Van Dusen learned later, was typical of Perls's style. Some people wailed; he took over meetings.

Van Dusen, a student of existentialism, was tremendously impressed by this elderly German psychiatrist. Perls seemed to be existentialism in action; he acutely observed what people were doing while they were doing it, directed their attention toward their actions, and in the process went straight to the emotional reality of their lives. Van Dusen made arrangements for Perls, who lived in New York, to return to California and serve as a training consultant at Mendocino State Hospital.

Eugene Sagan, a young red-haired psychologist in private practice in Berkeley, was struck by the gestalt thunderbolt about a year later, when he read *Gestalt Therapy*. He looked up Perls, then living in San Francisco and working with Van Dusen, and informally apprenticed himself, accepting an unpaid job as chauffeur in return for the privilege of learning about gestalt therapy firsthand.

Both Van Dusen and Sagan, with practical experience in gestalt work straight from the master, came to Big Sur intending to pass it on. They started out their weekend workshop by explaining some of the principles: the idea of working in the here and now, the goal of integrating the personality and raising awareness of sensory experience. The guests were intrigued, and nobody objected to the change of subject matter. When the leaders asked for volunteers, there was a quiet moment of expectancy in the lodge, a charged hiatus, and then Gia-fu raised his hand and stepped forward to become the first patient. Gestalt therapy had come to Big Sur, just a few weeks behind encounter.

The third major component, body work, arrived in several packages. First there was Gia-fu Feng, who in the mornings would give the guests lessons in the Chinese exercise system called Tai Chi Chuan. ("I remember," somebody once said about his first visits to Esalen, "that there was either a guy there named Gia-fu who taught Tai Chi or a guy named Tai Chi who taught Gia-fu.") There were programs concentrating on relaxation exercises and body movement. These were all proof of the shift away from the exclusively intellectual orientation of the first programs. But the most important development toward making Big Sur known nationally as a center of disciplines involving the body was a program that was organized later in 1963 by Eugene Sagan.

Gene Sagan had fallen in love with Big Sur on his first visit, both with the place and with what was happening there. He became another in its legion of friends and advisers. He was always coming up with new ideas for programs, often calling Murphy long distance—sometimes in the middle of the night—to share his latest inspiration. This time it was a conference entitled "Education of the Imagination"; it was sponsored by the University of California (Berkeley) Extension and was held at Big Sur. Sagan asked Perls to head the teaching staff, which also included Will Schutz, a psychologist connected with the T-group organization, NTL, and Charlotte Selver, a woman who taught a physical-training discipline called "sensory awareness."

It is an indicator of how little appeal human potential events had for the general public in December of 1963 that the program, offered to thousands of people through the university extension catalogue, did not produce the minimum couple of dozen customers and was canceled. Some of the leaders, including Schutz, dropped out. Sagan went ahead and put on a cut-rate version of it anyway.

Although the five-day conference at Big Sur was not an economic success—each of the paid leaders received only $100 plus room and board, and even then Murphy and Price lost money—it brought together an exciting combination of people and skills. Among those present were Murphy and Price, the two founders of Esalen; Perls, the father of gestalt therapy; Sagan, who for years had been using art, music, and psychodrama in his therapeutic practice; Bernard Gunther, a young patient of Perls's from Los Angeles, who had studied yoga and massage; and Charlotte Selver, who, with her husband, Charles Brooks, taught sensory awareness.

Perls had studied with Selver and Brooks in New York, but to the others sensory awareness was entirely new. The teachers used exercises, but these were not fast or strenuous; everything they asked the student to do was easy, relaxing, and gentle. Again and again participants were given permission to relax, pay attention, open up to the sensation, be quiet, and feel.

The discipline Selver and Brooks taught had originated with Elsa Gindler, a young calisthenics teacher in Berlin, who, after being stricken with tuberculosis in 1910, slowly taught herself how to control her own breathing so that she could allow the diseased lung to rest and heal while the other took over the primary function of breathing. After her recovery Gindler began to teach her methods to others. Charlotte Selver studied with her and, in turn, taught students of design at the Bauhaus. After immigrating to the United States in the 1930s, she attracted a growing band of followers in New York. A number of psychiatrists, among them Erich Fromm and Frederick Perls, studied with her in the 1940s. About 1950 she began to describe the work as sensory awareness. Alan Watts discovered her work in 1956, pronounced it to be the essence of Zen, and became a sponsor on the West Coast. In 1963, the year she made her debut at Big Sur, Charles Brooks, her husband and long-time student, a quiet graying man who had been a woodworker, became her co-teacher.

Several things happened as a direct result of the conference. One was that Selver and Brooks were invited back to lead more workshops, and Big Sur soon became the West Coast headquarters of sensory-awareness training. Another was that Bernie Gunther got the idea that he would like to learn more about sensory awareness and get a job at Esalen. The third, which would utterly transform the institute and its reputation, was Fritz Perls's decision to take up residence at Big Sur. This decision was inspired by Gunther, who had begun to take on the role of agent and impresario for Perls. Perls's instructions to him were

"You organize; I function." Gunther organized some lectures in Los Angeles, where Perls demonstrated gestalt therapy. Then Gunther started promoting a training program for prospective gestalt therapists, which led to trouble among Perls's small group of followers. Gunther, who aspired to become a lay gestalt therapist, arranged with Perls to become a trainee, free of charge, if he got the program going. But James Simkin, who had spent years as Perls's patient and student and was by then a successful gestalt therapist in his own right (in fact, Gunther had been his patient first), absolutely opposed letting somebody who wasn't licensed, who didn't even have an advanced degree, become a gestalt therapist. There was a lot of squabbling about this, and Gunther began talking to Perls about using Big Sur as his training center. Perls was not very enthusiastic about Big Sur, but Gunther had seen something there that had escaped Perls: The place had potential.

Perls considered this, and called Michael Murphy and worked out a deal. It was not in any way a big deal. Big Sur Hot Springs had a following of sorts, but it was really only a little resort, hanging on the edge of a California cliff, where a few dozen or so people congregated on weekends to discuss odd subjects. Fritz Perls was seventy-one years old; he had a following of sorts too, but he was a drifter and had never been able to stay long enough in one place to build a solid following for the therapeutic approach that seemed to many people to have such great value. Murphy and Price were a little surprised when Perls proposed to take up residence, but they talked it over and decided to give it a try: Perls would come stay through the summer and give three weekend seminars. Neither of them liked Perls much, but both were impressed and intimidated by him, and he was, after all, the founder of gestalt therapy. So they went along with it, and in the spring of 1964 Perls drove up the coast in his little Fiat. A brilliant, horny, and cantankerous old man, larger than life and not too far from death.

He wanted everybody to call him Fritz. This touch of California informality did not mean he had shed his Old World reverence for academic degrees; on his books he always identified himself as Frederick S. Perls, M.D., Ph.D., even though the Ph.D. was an honorary degree from an unheard-of college in Southern California. It was a matter of packaging: he had a feel for words, and he knew that "Fritz" was a much more zingy trademark than "Dr. Perls."

Once, when he was giving one of his lecture-demonstrations on gestalt therapy in a high school auditorium in Beverly Hills and was chain smoking, as usual, somebody pointed out to him that smoking was not permitted in the auditorium. "Maybe so," he replied, "but I am Fritz." And that closed the subject.

The most striking of Perls's many contradictions was his attitude toward other people's opinions. In one way he simply didn't give a damn what they thought: he would violate rules, behave outrageously, insult anybody, do whatever seemed to suit his own personal standards. But in another way he was hugely needy, mad for approval, forever striving to look good. His hunger for love and attention matched his hunger for many other things. He was like the man in Saul Bellow's *Henderson the Rain King* who marched through the world saying, "I want, I want, I want." The wanting, though, was always flavored with a bitter readiness to be disappointed. He craved closeness, but never counted on finding it. One can hear his bleak world view in a poem of his called the "Gestalt Prayer":

> I do my thing, and you do your thing.
> I am not in this world to live up to your expectations
> And you are not in this world to live up to mine.
> You are you and I am I,
> And if by chance we find each other, it's beautiful.
> If not, it can't be helped.

When Fritz was at the height of his fame in the late 1960s, that hard-nosed little message appeared in the poster shops, printed on huge portraits of Fritz as he appeared then, the human potential Santa Claus with white beard and twinkling eyes. Usually, though, the posters left off the last line of the "Gestalt Prayer," which nobody much wanted to think about. It was the do-your-thing part, the forget-about-other-people's-expectations part, the sometimes-we-connect-and-it's-beautiful part, that sold the posters, made Fritz a pop hero, and brought him hordes of followers. But those who tried to get close to him often failed, because, as it turned out, his own expectations were not easy to live up to.

A major ingredient in the culture that emerged in California in the 1960s, Perls himself was shaped by the culture of Germany in the 1920s and 1930s, another time of economic chaos, political instability, and intellectual ferment. Those were the years when Christopher Isherwood was gathering material for his *Berlin Stories,* Kurt Weill and

Bertolt Brecht were working on *The Threepenny Opera,* Walter Gropius and his associates at the Bauhaus were revolutionizing architecture, art, and design, and other Germans were marching at the front of such movements as existentialism and psychoanalysis.

Fritz, born in Berlin in 1893, got his M.D. from Friedrich Wilhelm University in 1921 (after an education interrupted by World War I and a period of military service in France) and went into training to become a psychoanalyst. Like Freud, he had artistic aspirations as well as scientific ones; in later years he would call the medical profession the sick road to the humanities.

Most of his fellow Freudians, perhaps seeking to offset the bizarre aspects of psychoanalysis itself, chose to adopt conservative, even stodgy, personal life styles. But Fritz went the other way, hanging out with the artists and writers at the Romanische Café, taking an interest in the politics of the feuding Marxist parties, and characterizing himself as one of the Berlin Bohemians.

In 1926 he went to Frankfurt. It was not as much of a cultural center as Berlin, but two of the leading German existentialists, Martin Buber and Paul Tillich, were there. And though there was no such thing as gestalt therapy yet, there was gestalt psychology, a body of experimental data and theory, mainly having to do with how the brain receives and organizes sensory inputs. Fritz worked with Kurt Goldstein, a gestalt psychologist, at the Institute for Brain-Damaged Soldiers. During this time, he began to develop the idea that a human being was not, as Freudian theory would have it, an ill-fitting assemblage of drives, instincts, and neurotic symptoms, but a functioning whole operating within his or her environment.

In Frankfurt he met Lore (later anglicized to Laura) Posner, a psychology student whom he later married. He did not stay in Frankfurt for long; the pattern of restlessness was already evident in his life. It was customary for Germans to describe some period of their youth as *Wanderjahre,* but Fritz's *Wanderjahre* never seemed to end. He left Frankfurt for Vienna, took a job in a clinic there, and continued his psychoanalytic training. After a while he left Vienna and went back to Berlin.

In Berlin he became a patient of Wilhelm Reich's. Reich, who had once been a young prodigy within the psychoanalytic movement, was then developing his own theory and methods of psychotherapy. He had a tendency to take Freudian ideas, raise them to new levels, and imbue them with new meanings, well beyond Freudian orthodoxy.

Where Freud had talked of repression of libido, Reich focused on repression of genital sexuality and said the ability to achieve a true orgasm was the equivalent of mental health. Where Freud had paid attention to the ways the unconscious manifests itself in small physical behaviors (tics, nervous movements), Reich began to look at everything the patient did for clues to hidden neurotic meaning. He would pay more attention to *how* a patient said something than to *what* he said. He talked of character as "armoring," a way of protecting oneself against reality, and saw orgasm as the healthy liberation of psychic energy from its character-forged chains. Reich was not only a Freudian renegade; he was a Marxist revisionist. He tried combining Freudian ideas with Marxist ones, an enterprise that soon got him expelled from both the International Psychoanalytic Association and the German Communist Party. In the early 1930s, when Fritz became his patient, he was working on his book *The Mass Psychology of Fascism,* which accused the German Marxists of being totally unrealistic in expecting the working classes to revolt and establish a socialist society. Reich insisted that political behavior was determined as much by character structure as by class status, and the character of the German masses, he said, was basically authoritarian as a result of sexual repression in childhood. Instead of becoming revolutionary, they became reactionary, whether it made economic sense or not. "Sexual inhibition," wrote Reich, "alters the structure of the economically suppressed individual in such a manner that he thinks, feels and acts against his own material interests." (In the early 1970s, Fritz used very similar arguments against the optimists who believed that a great humanistic transformation was about to blossom in America.) Reich had the idea (novel at the time, though it would become central to gestalt therapy) that it was more productive to pay attention to the patient's present actions and attitudes than to embark on archaeological expeditions through the past. And he always insisted that neurosis took up residence in the body as well as in the mind. He had his patients do breathing exercises, and he even, unthinkable for a Freudian, *touched* them with his hands to massage tensed and twisted areas of the body. (Years later, when Perls discovered Ida Rolf and her physical system of therapy, he recognized a spiritual descendant of Wilhelm Reich's.)

When Adolf Hitler became chancellor of Germany in 1933, Perls and Reich fled the country, as did many other Jews, intellectuals, and leftists. Fritz was, by that time, nearly forty years old, married, a father, living in a comfortable apartment, and building up his own psychiatric practice. He crossed the border into Holland with about $25 in cash hidden in a cigarette lighter, and was later joined in Amsterdam by Lore and their child. For a time they lived on charity in a loft crowded with other refugees. Then Fritz went to London to see Ernest Jones, Freud's close friend and biographer. Jones knew of an opening for a training analyst in South Africa, and Fritz took it.

Fritz had met and been much impressed by the progressive South African prime minister Jan Christiaan Smuts, who had socialized with the gestalt psychologists and existentialists in Frankfurt and in 1926 had written a book entitled *Holism and Evolution.* Fritz expected that South Africa would be a good environment for him, and the expectation proved largely correct. Within a year of his arrival in Johannesburg, he made a remarkable transition, from penniless refugee to wealthy psychiatrist. He built the first Bauhaus-style residence in South Africa, hired servants for the family, and in his spare time took flying lessons. He also established a new psychoanalytic training center, the South African Institute for Psychoanalysis.

All this success and prosperity was a direct product of the immense prestige then afforded Freudian psychoanalysis and of the status that Fritz had attained as a practitioner of it. This kind of respectability bound many a psychiatrist to the Freudian faith forever; it didn't work out that way with Fritz.

During the dozen or so years that he lived and worked in South Africa (the longest stretch that he stayed in one place during his adult life), he slowly moved away from psychoanalysis and toward a new and as yet unnamed therapeutic approach. One of the strongest causes of his drift away from Freudianism was a meeting with Freud. In all the years that Fritz had been involved with psychoanalysis, even during the time in Vienna, he had never had a face-to-face encounter with Freud himself. Then, in 1936, he finally did. It was a painful and in some ways historically significant meeting.

Picture a scene like this: Fritz, a prosperous psychoanalyst in his early forties, has come some four thousand miles by boat and train to give a paper at the International Psychoanalytic Congress and to visit Freud. Freud, then eighty years old, is in his study. Fritz is ushered to the door. Freud opens the door, and the two stand in the doorway for a few minutes and make small talk. Then Freud says good-bye, closes the door, and goes back into his study. Fritz leaves.

If you had been a spectator to that event, you would have said not much happened, and you would have been quite right, in a superficial way. For the rest of his life, Fritz carried with him the emptiness of that brief meeting. It was a classic example of what gestalt therapists would call "unfinished business." Fritz had wanted, and expected, signs of recognition from his famous mentor: to be taken into Freud's inner circle, given some attention or gratitude or approval, even love, from a person he admired so enormously. Instead, he got four tense minutes, and he never forgave Freud for that.

As a minor but significant sequel to the meeting with Freud, Fritz proceeded on to the Psychoanalytic Congress at Marienbad and read his paper, which was about oral resistance. Nobody liked it. The paper was criticized as being a digression from psychoanalysis rather than a contribution to it.

Fritz went back to South Africa, and although he remained a card-carrying psychoanalyst for some years to come, his heart was no longer in it; he was searching for something else. He took an interest in Zen, read some of the new books that were coming out of the European existentialist movement, and eventually began to write a book of his own, *Ego, Hunger, and Aggression.* Freud had gotten the world to pay attention to the psychological force of sex, and now Fritz proposed to get the world to pay attention to another basic process, the taking-in of food. He subtitled his new book *A Revision of Freud's Theory and Method.* He argued in it that neurosis is basically the avoidance of contact, and that one of the most fundamental forms of contact is eating. Eating without contact, the book said, becomes a metaphor for the deadened life: experience never tasted, hunger never filled.

Fritz had not entirely rejected psychoanalysis. Rather, he was trying to do with it what he thought people ought to be capable of doing with their food (and with every experience or idea): chewing it carefully and with awareness, keeping what could be assimilated and passing on the rest. And definitely not swallowing it whole. There are Freudian concepts in the book, but there are also traces of many of the other things Fritz had been absorbing over the years: existentialism, gestalt psychology, holistic philosophy, Reichian armor theory, and Oriental religion. Although the book showed that he had come a long way from orthodox psychoanalysis (the Princess Marie Bonaparte, a loyal follower of Freud's, read the manuscript of Fritz's book during a visit to South Africa and told Fritz that he ought to hand in his resignation), he was not yet quite ready to become the founder of a new school. Gestalt therapy was still about a decade away.

Fritz served as a medical officer in the South African army during

World War II and left the country not long after the war was over. His exit was about two years ahead of the political victory of the conservative National Party and the advent of apartheid. (In later years, Fritz boasted that he could smell fascism coming.) The Perls family came to the United States, via Canada, in 1946.

In New York, Fritz met Paul Goodman. He had read some of Goodman's writings while in Africa, and he was interested in finding out what Goodman thought of his ideas about therapy. Goodman thought highly of them; he became a patient and student of Fritz and Laura's and a collaborator on a book that would describe this new school of therapy they were in the process of inventing. Laura Perls has said that the three co-authors (Perls, Goodman, and Ralph Hefferline, a professor at Columbia University) were well into the book before they agreed on a name for it and for the philosophy that was its subject. They thought seriously of calling it *Existential Therapy*, but discarded that as being too closely associated with Jean-Paul Sartre. Fritz later said that he had a hard time persuading the others to accept the name *Gestalt Therapy*.

The book is an excellent presentation of the basics of gestalt therapy: a human being can be understood only as a whole and within his or her actual environment; neurosis consists in being out of touch with one's own feelings and sensory experience; and therapy is the recovery of awareness.

The publication of *Gestalt Therapy* in 1951 helped to establish gestalt therapy as a school of psychotherapy. The Gestalt Therapy Institute was opened on Central Park West, with the two Drs. Perls as its directors and Goodman as one of the trainees. It did not become, as Fritz may reasonably have expected, the launching pad for his ascension into the upper reaches of the psychiatric world. The main trouble with it, from his point of view, was that it was not exclusively his: Laura was a co-director, and a powerful woman who was quite capable of competing with him. Paul Goodman, whose stature as a writer made him much more than an ordinary trainee, didn't get along well with Fritz and tended to side with Laura. His best-known book, *Growing Up Absurd,* was dedicated to her. And he later claimed that Fritz was not a very disciplined writer and that he had actually written most of *Gestalt Therapy*.

So Fritz drifted again, after traveling a circuit of East Coast cities, teaching gestalt. He had a long affair with a woman in Miami, went to California, took a trip around the world, and returned to California.

He was looking for a place to settle down on his own. His marriage to Laura had lasted nearly thirty years, but it had become chiefly a professional partnership, and not a very smooth one at that. In 1964 Fritz was living alone in Los Angeles, with no commitments to keep him from doing something that most psychiatrists of his stature would have found neither appealing nor convenient: taking up residence at a little hot springs resort on a remote part of the California coast.

The summer-fall 1964 brochure carried the following offering:

INTRODUCTION TO GESTALT THERAPY—

Led by: DR. FREDERICK PERLS, Psychiatrist and author of *Gestalt Therapy*

Dr. Perls will explain the concepts underlying Gestalt Therapy, and will demonstrate some of the methods he has developed for extending awareness and healing destructive divisions of the self. These methods include the use of dialogue (between therapist and patient and between aspects of the self), and non-interpretive work with dreams. At times Dr. Perls will relate the techniques and philosophy of Gestalt Therapy to ways of artistic expression, working with Fritz Faiss, painter and sculptor, who will be in residence at Big Sur Hot Springs.

There will be three weekend programs: attendance at each will be limited to fifty, with first choice given to those who sign up for more than one weekend.

FEE (per weekend) $46 per person.

Originally, gestalt therapy, which Fritz had once called concentration therapy, was strictly between client and therapist, outwardly resembling classical psychoanalysis, couch and all. But during the 1950s Fritz had made great changes. Observing the emergence of the group approach, he had abandoned one-to-one work. He went to Moreno's psychodramas in New York and developed his own dramatic form of group therapy. The patient and the therapist would work together, within the group, and the patient would often play the part of the problem: be your father, be your mother, be your stomach, be your anger. But unlike Moreno, Fritz did not use other people from the group as actors in those little scenes; he thought that got in the way. (Later, when Fritz and his mode of therapy became famous, Moreno often claimed that gestalt was only a bastardized form of psycho-drama. Once, at a psychological convention in the 1960s, they appeared together on a panel. Moreno said to Fritz, "I don't mind you stealing my stuff, but you should have stolen all of it." Fritz replied, "Ah, Jacob, Jacob, when will you just accept your greatness?")

The object of gestalt work, Fritz sometimes said, was not to achieve a breakthrough; rather, it was to achieve a break-in, a sudden invasion of one's own privacy, a re-established contact with lost and deadened feelings. Fritz was confident that this could be achieved in a single session if the patient was ready to let it happen. He encouraged people to sign up for multiple gestalt workshops if they were seriously interested in working, but he was skeptical of prolonged therapy. "In therapy," he often told his audiences—many of whom were patients in therapy, and many of whom were therapists—"we improve and improve and improve, and nothing changes." Nothing changes, he said, because the patient really loves the neurosis and wants desperately to keep it; the therapist merely colludes in this by pretending to "help." Fritz had only scorn for "helpers," therapeutic bleeding hearts, and much scorn for patients who would try to trick him into being responsible for their progress. As far as he was concerned, it was up to them. His favorite description of the effects of his work was "I teach people to wipe their own ass."

Usually Fritz's sessions at Big Sur were held in the lodge. He would sit in an easy chair in front of the great stone fireplace. Next to him would be two straight-backed chairs, the essential props of gestalt therapy. A volunteer would emerge from the group and take the patient's chair, the Hot Seat. Fritz would then lead the patient into a session, which might last only a few minutes, or perhaps—rarely—as long as an hour. Often the session would begin with an account of a dream. Dreams, Fritz said, were "existential messages" from the unconscious. The messages were not there to be analyzed by the therapist, but to be experienced—received—by the patient. The patient would be instructed to play the parts of the various elements in the dream and would be encouraged to experiment with feelings and reactions—to *become* an object, emotion, or desire.

A man announces that he has dreams of an erupting volcano.
All right, says Fritz, talk to the volcano.
Patient: *You're just sitting inside. You're just sitting in there and most of the time I don't even know you're there—I just go on enjoying myself and every*

once in a while you just erupt and I end up shaking and sort of out of control, and I don't understand it.
Fritz: *Be the volcano.*
Patient: *Well, I'm waiting. I may erupt any time, you'd better watch out.*
Fritz: *Say this to me.*
Patient: *I may erupt any time, you better watch out.*
Fritz: *Huh?*
Patient: *(louder) I may erupt any time—you better watch out.*
Fritz: *I don't hear you yet.*
Patient: *(loud) I may erupt any moment—you better watch out.*
Fritz: *Okay, I'm ready.*
The patient gives forth a mighty roar of eruption, which gets a ripple of relieved laughter from the group.
Fritz: *What do you feel now?*
Patient: *(quietly) Shaky.*
Fritz: *Close your eyes. Enter your shakiness—enter your body.*
Patient: *It doesn't feel all that bad. I don't know why it's shaking. I don't know why I'm shaking.*
Fritz: *Can you allow the shaking to develop? I can give you the diagnosis— you suffer from over-control. So decontrol yourself—shake a bit . . .*[2]

The patient would be directed to see every object that appeared in the dream as a personal creation, a part of the self. He or she was also directed to pay attention to every physical action that manifested itself during the session. Fritz had sharp and perceptive eyes and ears. He would closely observe the patient's mannerisms and direct attention to them. And so, according to gestalt theory, the estranged fragments of the self were reunited into an integrated, fully alive human being. "The previously robotized corpses begin to return to life," Fritz wrote, "gaining substance and beginning the dance of abandonment and self-fulfillment; the paper people are turning into real people."[3]

The deadness in life, he believed, was perpetuated by the countless tricks that people had for cutting themselves off from the here-and-now reality of existence. They would intellectualize, they would talk about other things, they would be vague, they would distract themselves and others, to try to gain some distance from their own actions. Fritz developed tricks of his own (he called them "games") for bringing people back into contact. Sometimes he would have the patient talk to an imagined person—often a parent or spouse—visualized as seated in the empty chair. Sometimes he would have the patient play the roles of two parts of the self, moving back and forth between the two chairs to act out the dialogue of inner conflict. If someone made a movement or a gesture in a furtive or halfhearted way, Fritz would direct the patient to exaggerate it, carry it to ridiculous extremes, repeat it again and again. He would do anything to get people to own their feelings and take responsibility for their actions. If somebody said "I can't" do something, he would ask him to say "I won't" do something. If somebody used the word "it" too frequently, he would get him or her to use substitute words that did not double as convenient shields against true feelings.

Patient: *My hand is doing this movement . . .*
Fritz: *Is* it *doing the movement?*
Patient: *I am moving my hand like this . . . and now the thought comes to me that . . .*
Fritz: *The thought "comes" to you?*
Patient: *I have the thought.*
Fritz: *You* have *it?*
Patient: *I think. Yes. I think that I use "it" very much, and I am glad that by noticing it I can bring it all back to me.*
Fritz: *Bring it back?*
Patient: Bring myself back. *I feel thankful for this.*
Fritz: This?
Patient: *Your idea about the "it."*
Fritz: *My idea?*
Patient: *I feel thankful towards you.*[4]

Intellectualizing—thinking and analyzing—came in for much abuse in Fritz's sessions. He was not against rational thought per se, but it happened to be the form of avoidance that most of his patients used with consummate skill. "Lose your mind and come to your senses" was one of his favorite slogans; it was not so far from Timothy Leary's insistence that you had to go out of your mind in order to use your head. No wonder many people came to see gestalt as yet another assault on the rational mind.

Fritz's personal style was part of the drama of gestalt. He could be sarcastic, and often was. He could, and often did, permit his patients to make fools of themselves. That was the chance they took, the wild excitement of standing up and taking that long walk to the front of the room, to the chair in front of the fireplace where the old man with the German accent sat quietly, smoking a cigarette, waiting, offering no help.

Gestalt therapy, as Fritz developed and practiced it at Big Sur, was a vibrant and vital process. As therapy it was, of course, controversial. Some people considered Fritz to be the ultimate genius of therapy, able to come in minutes to the core of neuroses that had eluded other practitioners for decades; some thought he was a dangerous psychopath; and some thought he did impressive things that had no permanent therapeutic value.

Without question, the sessions were good theater. There was a truth about them. The people were real, the problems were real, and the emotions were real. One could say the same thing for what went on in the Roman Colosseum, of course, but the participants in those events weren't seen, the next day, smiling radiantly and declaring that their lives had been changed. Nor did the Romans in the stands live constantly with the question of whether it was time to become one of the gladiators, to march up there and confront the old man and the shadows of their dream life and the scattered shards of their existence.

Fritz found the experience at Big Sur to be, on the whole, satisfactory. The work in the groups went well, the place was pleasant, it appeared to be attracting people of stature. Perhaps Bernie Gunther had been right in thinking it might amount to something. When the initial series was over, Fritz told Murphy and Price he would return and continue giving gestalt workshops. He didn't ask them; he told them.

By 1964, Slate's Hot Springs, which Mike Murphy and Dick Price had renamed Big Sur Hot Springs, took on yet another name: the Esalen Institute. Murphy and Price had decided that the organization, such as it was, would take its name from the Esalen Indians who had once lived in the area. Big Sur Hot Springs remained the official name of the physical location, but the newcomers soon took to calling the place itself Esalen.

The necessity of creating a new name is an indication of the growing popularity of the place and its workshops. Joe Adams had moved to Big Sur and bought a place up the road, Redwood Lodge, that served for a short while as an annex to Esalen. The addition of Redwood Lodge made it possible to run concurrent programs. By 1965 you could spend a weekend discussing holistic depth psychology near the hot springs, or be at Redwood Lodge with S. P. R. Charpter, editor of the *Journal of Human Ecology*. You could talk about "Psychological Barriers to the Solution of Individual and World Problems" with Hallock Hoffman from the Center for the Study of Democratic Institutions, investigate the mysterious kundalini power of Indian yoga with Paul Kurtz, or discuss Zen with Paul Reps.

The little institute brought in a constant influx of new talent and offered a remarkable variety of programs. Ansel Adams and Imogen Cunningham led a seminar on Edward Weston's photography; Nicholas Roosevelt (an old-time local resident, the one Hunter Thompson had described as looking like a bum) organized a seminar on local land-use planning; a group of sociologists and political scientists participated in a panel about research on peace; economist Louis Kelso and labor leader Harry Bridges talked about unions in an automated society; Nobel Prize winner Linus Pauling led a seminar on relations between the United States and China.

S. I. Hayakawa, then a professor of English at San Francisco Sate College, was an Esalen regular in the 1960s. He led seminars on semantics, the intellectual movement that had been founded on the works of the Polish philosopher Alfred Korzybski. General semantics was concerned with the nonverbal and nonlinear levels of human experience that underlie words and concepts. Its thesis that the human potential was being thwarted by the habits of language fitted in reasonably well with the rest of the Esalen curriculum. It had helped Alan Watts in his efforts to elucidate the nonverbal meaning of Zen, and it had helped Fritz Perls in laying the foundations of his experience-oriented gestalt therapy. At Esalen, Hayakawa borrowed back from these sources, using Zen and gestalt to explain general semantics. His seminars were always well prepared, always very intellectual, but he was no dusty pedant. He liked to play the piano for songfests in the lodge, and one visitor to Esalen remembers seeing the future United States senator lead a group of seminarians in a snake dance across the lawn.

Joan Baez, who had traveled far in an eventful two years from her life in a cabin at Slate's Hot Springs, returned to Big Sur in 1964 and took part in a seminar on "The New Folk Music." She sang and talked about the songs of Bob Dylan:

> Come, mothers and fathers throughout the land,
> And don't criticize what you don't understand.
> Your sons and your daughters are beyond your command,
> Your old road is rapidly agin'.
> Please get out of the new one if you can't lend your hand,
> For the times, they are a-changin'.

A few months later, Ralph Gleason, jazz critic for the *San Francisco Chronicle,* and the folksinger Malvina Reynolds led another seminar on the new folk music that seemed to be helping to mobilize political action across the country. The message of these two weekends echoed Huxley's and Heard's proclamations about the vulnerability of society's status quo. The assertive new songs of protest and liberation, youth and love, were the sounds of a cultural and political revolution.

Although Esalen never became a truly political place—certainly not the hotbed of revolutionary thought that a few of its supporters hoped it would be and a few right-wingers believed it was—its programs reflected many of the conflicts that would sweep through the decade.

There were always more proponents of change at Esalen than defenders of the old order, but Esalen's policy of nonalignment with any particular school, sect, or discipline was flexible enough so that those with widely divergent views could frequently be found there. For instance, Baez, without whose voice no peace march or sit-in was quite complete, and Hayakawa, who later became the darling of the right for his audacious resistance to student protestors at San Francisco State, both led seminars within the same period of time in 1964.

The casual ways things worked at Esalen made it fairly easy, at least in the early years, for adversaries to take their turn, thus avoiding a direct conflict. A seminar leader would arrive for a week or a weekend, sometimes driving, frequently flying in from some part of the country to be picked up at Monterey Airport by Murphy or Price; the participants would usually begin arriving at the same time, most of them driving down the coast from the San Francisco area or up the coast from Southern California. There were repeaters, but the mixture was never the same. A group and a leader would come together, whatever happened would happen, and when it was over they would all disperse and make way for the next group. With everything in such flux, there was hardly any time or place for serious controversy to emerge.

And so the celebrities, causes, and currents of the time filtered through that small space like sand through the narrow neck of an hourglass. Ken Kesey, author of *One Flew Over the Cuckoo's Nest,* passed through for a weekend of group storytelling. Timothy Leary and Richard Alpert arrived for a seminar on "The Ecstatic Experience." Frederic Spiegelberg, whose lectures had put Michael Murphy on the road to Esalen, led seminars on Oriental religion and enlightenment. Albert Ellis, the feisty founder of rational-emotive psychotherapy, gave a lecture and demonstration of his techniques. Norman O. Brown, author of *Life Against Death,* lectured on sexual repression and sexual liberation. James A. Pike, the freethinking Episcopalian bishop of California, aired his views on new directions in religion. J. B. Rhine reported on his lonely and persistent efforts to bring parapsychology into the realm of respectable science.

Each leader drew a different kind of audience. By attending just one seminar at Esalen, you could not really get an accurate picture of what kind of people came there. Sometimes the character of the place changed in a few hours, as one detachment departed and another arrived to take its place; sometimes it was different on each side of Hot Springs Creek.

One of Michael Murphy's first real entrepreneurial triumphs was getting Arnold Toynbee, the renowned and respected historian, to give a lecture at Big Sur. It was only a one-day event, but, suitably publicized, it drew a sizable crowd. After the lecture Michael's parents gave a reception for Toynbee in the Big House. It was a terribly civilized gathering: Toynbee, university people, a smattering of socialites from Monterey and Carmel and Pebble Beach, assembled in the lovely old house by the ocean. At the same time, a workshop of Beat literati from San Francisco, who spent the evening shouting poetry at one another in a room heavy with marijuana smoke and four-letter words, was just getting underway at the lodge.

The wide variations in programming brought the existence of Esalen to the attention of a wide variety of people. You might have heard of it if you were a follower of the Beat writers or if you were interested in existentialism, T-groups, LSD, religion, or general semantics. The chances that you *had* heard of it increased as Esalen attracted more eminent thinkers and doers. Within a surprisingly short time from its beginning, Esalen could name among its leaders a number of world-famous people.

Paul Tillich spent a weekend at Esalen in 1965, the last year of his life. Tillich had a secure place among the intellectual movements that were flowing through Big Sur. As a professor at the University of Frankfurt in the 1930s he had known Martin Buber and Fritz Perls's employer, Kurt Goldstein. After he came to New York, in 1933, he joined the faculty of the Union Theological Seminary, where he was teacher and mentor to Rollo May and a colleague of Frederic Spiegelberg's.

He belonged at Esalen, a place dedicated to synthesis; he was the great synthesizer of the century, a philosopher who had been able to rise above the ideological warfare of his time and find connections between disparate movements and beliefs. Essentially he was a theologian, but he explored realms that other theologians declared off-limits: existentialism, socialism, psychoanalysis. He was the living bridge between the great German heritage of Protestant theology and the intellectual movements of the twentieth century. He was a powerful old man with a commanding presence. As Rollo May described him, he had "a large leonine head with a shock of bushy hair over a high forehead, high color, and a face constructed not in curves but in planes, like a portrait by Cézanne."

He chose as his theme for the weekend the synthesis that was nearest the Esalen heart: East and West. He talked about the parallels between the Oriental notion of self-transcendence and the Western idea of self-actualization. He talked about the Eastern and Western images of eternal life: Nirvana and the Kingdom of God. He talked about the possibility of an intellectual renaissance built on creative dialogue between Oriental and Occidental thought.

The presence of such eminent thinkers took Esalen irrevocably beyond the obscurity of Slate's Hot Springs. Murphy and Price were becoming proprietors of a successful business and found themselves in a position of influence and power. As Esalen expanded, they were confronted with new problems of many kinds, none of which they had anticipated.

There was, for example, the problem of Fritz Perls.

Ernest Hemingway used to say that some people were severely handicapped by the lack of a shit-detector. He would never have said this about Fritz Perls. Fritz had one of the world's most finely tuned shit-detectors; wherever he went he found some kind of shit to be exposed, shoveled through, or otherwise coped with. He used to say that there were three basic categories of shit: there was chickenshit, the cliché-ridden small talk that took up so much of ordinary everyday human interaction; there was bullshit, the explanations and rationalizations and phony games that he so often encountered in working with his patients; and then there was elephantshit, the high-level discussion of Great Subjects, like evolution and human growth. Fritz thought most of the Esalen seminars were in the elephantshit category. He said he didn't *object* to elephantshit. It was okay and seemed to be a necessary part of civilization, but it was shit, nevertheless. This point of view did not help his relationship with Michael Murphy.

Fritz and Michael made valiant efforts to get along with each other, but they didn't have much to work with. Michael was handsome and came from a prosperous family; he put great energy into being entertaining and kind, saying the right thing. Fritz was a gnarled old misanthrope from a poor Jewish background who had come to the conclusion, over the years, that most of what passed for social grace was either chickenshit or bullshit. Michael was a mystic who still, whenever time allowed, spent eight hours a day in meditation. Fritz scorned the supernatural. As for meditation, he had given it a sincere try during a stay in Kyoto, and had decided that sitting and doing nothing was one of the most stupid pastimes ever devised. Meditation, he used to say, was neither shit nor get off the pot. Michael, in his early thirties, was just venturing into sexuality; Fritz had been a dirty old man since he was thirteen. Michael was politically a middle-of-the-road optimist who saw signs of positive change everywhere; Fritz was a closet Marxist who thought America stood a good chance of caving in to some kind of dictator at any moment. Michael was all for openness to new ideas; Fritz thought this was the intellectual equivalent of bolting your food.

They were always pleasant enough to each other. Michael was a little afraid of Fritz. He kept thinking that if he really worked at it, he might make a breakthrough, establish a comfortable relationship between them. Fritz, who rarely went out of his way to be pleasant to anybody, did make the effort to get along with Michael. Undoubtedly he was partly motivated by his desire to remain at Esalen. He had approached the place in the same way he approached people—coolly, taking no chances, revealing no need—but it had gotten to him. He had come there in terrible health, thinking he had only a little time left to live. Then, much to his surprise, he began to feel better. As he did so, he thought that he might live a while longer after all, and that this might be a good place to do it. It could even become a kind of gestalt therapy institute, doing the organizing for him, providing a steady supply of patients and trainees. Meanwhile it provided him with regular meals, a place to hang out in the evening and play chess, and—among the patients and trainees—a never-ending flow of admiring females.

Fritz's efforts to be friendly with Michael were not made any easier by Dennis, who spent some time at Big Sur during Fritz's early years there. Dennis was one of the few people in the world Fritz did not intimidate. He was not a peacemaker like his brother; given a potential conflict, he would rather fight than make friends. He had many conflicts around this place he had known all his life, his family's property, which all these strangers were coming to and calling Esalen. He didn't much want them around, and often said so. He claimed to have no comprehension at all of whatever it was Michael was trying to do there; he said that, insofar as he could comprehend it, he didn't like it. And he especially disliked this cranky old man, who stomped about the place as though he owned it and seemed to terrify everybody.

So Dennis and Fritz clashed often, and Fritz, of whom so many people were terrified, usually lost. Once, when Michael and Dennis were standing together in the lodge, Fritz came up and started to say something to Michael. "Fuck off, old man," said Dennis. Another time, Dennis was sitting in his car in the parking lot in front of the lodge and Fritz put his head in through the open window to say something to Dennis. Dennis pushed the button and the window began to roll up, like a reverse guillotine, and Fritz withdrew in haste and confusion. Still another time, after a session in the bar with some of the Big Sur locals, Dennis got a bunch of them to pick up Fritz's little Fiat, carry it over to the lodge, and jam it against the main door. Dick Price angrily intervened and got into a fight with Dennis. He wrestled Dennis to the ground, and after he let Dennis up, Dennis found a piece of lead pipe and came after him. Dick ran around the lodge to escape, Dennis pursued him, and the seminarians inside, pondering that day's piece of evolutionary wisdom, looked out to see one of California's most promising young novelists chasing the cofounder of the Esalen Institute across the sun deck, brandishing a length of pipe.

Fritz had his problems relating to Michael, had his recurrent hostilities with Dennis, and he did not get on well with either of the other two residents. He thought Bernie Gunther, who had worked out a deal of his own, which gave him the opportunity to live at Esalen and earn his keep as a free-lance masseur and yoga teacher, was turning into a hustler. Nor was he fond of Gia-fu, although it is hard to imagine anyone not liking the congenial keeper of the baths. It may have had something to do with Fritz's general antipathy toward mysticism, which surfaced frequently. When an unknown young graduate student named Carlos Castaneda came to Esalen in the early sixties to help lead a seminar on Indian shamanism, he told some wild stories about his encounters with a medicine man in Mexico called Don Juan. Fritz dismissed this as nonsense. Nor did Fritz care much for Peter Hurkos, the Dutch clairvoyant who came to Esalen to demonstrate his abilities. When Fritz stood up in a room filled with about fifty people and publicly denounced Hurkos as a charlatan, Hurkos was so badly shaken that he was totally unable to perform.

It was only much later that Fritz found a student and ally at Esalen in Dick Price, who was one of the first people there to become close to him. But that happened gradually. At first Price thought, along with Murphy, that Fritz was a finicky and disagreeable old man, and he avoided him as much as possible.

* * *

Another problem that began to plague Murphy and Price was the matter of drugs. It was rapidly growing into a major national issue, inspiring euphoria in some parts of the body politic and hysteria in others. Officially, drugs were not a part of the Esalen experience. There were seminars about the psychedelics, of course, but these were ostensibly discussions, not demonstrations. The brochure announcing the appearance of Timothy Leary and Richard Alpert explicitly stated, "No drugs will be used." This was fine as a statement of policy, but did not make much of an impression on the seminar participants. Murphy sat in on the seminar for a while and, looking around at the audience, decided that one and all were zonked out of their minds. He said it reminded him of a science fiction film he had recently seen, about Earth invaded by wide-eyed, catatonic beings from outer space.

Murphy and Price really didn't mind some use of psychedelics around the place, nor was there much they could have done if they had minded. Esalen was, after all, open to the public as a resort, with a bar and a restaurant. They were not about to start searching cars and rooms. People seemed to behave themselves, and only occasionally was there a bad trip to be dealt with.

This easygoing attitude prevailed throughout the decade, but it was often under severe strain. Rumors circulated wildly. Some of the staff members believed there were undercover narcotics agents about the premises, perhaps sitting in the audience, taking in Zen and gestalt therapy and getting ready to return with a warrant that would put the place out of business. Willis Harman, who was engaged in legal LSD research and was often in touch with government officials, called up several times and warned that a massive drug bust was about to take place. Each time Murphy and Price warned the staff, good grass and acid were thrown over the cliff in anticipation, and nothing ever happened. After a while, a sign was posted, announcing that illegal drugs were not permitted. It is hard to believe this made much of an impression on anybody, but at any rate the great drug bust never materialized. The forces of law and order cannot have been trying very hard.

As Esalen's programs expanded, and the content became increasingly experiential and experimental, other problems began to surface, from hiring personnel to more complex matters concerning the skills and egos of the professionals and staff members.

Each of the disciplines that turned up in the programming had its own standards and methods. As students went on to be leaders, the materials or methods were adapted, changed, and altered. As new and wider audiences were reached, some of the founders or original practitioners of the various disciplines became concerned about who was qualified to teach what.

One day Bernie Gunther came to Murphy and proposed that he introduce the leaders at the beginning of each seminar. Murphy or Price had usually done this, but both were glad to pass on the responsibility to Gunther. His idea was that he could also do a little audience warm-up, a sensory-awareness icebreaker, using some things he had picked up from Charlotte Selver's workshops, in addition to some of his own inventions. People touched each other in simple massagelike exercises, relaxed their bodies a bit, and got over their discomfort. Gunther made it easy and fun, and people enjoyed his manner.

When Selver and Brooks returned to Esalen, they were dismayed to discover Gunther practicing his own version of sensory awareness. One morning Murphy came downstairs from his room at the Big House to find Charlotte Selver, usually so pleasant and calm, close to tears. She said she had been awake all night. It was this business of letting Bernie conduct sensory-awareness exercises. She had been doing the work for thirty years and, in all that time, had allowed only one other person—her husband—to become a teacher. *Her* teacher, Elsa Gindler, had always said that the work should be very thin and very deep. But Bernie, she said, was very broad and very shallow.

Together, the concerned parties, with the help of Murphy and Price, managed to negotiate a settlement. Gunther agreed that he would no longer call his work sensory-awareness exercises. For a while he called it sensing experience, and, later, sensory awakening. Selver and Brooks, meanwhile, maintained the integrity of their own teachings.

This was only the first of many crises about who should do what and how it should be labeled. Rivalries and sensitive egos were not unfamiliar in academic and corporate circles. But in the free-flowing spirit of Esalen, where so many people were forging new disciplines from myriad sources, these tensions seemed especially awkward and painfully at odds with the prevailing mood. Yet they were also inevitable, given Esalen's rapid growth in popularity and reputation. Careers, even cults, would be made and broken here. Michael Murphy and Richard Price, at first unaware of their powerful influence in resolving these conflicts, would come to realize that their decisions not only influenced the actions of individuals, but affected what reached the mainstream of American culture.

All of these problems were growing pains. Everything at Esalen metamorphosed with amazing speed. It had been in business for scarcely a year before it began to turn into a dispensary of new methods of psychotherapy and bodily development, and soon moved into yet another phase with the arrival of the first resident teachers. Either of these transitions was as much as a small organization might be expected to digest in a decade, but at Big Sur there was not even a pause for catching breath. Things moved on, and an even greater transition began to take form: Esalen became not just a forum, but an activist organization. It was out to change society.

This transition—it was the biggest one of all—took shape within a general climate of belief that something very big and wonderful was about to happen. The belief was never articulated like the predictions of those cults which have sprung up at so many times and places in history, built on the expectation of a coming disaster, a millennium, an Armageddon, or a messiah, but it was a recognizable cousin to them, with a similar supercharged energy and a comparable hunger for favorable signs and portents.

It is hardly surprising that such a belief should develop at Big Sur, what with the philosophizing about the evolutionary transformations of humankind and the almost daily evidence of personal breakthroughs. ("Three women just have spontaneous orgasm," announced Gia-fu one day, charging into the lodge with a report from a current workshop.) People were embracing new and noble ideas, not only by thinking about them, but in many cases by setting forth to build their lives upon them. They were regularly, in gestalt and encounter sessions, opening up to new regions of feeling. They were experiencing massage, sensory awakening, and other liberations of the body. In the baths, middle-class Americans were finding they could be naked in the presence of people of all ages and sexes and, after the initial ordeal of disrobing and marching in vulnerable nudity down to the tubs, enjoying the mingled delights of hot water, naked bodies, surf, and sea breeze. In the cabins, late at night or during the long quiet afternoons, they were shedding their sexual inhibitions and venturing into the new worlds of psychedelia. Hovering over these hedonistic pursuits was a kind of spirituality that would have been scandalous to a conventional minister but would have been perfectly recognizable to a denizen of the old Big Sur Bohemia. It was a religious vision that harmonized with the themes of self-actualization, human potentiality, and transformation; it saw the coming cultural change as an awakening, a new phase in human evolution. There was much talk of evolution in the seminars; the source most often cited was not Darwin, with his bleak notions of survival of the fittest, but the scientist-theologian Teilhard de Chardin, with his ideas of the onward-and-upward spiraling of the human spirit.

The belief system that formed at Esalen was not to be found in a single book or learned in a weekend. You discovered it in bits and pieces, from things you read and heard and experienced.

In another era, perhaps, such exposure would not have led to the same excited anticipation of a new order. But in the mid-1960s, political, cultural, and technological revolutions were underway. Earlier in the decade, Lyndon Johnson had decisively taken over the White House, pushed through a package of civil rights legislation that offered the promise of new lives for America's minorities, launched a war on poverty, and roundly defeated his Republican opponent, Barry Goldwater, in what could easily have been read as a victory for the forces of progress. The opposition to the war in Vietnam was on the horizon. In Berkeley, students had won major concessions from the administration regarding political activism on campus, drawing California once again into the national spotlight and touching off comparable demonstrations across the country. And it escaped no one's attention that these civil and political changes were accompanied by a major shift in sexual mores, away from monogamy, premarital celibacy, and rigid sex-role differentiations.

Riding the crest of every change was a movement: the civil rights movement, the free speech movement, the peace movement. The sexual-freedom movement even had a Sexual Freedom League, headquartered, of course, in California. For those who were uninspired by free speech and sexual freedom, there was another kind of movement—the exploration of space—that was also a part of a romantic evolutionary vision.

Heard had spoken of a "psychological revolution"; Michael Murphy often referred to what was happening at Esalen, and the upheavals of the era, as a "consciousness revolution," which encompassed the spiritual and the scientific as well as the psychological. He frequently signed his letters "in the spirit of the revolution."

Murphy was more than the primary creator of Esalen; he was its major product, the embodiment of the diversity and enthusiasm of the place. He attended every seminar that was held at Big Sur in the early years, and was able to extract ideas also from the movements and rumblings that were shaking the foundations of society in the 1960s. Murphy avidly followed the doings of the astronauts and cosmonauts. Their ventures into the unknown excited him more than the doings of campus radicals and progressive politicians.

Murphy was constantly searching for more expressions of the Vision and for other seekers of it. He attended many psychological conventions, not only to scout for new seminar leaders and to hear new ideas, but to reassure a profession growing nervous about the kinds of therapies offered at Esalen that the new developments could co-exist with the established therapies.

At a psychological convention in Los Angeles in 1964, Abraham Maslow, already known and respected in his field, considerably aided Esalen's credibility by offering this recommendation to his colleagues: "I want to tell you about Big Sur Hot Springs. The operative word is *hot*. This place is hot."

But it was Murphy himself who was Esalen's most visible asset. In his early thirties now, he still had a boyish personality: earnest, respectful toward older people, full of enthusiasm, and—among those he knew well—able to break into wild, mischievous playfulness. Like his mother, he had the gift of joy. Even if you didn't know him well, you could not help noticing that he *looked* happy. And he had a way of disarming potential opposition. People who started out disapproving of Esalen often found that Murphy, in a sequence of movements as gentle and effortless as a bit of Tai Chi with Gia-fu Feng on a cool Big Sur morning, transformed them from antagonists into mentors. Murphy didn't go around telling people what *he* was planning to do at Esalen; he asked them what *they* thought he ought to do. Once asked, they inevitably gave advice, and in the process of giving advice developed a personal investment in the enterprise's future success.

The physical beauty of its setting was Esalen's other major asset. Murphy was forever inviting people to come to Big Sur as the institute's guests, either to attend a seminar or merely to stay there for a day or so. These visits had their own kind of persuasiveness. The place made converts of many who spent a couple of days there, soaking in the hot tubs, perhaps getting a massage, eating good meals, and taking leisurely strolls along Hot Springs Creek. Most of the visitors brought their spouses or companions, but some came alone and found somebody among the staff or the guests to help them pass the time. One nationally famous East Coast psychologist who became an occasional seminar leader was known to have only the slightest interest in Teilhard de Chardin but a strong commitment to the masseuses and the long-skirted young waitresses in the lodge. Such pleasures as these encouraged many visitors to return and softened their feelings toward this interesting educational venture.

James F. T. Bugental was one significant new convert. Then in his mid-forties, with a crew cut and a mustache and horn-rimmed glasses, Bugental was a major link to Southern California and to another movement that was beginning to look like a psychological revolution unto itself: the explosion of group psychotherapies. It had been happening in many places—New York; Bethel, Maine, where the National Training Laboratories were located; Chicago, where Carl Rogers first began to connect group methods to his client-centered therapy; most of all, Southern California. Los Angeles was becoming the Vienna of the group therapies. It had always been a therapy-prone region (Beverly Hills had more psychiatrists per capita than any other city in the world), and the new group approaches flourished there. Los Angeles needed them. This was one of the fastest-growing urban areas in the country, and many of the new arrivals were affluent, educated, young. They had cut loose from their original communities and had come to a place where people were forever arriving and departing, where there was always a moving van on the block, where friendships, love affairs, marriages, and jobs came and went as easily as the people. If, in fact, groups are an organized response to alienation, then you have a good explanation of their popularity in Los Angeles. In addition, Southern California businesses and industries—the aerospace firms, especially —had gone in heavily for sensitivity training, and this nourished the growth of such centers as the Western Training Laboratories (connected to NTL), the Western Behavioral Sciences Institute in La Jolla (where Carl Rogers was a resident fellow), and the UCLA School of Business Administration, which was the major academic resource for the mixture of management with encounter. Bugental had taught at WTL and UCLA, was the first president of the American Association for Humanistic Psychology, and a partner in Psychological Service Associates, a firm that based its practice on existential-humanistic theory and new group methods. He would prove a valuable resource for Esalen.

Murphy had written to Bugental in 1963, telling him about Big Sur

113

Hot Springs and inviting him to visit and/or give a seminar there. Bugental read the letter with profound suspicion. There were getting to be too many institutes, some of them of doubtful character, and the people connected with reputable centers like WTL and WBSI feared that the rapidly expanding group-therapy field might be invaded by charlatans. Bugental put off answering the letter and asked around to see whether anyone had heard about the place at Big Sur Hot Springs. By chance, his son had met Murphy at a party in Los Angeles, and said he was a great guy. Then one of Bugental's partners visited Big Sur and returned with a favorable report. Eventually, Bugental and his wife gathered up their cameras and drove to Big Sur to attend a photography workshop. It was an agreeable but sedate weekend—no encountering, no philosophizing, either—led by four photographers: Ansel Adams, Imogen Cunningham, Cole Weston, and Jack Welpott. And it was about photography, nothing else. Bugental and his wife understood there were baths on the premises, but they never got around to visiting them.

They found the place beautiful and relaxing, felt welcome there, and during the weekend became acquainted with Murphy. He was, as usual, attending the workshop. Murphy had read Bugental's book *The Search for Authenticity,* and said it was wonderful. He asked Bugental for advice about future seminars. Before the weekend was over, Bugental was another Esalen fan. Soon he was returning to Big Sur to lead seminars and encounter groups; by 1965 he was a member of Esalen's executive committee, the institute's semihonorary board of directors. Other members of the committee were Virginia Satir, of the Mental Research Institute in Palo Alto; Frank Barron, of the Institute for Personality Assessment and Research at Berkeley (probably the best-known national authority on the psychology of creativity); and George Leonard, editorial manager of the West Coast office of *Look* magazine.

George Leonard had come on the scene early in 1965, bringing a heady rush of new energy and big-media power. He would play a most important role, as Murphy's close friend and Esalen's spokesman and theorist, through the remainder of that lively decade. He was, when Murphy first met him, forty-one years old, a tall, slender man with a resonant voice and a Georgia accent. He had been reluctant to go to California when *Look* first asked him to, but soon found much of interest in his new homeland. He became one of the most energetic promulgators of the news that there were Big Things happening on the

West Coast, and wrote one of the first national magazine articles about the Beat movement and one of the first about the emerging youth culture. ("The tempo of history has been doubled and redoubled, and social changes that once took decades are now happening overnight," he wrote.)[1] In 1962 he edited a special issue about California that suggested the populous state was developing a new kind of society and perhaps "a new kind of person" able to cope with it.

Leonard had a marvelous ability to look at the confusing incidents of his time and to discern in them a pattern of positive transition. He carved out a special place for himself as a star reporter on cultural change. Many stories of this kind were breaking, and Leonard approached them all with great optimism. He wrote award-winning stories on new developments in education (learning machines, behavior-modification psychology) with reassuring confidence that great progress was being made. When the civil rights action began to heat up, he returned to the South to cover the major demonstrations. Here, too, in the turmoil between black and white, he found signs of a dawning new era.

In 1964 Leonard began working on an article, an outgrowth of some of the education pieces he had written earlier, that was to be entitled "The Human Potential." The article became the largest he ever undertook for *Look;* he worked on it, full time, for about eight months. Although it drew on some of the same sources as Esalen had, it was not written about or with Esalen. Leonard had already skimmed extremely close to the Esalen orbit without quite intersecting it; he had interviewed Huxley, Hayakawa, and Bishop Pike for the California article. For "The Human Potential" he interviewed behavior psychologists and brain researchers. The article grew until it was twenty thousand words, a gargantuan size for a *Look* piece. Leonard kept honing it and polishing it, showing copies of the manuscript to friends and asking them for their comments.

One of the people who read the work-in-progress was Lois Delattre, who was then working in a hospital with Leonard's wife, Lillie. Lois was a bright, attractive, restless young woman who was in touch with most of the things Leonard was writing about. She had been married to a minister, Pierre Delattre, who had operated a bread-and-wine mission in North Beach during the height of the Beat era and had then become a writer himself. With Herbert Gold and some other local literati, he had led an Esalen seminar on "The Expansion of Consciousness Through Art" in 1963. Lois and Pierre had separated, and Pierre

115

had left San Francisco and the ministry. But Lois stayed on and kept in close touch with Esalen. After she read the draft of Leonard's article, she told him, one day when they were having lunch at the Palace Hotel, that he *had* to meet Mike Murphy. Murphy, as it happened, was coming up from Big Sur that night and was going to have dinner at her house. So Leonard went to the dinner party, a small gathering, and was introduced to Murphy. The two immediately launched into a marathon conversation.

"We started talking," Leonard recalled later, "and it was the most amazing dovetailing of interests. It was almost like the beginning of a love affair." They talked all though the dinner party, then drifted off to Leonard's house in Pacific Heights, and at 2:00 A.M. were still talking. The conversation was a feast of agreements: they agreed that majestic changes were underway; they agreed that the 1960s were one of the watershed eras of human history; they agreed that a profound shift in consciousness was in the making. Each brought different perspectives to bear on this: Leonard had chronicled social movements, behavioral psychology, and brain research; Murphy had studied Eastern religions, humanistic psychology, and the new group therapies. The more they talked, the more they were convinced that all these pointed in the same direction. Some time that morning, Murphy, leaning against the marble fireplace in the high-ceilinged living room, said, "George, let's fire a shot heard round the world." And Leonard replied, "Okay, Mike. Let's do it."

7

A shot heard round the world. Such an aspiration requires a richness of resources and a clarity of purpose. If you had received the Esalen brochure for the fall of 1965, as thousands of people on the ever-growing mailing list did, you would have seen that Esalen had both. The richness of resources was evident in the membership of the executive committee and the Ph.D.–laden advisory board. It was evident in the seminars, which included some of the nation's leading theorists, psychotherapists, philosophers: Rollo May, talking about "frontier problems in psychotherapy and human development"; Alan Watts and Bishop James A. Pike, talking about "Christianity in revolution"; Gardner Murphy, of the Menninger Foundation, talking about "the countless occasions on which man has outgrown his image of himself long before he has been able to find a new image"; B. F. Skinner, on "deriving values from a scientific account of human behavior"; Frank Barron, discussing "the psychology of creativity"; J. B. Rhine, discussing "parapsychology and the nature of man." Philosophical weekends were not all that was offered. There were concerts of music and dance, encounter groups, experiential sessions of therapy and meditation.

The purpose was stated in the brochure's general introduction, which George Leonard had contributed. It began:

> Within a single lifetime, our physical environment has been changed almost beyond recognition. But there has been little corresponding change in how we, as individuals, relate to the world and experience reality. Such a change is inevitable, however—indeed, it is imminent. New tools and techniques of the human potentiality—generally unknown to the public and to much of the intellectual community—are already at hand; many more are presently under development. We stand on an exhilarating and dangerous frontier—and must answer anew the old questions: "What

117

are the limits of human ability, the boundaries of the human experience? What does it mean to be a human being?"

Murphy and Price had always searched for phrases to describe what Esalen was about. Leonard gave them the phrases. His elegant, gracious prose expressed both the sense of impending transformation and the belief that the means for bringing it about were near at hand, marvelously converging right there in the meeting rooms at Big Sur. They had the phrases now, and the phrases had them as well; because unless those words meant nothing at all, they declared to the world that Esalen was enlisted in the service of one of the greatest transitions in all of human history, knew something of how to make it happen, and anticipated results soon. The phrases gave Esalen's followers a bright promise, and gave its potential critics something against which to measure its performance.

In the event that the reader missed the point of Leonard's introduction, some lines of poetry on the first page of the brochure, a passage from Christopher Fry's play *A Sleep of Prisoners,* said it in a different way:

> Dark and cold we may be, but this
> is no winter now. The frozen misery
> of centuries breaks, cracks, begins to move,
> the thunder is the thunder of the floes,
> the thaw, the flood, the upstart spring.
> Thank God our time is now when wrong
> comes up to face us everywhere,
> never to leave us till we take
> the longest stride of soul men ever took.
> Affairs are now soul size.
> The enterprise
> is exploration into God.[1]

Murphy and Price both believed in Esalen's declared purpose, but they had different ways of believing. They were two quite different people. They had mutually honored this difference in their first division of labor: Murphy planning the seminars, Price managing the resort. At first they had shared these responsibilities, meeting daily, each a consultant to the other; but as the scope of the whole operation expanded, each became increasingly occupied with his own concerns. Their basic managerial division of labor did not change, but the volume of work increased: on Murphy's side more programs to be planned, leaders and ideas forever to be sought out, new projects and expansions to be considered; on Price's side a more complex business operation, reservations to be made, guests to be housed and fed, staff and seminar leaders to be paid, grounds and buildings to be maintained and improved. It became difficult for them to work together as closely as they had in the first few years.

The differences of personality and style became more apparent with the passage of time. In the early 1960s, people who came to Big Sur found them scarcely distinguishable: a couple of amiable and presentable young men, about the same age. Murphy was perhaps a bit more visible, more likely to be the one greeting the arriving seminar leader or attending the sessions; nothing more than that. But as Esalen became better known and as Murphy expanded into his role, a certain mystique began to grow up about him. He was from an old California family (you heard about the John Steinbeck connection); he had gone to Stanford and then had lived in an ashram in India (you didn't run across many ashram alumni in the early 1960s); and he meditated. Many people were just beginning to discover meditation as a spiritual practice or as a form of psychotherapy or even as an approach to relaxation and physical health. They practiced it for fifteen minutes or a half-hour at home, when they remembered, and visited yoga teachers and Zen centers for more regular and disciplined experience. But here was a man who, it was said, meditated for eight hours a day and had done so for years: an awesome piece of personal information. And yet he was so outgoing, so devoid of heavy-handed spirituality. Esalen strove to synthesize the best of East and West; Murphy seemed to do that in his own person, to be simultaneously the Eastern contemplative and the Western entrepreneur. It was a time when old values and beliefs were being challenged everywhere, and many people felt deeply threatened. Murphy personally eased the transition for anybody who knew him. He had all the pep and presentability of a 1950s college boy, but he was at the same time a spokesman for the things of a new era: Eastern religions, psychedelic drugs, group therapy.

There was less charisma about Price. He was a personable and intelligent, maybe even brilliant, person, but the pieces of his life did not make legend. There was, perhaps, a certain mythic quality to his having spent some time in a mental hospital—a sense of an ordeal completed, of dues paid—but it lacked the glitter of Steinbeck and India. For Murphy, the mid-1960s were a time of euphoric expansiveness; for Price, they were a more complex and conflicted time. He was enjoying the activity at Big Sur, the comings and goings of interesting people, the challenge of running a business, the joy of doing something that he believed worth doing—but there was also suffering in his life. He still felt the aftereffects of his hospitalization: an almost constant physical discomfort, which he attributed to the insulin shock treatments, and a lingering sense of grief and rage over the empty months he had been forced to spend at the Institute of Living in Connecticut. He hoped that in time Esalen might evolve into a place that would have something to offer to people who had been through such experiences, and he kept a close eye on the new disciplines that turned up at Esalen, in the hope that he might find something for himself.

Differences of style carried the men in different directions. Murphy, who had grown restless at Big Sur even during the summer vacations of his childhood, was always finding reasons to go somewhere else. Price, who had no family connection to the property, became very much at home there and seldom left. The main woman in Murphy's life was Patricia Felix, who had came to Esalen as a guest in 1965 to attend a weekend seminar; she lived in San Francisco.

Murphy and Price differed as well in their sense of timing. Murphy agreed with Leonard that something very large was going to happen very soon, and that Esalen should forge ahead into new territory as speedily as it could. Price was less sure of that; he was more inclined toward incremental change and was in no great hurry for Esalen to do more than what it was already doing.

Such differences should have produced occasional fights, chronic conflict, even a collapse of the whole enterprise—other enterprises have foundered on smaller things—but that didn't happen. Through all the changes and transitions, Murphy and Price never had a single serious argument. Esalen saw more than its share of battles, and often Murphy and Price were caught up in them, but they managed to get through such things without ever once having a major dispute between themselves.

Later, when the media began to discover Esalen, Murphy was the one who ascended to a certain fame along with the institute. Many people said, then, that Price resented this. If he did, it was a secret he managed to keep from Murphy and from himself. He never made any effort to put himself in public view, was never to be found socializing at conventions, making speeches, giving interviews, or in any way attempting to take credit. He used to say of himself that he was not much interested in getting credit and, for that matter, not much interested in giving it.

The friendship between Murphy and Leonard flourished. A couple of weeks after their first meeting, Leonard and his wife went down to Big Sur, stayed at Joe Adams' house, visited with Murphy and Price at Esalen, and got a private sensory-awareness session with Bernie Gunther. The weekend after that Murphy went up to San Francisco again. That became the pattern for the next couple of years, more often than not with Murphy in San Francisco. He would turn up at the Leonards' house around sunset on Friday afternoons, and he and George would spend the weekend brainstorming, talking about what was happening in American society, and what could perhaps be made to happen. These were glorious times of great expectations and high possibilities. As they talked, they would make notes, covering page after page with phrases, scraps of ideas. Sometimes they would spread the papers on the floor of Leonard's basement so that they could survey them and reshuffle the piles. In one of these sessions, half-seriously, they talked about what form their kind of thinking would take if it were a movement like the civil rights movement or the peace movement. The phrase "human potential movement" got written down on one of those pieces of paper. (Leonard liked it; Murphy wasn't too sure about it.)

The idea that came to dominate these meetings, and soon became the chief vehicle of Esalen's next stage of development, was the residential program.

Murphy had always had, in the back of his mind, his own notion of how Esalen might evolve. It could, in time, become a kind of ashram—a small college of consciousness, he would sometimes say, similar to the Aurobindo ashram, but without that paralyzing fixation on a single teacher. This had been a half-formed, long-range idea, but in the mid-1960s it converged with other agendas, inhaled the spirit of the times, and turned into a top-priority project. It might be the first salvo of the shot heard round the world, and it might do something about a problem that had troubled Murphy very much: the temporary nature of Esalen's affect. People came to Esalen for a weekend or a week and some had marvelous moments of great joy, new insights, and a heightened sense of the possibilities of life—moments precisely like those which Maslow in his writings called peak experiences—but when they went back to their families and their jobs, the dust would settle on their memories of Big Sur, old problems and old ways of being would return, and things would be as they had been before—or worse. Too often, people would experience profound letdowns. Perhaps a sustained program, combining all the Esalen disciplines, could produce a lasting personality change that would hold up in an as yet untransformed world.

Such was the climate of thought within which the planning for the residential program took place. The actual locus of the planning was wherever Murphy happened to be at the time; mostly it took place at the Leonards' house in San Francisco and at the offices of Psychological Service Associates on Westwood Boulevard in Los Angeles. Out of these meetings there had emerged, by late 1965, a detailed plan for what was at first called the Experimental College. It would have about twenty graduate-level fellows, two full-time faculty members, and a rotating part-time faculty of specialists.

The curriculum would consist of meditation, encounter, sensory awareness, creativity, movement, emotional expression, inner imagery, dream work, and peak-experience training. There would be special sessions with the leaders who came to Big Sur to give seminars for the public, and there would be continuing work with the Esalen residents: sensory awakening with Gunther, gestalt therapy with Fritz, and Tai Chi sessions with Gia-fu in the mornings. The prospective faculty was an eclectic group that included psychologists and artists and priests and even the Stanford track coach.

The project was not much like a college, despite the talk of curriculum and faculty; it was, indeed, much more like an ashram for the New American Yogas. The fellows would rise in the morning and meditate together, and their days would be filled with the work of developing their innate human potentialities: using dream work and inner imagery and meditation techniques, they would send tendrils down into their undiscovered inner selves, and in the arts and psychodrama they would express freely what they had found. Encounter would teach them to relate effectively with others, and gestalt and sensory awareness would put them in touch with their bodies. They would develop their spiritual selves, their creativity, their physical grace and strength. They would begin to understand how to deal with personal crises and uncertainty, how to enter productively into different states of consciousness, how to be fully alive in the here and now.

Each fellow would work on some project during the time of the residential program—nothing so formal as a dissertation, but *something* concrete. The planners assumed that the experience would have great payoffs back in the work milieu. An outline Murphy and Leonard wrote suggested that:

> An architect would have a richer sense of significant form and its relation to people's moods; he would be more willing to permit divergent solutions to problems, with more sense of what his client really needed for enhanced living and working. Or, a philosopher would have a richer sense of the stuff of real life with which to inform his theorizing and generalizing about significant human problems; the range of his thought would be broadened by his extended experience. Or, an educator would have a new world of areas to be educated and means for doing so opened up to him.

The project was anticipated with vigorous optimism. Bugental called it "the equivalent of the Mercury or Apollo Projects, solidly grounded, 'all-out' efforts to explore entirely new regions of human experience. From among the 'psychonauts' . . . may come the first real breakthrough into 'inner space' that may well change the entire conception and nature of the human experience."

There would also be a research program to gather hard evidence that would *prove* to the world such transformations had truly taken place. Two first-rate psychological measurement experts, George Brown of the education department at the University of California at Santa Barbara and Frank Barron of Berkeley's Institute of Personality Assessment and Research, agreed to design a battery of tests and supervise the research work. An additional $10,000 was penciled into the budget for this.

The budget was already substantial. It looked like at least $150,000 would be needed. If each fellow paid $3000 a year for room and board, that would leave a shortfall of $90,000 to be made up. Some thought $200,000 was a much more likely bare minimum if they were to get the kind of people they wanted for the visiting faculty. Lists of foundations, government agencies, and potential fat cats began to be drawn up, and phone calls were made to foundation executives by those who had some contacts in the money world.

An ally emerged—new allies were always emerging—who knew how one went about these things. This was August Heckscher, an amiable white-haired gentleman who was then head of the Twentieth Century Fund. He understood, and explained to Murphy, that foundation executives needed to be impressed, and that if Esalen and the human potential movement were to make the right kind of entrance, a bit of showmanship would be in order. They held a series of luncheons in New York for the heads of about thirty of the major foundations and got some of their heaviest guns from the psychology world—Maslow, Skinner, Gardner Murphy—as speakers. It was impressive, and some of the foundation people, in the clubby mood the luncheons generated, said yes, they would be most interested in proposals from Esalen. One woman told Murphy she particularly liked the phrase "human potential movement," which had been mentioned during the luncheon speeches; she said she was sure it would have a great impact in the future.

Back on the West Coast, plans for the program went through some minor changes and adjustments. At one of the Los Angeles meetings, the planners decided to stop calling the program the Experimental College; they thought "experimental" sounded too uncertain and "college" too academic. They decided to call it simply the residential program.

A faculty-selection committee was appointed, with Virginia Satir as its chairperson. She was extremely enthusiastic about the residential program, and somewhere along the line she volunteered to be one of the full-time faculty members. Some of the advisers had their reservations about this; they thought she was a splendid person, but she was a family therapist and had had very little experience with the disciplines that were expected to form the core of the program.

Although family therapy was not quite what Esalen was about, there was no doubt that Satir's way of going at it, which had brought her to a position of national prominence in her field, was somewhere in the human potential mainstream. She worked with entire families, even groups of families, at the same time and had developed a repertoire of fast-moving psychodrama-style exercises for getting people in touch with different family roles: flop on the floor like a limp pile of spaghetti and be the eternal placator, or stand up with a pointing finger and be the blamer. She theorized that a family was basically a communications network, and her work was aimed at helping people become more aware of how they functioned in the family setting and more capable of communicating their needs and feelings to its other members. She talked of healthy, fully functioning families in much the same way that Maslow talked of healthy individuals. And she was full of life and energy and good humor. One day Murphy and Bill Quinn and Virginia Satir turned up at Bugental's house in Los Angeles, drunk with laughter. They had just been to a department store to accompany Virginia while she bought a girdle. They had concocted this story that Virginia was a famous Russian lady cosmonaut—an interesting choice of role—and that Murphy and Quinn were her translators. The three of them would wave their arms at one another and shout in pseudo-Russian, and then Murphy and Quinn would speak to the salesclerk in accented English while the lady cosmonaut looked on imperiously. One thing they were sure of: with Virginia Satir running the residential program, it would not be dull.

Virginia was certainly lively, but perhaps not the most reliable candidate to manage a program of such scope as the residential program. Although she had tremendous skill in helping families become solid, cohesive, and stable, she was somewhat unpredictable herself. There was a Mr. Satir somewhere in the past, but nobody knew much about him. Virginia was forever on the move, charging around the world, maintaining residences in half a dozen different places. Sometimes it would take weeks to locate her if you didn't keep carefully posted on her quickly changing schedule. She did not seem to be the kind of person who would settle down and spend nine months on Esalen's little postage stamp of real estate. But Virginia had made a commitment; she was even planning to buy some property at Big Sur. Anyway, it seemed somehow unhumanistic to go looking for things that might go wrong. So many things had gone so right; Esalen's history was filled with marvelous coincidences and serendipity. Surely things would work out.

In the fall of 1966, the residential program began. The preparations for it had been underway for more than a year. There had been a couple of hundred applications, and out of that they finally ended up with seventeen people. Among them were an engineer, a Jesuit brother, a junior college art teacher, a psychologist. There was Lois Delattre, who had brought Leonard and Murphy together and had been a close friend of Esalen's since its first programs five years or so earlier. There was Edward Maupin, for whom they had especially high hopes. He was a handsome young psychologist who had written a doctoral dissertation on meditation at the University of Michigan, the first on that subject ever accepted by a major university's psychology department. Maupin had been working in the Neuropsychiatric Institute at UCLA when he heard about the residential program, and left his job when he was accepted as one of the fellows. He came from the town in Ohio where John Glenn had been born, a detail that Murphy and Leonard liked: they said he would be Esalen's first man in space. It looked like the right kind of group. Most of them were in the early thirties, young enough to be adventurous but old enough to have had some life experience—a bunch of bright, seeking, idealistic Americans.

The program was considerably scaled down from what it had been on paper. Although the foundations had professed cordial interest in the human potential movement, no grant had been obtained in time. For a while the secretary of health, education, and welfare, John Gardner (who had written a book called *The Pursuit of Excellence*), took an interest in the project, but nothing came of that, either, and some of the Esalen people were much relieved that there would not be a bunch of Washington bureaucrats scrambling about Big Sur with evaluation forms. So instead of two permanent faculty members there was only one, Virginia Satir. The plans for visiting faculty had been dropped; there would be no Stanford track coach. There was no research project.

Even without those embellishments, it looked good. It felt like a time of great promise when the residents assembled that fall and moved their belongings into the row of little box cabins that had once been the home of the followers of the First Church of God of Prophecy. The energy was so high, the people so intelligent and interesting, the first meetings so sparkling, that nobody could quite comprehend the reality of what happened in a few weeks, when, in fact, the program collapsed.

Suddenly, Virginia Satir left. It became apparent to her that this was not what she wanted to do after all, and one day she simply moved on. She did not tell anybody why she was leaving or when she would be back, so the precise nature of the disaster was not clear to anybody. The rest went cheerfully about their business, had regular meetings, gossiped about what might happen next. They did have Tai Chi sessions with Gia-fu, sensory-awakening exercises with Bernie Gunther, and several days of gestalt work with Fritz. When Alexander Lowen, who specialized in neo-Reichian bioenergetics therapy, came in for a workshop, they all participated in that, and some of them got to sit in on seminars with other notables who passed through, people like Joseph Campbell and Ashley Montagu.

The rest of the time, they more or less made up their own program. Ed Maupin emerged as an informal leader. He came up with the "group mind" project: six members, for three days, tried acting as if they were a single being. They called it Symbo, short for symbiosis. There weren't any rules they knew of for how to be a group mind, so they had to make them up as they went along. At first, until they decided the process was too awkward, they experimented with a different kind of language. Instead of starting sentences with "I," as in "I am hungry," they would say, "This part of Symbo . . ." It was "This part of Symbo is angry," "This part of Symbo has to go to the john," and so forth. After they gave that up they decided to try operating on the assumption that the task of all the members of the organism was not to change anything, but to accept the present state of the organism. The experiment went through several stages, and those who participated in it were solemnly convinced that it was, sure enough, another breakthrough in human relations. Ed Maupin later ran workshops based on the Symbo experiment and wrote an article about it for *ETC.,* the general semantics publication.

All these activities and entertainments helped distract attention from what a failure the program actually was. Nobody was willing to call it that except Fritz, who had kind of hoped it would work out that way. For all the others, it was impossible to admit that the reality was so far from the expectations. The residents valiantly made the best of it, and Murphy turned to the work of planning a second residential program, which turned out to be much more eventful and much closer to what everybody had expected, though it held its own surprises and a measure of tragedy.

Price thought the residential programs were premature; that Esalen was not quite ready to move into something so ambitious. He did not object to Murphy's wanting to move ahead with them, but neither did he get involved in their planning. He was busy with other things, most of all with gestalt therapy and Fritz Perls.

Price had attended Fritz's first gestalt therapy workshop and had been unimpressed. Obviously, Fritz possessed a great skill, but Price found his manner uninviting. Nor did he care much for Fritz's appearance. Fritz was gaunt, goateed, and carried his head thrust forward, like a vulture's. He acted and looked like what he was—an aging, embittered, and not very healthy German-Jewish psychiatrist—and he reminded Price of the unyielding doctor who had worked him over at the Institute of Living.

Then in January of 1966, more than two years after Fritz's first appearance at Esalen, Price dropped in on another gestalt workshop. Jean McGowan, the woman he had been living with, had left him, he felt lonely and in need of help, and Fritz was available. It seemed worth a try.

Fritz began by doing some simple gestalt exercises, directing the participants to pay attention to whatever was happening in their own experience of the moment, to the flow of thoughts and feelings. It was one of the simplest and most basic items in the gestalt repertoire, and Price found it oddly effective. This, he thought, is what therapy should be—something that starts with who you really are, what and where you are, just now. So began a therapy, a friendship, and an apprenticeship.

The first stage of Price's relationship with Fritz began with Price's discovery that Fritz, and his style of therapy, really had something to offer. Fritz had come riding in on the advance publicity for gestalt therapy, which, if closely examined, seemed to depend mostly on the enthusiasm of Aldous Huxley and Alan Watts for *Gestalt Therapy*, written, in large part, by Paul Goodman. Fritz clearly did impressive things, but neither Murphy nor Price had really trusted him.

That Dick Price discovered Fritz when he did is explained partly by his emotional state the day he walked into the lodge, carrying the hurt of a collapsed love affair. But it also has to do with changes in Fritz that made him more approachable than he had been before. Fritz was still tough, but he was mellowing. He was, in fact, going through a personal transformation that was at least equal to those of all the legions of people who came to Esalen over the years. In the rambling autobiography he wrote at Big Sur, the one he entitled *In and Out the Garbage Pail*, he said of his coming there:

> The target Esalen scored a bull's-eye with the arrow Fritz Perls. A landscape comparable to Elath; beautiful people on the staff as in Kyoto. An opportunity to teach. The gypsy found a home and soon a house.
> He found something else as well: a respite for a sick heart.[2]

In the gestalt system body and mind are a functioning whole, and the heart is not only the pumper of blood but, much as it is viewed in our folklore and love songs, a true locus of emotions. Before Fritz came to Esalen, and through the first year or so that he was there, he was suffering from intense angina pectoris near his heart and in the left arm. He had consulted a cardiologist in Los Angeles, who prescribed medications, which he took but which did not end the pain, and advice to quit smoking, which he did not take at all. He often thought the time would come soon when he would kill himself to end the agony in his chest. And he was old, and there was no love in his life.

When he first came to Esalen he thought the baths might help—he had enjoyed the German spas in his younger days—but after a try he found the mild pathway that connected the baths to the lodge too steep, and for a long while he stayed away from them. He would have made less of a mark on Esalen and on the world had he not experienced a surprising recovery from his heart trouble, which he attributed entirely to the efforts of Ida Rolf, a lady who had developed a bruising therapy technique that invaded the body with knuckles and elbows.

Ida Rolf, born in New York, was a woman of about Fritz's age who had developed an approach to physical healing that she called structural integration. Also known as Rolfing, the practice was built on a foundation of hatha yoga, osteopathy, and the Alexander technique, a method of physical re-education that Huxley had mentioned in his Human Potentialities lectures.

Like Fritz, she had had a hard time making a place for herself and for her work. Although she had a solid academic background (a Ph.D. in biological chemistry from Columbia) she had, from the time she first began to try working directly on people who had severe impairments of their ability to use their bodies, moved into a professional twilight zone. Chiropractors and osteopaths were interested in her way of working—she would probe deep into the muscular tissue to break down the fascial covering and bring about subtle changes in the body's structure—but they merely wanted to incorporate it into their work. She did not want to be integrated into an already established discipline; she insisted on staking her own claim to a piece of the terrain. Over the quarter of a century that she practiced, she found enough clients to provide her with an income and a few students to offer some hope that the methods she had developed would not expire with her. But her work had not had much of an impact, and it seems likely that had she not intersected with the path of Fritz and Esalen, the world would never have heard of her.

Fritz first got a sample of Rolfing in Los Angeles. A student of Ida Rolf's attended one of his lecture-demonstrations, saw that he was in intense physical pain, and offered him a first hour. (Rolfing sessions are done in "hours" that in actual practice last longer than sixty minutes each.) Fritz wanted to arrange to do more work with her, but she told him his case was too serious and suggested he contact Ida Rolf in New York. He wrote to her and invited her to come to Esalen. She came out for a week and gave him a Rolfing session each day. They had what they both considered a breakthrough in the seventh hour, when Fritz passed out. This caused her an anxious few minutes—it is no light matter to have a seventy-year-old heart patient become unconscious while you are in the process of "reorganizing" his neck—but Fritz came to and said that the experience had taken him back to a time when his neck had been painfully twisted by an anaesthetist when he was under surgery. (It is part of the theory of Rolfing that the memory of physical and emotional traumas can be triggered by the manipulation of the affected part of the body.) Fritz became an avid supporter of Rolfing and of Ida Rolf. She returned to Esalen regularly after that and, in addition to giving Fritz many more Rolfing sessions, made Esalen the West Coast center of Rolfing, much as Fritz had made it the West Coast center of gestalt therapy.

Fritz was also experiencing more subtle forms of healing at Esalen. Even without going to the baths he was often outdoors, reveling in the scenery and the atmosphere, and he was eating well and was working. It was the opposite of a retirement. Instead of tapering off, he was working more intensely and more effectively than before. He had no associate or assistant therapists, and when his programs were in session he would work several hours a day, often in the evenings as well. Sometimes there would be a weekend workshop followed by a five-day workshop followed by another weekend workshop, with no days off. He loved it. The workshops were a kind of theater, in which the patient became for a while a center of attention. But Fritz was *always* a center of attention. For somebody who had once yearned to be an actor, it was a great life. He was watched and admired, and among those who came to watch, admire, and learn from him was a growing band of professionals, many of whom became dedicated gestalt therapists. The word was spreading, more rapidly and more easily than it had ever done during those years in New York when he had tried to make it happen. Suddenly there seemed to be no limit to how far it could go. "Perhaps," Fritz said to a group of his students one day, "I am to become one of the gods of therapy after all."

Fritz grew a full beard and took to wearing the one-piece jumpsuits that became a kind of trademark of his, as was his ever-present cigarette. Fritz's smoking was one of the more conspicuous failures of gestalt therapy and the source for much of his thinking about the two psychic forces he identified as the "top dog" and the "underdog"—the inner policeman who was always striving for self-improvement, and the sneaky self who always managed to win out in the long run. The jumpsuits were for wearing around Esalen, and especially for going to the baths; they were easy to get on and off and easy to hang up on the sometimes-crowded clothes pegs. Fritz was going to the baths regularly now; that was where he put on some of his best performances as a dirty old man. (He liked to refer to himself as a dirty old man, and often introduced himself as such; it was a good way to get a relationship launched in an interesting direction. Once he approached a beauty at a party at the Big House and warned her that he was a dirty old man. She replied that she was a dirty young girl, and they took it from there.) At the baths, where the nudity was casual and most sexuality curiously subdued, Fritz preferred to let his sexuality be overt. He had a compulsive need to touch women's genitals, and he indulged himself freely with whoever would permit it. Usually somebody would permit it. And if he got an erection or some semblance thereof, he made no effort to conceal it.

Fritz often claimed that he was happier than he had ever been in his life, thanks to his growing popularity, the free-spirited Esalen environment, and the healing elbows of Ida Rolf.

This is not to say that Fritz suddenly became friendly, courteous, or approachable; nobody has ever described Fritz as "nice." People were always trying their luck with him, in the sessions and outside of them, hauling out whatever kind of charm they had to try to impress him or gain his approval. It was a dangerous game. He would insult you by describing you, to your face and in front of a roomful of people, with any of the inelegant terms he had available to describe ways of being phony: bitch, shithead, weeper, mindfucker, crazy-maker. If you bored him, he might fall asleep in his chair. Or he might just ignore you. Sometimes when he was eating alone at one of the tables in the lodge, people would come up and start talking to him, and he would merely sit there and continue chewing, looking off into the distance and perhaps letting a morsel or two tumble gently down his beard. Yet if he thought you were being straight with him, if you revealed your feelings in what seemed to be a genuine way or simply related to him straightforwardly, without trying too hard to win approval, he would respond—directly, even with warmth and sympathy. And on rare occasions, among close friends, he would permit himself to become downright sentimental.

Wherever Fritz went, he was the center of a little solar system of people trying to get his attention or his approval or to learn something from him personally. Most were rebuffed in their attempts, but there were a few, smarter or more authentic or more persistent or just better operators, who found their way into his circle of personal friends and disciples. To the gestalt true believer—and there was a growing number of these—everything that Fritz did was therapy. Hence, if he was rude to you, it was because you were acting phony or being manipulative; if he was polite or friendly, that was the badge of your authenticity.

There were no particular rules about becoming one of Fritz's students; it was existentialism in action. If you decided that you wanted to learn gestalt, you went to Esalen or you went to see Fritz when he turned up, as he often did, at professional conferences or workshops around the country. You put in some time in the Hot Seat, because a gestalt therapist who had never occupied that chair was as spurious as a Freudian who had never been analyzed. You read *Gestalt Therapy* and, if you could find it, *Ego, Hunger, and Aggression,* the book Fritz had written in South Africa and that was republished by a small San Francisco company in 1966. You listened to his occasional lectures on theory, which were rare and brief. Mostly you watched and figured it out. Or, if you didn't quite figure it out, you went back to your patients and pretended you were Fritz.

They built a house for Fritz, and this was another one of those things that didn't work out exactly according to plan. The idea was that Esalen would provide the property and Fritz would pay for the actual cost of building the house, which would then be his for life. Construction cost was estimated at $10,000. Fritz put up that amount and then took off on one of his trips to Europe. While he was gone, Esalen's building crew and miscellaneous subcontractors went to work. The site chosen was a spectacular spot on the edge of a cliff just above the baths. The builders poured vast amounts of concrete for the foundations and made most of the house from hand-hewn stone. The cost went well above the estimate, and Price wrote to Fritz, asking for more money. Fritz wrote back to say he wouldn't give another nickel, and the work went on anyway. It finally cost Esalen about $40,000, at the time a huge sum for a small two-bedroom house on land already paid for. Fritz came back from Europe, found it satisfactory, and moved in.

Fritz became an institution within the institute. His gestalt programs (weekend seminars, five-day workshops, longer training workshops for professionals) were listed separately in the brochure. He had his own private house, his students, patients, friends, and admirers—and he had his own idea about how Esalen ought to be developing. He did not think much of the rhetoric of evolutionary transformation, nor did he think much of any set of blueprints for how a person or a society ought to be. He belittled all this talk about society changing: the only way to change was to be what you were. The best thing Esalen could do, he thought, would be to develop itself into a good vehicle for gestalt therapy—and maybe Rolfing.

Despite his favored position, Fritz remained insecure, jealous, and combative. He was critical of other seminar leaders, of other therapists and psychologists, of visionary ideas. He called them "elephantshit," or "anastrophic expectations." He had often said that some people escape from reality into fantasies of horrible things that were going to happen to them—catastrophic expectations—and at Esalen he invented a new word—anastrophic—to describe the contrasting syndrome, which he found in abundance. When he heard about the residential program, he immediately became suspicious. He didn't like the sound of it, even though Murphy assured him that gestalt therapy would be part of the curriculum. He was not interested in being part of something, another sideshow, along with Tai Chi lessons and sensory-awakening exercises. Most of the planning for the residential program seemed to be happening somewhere else, and he was not being invited to the meetings. (Perhaps he suspected the truth, which was that one of the reasons the planners held the meetings elsewhere was to get around having to invite him. Everyone knew he attended meetings the way Napoleon visited countries.)

Fritz was Murphy's greatest problem. He was hard to handle, and he would not get in step with the human potential movement, even though everyone recognized that gestalt therapy was a principal ingredient of it. Fritz's waywardness was most dramatically demonstrated one weekend early in 1966, when Abraham Maslow came to Esalen to discuss his concept of a "being language."

Maslow, exploring new avenues in his work on healthy, self-actualizing people, theorized that there were really two entirely different sets of basic motivations: those stemming from a sense of deficiency and those that expressed the full and natural human being. He called them "deficiency motivations" and "being motivations," or, for short, D-motivations and B-motivations. He saw strong differences between D-values and B-values, and between D-love and B-love. He even began to suspect that among self-actualizing people there was a superior form of expression—more true, open, and affirming. He called it B-language. He thought that if he could bring together a group of people who understood this, who were themselves healthy and growing people, they would be able to detect the presence of this language, lying heretofore undiscovered, like a jewel in the rough underbrush of ordinary conversation, and bring it into a fuller existence. He was deeply convinced that practically everything that took place in the society, including ordinary talk, was a conspiracy against the potentialities latent in the human mind and spirit. If only the conspiracy could be brought into the open, if the obstacles to full humanness could be understood and removed, then, he was sure, a great step in human progress would be made.

Murphy obligingly gathered together a group of scholars, therapists, and Esalen staff people for this meeting, and also invited some Esalen well-wishers to come as spectators. The most prominent in the latter category was the Academy Award–winning actress Jennifer Jones, widow of the film mogul David O. Selznick. She had become an ardent admirer of the human potential movement. Fritz came, too. They had to invite him; he would have come anyway.

Even before the meeting started, it was in trouble. Maslow went down to the baths before dinner on Friday, had a nice soak and a massage, and came back feeling splendid. He spoke of the Esalen masseuses as young priestesses. It had been a peak experience, sublime and nonsexual. "Bullshit," said Fritz. "You are just turned on." This offended Maslow, and they bickered about it in the dining room. To Maslow, it was a betrayal of the human spirit to reduce a sublime experience to a sexual one; to Fritz, it was a betrayal not to do so.

The meeting assembled in the lodge after dinner, the invited participants in a little circle in front of the fireplace and the observers seated, audience-style, around the outside of the circle. Murphy said a few words of greeting, then turned the meeting over to Maslow, who reviewed some of his ideas about the two kinds of motivation and then plunged directly into the work. This was confusing to some of those assembled; the invitees did not all have a clear idea of the purpose of the meeting, and some had come just because they thought it would be nice to hang around Big Sur over the weekend and be vaguely humanistic together. Suddenly, here they were, in the midst of a most abstract and difficult discussion. Maslow, they realized to their amazement, really planned to *do* this. He was prepared to sit there all weekend, march through the whole English language, one piece at a time, and figure out how to define things in B-language. "Take 'duty,' " he said. "Now, how would you define duty in a nontraditional way, a psychological meaning that conveys self-actualization or health?"

Hobart Thomas, who had organized an existential psychology conference up in Santa Rosa a few years before, was one of the participants. Duty, he suggested, could be thought of as the fulfilling of one's own personal destiny, becoming what one could become.

"Right," said Maslow. "That's a good example."

"This is just like school," Fritz said. "Here is the teacher, and there is the pupil, giving the right answer."

Maslow pretended to ignore this. Getting into arguments was not his thing; he preferred to have friendly high-level discussions about humanistic psychology. He lowered his head and plowed on into the subject of being-language—and the ordeal continued through that evening and through the next day. Although the meeting took some time to attain the status of a real disaster, it was never, even for a few minutes, a success. The dominant fact in the room, overshadowing everything else, was the conflict between Fritz and Maslow. To those who had had experience with T-groups, it was obviously necessary to recognize the conflict and deal with it. Several of them suggested this. But Maslow was not about to let go of his agenda for the meeting and sail into the uncharted waters of group process. Fritz was not playing T-group rules, either. He was not talking about his true feelings or seeking a straightforward confrontation with Maslow; he was choosing to sit around and drive Maslow crazy. At one point Thomas suggested that it might be a good idea to take a break and do some kind of movement to relieve the tension. Fritz asked him what he wanted to do.

"Anything," Thomas replied desperately. "Dance, maybe."

"Good," Fritz said. "Let's dance." He got up and gathered the surprised Thomas into his arms, and for a few minutes the two of them swept about the circle in a burlesque ballroom waltz while Maslow watched in monumental disappointment.

Mike Murphy had been trying to act as chairman of the meeting, but he had no delusions about being a group leader, and he felt that whatever it was that needed to be done to ease the tension, he was not the man to do it. During the Saturday dinner break, before the evening meeting, he persuaded John Levy to take over as chairman. Levy, a member of Esalen's executive committee and the executive officer of the Association for Humanistic Psychology, was a quiet, solid man whom they all knew and trusted. He agreed to chair the evening meeting. And that was the worst part.

After Levy convened the meeting, Maslow took over again and returned to the subject of being-language. Most of those present were personally fond of Maslow, and they kept trying to do what he wanted, but the conversation developed a stilted, deadly quality. A man from Southern California, who represented a philosophical society that had been founded by a famous Indian yogi, delivered a long and very obscure speech. After it had gone on for a while, Murphy looked over and saw that Fritz was sliding down from his chair onto the floor. In a few seconds everybody else had noticed, and the whole group watched in horrified silence as Fritz slithered across the floor toward the philosopher, reached one supplicating arm toward him, and said, "Come down here with the rest of us; get down with the common people."

Maslow told Fritz he was being childish, so Fritz proceeded to be childish in gestalt therapy style: do it all the way, invest yourself in it, get fully in touch with it. He crawled around on the floor and made whining sounds and hugged Maslow's knees.

There sat kindly Maslow, a professor at Brandeis, the father of humanistic psychology, rigid as a rock in his crew cut and cashmere sweater while this crazy old man in a jumpsuit hugged his knees and made baby noises. "This begins to look like sickness," Maslow said.

Levy could not resolve the confrontation—probably no one could have—and the meeting broke up in confusion. Maslow was furious and said he was going to call a taxi to come down from Monterey and take him to the airport so that he could catch the next plane for the East Coast. Levy followed Maslow about and finally got him to calm down and agree to stay over until the next day. Others went to Fritz and found him weeping—not playing the child, but sobbing in his own frustration. Murphy escaped onto the porch for some fresh air, and Jennifer Jones stood there, her faith unshaken. "These wonderful men," she sighed. "How brave they are. What chances they take."

The next morning, while Thomas was eating breakfast in the lodge, Fritz sat down next to him and handed him a piece of paper, on which he had scrawled a few lines of poetry. "Here," Fritz said. "Here is the language for being." The poem went:

> I'm not a lady who perfumes her farts
> I am a scoundrel and a lover of arts
> I am what I am,
> And I fuck when I can
> I'm Popeye the sailor man.

They assembled for a final meeting that morning. Maslow had regained his composure, but he was still deeply upset. He spoke of the seriousness of their purpose, of saving the world, of the urgent need to understand things and get them down in writing so that they would be accessible to others. He also lectured Esalen about the need to maintain the good will of people in the academic world whose support was important but could easily be alienated. It was obvious whose good will he was talking about. Fritz called Maslow a sugar-coated fascist. Murphy did not say anything, but Price said it sounded as if they were being threatened, and he resented it.

The being-language conference had indeed been several thousand miles short of a success, but it was a heroic sort of disaster. Jennifer Jones was right: they were brave men, and they did take chances. Maslow went on with his efforts to carry a humanistic vision into psychology and into the culture as a whole, and had some success with it. Fritz stayed with his earthier view of the human potential, and had some success with that. Both remained connected with Esalen. Murphy, who had youth and resilience and a sense of humor, recovered quickly from the conference and later loved to regale friends with his description of Fritz crawling around on the floor and Maslow saying, "This begins to look like sickness."

Jennifer Jones was undaunted by the shortcomings of the being-language conference, and went ahead with a project of her own. Her idea, which she had discussed at length with Murphy, was to put on a party that would be more or less the Southern California equivalent of the luncheons that had been held in New York City for foundation officials, except that this would all be done in one wonderful event, and, instead of foundation people, the guests would be top people from the film world. They would come and learn about the human potential movement and meet some of *its* top people and, having been favorably impressed thereby, would become staunch friends and supporters of Esalen and of research in humanistic psychology.

Originally it was to be a small party. But Jennifer Jones had been out of circulation socially since Selznick's death, and she became more and more enthusiastic about this party, which would announce her return. The list grew until the number of dinner guests was around ninety, including dozens of famous film stars, like Jason Robards, Jr., Natalie Wood, Eddie Albert, and Rock Hudson. The human potential delegation included Carl Rogers and Richard Farson from the Western Behavioral Sciences Institute; Mike Murphy, George Leonard, and Fritz Perls from Esalen; John Levy of the American Association for Humanistic Psychology; and Abraham Kaplan, a professor of philosophy from the University of Michigan who had recently taken an interest in Esalen and humanistic psychology. It became much too large for the kind of convivial gathering of stars and scholars that had been envisioned at first, but everybody was so excited about bringing together such an interesting group of people that no one seriously considered the possibility that the party might be too glamorous for its purpose.

It didn't really *look* like a little intellectual soirée that evening as the sports cars and Lincoln Continentals began pulling up in front of the Selznick mansion atop a hill in Bel Air, to be taken over by the hustling, red-coated young parking attendants while the guests walked up the driveway under swinging Japanese lanterns to be greeted at the door by their beautiful hostess. It looked like a big Hollywood bash.

It took a long time for all the guests to arrive, and while they were assembling, cocktails were served in the huge, wood-paneled living room. George Leonard, who had been selected to serve as master of ceremonies, gave a little introductory talk about the movement and introduced the guests. He was good at this sort of thing; his talk was easy to understand, and it communicated some of his enthusiasm for the great things that the human potential movement hoped to accomplish. It all went quite well, except for occasional interruptions by

Jason Robards, Jr., who had had a few too many drinks and wanted to do gorilla imitations.

After the talk and the introductions everybody was herded in to dinner, which was served with wines, champagne, and liqueurs; and after the dinner the Esalen contingent prepared to show a rough cut of a film entitled *Journey into Self,* a documentary of an actual encounter group. It was late by this time, and the projectionist had some trouble getting the projector to work. Finally he got it going and showed the film, an unadorned documentary of a rather quiet group led by Rogers and Farson. There were touching moments in it, but they were subdued. The whole thing was a polite, even staid example of an encounter group, and it was quite unsuitable for that particular audience, most of whom would have been unimpressed by a boisterous one. They were professional film people, who spent their lives working on technicolor slam-bang adventures, romances, and comedies, and they had little tolerance for this plain little black-and-white thing in which a bunch of people sat around and *talked* to each other. Nobody paid much attention to the film, anyway. In a dark corner of the living room, to one side of the screen, a director and one of the most famous blonde movie queens of the decade were doing something interesting on a couch. It was too dark in the room to tell exactly what it was they were doing, but whatever it was, it was more interesting than this film, and that was what everybody watched.

After the film was shown, Carl Rogers stood up. A gentle, balding man with an unassuming manner, he told the guests that they had just seen a film of an actual encounter group. For those who were interested in finding out what it was actually like, he was prepared to lead a group. He was very matter-of-fact and very un-Hollywood: no hype, no effort at persuasion. He merely said he was going to go down the hall to another room, and anybody who wanted to participate in the group could follow him. Having said this, he walked across the living room and down the hall. Nobody followed.

In the living room the guests milled about and got more drinks. A producer's wife asked John Levy what the movie they had just seen was supposed to be *about.* He tried to explain something of the theory of groups, and asked her—in a Rogerian manner—what the message had been for *her.*

"All I could figure out," she said, "was that if you shut a bunch of people up in a room and keep them there long enough, sooner or later somebody starts to cry."

Outside, by the swimming pool, Fritz had set up a few chairs and was preparing to give a demonstration of gestalt therapy. This did not go over much better than Rogers' encounter group, although at least a few people did participate. Natalie Wood tried a bit of work in the Hot Seat, but didn't like it at all when Fritz told her that she acted like a spoiled child; she left the party in a huff. Tuesday Weld tried it and was equally unimpressed. Fritz had been on his best behavior all evening, but in a few brief minutes he managed to alienate two actresses who later appeared in movies that spoofed the human potential movement: Natalie Wood was one of the stars of *Bob and Carol and Ted and Alice,* which lampooned a growth center very much like Esalen, and Tuesday Weld later starred in *Serial,* a satire of the hot-tub ethos of California's Marin County.

As a party, the party was a great success. A few conflicts and unpleasantnesses are common at such events, and nobody was particularly troubled about the little gestalt therapy poolside scene. The great majority of the guests, in fact, never knew about it. Most of them stayed late. Dennis Murphy, who was then in Hollywood writing the screenplay of his novel *The Sergeant,* showed up some time after midnight and helped keep the party going until morning. Everybody except Fritz's patients had a good time, and it went into history as a sparkling piece of Hollywood social life. Murphy and the Esalen–humanistic psychology contingent had enjoyed their brush with the great and the near-great of the film world, but the event produced no tangible contributions toward Esalen's progress.

Years later, looking back, John Levy saw the party as a great missed opportunity. He thought the Esalen delegation should have taken a more active part in the planning of it, exerted some control over the size of the guest list, and taken care that the message they wished to communicate would not be engulfed in glamour, booze, and confusion. Instead, they had gone into it like a gaggle of starlets, expecting to be discovered.

Perhaps they should have been more aggressive in pursuing this opportunity, but it would have been entirely out of character—even contrary to the philosophy that formed the foundation of Esalen's activities. Esalen's goals were certainly not small; it was out to change the world, although that in itself was not unusual. In the mid-1960s, you could hardly walk down the street without meeting someone who was on his (or her) way to change the world. The difference lay in the way Esalen went about it. Political movements, such as the civil rights movement and the peace movement, were forces of opposition and resistance; their adversaries were numerous, tangible, and organized, and their followers were forever being urged to hurl themselves against the barricades.

The human potential movement, as it issued forth from Esalen, had a much more Oriental tone; it was derived from the Taoist principle of *wu-wei,* which had to do with acting by not placing oneself in frontal opposition to the direction of things. Alan Watts had often written and spoken of this, and that summer he gave a seminar at Esalen entitled "Being in the Way," which was about the different meanings of that phrase—being an obstacle or being in the flow of life. The Esalen approach to changing the world was to be in the flow: to achieve harmony with that which was bound to happen and to join whatever seemed to be moving in the right direction. Its progress thrived on pleasantly fortuitous happenings (such as Abe Maslow turning up at Big Sur) and was nourished by the continual appearance of new allies who opened new doors. And when somebody came along with what seemed like a worthwhile project (Maslow's being-language conference, Jennifer Jones's party, the residential program), nobody was inclined to scrutinize every detail and control the exact outcome. Out of this came Esalen's greatest successes and its greatest failures, and several things that were a little of each.

Esalen had been introduced to many groups: the psychological community, the foundation world, Hollywood society. George Leonard opened what was perhaps the most important door of all, and brought Esalen to the attention of the American public.

At the same time that the Esalen residential program was being outlined, Leonard was busy planning another special California issue of *Look.* He took part in starting the residential program, and Murphy helped with the *Look* issue: discussing it often with Leonard, sitting in on idea sessions in San Francisco, accompanying Leonard to the *Look* offices in New York, and participating in an experiment on the use of LSD as an aid to journalistic creativity.

Leonard had not yet had any personal experience with psychedelic drugs. He had interviewed several of the people who were then doing research with them, but he had never quite been convinced of their value and had expressed doubt about them in his article on human potential. Lois Delattre challenged him about this the day they had

141

lunch at the Palace Hotel, the same day she invited him to her house to meet Murphy. She directed his attention to the people who were at the surrounding tables in the Garden Court, the large and elegant glass-ceilinged central dining room. It was the usual crowd of business executives, wealthy tourists, socialites, and local politicians (the mayor was a few tables away). She asked Leonard if he could see a single person in the room who couldn't do with an LSD trip. He looked around and had to admit that he couldn't. Nevertheless, although LSD and other psychedelics were then legal and available, he made no effort to try any of them until the *Look* meeting.

This session was conducted under the auspices of the International Foundation for Advanced Study, the research organization that had been set up by Myron Stolaroff and Willis Harman. They had been administering LSD to people in various fields and monitoring them to see whether it affected their creativity and efficiency. The whole thing was conducted with great care and attention to detail: on the night before the session, the participants were given a preparatory lecture by Stolaroff and Harman. The next morning they gathered in a large room at the institute's offices in Palo Alto, near the Stanford campus. The research subjects were Leonard, Murphy, *Look* photographer Paul Fusco, and James Fadiman, a psychologist. The observers were Harman, Stolaroff, and a psychiatrist. The subjects were given a brew consisting of lithium, a tranquilizer, and LSD.

For about four hours they listened to music through stereophonic headsets, and some of them were so deeply moved that tears streamed down their faces as they sat quietly in the big room's overstuffed chairs. Then they took off the headsets and started talking about California.

The ultimate product of that discussion, the second *Look* special issue on California, came out in the summer of 1966. About twenty *Look* staff members worked on it, including Fusco, Leonard, and T George Harris, who would later become editor of *Psychology Today*. It drew on more than an afternoon's acid trip, and it peered into virtually everything that was new on the West Coast, from topless cocktail bars to the charred streets of Watts.

The issue brought together many themes: youth, the future, revolutionary change, inner exploration, psychology, the human potential movement (a phrase that was used several times), and California. It declared that those themes were converging. It proclaimed that California was the viewfinder through which the rest of the country could see its future, and that the future was a new game with new rules:

> The game is no longer to explore and control your physical environment, not to build empires on the face of the earth, but to explore and expand yourself, your institutions and all of human possibilities, to seek ever-receding frontiers in the infinitely rich and varied common countryside of humanity. The rules include a surprising openness in personal relations, a radical shift in the morally admissible, an expanded definition of education . . .

Esalen was mentioned in the caption of a large photograph of Michael Murphy. The photograph, which appeared on a photo spread headlined TURNED-ON PEOPLE, showed Murphy jubilantly flinging his arms against a background of Big Sur sky, his head thrown back in exuberant, self-actualizing laughter. ("It took a lot of film to get that shot," he once said.) The caption also mentioned some of the leaders who had appeared at Esalen in the past and referred to a new project, "a spirited experiment in education, a residential program to train graduate Fellows in aspects of life that most schools neglect or completely ignore."

Although Esalen was referred to explicitly only once, its influence was visible throughout the magazine; much of the copy was an update of material Leonard had first written for his article on "The Human Potential" (which *Look* never published), but was modified by a new interest in human relations training groups (". . . our nation has passed through the opening stages of a largely unreported revolution—there is no other word strong enough—in how people get along together.") and a new tolerance for LSD.

> Many Californians, among them honor students and leading professionals, have used the drug in a most "serious" manner, under careful controls. These people have tried LSD neither for kicks nor for therapy, but to gain glimpses of new and rich worlds of consciousness. They may be likened to the proper Britishers of some generations ago who ended their formal education with a Grand Tour of the Continent and the East. The young Victorians might return to the rigidities of their own society, but—simply because they saw other cultures, other ways of doing things were *possible*—they would never again be quite the same, never quite so

dogmatic, never quite so willing to reject unfamiliar approaches out of hand.[3]

This was the message that went circulating out through the news-stands and mailboxes and libraries and reception rooms around the country in the summer of 1966—two years after the Berkeley Free Speech Movement, one year after the Watts riots, one year before the Summer of Love.

Fritz Perls, circa 1962. (JACK GAINES)

Aldous Huxley at Big Sur, 1962. (F. FLORIAN)

The Big House, built as a residence by Michael Murphy's grandparents and now used for guest lodging and meetings. (KATHY THORMOD)

Robert Schwartz, Will Schutz, Michael Murphy, 1966. (Schwartz was a visitor.) (MORT KAYE STUDIOS)

Richard Price, 1966.
(MORT KAYE STUDIOS)

Gia-fu Feng, 1965. (PAUL HERBERT)

Gia-fu conducting Tai Chi class on the swimming pool deck, 1965. (PAUL HERBERT)

Buckminster Fuller at Esalen, 1967. (PAUL HERBERT)

Abraham Maslow, mid-1960s. (PAUL HERBERT)

Ali Akbar Kahn concert in the main lodge, 1965. (PAUL HERBERT)

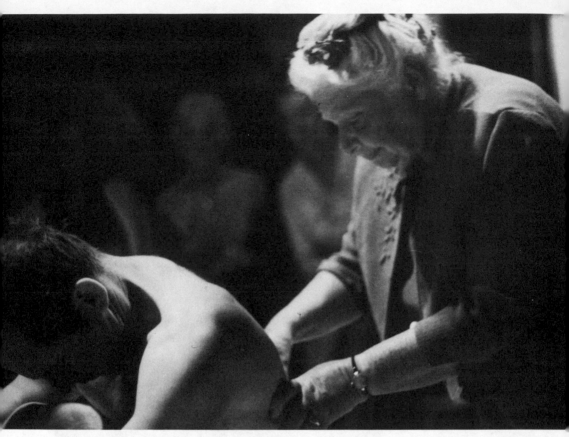

Ida Rolf, 1966.   (PAUL HERBERT)

Charlotte Selver and Charles Brooks, 1977.   (JACOB GAINES)

Alan Watts, 1970. (PIRKLE JONES)

Fritz Perls in the lodge, mid-1960s. (PAUL HERBERT)

In 1967 the proprietor of the little restaurant and gas station at Lucia, just south of Esalen, hung a sign on the door, saying, "We do not serve hippies or beatnicks." This was one local's deeply felt, if slightly misspelled, response to the latest surge of media-assisted rebellion against mainstream American culture. In some ways it looked as though the Beat Scene of the 1950s was being made over into a bigger and noisier and more crowded spectacular, with rock music instead of jazz and poetry for its sound track. This outburst of youthful restlessness was bubbling toward some sort of a climax in the summer of 1967—the Summer of Love, as it was beginning to be called. The most frequently heeded set of directions for how to play the hippie game was Timothy Leary's: "Tune in, turn on, drop out." He had left out only one item: Go to California. The Haight-Ashbury district in San Francisco was where the greatest numbers of hippies assembled, but the Sunset Strip of Los Angeles was not far behind. Any place on the West Coast was an acceptable place to be that summer, and there was much migrating up and down Highway 1. The Big Sur area, which had been a congenial Bohemian hangout since before the hippies were born, underwent a population explosion. Far back in the hills, at the ends of dirt roads once known only to the most intrepid of the Big Sur Heavies, there were communes with two or three hundred people, nearly as much as the usual permanent population of the entire Big Sur coast. And there were smaller encampments wherever anybody could find room to put up a tent or a lean-to and build a campfire out of sight of the road.

The wooded hills around Esalen were filled with squatters. Just inland, in the misty, redwood-shaded canyon through which the Hot Springs Creek trickled, there were pup tents and bedrolls and sleeping bags and, here and there, marvelously constructed little shacks, some of them decorated with altarlike structures or colorful woven Gods' Eyes hanging from the trees in front of their entrances. The canyon had a mysterious, otherworldly aura; although it was only yards from a California highway, where traffic rumbled north and south across the bridge, it felt like a land that belonged to the Grimms or Tolkien.

A great sense of change trembled in the air along the California coast that year, an undefined yet powerful feeling that the old was precipitously giving way to the new. The hippie scene was only a part of this, but it was a part that everybody saw, worried about, and tried to understand. It seemed to signal a truly revolutionary change in society: if a whole generation was exiting from conventional morality, what vast changes might the future hold?

It reverberated through countless individual lives, stirring feelings of restlessness and opportunity among the middle-aged and middle class. Since youth seemed to be the focus of this new energy, people tried to act or look younger, hoping that a little of the exuberance of the hippie scene would rub off. It was a time of Indian summers, when many marches into gray adulthood and middle age were temporarily reversed. Bob Dylan, the poet laureate of the decade, sang,

> Ah, but I was so much older then
> I'm younger than that now.

Esalen seemed to have something to say about all this. It appealed to those who were trying to make sense of what was happening in society and to those who were interested in making more personal and immediate changes in their own lives: rediscovering their bodies, opening up their senses, learning to feel and communicate their desires. Such programs brought the adult and the employed to Esalen, and there was a definite complementary relationship between the earnest seminarians who did their thing in the meeting rooms and the young who wandered the highways and lived in the hills above Big Sur.

In hippie circles, Esalen became known as "the country club." Every day the hill dwellers would come down out of the woods and pass the time hanging around the lodge. Murphy and Price were not pleased by this, but they let it happen. The hippie movement was as much a surprise to them as it was to the rest of the country. But it did seem possible that these young people were, in some way, harbingers of the very transformation Esalen was dedicated to helping bring about. So the hippies wandered freely and pointlessly about the premises, like sacred cattle shambling through the streets of an Indian village.

There was still a lingering homy obscurity about Esalen then. It was well known, its programs well attended, but it did not yet have a national constituency. It was primarily a California place. Nor had the image of Esalen as a hotbed of encounter groups yet been established. Group workshops, sometimes identified as encounter, were a regular but decidedly minor part of the programming. If you had heard of Esalen, you were as likely to identify it with existential philosophy, humanistic psychology, gestalt therapy, or Zen. Even if you came to Big Sur for an experiential program rather than an intellectual one, you would probably drop in on a Selver-Brooks sensory-awareness seminar or perhaps one of Bernie Gunther's increasingly popular weekends of sensory awakening, body movement, meditation, and massage. These did epitomize one kind of human potential experience, the kind known as "touchy-feely," but they had little resemblance to the truth-dredging and emotion-purging encounter sessions that soon came to be seen as the very essence of Esalen.

But many things were in motion that summer, changing both the reality and the image: Murphy moved to San Francisco to open an Esalen branch in the city and launch a batch of new projects, Will Schutz moved to Big Sur to make Esalen the headquarters of his style of encounter, and George Leonard launched a program to use encounter as a weapon against racial prejudice.

This was a time that Murphy always looked back on as the craziest period of his life. Esalen was expanding in a burst of feverish activity; hippies were everywhere; people were striving to change their life styles, blow their minds, improve themselves, liberate themselves, solve their problems. His personal life was also full of uncertainty. He was passionately involved with Patricia Felix, and just as passionately ambivalent as to what to do about it. Patricia was a striking and intelligent woman, three years older than Murphy, twice married and divorced. She had moved to Esalen in 1966 to be with Murphy during the first residential program, and rented a place on the property called the Farm House. Murphy often stayed there, but he still kept his own room in the Big House, a symbol of his reluctance to commit himself fully to the relationship. It was a stormy affair, with many highs and lows. He would often ask people, in that earnest manner of his, what

147

they thought he ought to do. Most of them told him he should break it off. He got a million dollars' worth of advice, from some of the best psychologists in the country. None of it helped.

It was while Murphy was becoming increasingly restless at Big Sur that he thought about opening an Esalen branch in San Francisco. Already there were "growth centers," modeled on Esalen, springing up elsewhere. The first, started by a young man named Bob Driver, was known as Kairos. It was in a resort motel near San Diego, in a horsy region full of white fences and retired admirals. But others, like Oasis in Chicago, and Aureon in New York, were in cities, demonstrating that the resortlike setting was not a necessity. In some ways, in fact, it was a disadvantage, since it meant higher costs for the customers, who normally were charged for room and meals. An urban center could offer its programs at lower prices, be accessible to more people, and thus be less vulnerable to the charge of serving only the white, the wealthy, and the college educated—a damaging charge in these politically touchy years.

Murphy discussed the idea with many of Esalen's advisers, who encouraged him to proceed. George Leonard was a strong advocate of a San Francisco branch. So was James Pike, who offered Esalen the headquarters of his diocese, magnificent Grace Cathedral on Nob Hill, for its programs.

Pike had been a staunch early supporter of Esalen. He liked its freedom from subservience to any particular orthodoxy and thought its mixture of religious, philosophical, and psychological inquiries was valuable for the rethinking of the Christian faith that he was trying to bring about. He led seminars at Big Sur with Alan Watts and James F. T. Bugental, and brought other Christian renegades there, such as Bishop John Robinson of England, author of the controversial *Honest to God,* and Harvey Cox, author of *The Secular City.*

Pike had come into the priesthood late. He left a brilliant career as a lawyer to enter Union Theological Seminary, where he studied under Paul Tillich. In San Francisco he had befriended Beat poets and Zen mystics and was on good terms with Alan Watts, whose high-spirited theology he greatly admired. He was, if anything, even more radical than Watts, embracing civil rights activism in the 1960s, advocating the ordination of women, and challenging church dogma. He publicly repudiated the doctrine of the Virgin birth, and called the concept of the Holy Trinity "outdated, incomprehensible, and nonessential." Each time Pike made one of his iconoclastic pronouncements, it sent shock waves through the church. The Episcopalian Church of America was, indeed, nearly as open minded as its English counterpart (as Watts had discovered), but Pike severely tested its limits. He wanted the church to establish some sort of a religious think tank to discuss religious and social issues and to explore the connections between Christianity and the new movements in psychology, philosophy, the arts. He thought a branch of Esalen, located in Grace Cathedral, might fill this role.

At the time this project surfaced, Pike was already in trouble because of his theological views and his activities as spokesman for radical causes. He was always making speeches, being interviewed, showing up on television—intense, articulate, and contentious, smoking and waving his cigarette around like Bette Davis. Some of his fellow clergymen were tired of hearing about him, and, scandalized by his thoughts on the Virgin birth and the Holy Trinity, a group of them launched a move to have him tried for heresy. Avidly reported in the national media, this action was most embarrassing to the leaders of the church. On the one hand, they did not want to become involved in anything so medieval as a heresy trial, especially of a priest who had a large personal following and who also happened to be a damned good lawyer. On the other hand, they could not condone his views. The matter simmered along throughout 1967. Finally, Pike's colleagues formally rebuked him for "irresponsible" teachings. By that time, however, he had resigned his bishopric and had become a fellow at the Center for the Study of Democratic Institutions in Santa Barbara.

His successor as bishop was friendly to the Esalen project, but some other church officials and members of the Grace congregation were not. After much discussion, the cathedral chapter approved an arrangement whereby Esalen would be permitted to hold programs in the cathedral's meeting rooms, but have its offices elsewhere. Murphy rented some space, at low cost, in a house that belonged to a cousin, and made plans to hold some of the Esalen–San Francisco events in other locations in the city.

The San Francisco branch was inaugurated in the fall of 1967, in a spirit of synthesis that harked back to Esalen's original goals of blending East and West, science and religion, psychology and philosophy. It was also resoundingly ecumenical. The commencement proceedings started with a celebration led by Sister Mary Corita, an artist and a Catholic nun of the Order of the Immaculate Heart. That night Abe

Maslow gave a lecture at the First Unitarian Church on "The Farther Reaches of Human Nature." The next night at the same church Alan Watts put on a service that he called an "ecumenical liturgy." This was the sort of thing he did brilliantly, and it is probably just as well that it was not held in the more sedate Grace Cathedral. It was a splendid evening of religious razzmatazz that included Buddhist, Hindu, and Gregorian chants, conga drums, Indian music, incense, and fire. The robed assistants at the ceremony were several of Watts's cronies from Beat and psychedelic circles, including Timothy Leary, and Watts preached a sermon entitled "Joy to the World." A few days later, at Grace Cathedral, there was a series of panels on "The Scope of the Human Potential." Among the panelists were Willis Harman, Richard Farson, B. F. Skinner, and Price Cobbs, a young black psychiatrist.

Murphy attended all the opening events at San Francisco, as he had all the seminars during the first years at Big Sur. Patricia was with him. She had moved to San Francisco, where she had an apartment. Murphy had a room next to the office in his cousin's house. He was still powerfully attracted to her and still uncertain as to what to do.

One night he took her to see *Zorba the Greek.* The film's zest for life captivated them both, and they came out of the theater in a kind of euphoria. Walking down the street to Murphy's car, they decided to get married. They drove directly across the mountains to Carson City, where they found a wedding chapel presided over by a short and balding man whom Murphy, already having misgivings, thought looked like a ringer for one of Esalen's seminar leaders, Buckminster Fuller.

The next day they returned to San Francisco, and Murphy caught a plane to the East Coast for one of his foundation expeditions. He stayed with the Maslows, Abe and Bertha, Esalen's long-suffering Jewish grandparents. It would have been the most natural thing in the world, of course, for Murphy to tell them immediately that he had just been married. Maslow had met Patricia in San Francisco and had liked her; it was the sort of news he and Bertha would have liked to hear. But for some reason Murphy didn't get around to telling them right off, and having let the first opportunity pass, he never managed to find another one. He spent a few days with them, and all the time he kept saying to himself, "I'm not telling them, I'm not telling them."

He didn't tell them, and he didn't tell anybody else. Even the people who worked in the office next to his room didn't know he had married. It came out, finally, at Big Sur, when he and Patricia were on a hiking trip with the Leonards and another couple, taking the trail that goes eastward over the hills to the Tassajara Zen Center. Along the way Pat told Lillie, Lillie told George, and Michael admitted it was true. But making the marriage public did not make it successful, and after another tumultuous year they were divorced.

Although this was one of the most difficult times of Murphy's life, he never lost that *Zorba the Greek* spirit, that willingness to take a leap. He felt quite at home in a state of euphoria, and transacted much of his business there. That was one of the things that attracted people to him. People who worked with him recall with fondness those moments when, considering some new idea, he would get caught up in the possibilities and say, "Let's *do* it!" And in those moments it seemed that almost anything could be done.

Esalen's managerial style was positive to the point of being downright whimsical. Projects were launched with little or no thought given to how they might fail or go wrong, and personnel decisions were made the same way. Fritz was at Big Sur because he had chosen to come there, not because he had been sought out for the post of resident teacher. Virginia Satir had decided she would like to lead the first residential program, nobody objected, and she had the job. In view of this record of management by *wu-wei*, it is somewhat surprising that one of the major shapers of Esalen's history, William Schutz, took up residence there in response to an invitation, extended after some years of communication between him and the organization. He was probably the best-qualified person in the country for the position he assumed at Big Sur in 1967.

He was solidly built, muscular (like most human potential leaders he believed in physical fitness), and balding. He had a hard edge to his personality that frequently intimidated people. Although he practiced the encounter style of relating that he preached—was straightforward, expressed his feelings, asked for what he wanted, told the truth—it was not a style that generated intimacy. There was a strong strain of machismo about him that showed up in his choice of group methods, and it colored his personal relations. Men were often a little afraid of him or were inspired to compete with him for leadership of the group, a challenge that he seemed to enjoy. Dick Price, who had to deal with Schutz on various administrative matters, found him demanding and difficult, yet in his own way agreeable and reasonable enough. There grew up between the two of them a guarded relationship, polite and respectful but with little warmth. Women were often attracted to Schutz, to his leadership, his muscular style, and his flashes of vulnerable openness. Others found him too macho and too much on the make.

In his professional training, Schutz had touched all the bases. As a young social psychologist coming up through his field in the 1950s, he had recapitulated the history of the evolution of modern group therapy, from group-dynamics research through T-groups to an eclectic form that became generally known by the name he gave it: open encounter. Coming out of UCLA with his Ph.D. in 1951, he went to work at the University of Chicago, where some of the early group-dynamics research was being conducted. Then he was recalled into the navy and put in charge of a project to figure out how to select a group of men who could work together in a ship's combat information center (a busy and crowded room where intelligence data, mainly from radar, were received, evaluated, and disseminated) and not end up fighting one another instead of the enemy. In the process he developed personality tests and theories about compatibility that were eventually written up in a book entitled *FIRO: A Three-Dimensional Theory of Interpersonal Behavior.*[1] (FIRO, which became Schutz's intellectual trademark in his early years as a research psychologist, stands for "Fundamental Interpersonal Relations Orientation"; it has to do with the idea that every person has characteristic ways of orienting toward other people.) Some of the FIRO research was done in the social relations department at Harvard, the same department in which Dick Price had been a graduate student a few years before.

Schutz taught at Harvard for four years, and there made his first cautious venture into actually running a group. Until that time his work as a social psychologist had been strictly research. But in the late 1950s he started teaching the group-dynamics seminar as a modified T-group, in which the students spent part of their time analyzing their own interactions. This was pretty academic, with much note-taking and reference to theories of social psychology, but it is interesting to note that Harvard was the site of the first Schutz encounter group. He has said that when he sat down and started that meeting, he felt absolutely at home, as though he had been doing it all his life.

In 1958 he went west to teach at Berkeley, and began going to summer workshops with the Western Training Laboratories group at Lake Arrowhead. A few years later he began to hear about Esalen. A graduate student who was in one of his group-dynamics seminars (he was calling them T-groups by this time) came back from a weekend and told Schutz he ought to go down there, because they were doing the same sort of thing he was doing. Schutz did not follow through on that suggestion, but the courtship had begun. A few weeks later he got a letter from Murphy, inviting him to conduct a seminar. He declined, but he did accept Gene Sagan's invitation to be one of the faculty for the "Education of the Imagination" conference Sagan was organizing, which was held at Big Sur in 1963 with Fritz Perls, Charlotte Selver, and the others. Schutz was one of those who dropped out of this project when it was canceled by the university for lack of enrollees, so he did not participate in the cut-rate version of it that brought Fritz and Bernie Gunther to Big Sur for the first time.

He might have become involved with Esalen at that time anyway; since he knew a lot of the people, mostly young psychologists of the T-group persuasion, who were interested in what was going on there, but his introduction was postponed for a while when he accepted an appointment at the Albert Einstein School of Medicine in New York.

Over the next few years, Schutz synthesized, from several different methods and approaches, a new form of group therapy. He did this partly as an outgrowth of experimental work with T-groups at the National Training Laboratories in Bethel, Maine, and partly in response to what was happening in the more conventional surroundings at Einstein. For a couple of years he commuted between the two, and found them immensely different. Bethel was a lively place. The T-group process had become rigid in the late 1950s, a victim of its own success, but NTL was now looking for ways to loosen it up, and he was one of a small group of trainers working on the project. This loosening-up was being allowed to proceed with extreme caution. NTL's management was willing to adopt some new approaches, but they were always nervous about the possibility that things might go too far and charge off into unexplored emotional territory. To guard against this possibility, they arranged to have a man from the front office sit in on all the personal-growth groups. However, the man from the front office turned out to be considerably wilder than Schutz then was, and he gaily supported experiments with things that people in T-groups had never done before: they drew pictures, tried group fantasies and nonverbal exercises, tried "happening" sessions with no prearranged structure, just making things up as they went along. They got rid of the huge oak tables that had been a standard feature of

T-groups and sat in a circle of chairs. Then they got rid of the chairs and sat on the floor. The people changed along with the process. Will Schutz was not only loosening up NTL; he was also loosening up himself, becoming less conventional and more open to new ideas and experiences.

While this was happening he was still holding down his regular job at Einstein, where things were not so lively. The version of group therapy there usually involved the appearance of a psychiatrist, suited up in coat and tie, usually puffing on a pipe and carrying a briefcase or a stack of important-looking papers. He would sit down with some mental patients and announce that group therapy had begun. Then he would wait until one of the patients said something or did something so that he could explain to the patient the meaning of what he or she had just said or done. The medical school also conducted diagnostic rounds, much the same as in other hospitals. A small band of psychiatrists, psychologists, residents, and interns would go around and look over the patients and argue about the precise nature of the illness: he's a hebephrenic schizophrenic. No, he's a paranoid with schizoid tendencies. No, he's a hysteric. Having come to an agreement, they would talk about the mode of treatment, what would be done *to* the patient. Although it was an axiom that successful psychotherapy required the patient's active effort to improve, the patient's role was, in fact, an entirely passive one.

Schutz had not come into this situation with different views on how psychotherapy should be practiced. He was a social psychologist, and although he was a member of the faculty, he viewed this job as an extension of his own education, an opportunity to get some experience in clinical work. Also, psychiatric clinics are extremely hierarchical organizations, with psychiatrists at the top and patients at the bottom. Psychologists are well above the patients, but they mainly do research and personality testing. Psychologists do not generally tell psychiatrists how to do their work. They may do counseling work with patients, but real therapy is understood to be done by real doctors, that is, M.D.'s. Schutz comprehended this and kept his feelings of discomfort to himself, but began exploring around in his spare time to find out what there was in the way of alternative approaches to therapy.

There were, as a matter of fact, plenty of new methods. New York was the national capital of the Freudian establishment, but it had a thriving underground of therapeutic variations. Schutz went rambling through them. He went to the Psychosynthesis Institute and learned about the work of Dr. Roberto Assagioli of Italy, whose psychology had a strong religious dimension and who employed such techniques as guided fantasy in his therapy. He discovered Alexander Lowen, who had been a student of Wilehm Reich's and had developed a body-oriented form of therapy called bioenergetics. He went to the Psychodrama Institute and sat in on psychodrama sessions with Moreno's students. He watched Paul Goodman demonstrate something called gestalt therapy, and he got Rolfed.

He experimented cautiously, at Einstein, with the introduction of techniques adapted from his explorations, such as the standard bioenergetic technique of having patients pound on pillows to release anger. He tried arm-wrestling with a young schizophrenic boy whom he had talked to for six months in one-to-one therapy sessions without a sign of contact, and found that after the physical contact, they could truly talk.

He experimented, less cautiously, up at Bethel during the annual summer T-group sessions. He tried introducing imagery work from psychosynthesis, emotion-releasing techniques from bioenergetics, and action methods from psychodrama. He picked up techniques from others who were also involved in the T-group innovation process, and together they made up new ones. There was, for example, the one they called "high noon": a couple of people who were having a conflict would stand at opposite sides of a room and start walking toward each other until they met in the center, at which point they were to do whatever they felt like doing, anything that expressed the truth about where they were with each other at the moment—wrestle, embrace, shake hands, whatever. Such exercises, he discovered, had a powerful ability to cut through verbal logjams. In a conventional group, people could haggle over an interpersonal conflict for hours, draining the energy of the leader and the other members of the group. But switching from talk to physical action had a way of moving the group with breathtaking speed toward new levels of insight and resolution.

Soon Schutz came to realize that this kind of group work was something new and quite different from either the classic T-group or any kind of group therapy that he had seen. The verbal interaction, the group process itself, was merely the matrix, which could be filled with virtually anything the group leader had at his disposal. The content was no longer restricted to what was expressible in verbal exchanges, but could expand via psychosynthesis into the world of inner symbolism and spiritual aspirations, via bioenergetics and the other neo-

155

Reichian approaches into direct work with the body, via psychodrama into an exploration of all the relationships with people who were not present in the group. It could also shift gears abruptly from verbal interaction and move into physical confrontation. It had its growing vocabulary of "exercises" and nonverbal interactions: high noon, the trust exercise (a person stands behind you, and you see if you can fall backward, trusting that you will be caught before you hit the floor), arm-wrestling or even body-wrestling between people in conflict. This added up to a lively and fast-moving group process that seemed to get to the core of things and that was, more often than not, fun. It also created a new concept of the group leader: in this kind of a group he or she was neither the all-knowing doctor of clinical group psychotherapy nor the social-psychology technician of the T-groups, but rather a ringmaster, continually introducing new acts. The line between "personal growth" and "therapy," which was never distinct anyway, completely disappeared. Schutz favored the "growth" perspective (he described it as a matter of taking people from minus to plus rather than the conventional therapeutic goal of minus to zero). There were, however, occasions within this group setting when the group leader was actually doing therapy, perhaps using unconventional techniques like massage or bioenergetics. But it was therapy, nonetheless.

During the mid 1960s, when he was developing his new group approach, Schutz thought about finding some new name for it to distinguish it from T-groups and sensitivity training. He liked Carl Rogers' term "basic encounter" and eventually began to call his own process "open encounter," meaning that it was fundamentally an encounter system, but open to the use of other methods.

Several significant events accompanied his fortieth year: he broke up with his second wife, started writing a book about his new methods, and agreed to lead three Esalen seminars at Big Sur in 1966. The next year, Schutz was invited to come out as an associate-in-residence, and he accepted.

Some of Schutz's colleagues could not comprehend why he would want to leave New York, give up a teaching position at a prestigious institution, and go to Esalen. It was perfectly all right to give a weekend seminar there, if that happened to be the sort of thing you went in for, but reputations in academia were not to be built out there, among the hippies and the hot tubs. Even after he became famous, some psychologists continued to regard him as a dropout. "Schutz could have had anything," one said. "He could have been doing major research work. He could have been a clinical psychologist, if he wanted to go that way. He could have had a tenured teaching position."

Schutz may well have been interested in scholarly prestige, but he gave it up in favor of simpler things, such as money, fame, happiness, sex, and power. He was, in fact, a very ambitious man, and frankly admitted as much. His going to Esalen did indeed have a what-the-hell spirit to it, but he knew what he was doing. He always thought of his move afterward as the best one he had ever made. It provided him with a working base but left him free to continue free-lance group-leading work around the country—a profession that was fairly lucrative and in which he was well established. It put him in the middle of the human potential movement, which was just on the verge of becoming nationally known, and it put him in a place that was beautiful, full of interesting people, and fed by an unending stream of new women. He was candid about his interest in that, too, and frequently spoke about it to participants in his encounter groups, making a point of letting them know if he had had an affair with a woman in the group. And he had a cause, to which he became increasingly dedicated during his years at Esalen: he wanted to bring encounter to the world. He thought society as a whole was badly in need of the very qualities the encounter experience sought to cultivate: openness and honesty, a willingness to take personal risks and accept responsibility for one's acts, a deeper capacity for feeling and expressing emotions, greater freedom from false morality, an enhanced sense of the body. He was looking for a platform, and he made the observation—precisely the same one Fritz (with Bernard Gunther's help) had made earlier—that going to Esalen was an admirable substitute for establishing and managing one's own institution. The more famous it became, the better it served as a launching pad for techniques and philosophies. And encounter, for Schutz, was both.

Schutz's book about his unique approach to group encounter was published in 1967, not long after he moved to Esalen. It was entitled *Joy: Expanding Human Awareness,* and it was a guided tour through the open-encounter method. It talked about Rolfing, bioenergetics, fantasy, psychodrama, and all the games and devices of the group process. But it was more than just a collection of therapeutic hardware. It had a message that represented a progression in the human potential movement. Aldous Huxley had suggested in 1960 that certain techniques might be used to enhance human potentialities. George Leonard had announced in 1965 that some of these methods were ready for the public and that more were on the way. Will Schutz boldly claimed in 1967 that they were here and they worked. His language was not obscure or metaphorical or academic. He did not talk about self-actualization. He talked about feeling good.

> The theme of this book is joy. The theories and methods presented here are aimed at achieving joy. Joy is the feeling that comes from the fulfillment of one's potential. Fulfillment brings to an individual the feeling that he can cope with his environment; the sense of confidence in himself as a significant, competent, lovable person who is capable of handling situations as they arise, able to use fully his own capacities, and free to express his feelings.[2]

Joy was a huge success: Schutz appeared on the major TV talk shows, carrying the good news of Esalen and joy to millions of Americans. All this added up to what was by far the greatest amount of publicity Esalen had yet received.

Joy had been written in New York by a man who, at the time, had no formal connection with Esalen and had gathered his material mostly on Manhattan Island. Nevertheless, it was perceived, by both its admirers and its critics, as a product of West Coast culture. Furthermore, it was generally taken to be a report on a form of group process that had been developed at Esalen and was the stock-in-trade there. This wasn't true. The first residential program had been expected to put all these pieces together, but that hadn't really happened. Various group leaders had experimented with syntheses of the different methodologies that circulated through the Esalen ambience, but nobody had systematically exposed himself to several disciplines over a period of years, as Schutz had done, nor had had the opportunity to get extensive experience at putting them together in practice. But although the open encounter–Esalen equation was not true, it soon became true. In the summer of 1967 Schutz began running "More Joy" workshops at Big Sur, and his recipe for open encounter became the foundation of the second residential program.

Nor had it been part of the initial arrangement, when Schutz took up residence at Esalen, that he would lead the residential program. The arrangement was simply that he would rent the Farm House, the small cottage on the Esalen property that Pat Felix had lived in, for $250 a month, run a few workshops, and be free the rest of the time to zip around the country, appearing on Johnny Carson's show, consulting, and leading groups. He did do all those things, but he also ended up running the residential program.

Ed Maupin, who had taken on the leadership role in the first residential program after Virginia Satir's disappearance, was supposed to be in charge of the second program. But Schutz was extremely interested in it, so it was arranged amicably that he would lead it jointly with Maupin. Yet it must have been obvious to one and all from the time the participants gathered together for their first meeting—in a room that had been named FIRO, in anticipation of Schutz's arrival— that Schutz was in charge. It was obvious to Maupin, who discreetly retired to a secondary status and let Schutz take over.

It was a sizable group that assembled in FIRO that first night, sitting in a wide circle of folding chairs. Abe Maslow was there to give them a fatherly pep talk. There were over twenty people in the program. Among them were John Heider, a psychologist and the son of the famous gestalt psychologist Fritz Heider, and John's wife, Anne. Heider would later become an Esalen group leader himself. So would Betty Fuller, a large woman who wore flowing dresses and looked like a Hawaiian queen. There was Stuart Miller, short and elegantly dressed, who later wrote about his Esalen experiences in *Hot Springs: The True Adventures of the First New York Jewish Literary Intellectual In the Human Potential Movement*.[3] There was Ben Weaver, one of several former Peace Corps volunteers in the group. There was Marcia Price, who had been a patient and a lover of Fritz's, and who became Esalen's first suicide. There was blond Steve Stroud, who in 1970 joined the delegation that went from Esalen to study under the Chilean Sufi master Oscar Ichazo. There was Art Rogers, who taught psychology at San Jose State; he was another future suicide. There was quiet, dark-haired Pamela Portugal, one of the prettiest women in the group, who later became Schutz's girl friend.

Maslow's presence impressed them with a sense of the importance of the occasion. He had recently been elected president of the American Psychological Association, and he was on record as having said that Esalen was one of the most important educational institutions in the United States. The fact that he had come there to be with them that night supported the impression that they were the true shock troops of their generation, who would, under such expert guidance,

159

work their way to the promised land that was being vaguely sought by all the protestors and peace activists, the hippies in the hills, and all the young people who had flocked to San Francisco with flowers in their hair.

After the opening meeting the group plunged immediately into a strenuous regimen of encounter sessions—morning, afternoon, and evening. Schutz was a strong, energetic, demanding leader, but this is not to say that he was in absolute control of the group. It had an energy all its own, and he led it by helping it plunge along in its own direction. On the third day of the program the group decided to remove the chairs from the room and sit on the floor. Schutz assented readily to this, having learned at NTL that changing the furniture changed the dynamics of the group. On Friday of the first week, one of the members of the group stood up and without any prior announcement took off all his clothes.

By making his style of encounter the central discipline of the residential program, Schutz automatically made it a major part of Esalen as well. Visitors to Esalen heard the residents referred to as trainees, noted what it was that they were being trained in, and reasonably concluded that the institute was in the business of producing encounter leaders. That, in fact, turned out to be the most tangible outcome of the residential program: several of the graduates became well-known group leaders, drawing heavily in their work on what they had learned from Schutz; some of them became administrators at Esalen; some of them led later residential programs that trained still more encounter-group leaders.

While plans for the San Francisco office were being made final, and encounter was fast becoming a major Esalen ingredient, George Leonard and Price Cobbs started conducting interracial encounter groups. In the two years that Leonard had been connected with Esalen, he had become convinced that groups could do much more than merely improve communications or smooth out the working of organizations. "In California and throughout the nation," he wrote in *Look*, "churchmen, educators, statesmen are gathering in these intense little circles to break through the ancient misunderstandings that have separated tribe from tribe, race from race, nation from nation." Race from race. Was it possible that the group process could clear a path through such a complex interpersonal tangle as that one?

Leonard proposed to try. He was one of those fervent rarities, a white Southern integrationist. A member of an old Georgia family, he had grown up in Atlanta and had passed the summers of his childhood in Monroe, a hot, Faulknerian little Southern town that had a square with a Confederate soldiers' memorial, old men sitting around playing checkers with Coca-Cola bottle tops, and a shadowy population of blacks who moved apologetically through the streets on their way to work. The dominant belief that governed this society—its paradigm, as Leonard would say now—was that the darkies were happy. Young George rode out sometimes with his grandfather, who was a land-owner and a state senator, to visit the black tenant farmers. They were, his grandfather assured him, contented. But one day he saw a mob try to break through a cordon of police to seize and lynch a young black rape suspect in front of the Monroe courthouse. It was at that moment, when he looked the terrified prisoner in the eye, that he first doubted things were as he had been told. "Never again," he wrote of this event, "could I believe what my elders said about Negroes. They did not sleep like babies. They never really slept. They spent their nights in passion and waiting and terror, their eyes white in the darkness."[4] Other events and experiences weakened his faith in the Southern view of race, and by the time he returned to the South to finish college, after a period of World War II service in the army air force, he was no longer seeing the South the way other white Southerners saw it. Later he thought that his interest in the human potential movement and Esalen and all that was related to his thinking about the racial issue. Having discovered that his society and its authority figures could be wrong on something as important as race, he remained open to the possibility that they could be wrong on other subjects, as well. There might be entirely different ways of looking at almost anything.

In the early 1960s, as a journalist, Leonard had other broadening adventures. The civil rights movement and the explosion of new ideas about psychology were happening at the same time, and Leonard was in the unique position of being able to observe both at close range. He discussed human potentialities with Aldous Huxley, behavior modifi-cation with B. F. Skinner, and racism with Martin Luther King, Jr. He was present at the confrontation at Ole Miss when James Meredith became the first black to enroll in that fortress of white Southern culture and had marched with Dr. King on Selma in 1965. When the riots exploded in the Watts section of Los Angeles in the summer of 1965, he and Murphy were brainstorming the future of the world in his house in San Francisco. Later, after the riots, Leonard toured Watts, contemplated its charred remains, and knew that the great social transformation he had written about so glowingly in *Look* in 1964 would have to include a closing of the gap between black and white.

He read an article in a San Francisco newspaper about the difficulties that Price Cobbs, a black psychiatrist, and his wife were having because they had moved into what had been an all-white neighborhood in San Francisco. Leonard sent a copy of the piece to his editors in New York and got *Look* to assign a writer to do an article about it. In the process, he and Cobbs and their families became friends. It is possible that Leonard was interested in taking on a suitable black friend to demonstrate his own liberalism; Cobbs had some doubts about this himself. But he became convinced that Leonard was really trying to comprehend racism—his own and that of others—and get past it.

When Leonard started talking about running some kind of an interracial encounter group, Cobbs went through still another round of doubts. He knew of Esalen, and identified it as a playground of middle-class white dilettantes. It was all right for his friend George to be caught up in this, but he didn't think it was for him. He wasn't even sure, at that point, that he was interested in improving relations between the races. Black activist thinking was rapidly turning away from the quest for integration; more and more, its focus was symbolized by such slogans as "black power" and "black is beautiful." This line of thinking, if carried to its ultimate conclusion, dictated that the first priority of a black psychiatrist was to lessen the suffering of blacks, not to resolve the confusion of whites. Cobbs remained ambivalent about the issue. Even after he had agreed to do the workshop with Leonard, he was tempted to cancel out and go instead to a black-power convention on the East Coast. His wife persuaded him to honor his original commitment.

It was a large group that assembled at Esalen for the workshop that Leonard, with his customary reckless optimism, had entitled "Racial Confrontation as Transcendental Experience." There were about thirty-five participants, plus Leonard, Cobbs, and his wife, Vad, who acted as a third group facilitator. It was racially mixed, but not racially balanced: there were more whites than blacks, more black men than women, and a few Orientals. It was overwhelmingly middle class, with a strong representation of counselors and teachers.

It was a heavy weekend. Cobbs had a tough, confrontational style. He was writing a book entitled *Black Rage,* and he knew his material.

After the introductions and preliminary skirmishing the weekend was dominated by the conflict between blacks and blacks. There was the merciless exposure of the games that black people played: the militant game, the middle-class-brother game, the hip-dude-out-to-make-the-white-chicks game, and all the rest. The blacks tore into each other and then began to coalesce, feeling a strong sense of unity as the whites expressed envy of their ability to fight and yet hold on to a deeper solidarity. Then the alignment shifted to blacks against whites, with strong white-against-white undercurrents. The whites, progressive and liberal, told of the black guests who came to their parties and the courageous things they had done to get blacks hired and promoted in their companies. Some of them had driven here, hundreds of miles from San Francisco or Los Angeles, with black colleagues and friends, to whom they turned now in a desperate search for affirmation of their goodness. They did not get it. Black rage was suddenly real. Interracial friendships crumbled on the spot as the blacks acknowledged their resentments and the more subtle forms of racism—the white good-guy liberal varieties—were exposed. Later, it became a maxim of Leonard and Cobbs that no white was free of prejudice and no black was free of anger.

The two men had brought blacks and whites together to vent lifetimes of racial stress in one weekend, and then had made it into a marathon. There was a first meeting on Friday night after dinner, a break until morning, and a long haul from Saturday morning through Sunday noon, with time out for meals and a visit to the baths on Saturday evening—but no sleep.

The all-night encounter session from the bath break onward was the really rough part, a time of utter desolation. The anger rolled on and on without end, and by 3:00 A.M. it was mixed with a general sense of depair. The anger was no longer a form of communication; it was only a sterile outpouring of bitterness. It led nowhere. Everything, it seemed, had failed: the weekend was a failure, the people themselves were failures, and the prospects for tearing down the barriers between races were nil. Leonard and Cobbs both felt that they were presiding over a disaster. Once or twice their eyes met across the room in an unspoken, mutual acknowledgment that they had made a terrible mistake.

This was very likely the toughest encounter session that had ever been convened at Esalen. There was never any guarantee in encounter groups that a resolution would be reached; some encounter groups never broke through, they only broke up. Yet when something positive did happen to transform the collective mood, it could be a deeply moving, unforgettable experience. And that happened to this group, some time after the sun rose.

It began with a white woman who said she dated black men exclusively. This was taken by black and white alike to be another sleazy piece of white liberal trickery, and the members of the group, especially some of the black men, were pressing her for an explanation of why she *really* did this. She began to cry, and said, "Because I've given up on white men." She sat there, weeping and alone in a roomful of tired people, and then a black woman went across the circle and embraced her. They wept together and everything changed in a simple, nonpolitical moment of human compassion. For some minutes there was absolute silence as a feeling of something powerful beyond words welled up among them. People looked around the room and saw other faces with eyes that were full of tears. Somebody hugged somebody else. Then the whole room was full of weeping and embracing people. Tears and hugs were often in plentiful supply at encounter groups, but there was nothing facile about these: they were hard won and real. The whole development was enormous and astonishing, and perhaps the most unexpected thing of all was that blacks were weeping for whites.

They had another hour or two in which to come back down and attempt to make sense of what had happened. They knew that all the old problems were still there, but somehow the ground had shifted. They had glimpsed a commonly shared substratum of humanity. The workshop's title, "Racial Confrontation as a Transcendental Experience," was human potential hype at its worst, but they had had, in fact, a transcendent experience. They talked, using words to pull themselves back into the everyday world, and when it was time to end the weekend there were more hugs and tears, and then they all went down to the lodge together and had lunch.

It was a euphoric drive up Highway 1 that afternoon for Leonard and for Vad and Price Cobbs, randomly remembering and discussing bits and pieces of things that had happened during the weekend, sharing the conviction that they had tried something impossible yet worthwhile, and it had worked. Late that night Cobbs called Leonard and said, "George, we've got to take this to the world."

The interracial encounter groups became a regular feature of Esalen San Francisco, a valid response to a social issue, and for a time they were extremely successful. Leonard and Cobbs ran the groups with the assistance of two black psychology students, Ron Brown and Michael Brown (not related to each other). Most of the sessions resembled that first weekend at Big Sur: the same modified marathon format, the same cycles of anger and despair and ultimate reconciliation.

And so, for a while, Esalen had yet another purpose, that of serving as a center for the resolution of interracial conflict.

9

Esalen, in the late 1960s, was like the man in Stephen Leacock's poem who flung himself upon his horse and rode off madly in all directions. Its let-it-happen style allowed for many things to be going on at once: Leonard and Cobbs running their interracial groups, Fritz doing his gestalt thing, Schutz promoting encounter. All these were humanistic and presumably harmonious goals, but as it advanced into national prominence, Esalen began to experience its first serious conflicts.

As director of the residential program, author of a popular book, and featured workshop leader, Schutz quickly emerged as a major figure in the human potential movement. It was a time—briefer than anyone knew—when several such figures, at the height of their powers, were often at Esalen. Fritz Perls and gestalt were still prominent. Bernie Gunther's sensory-awakening sessions remained popular. Ida Rolf was occasionally in residence, and Alan Watts was still among the regulars.

Inevitably, with so many titans circulating, there was bound to be friction. Somebody once observed that Esalen in this period was like the Wild West. There was no sheriff in the territory, so people made up their own laws. Whenever differences arose, they would lead to shootouts.

Clearly the most trigger-happy person around was Fritz Perls. He had for years been taking potshots at Gia-fu, Bernie Gunther, and many others. Some of his fights had made it into Big Sur legend, but none was as long or as fierce or as famous as the rivalry between him and Schutz. Murphy and Price referred to it as a game of capture the flag; it was both a personal feud and a dispute over whether encounter or gestalt was the best remedy for what ailed America.

It is perhaps misleading to characterize the feud as a shootout, because, ironically, there was never a direct confrontation or face-to-

167

face discussion of differences between these two giants of existential encounter. Nor was there, for that matter, any indication at first that their relationship was to be anything other than an alliance of colleagues. Fritz welcomed Schutz to Esalen, made it known in various ways that he considered the newcomer to be a solid professional—not one of the wooly-headed mystics that spooked the premises—and even the right kind of professional, a rebel against old-fashioned psychotherapy. Possibly Fritz expected Schutz to become a student of gestalt. To enter into gestalt apprenticeship with Fritz was a strange rite of passage that took place without any explicit arrangement being negotiated between student and teacher. The student merely made the decision to study and started attending gestalt workshops; Fritz went about his business, accepting no responsibility and conferring no certificates. You did your thing and Fritz did his. Schutz did not give any sign, however, of intending to move into this sort of relationship. He brought the people in the residential program around for some gestalt sessions but did not become a regular at Fritz's seminars. Nothing was said about this, of course; nothing would have been said if he *had*.

Instead, Schutz became, in a very short time, a resident superstar whose reputation was the equal of Fritz's, not only within his profession, but out there with the vast American public that was just beginning to discover Esalen's existence.

In September of 1967 *Time* published an article about Esalen. It was an important milestone in Esalen's progress, and it was significant in shaping the public's perception of what Esalen was about. The magazine was scanned in the lodge at Big Sur with the same kind of excitement and attention to detail with which a Broadway cast reads its reviews: Who got mentioned? What did it say? Was it favorable or unfavorable?

In general the article was quite favorable. It described Esalen as a center of "sensitivity training," whose purpose was to help people become more aware of themselves and others through sensual and physical experiences. The specific Esalen teacher it talked about the most—a detail that escaped no eye—was Bernard Gunther. There was a picture of Gunther running one of his body-awareness groups, with a couple of dozen people out on the grass in front of the lodge. The article also spoke briefly of "Social Psychologist William Schutz," who gave workshops on joy. It mentioned, somewhat obliquely, that the form of sensitivity training practiced at Esalen drew on the "interaction emphasis of Gestalt psychology," but there was no mention of gestalt *therapy* nor of Fritz Perls.

Not long after that, people began to notice that whenever Fritz gave a talk about gestalt, he managed to throw in a few disparaging words about ersatz forms of group work that were being practiced. He didn't usually say exactly *where* this spurious activity was going on, or exactly who was doing it, but it hardly took a detective to discover that when he talked about "joy boys" and "turner onners," he was gunning for Gunther and, frequently, Schutz. Nobody ever found out precisely why Schutz worked his way so quickly to the top of Fritz's lengthy shit-list, but it is not hard to imagine why. Unlike Gunther, who was a former patient of Fritz's, with no higher degree or professional status, Schutz had an impressive background as a research social psychologist and an eminent position as a trainer in the T-group world. Large numbers of people were signing up for his workshops at Esalen (both men paid close attention to who drew the biggest groups), and he had a special position there as the leader of the residential program. There may also have been sexual jealousy involved. Schutz pursued the female visitors as enthusiastically as Fritz did, and he was thirty years younger. There was never any overt conflict over a particular woman, but it seems likely that Fritz may have been bitter about this terribly important matter. He was getting old and knew that his sexual powers were not what they once had been. ("I like my reputation as being both a dirty old man and a guru," he said in *In and Out the Garbage Pail,* the book he was then writing. "Unfortunately the first is on the wane and the second is ascending."[1]) Schutz's powers, however, appeared to be in pretty good shape.

Whatever the etiology of the conflict, there was a vigorous rivalry between two articulate and strong-willed men on a piece of land no bigger than the tiniest of villages. No corporation, university, or small town is without similar rivalries, but you will rarely find a comparable snit between people of growing national reputations on such a minuscule territory. The place was not, as they used to say in the Western movies, big enough for the both of them. As it happened, their residences were about as far apart as possible in that small area: the house that had been built for Fritz was on the southern fringe of the Esalen property, and the house that Schutz rented was on the northern extremity, across Hot Springs Creek. But that was only a few hundred yards' difference, and neither man was given to hiding out in his house. They were out around the premises, going to the baths, and taking their meals in the dining room at the lodge.

The casual visitor to Esalen, one who passed through the place without being privy to its domestic intrigues, probably would not have noticed anything amiss. Someplace in the dining room there would be Fritz, a white-bearded old man in a jumpsuit, usually accompanied by a few of his students, perhaps with Dick Price. Somewhere else there would be Schutz, with his balding head and trim black beard, usually wearing a bright-colored shirt and accompanied by a few of *his* students. Most of the time they went their separate ways. Once in a while they would speak to one another, briefly. On a couple of occasions, when Schutz workshops were in progress, Fritz would come up to Schutz in the dining room and comment that everybody seemed to be having a good time—a remark that only Fritz and Schutz understood to be what it was—an insult. Fritz was saying that everybody came to these joy workshops and just had fun. They were not serious.

Schutz resented this. As far as he was concerned, people in his workshops worked just as hard, goddamn it, as they did in Fritz's. He was not just running feel-good weekends. Once, he got Murphy and Price to arrange a meeting that was to be a real encounter about this issue. Murphy, Price, Fritz, and Schutz sat down together at the Big House one evening. Schutz said frankly that he was tired of hints that he was a therapeutic lightweight; he wanted Fritz to come to one of his encounter groups and see for himself what they were like. Fritz said he didn't want to do that. Dick Price pointed out that it was not entirely logical to refuse such an invitation. "I am not always logical," Fritz said, and left.

But, in a curious way, Fritz *was* being logical. He knew enough about what went on in Schutz's groups to know that they were *not* touchy-feely turn-on sessions. In fact Schutz's approach was much like his own. There were, it is true, great differences of style, but the underlying philosophy was the same. Both drew their ideas from the existential literature that sang of the authentic individual. Both were members of the therapeutic lineage of Reich and Moreno, men who saw therapy as a way to liberate people from the stultifying effects of social conditioning. Both tried to detect the repressed emotion and bring it out into the open. Fritz went at this chiefly by relying on his remarkable powers of observation. He would catch the tremor in the voice, the motion of a finger, the recurrent phrase, and try to get the

170

patient to "own" that piece of behavior and openly express its true message. Schutz relied more on the group process, trusting the principle that one's characteristic ways of relating to people will come out in every social setting, but he was basically after the same game: recovering the deadened feeling, increasing the individual's ability to be open and honest. It was a toss-up as to which process was the more to be feared if you had something that you were not at all sure you really wanted to deal with. Schutz was equally committed to the basic notion that anything, *anything,* could be exposed in the group, and to the equally unsettling principle that the real responsibility for what happened was the participant's.

Fritz knew all this, and if he had spent any time in one of Schutz's workshops he would have had to deal with the fact that they resembled his own work much more than they resembled Gunther's amiable sensory-awakening sessions. By staying away from Schutz's workshops, he could deal with Schutz purely on the basis of Schutz's image and style, where he was more vulnerable. If one wrote books entitled *Joy* and held workshops entitled "More Joy" and ended his weekends, as Schutz did, by playing a phonograph record of "To Dream the Impossible Dream," he could hardly be entirely outraged when somebody started calling him a joy boy. Even here, however, the difference was not quite as great as Fritz made it out to be. Fritz was also capable of rhapsodizing about the delights that lay in wait if you could only break through your own shell; there was a fair amount of joy-boy hype in the lines he liked to use in his little talks about gestalt: "The previously robotized corpses begin to return to life, gaining substance and beginning the dance of abandonment and self-fulfillment; the paper people are turning into real people." But Fritz did not *want* to discover the points of similarity between himself and the other Esalen luminaries. He wanted to emphasize the differences. Always a loner, he was never quite at home in the midst of any movement, even though it seemed to be surging approximately in his direction. His task in life, as he saw it, was to build a gestalt therapy movement, and he did not have much time.

He anxiously watched each step of Esalen's progress into national prominence, and was not pleased by what he saw. The next big break after the *Time* piece was a lengthy article in the *New York Times* magazine by Leo Litwak, a San Francisco State English professor. The title of the article was "Joy Is the Prize," and although it *did* mention Fritz, it was mainly an account of the author's experiences in a Schutz More Joy workshop. Its major illustration was a picture of Schutz working in a group. A few weeks later *Life* sent a reporter, Jane Howard, to Big Sur to attend one of Schutz's workshops and write an article about it. Fritz was especially nervous about this one, because it was his greatest ambition to have his photograph on the cover of *Life*. He told several people this, including the *Life* photographer, who obligingly took pictures of him. Fritz didn't make the cover, but he did show up in a large photograph in *Life*'s story on Esalen, talking to a patient and shaking a fresh cigarette out of a pack.

All of this competitiveness and publicity-seeking could be dismissed as plain personal vanity. Certainly there was plenty of that around. But there was more to it than that, and Murphy and Price were right when they called it a game of capture the flag. Except that it was not merely a struggle for the power to define Esalen. There was no telling where all this might lead. Perhaps it would lead onward to a future society as deeply informed by the ethic and world view of Perls as the past one had been by the ethic and world view of Freud. If you allowed yourself to believe even for a second that this was possible, and if you were an old man suddenly surrounded by the representatives of those huge, fame-giving mass magazines, you just might become unhappy when they paid more attention to one of your former patients and to a psychologist who looked like a wrestler and wrote books about joy.

Esalen did, in fact, generate a great amount of joy, and many kinds of it: the bliss of meditation; the serenity of moments alone with the trees and surf; the breaking through conflict to new closeness with others; the stunning discovery, after a massage or a sensory-awakening session, that the human body could be simultaneously relaxed and alive with energy and sensation; the sweet conversion to the belief that great things lay ahead for every human life. And, Fritz's disapproval notwithstanding, those in the second residential program were discovering the wild joy that comes with a falling-away of inhibitions, with the realization that they were free to do anything they really wanted to.

"Mother Esalen," Ed Maupin often said, "gives permission." The resident fellows had come from institutions that doled out permission in extremely small spoons. Here there was permission in abundance. Schutz, who was the chief lawgiver, took the position that you could do whatever you were willing to take responsibility for. This attitude converted rather easily to an operational assumption that you could do whatever you could get away with. Since such outside temptations as money or power did not have much pull on the residents, most of their interest focused on sex and dope.

These were readily available. There was a good deal of pairing-off and passing-around of sex partners within the group, and the lodge was a rich hunting ground traversed by a bountiful river of seminarians and tourists. The river of psychedelic chemicals that also moved through Big Sur was equally copious. Few substances that were known did not get sampled: LSD, mescalin, magic mushrooms, and marijuana were high on the list, with all manner of uppers and downers and lesser-known mind-scramblers farther down. The infiltration by narcotics agents that had been predicted and feared for years never came to pass, and, in retrospect, one can only wonder why. Any undercover agent who had taken the trouble to get into an Esalen residence program would have found plenty to work with.

The official policy at this point was that the institute was dedicated to the discovery of methods of consciousness expansion other than drugs and was based on the understanding that illegal drugs were not to be used on the premises. Residents took this to be strictly for public consumption; their own practice was to experiment freely with drugs, to find out what it was like to participate in an encounter group while high on marijuana or LSD. For some of them the first months at Esalen were, as one member of the residential group put it, a search for the perfect chemical hit. "We believed," he said, "that if we could find the right combination we would get the permanent Sanforized satori." Nobody found that, but it was not for lack of trying.

The most daring adventurers were Ed Maupin, John Heider, and Steve Stroud, the "psychedelic madmen," as they called themselves. They were also always searching for ways to create psychedelic experiences without chemicals. One procedure they invented became known as the Blowout at the Baths. In order to undergo it, you first sat in the hottest tub at the baths for a half-hour or so while breathing rapidly in order to hyperventilate. When you were sufficiently giddy, you would be lifted from the hot tub, quickly plunged into a tub filled with fresh bone-cold water, and held there—sobbing and screaming and gasping for breath—then helped out and allowed to lie down on one of the massage tables while you savored the experience. This was said to put you in touch with deep feelings of peace and gratitude, some of which undoubtedly had to do with the fact that it was over. The Blowout was tried by most of the residents, and later offered as an optional extra to the customers in some of the encounter workshops.

The daily work in the group meetings was intense, relentless, exhausting. Little was held back, since it was deemed unethical to hold things back. Out there beyond the green coastal hills was a society in which people held things back so much that most of them no longer knew what they were repressing. In corporations, universities, government agencies, and even families, people devised elaborate systems of lies that they called diplomacy or courtesy, and they built up catastrophic expectations of what would happen if anybody told the truth. This was the pattern of behavior that Schutz and the residents intended to render obsolete through the medium of encounter.

The effort in group work frequently became angry and hurtful, even violent. Schutz believed in allowing anger to be expressed in physical combat. There were moderate constraints: when people wrestled and pushed one another about, they were not trying to kill or maim, and, in a large room furnished with nothing but pillows, and with the other members of the group standing in a protective circle, there were certain limits. Even so, it could be dangerous. The most serious incident of physical violence involved Art Rogers, a man who had no flair for releasing his emotions and who had never entered any of the encounter wrestling matches. Rogers was assailed by the group for being a square, smiling, pipe-smoking psychologist who treated everybody like a patient. He violated all the unwritten rules of encounter: he intellectualized, refused to show his feelings, professed to like everybody. Nobody suspected—he gave them no reason to suspect—that he was a deeply tormented person. They thought he was merely uptight and believed it would be a service to help him "open up." They taunted him for his phoniness. A woman snatched his pipe away from him and broke it. A bunch of the men chased him out of the meeting room, threatening to beat him. That same afternoon he came into the group again, still smiling infuriatingly, and they began chanting, "Art, Art, Art, Art," until he lunged across the room and threw Ed Maupin through a window in a rain of shattered glass. Fortunately there was a curtain in front of the window, and neither man was physically harmed. The incident momentarily sobered the group—somebody could easily have been hurt or even killed—but in the end it was generally pronounced a success. Art had gotten in touch with his feelings.

They all understood that taking risks was part of the adventure. They may not have had any explicit instructions about what risks they were to take, but they knew that they were there to push at the limits. In the group sessions, they pushed at the limits of self-disclosure and confrontation. They pushed at the limits of sex. The members of this residential program never reached the point of group sex in the meeting room, but the idea came up a few times, and some of them had lingering regrets for not having tried it. Ed Maupin believed the residents had fallen far short of any real effort to, as he put it, clean up their sexual karma. He said, disapprovingly, that the sex was only the conventional pairing-off of males and females. He thought the experience would have been more rewarding if they had pushed the limits much, much farther.

Dan Panger, a tall, intense man who was then writing novels (he later became a Unitarian minister), came up with an area that the group had never confronted. He approached Schutz one day and said that, having given the matter a good deal of serious thought, he saw where the group's experience fell short: they had looked at sex, they had looked at dope, but they had not looked at death. He proposed to initiate them into an experience that would remedy this deficiency. They would all go down to the baths at night and be wrapped in wet sheets so that they could not move or escape. Lighted candles would be placed around them, and there would be reading of poetry about death and beating of drums. They would lie captive in the sheets all night long, while Panger passed among them carrying a long knife. Schutz asked what the knife was for. Panger would not tell him; that was part of the necessary sense of mystery.

Schutz had his doubts about this particular growth experience, but he allowed Panger to propose it to the group. They solemnly discussed the proposal, and some of them professed to be eager to proceed. But in the period before the event took place—a time during which they were supposed to meditate on death—the consensus crumbled. One by one, people began coming to Schutz and saying they were not so sure about this. Some of them confessed they did not trust Panger, this tall man with the large dark eyes, who boasted that he could captivate women merely by staring at them across the dining room. They were not too sure about the religious experience he said he had had a week or so before, which had inspired the proposal. Panger was a bit conten-

175

tious, a leader of a faction that was in conflict with Schutz and the psychedelic madmen. He had encouraged Stuart Miller to go up to San Francisco to notify Mike Murphy and George Leonard that Schutz was a fascist. Perhaps, Heider suggested, it would be better if he and Stroud were to stay up with Panger to guard the guardian. Finally, after an unsuccessful effort to resolve the differences within the group, the death-confrontation project collapsed. It was the first time the group came eyeball to eyeball with the unknown and blinked.

It was an intense, frightening, euphoric autumn, a crowded smorgasboard of experience. The residents spent long hours in the groups, and in the lodge they were lionized like young princes and princesses, treated with reverence by the visiting seminarians, and appropriately resented by the less fortunate young people who worked in the kitchen and the lodge and on the grounds. They were interviewed by reporters from national newsmagazines, and when Jane Howard's spread on Esalen came out in *Life,* there were a couple of them, bareass naked, doing yoga on the massage tables at the baths. They had personal contact with all manner of human potential celebrities, including an early pep talk by Abe Maslow, gestalt sessions with Fritz, bioenergetics work with Alexander Lowen, explorations of mythology with Joseph Campbell, and conversations with Buckminster Fuller and Alan Watts.

Soon after the program began, it became necessary to find ways to dilute the intensity of the group's work. Schutz worked out an intern program in which members spent one week out of four serving in clinics, mental hospitals, schools, halfway houses. Maupin came up with a program of afternoon yoga and meditation sessions, which injected a precious respite of silence and relaxation into their overheated days. Even with such escape valves, the pressure of these all-day daily encounter meetings was too much. Some people stopped attending them regularly. Stuart Miller and Dan Panger stopped attending them altogether, and spent their days lolling about the lodge, drinking coffee and checking out arriving females. After a while Panger formally dropped out of the program, as did Art Rogers, who returned to his teaching job at San Jose State. The remaining members decided to take an extended break and to discontinue the encounter meetings over the Christmas and New Year's holidays. The daily meetings stopped. John Heider went off to Duke to finish up some work on his doctorate; others went to visit relatives. Some stayed around the campus, as they were then calling Esalen, enjoying the infinite peace that came with

176

not meeting in encounter sessions every day, resting, healing, and assimilating. Esalen had one of its periodic financial crises, and many of them took on part-time jobs. The fact of the matter was, although nobody knew it then, that the residential program was basically over. After that time came a long phase of anticlimax. For some three months they had been through the most strenuous regimen of human potential work that any group of people had ever experienced, and that was enough. A decision was being formed, in the way most decisions are formed at Esalen—by a less-than-clear consensus emerging from the random acts of separate individuals and the influence of external circumstances—that the program would not resume in its previous form.

For some of the psychonauts, the program had been a disappointment and a disaster. For others, the experience had been, on the whole, a positive one. It had been something of an ordeal for everyone. The human organism craves ordeals, yet people can never say honestly, afterward, that the experiences were satisfactory. Often, they content themselves with the knowledge that a certain ordeal was, if nothing else, intense. Something had happened; they had not missed out.

"There may be one of us for whom that was *not* the most significant time of our lives," John Heider said years later, "but for most of us this was the crucible. This was our World War II. This was our place of coming of age. I don't know anybody, even those of us who were badly hurt, who would wish they'd been at a place of safety that year."

The sense of hazard was, in fact, essential to Esalen's appeal and its notoriety. Joy, if it was to be achieved at all, was to be achieved through the taking of risks. Schutz made this his public creed. People, he would say, were capable of much more than they suspected, and to take risks was to uncover new strengths, greater depths, unsuspected capacities for life. The creed suited his personality—it was confrontational, demanding, and frugal with sympathy—and it also helped Esalen deal with a tough ethical problem. Traditional psychotherapists complained that growth centers should not be offering psychotherapy when they had no way of following through, no way of taking responsibility for what happened to their clients. One popular answer to this was that the programs were growth experiences for healthy people, not therapy for the mentally ill. This harmonized happily with Maslow's theories of self-actualization and with the emerging theology of personal growth, but it did not square with the daily realities of running a center like Esalen, since some of the souls who turned up there were profoundly troubled, and some of them were certifiably crazy. Schutz responded by saying that if you came to an encounter group, you took your chances, and what happened in the process was pretty much up to you. Like Fritz, he made the taking of responsibility for a client sound like a betrayal of the human potential.

This frightened away some people and appealed strongly to others. In time, it became a part of the Esalen mystique, no less seductive than the baths, the bodies, and the coastal breeze. An encounter or gestalt workshop was approached with a delicious sense of fear, with the knowledge that it would be at least a challenge and quite possibly an ordeal. Some people came there intending to prove to themselves (or to someone else) that they were brave enough to do it, and some people came because they knew they needed help and reckoned the risk to be worthwhile. All manner of tragedies and triumphs emerged from these adventures, and those who were the most fortunate were the ones who not only succeeded in taking risks while at Esalen, but managed to return home with some part of the encounter ethic and put it to work in their everyday lives.

Consider a couple, here called Kevin and Janet, who attended a workshop in the middle of 1968, when the Schutz mode of encounter was at its risk-taking prime. This workshop was described in the brochure as a four-week intensive, and Schutz was assisted by two of the more promising graduates of his residential program: young Steven Stroud, who had come out of his training with an awesome ability to tell the truth to anybody about anything; and Betty Fuller, who had not solved her weight problem but who was, some said, the best encounter group leader of them all. There were about thirty participants, divided into three groups: one for couples, one for single people, and a training group for professionals.

Kevin and Janet took the couples group. They were middle-aged, each divorced, had been going together for about a year and a half, and hoped the workshop would help them decide on their next step.

The group began with Schutz leading a few warm-up exercises—some milling around, some touching and stretching and breathing, a few group shouts to get the energy flowing. Almost casually, Schutz gave them a preliminary assignment. He said he wanted each person to pick three secrets—big, dark, shameful secrets which the relationship could not possibly withstand—and tell them to his or her partner.

He did not specify just how or when this was to be done, but suggested that the sooner the better.

Kevin found when he awoke the next morning that his voice was gone, thanks to his overzealous participation in the shouting. Whispering, he revealed the three things he had determined during the restless night to be the ones that best met Schutz's criteria. The hardest was that he had once had a homosexual affair. It was especially hard to tell Janet this because—as he knew—her first husband had been bisexual. Janet had suspected none of this, and later, in the group, she went into a wild fit of screaming, kicking, and sobbing.

As the month progressed, other couples' secrets were revealed. Extramarital affairs and homosexuality topped the list. They had encounter sessions six days a week, often far into the night, and tried all the techniques and games. Sometimes couples got into fights in the meeting room—one woman tore her husband's shirt off and put bloody scratches on his face. Couple by couple, they took their turns with the Blowout at the Baths; the Freakout at the Baths, they called it. The ordeal of hyperventilating in the hot tub and then being immersed in cold water was no less an adventure than the secret-sharing had been, especially for Janet, who felt utterly betrayed by all men in the moment that Steve Stroud and Kevin lowered her into the cold tub. A few minutes later, lying on a massage table with a gentle wind blowing across her skin, she felt her emotions run precisely the opposite way—felt cleansed, trusting, loving, forgiving of all sins. It was a wildly gyrating month, full of dramatic highs and lows. At the lowest point of all, about two-thirds of the way through, Kevin and Janet got into a bitter fight late at night in their cabin. Kevin hit her—the only time he had ever done that—and she decided to pack her things and leave right then. She probably would have done so if Betty Fuller had not heard the racket and personally intervened, two-hundred-plus pounds of straight talk and compassion, to work with them until they were through the impasse.

In the last week of the workshop, one evening while they were sitting on a rock and watching the sun go down over the Pacific, they finally came to the subject that had been truly taboo between them: marriage. They had both been thinking of it for months, each had gone to considerable personal hardship to come up with the $785 cost of the workshop, they knew that was what they were there to decide—but they hadn't talked about it. They were both too shell-shocked by their previous marriages to bring the subject out into the open. Finally, scarred yet united by the month's risk-taking, they decided to get married; they announced their decision later that evening to the cheers and applause of the other members of the group, some of whom were in the process of deciding to get divorced. And on the last day of the workshop the group had a party at Nepenthe, a restaurant up the coast from Esalen, and Kevin and Janet bought a ring in the gift shop there.

Fourteen years later they are still married and firmly convinced that the ways of interacting in which they had been schooled at Esalen—taking risks, telling truths, accepting feelings—had helped them become healthier people in a stronger relationship. Through them, and through countless other Kevins and Janets, the encounter ethic flowed forth from Esalen and other such academies into American society and—converging with other forces of the times—made a difference in how people led their lives.

As more and more people took notice of Esalen, Murphy found himself being held accountable for things like drugs, encounter groups, and sexual freedom that he was not entirely sure he wanted to defend. He had reservations about many of these, and he did not feel comfortable in the role of spokesman for every deviation from the American norm.

Something happened in January 1968, a few months after the opening of the San Francisco branch, that was in a way the most serious setback Esalen had faced, the most unsettling problem Murphy had to deal with. There had been plenty of disasters and difficulties, such as rivalries between workshop leaders, problems with the guests, recurrent money crises, and incidents like the Language of Being conference. But all of these things had their funny side, and one of the most winning characteristics of Esalen people was their willingness to look back and have a laugh. Murphy had such a lust for the ludicrous that some of his friends suspected he had fun even when things went wrong, that precisely in the horrible moment when Fritz began inching across the floor in front of Maslow, a renegade corner of Murphy's mind was already telling the story.

But this couldn't be laughed away, there was no way to make it fun, and even though it did not happen at an Esalen event or concern any of its celebrities, it felt like something central and important.

Lois Delattre, who had introduced George Leonard to Michael Murphy and had been a graduate of the first residential program, had gone to work in Esalen's San Francisco office. Like so many other bright young people of her time, she had tried LSD. Then she heard about MDA, a psychedelic drug of the amphetamine group, chemically related to "speed" and other stimulants. But where other amphetamines had unsavory reputations, and were likely to be taken only by the more careless, self-destructive, or uneducated members of the drug culture, MDA was reputed to be different. Sometimes called the "love drug," it produced no hallucinations, but rather a feeling of euphoria combined with a heightened sense of touch and emotional openness. It brought, so the rumors went, closeness and communication. Lois kept asking around and finally located enough MDA for herself, a male friend, and another couple.

Soon after the four of them took the MDA, Lois became very agitated. Then she became very quiet and left the room to lie down on the bed. Her companions came in to see how she was, found her breathing deeply, as if she were in a trance, and left her alone. After a while they went in to check on her again, and found her dead.

Some people held Esalen responsible for Lois' death. She had been through the residential program; she had worked in the office. The connection between Esalen and some of the leaders of the drug culture (such as Alan Watts and Timothy Leary) was uncomfortably close.

Murphy, Leonard, and others who had known her felt a great sorrow at her death and a great need to convince others (and perhaps themselves) that Esalen was not the cause of her death. Murphy often went to great lengths to explain that when Lois had asked the manager of Esalen's San Francisco office, David Barr, to help her find MDA, he had refused. Moreover, Lois was an adult, and nobody could have prevented her from obtaining or trying a new drug.

Lois' death was a shock to those at Esalen. They had always been serious about exploring new and perhaps dangerous realms of consciousness. But they had never thought that anyone might actually die in that quest, and they had not expected that part of spreading the word about Esalen would include defending it against a charge of catastrophic, fatal irresponsibility.

10

Nineteen sixty-eight was the beginning of Esalen's most expansive stage, a period that lasted for about five years. The institute was holding programs in both San Francisco and Big Sur, sometimes as many as three at each place. At Big Sur there were four meeting rooms, and Fritz often held gestalt workshops in his house up on the cliff. The only limit to the number of people at Big Sur was how many could be accommodated in the cabins and fed in the dining room. In San Francisco, programs were held in various meeting rooms in Grace Cathedral and other churches, and at a religious-oriented growth center called the Berkeley Center for Human Interaction, located across the bay in a theological seminary district of Berkeley known as Holy Hill. (For a hotbed of countercultural activity, Esalen was remarkably cozy with churches.) Meals were rarely served in connection with the San Francisco program, and accommodations were not provided at all, so for the most part the size of enrollment was limited only by the capacity of the meeting room.

All this allowed for a rapid growth in the volume and variety of programming. In 1965 Esalen's catalogue had had twelve pages, offered a total of twenty programs, and listed eight members of Esalen's executive committee. By the fall of 1968, the catalogue ran to twenty-eight pages and listed about 120 programs. There were now six "officers," nine "associates-in-residence," two "education research associates," seven staff members, nine "advisory committee" members, and thirty-eight "advisers."

In August 1968, the American Association for Humanistic Psychology held its annual meeting at the Fairmont Hotel atop San Francisco's Nob Hill. Few other events reflect more vividly the giddiness

183

and agony of the times. The Fairmont is a short block away from Grace Cathedral, which was then living a double life as headquarters of the Episcopal Diocese of California and showcase of the Esalen Institute. Esalen was much in evidence at the AAHP meeting; so were the humanistic psychology movement's growing pains; so were the turmoils of American society itself.

Humanistic psychology, increasingly linked in the public mind with Esalen and the human potential scene, had started out to be a purely intellectual movement, a crusade of scholars. It had political and social overtones, but it was basically an effort to break the ascendancy of Freudian and behaviorist theories in the world of psychology and to substitute a more expansive vision of human nature. Before it became an organized movement it had been a loose aggregation of splinter groups, whose unity consisted mainly in their shared opposition to the Freudian and behaviorist establishments. Maslow numbered among this band Rankians, Adlerians, Jungians, neo-Freudians, gestalt psychologists, and gestalt therapists, as well as such renegades as Herbert Marcuse, J. L. Moreno, Thomas Szasz, and Norman O. Brown.

Maslow was the great shepherd of the "third force," as he called it, and worked hard to create some sense of shared interest among its members. He maintained a huge mailing list of people to whom he sent out papers, his own and those of others, to keep them informed of new theory and research that contributed something to the advancement of the cause. In the late 1950s he enlisted the support of Anthony Sutich, a remarkable man who had been totally immobilized by rheumatoid arthritis for all of his adult life. He had managed to keep active in several fields and had a full-time practice as a counselor, despite the fact that he was able to do little more than lie on his back, read, and speak. Together, Sutich and Maslow launched the *Journal of Humanistic Psychology,* which commenced publication in 1961, and the American Association for Humanistic Psychology, which held its first national convention in Philadelphia in 1963.

This movement was chiefly but not exclusively psychological. The original board of editors of the *Journal* included psychologists—like James F. T. Bugental, Rollo May, Abraham Maslow, and Carl Rogers—and humanists like Aldous Huxley, Arthur Koestler, Lewis Mumford, and Michael Polanyi.

It was conceived as an intellectual society, not as a guild of group therapists. Its chief concern was to be theory. Its activities would be panels, discussions, and exchanges of papers. Yet so rapid were the currents bearing it along that by 1968 you could easily have formed the impression that humanistic psychologists were those people who did groups. And you could have been forgiven, also, for thinking that humanistic psychology and Esalen were roughly interchangeable terms.

The panels had such titles as "Techniques of Emotional Release" and "Conditions Influencing the Nature and Development of the Encounter Group Movement." Among the panelists were Murphy, Schutz, Satir, and Watts. Other sessions were not panels, but "experiential" events. This once obscure word had become absolutely essential to the organization's vocabulary. It connoted a session in which something happened, in which you were expected not only to listen, but to participate. Fritz's demonstration of gestalt therapy in one of the larger meeting rooms was experiential, especially for the female psychologist who got up and worked on her dream life in front of a few hundred of her colleagues. Bernie Gunther's demonstration of sensory awakening was even more experiential, because *everybody* participated.

Just as Esalen's clients had demanded the opportunity to feel and to own for themselves some part of the evolutionary change that its thinkers envisioned, so did the members of this rapidly growing psychological organization—one that democratically accepted not just psychologists, but anybody who wanted to join—clamor for more than just talk. There had been enough of abstract dissections of the psyche, and the pendulum was swinging the other way. It was becoming unacceptable to think or analyze without having experienced. It was all right, however, to experience without thinking or analyzing; frequently you would be asked to do precisely that.

Other organizations begin their conferences with a presidential address. The 1968 AAHP conference began with a presidential experience. The president was Jack Gibb, a leading T-group psychologist who had been developing techniques for working with large groups in a short period of time.

The experience took place in the gilded and spacious Grand Ballroom of the Fairmont. The room had been built for banquets and cotillions, yet it served admirably as the space in which about nine hundred therapists, educators, and miscellaneous seekers padded about in their stocking feet on the perimeters of the new social frontier. The conference program had given notice that this would be "an experiential session that will involve movement, sitting on the floor, and working in small groups," and as people wandered into the large room, they obligingly complied with the request to take off their shoes and to leave their coats, briefcases, purses, and other encumbrances on chairs near the walls so that the main floor space would be open. When this was done, with the outskirts of the elegant room looking like a huge remnant sale, and with the participants milling about in expectant confusion, Gibb gently began to direct the flow of activity. He was standing off to one side of the ballroom with a microphone. At the beginning he kept everyone walking about, exchanging brief greetings with others, sometimes picking one other person to join with in a brief exercise—a bit of dancing, a conversation with a stranger. He kept everything in motion, with never too much time for anyone to agonize about whom to choose for whatever came up next.

At the end of an hour or so of moving about, occasionally forming into pairs and occasionally into larger groups that stayed together for a while, the participants were asked to stand together, join hands, and make a humming sound. It was a magical few minutes, as all those voices softly rose and fell according to their own rhythms, like a huge choir in which everybody was a member. All the little exercises had been quite simple, and so was this finale, but the total effect was powerful proof that even such a ponderous and alienating event as a professional convention could be turned into something friendly and, yes, humanistic.

People walked out of the room smiling at one another, their faces glowing. Throughout the conference there was a playfulness that is not at all common to such meetings. Unfortunately, there was also a certain look-at-me quality that did not ring true. You do not, for instance, play patty-cake in the lobby of the Fairmont Hotel—as some of the conferees did one afternoon while the bellboys looked on nervously and Fritz strolled past in an embroidered guru shirt, dribbling cigarette ashes on the rug—merely because you happen to feel like it. You do it in part because you want to be *seen* feeling like it.

The meeting teetered constantly on the edge of respectability and frequently fell over it. Very little of it had the feel of an average luxury-hotel professional convention. There was a workshop entitled "Creative Risk-Taking." Creative risk-taking turned out to be approximately the same thing as anarchy. The leader announced at the beginning that the essence of the whole thing was to make it up yourself. No doubt different groups would have responded to such an opportunity in different ways: some would have sung songs or started fights or held a meeting; some would have sat there; some would have left.

This group moved into a carnival of adult playfulness of the sort that was then common on the human potential circuit. They did things they had learned from Gunther and Schutz: back-patting, neck-rubbing, and throwing people up in the air. One detachment went outside and captured an unresisting man who happened to be walking past the hotel. They brought him back into the meeting room, where he observed the odd proceedings. At the end of the creative risk-taking session there was a brief discussion of what had happened; the man introduced himself and said he hadn't the vaguest idea of what was going on but thought it looked like fun. All this was amiable enough, but there was a general feeling of near-riotousness about it that seemed to stimulate some people and frighten others.

On the same day the creative risk-taking session was held, Price Cobbs and George Leonard presented a report on their interracial encounters. This was a subject that interested many of the members, especially those of a more political bent, and it drew a good-sized audience. As Cobbs and Leonard started their presentation, they were repeatedly heckled by a young man in the audience who was a leader of a local activist group called the Diggers. In the Haight-Ashbury of 1968 there were more clusters of divergent radical activism than you could have found in St. Petersburg in 1910, and in these circles the game of radicaler-than-thou was played hard. Again and again, as Cobbs and Leonard tried to make their presentation, the young man rose to denounce their program as a counterrevolutionary cop-out. The well-meaning white liberals in the audience didn't know how to deal with this interruption; Cobbs, less troubled by such inhibitions, called on two of his assistants to throw the guy out. The young man screamed and protested as the two psychology students, one white and one black, obligingly bounced him from the session. He screamed all the way—calling for help, protesting that his back was being injured, that he was being attacked by psychiatrists—as they carried him out through the lobby and dumped him on the sidewalk in front of the hotel amid a stunned cluster of doormen and arriving guests.

This incident, more than any other, turned the management of the Fairmont toward thoughts of canceling the whole conference and letting the winds of change blow somewhere else. In fact, the management had become so disgusted with the spontaneous goings-on in their hotel that they threatened to throw the whole conference out unless something was done. AAHP executive officer John Levy agreed to hire uniformed guards to police the lobby and the meeting rooms.

The word went out among the membership, and for the last day or so of the conference the spontaneity level subsided. The varying reactions to Levy's action by AAHP members reflected the divergences within the organization itself: the radicals chuckled over the uptight hotel management, the middle-of-the-roaders thought the exuberance was a necessary awkward stage along the path of social change, and the more serious members, who were embarrassed by the near-eviction, took it as further evidence that the movement they had conceived of as a force for the affirmation of human dignity was turning into a circus. They particularly disliked the increasing identification of humanistic psychology with the let-it-all-hang-out encounter and touchy-feely awareness activities, a development that Esalen had helped bring about.

At the very moment that humanistic psychology was becoming more experiential, as evidenced by the irreverent nature of the conference, the protest against the wilder aspects of the human potential movement was already being sounded from within. Rollo May was so disgusted with the proceedings of the organization he had helped to found that he left before it ended. Humanistic psychology was having its own game of capture the flag, one in which the humanists, the embattled idealistic scholars and theoreticians, appeared to be losing ground rapidly to the promoters of experience and catharsis—losing ground, but fighting back. Even Joe Adams, one of Esalen's first allies, was to be found among the critics of what he called "the new emphasis on pure feeling and visceral experiencing—the new anti-intellectualism." He presided over a panel that discussed these issues, under the general title "Is Unstructured Affect an Expression of the Disintegration of the Culture?"

After a day of pondering such matters, the psychologists could go to their hotel rooms and turn on their TV sets to watch the news from yet another convention, the 1968 Democratic National Convention in Chicago, where the idealistic Eugene McCarthy peace campaign was being overrun by the Democratic Party machine while outside in the streets the demonstrators, the forces of unstructured affect, battled police.

Esalen was polarized in so many directions, it is no wonder the journalists had a hard time telling the world what it was about. It was religious and hedonistic, intellectual and anti-intellectual. You could take as its ethic the tough wipe-your-own-ass canon of gestalt and encounter or the kindly humanism of Maslow. It hankered for respectability, but steadfastly maintained its Beat-hippie-counterculture connections. One of its founders aspired to fire a shot heard round the world, and the other wanted to cultivate his garden.

Some of these differences complemented one another in a kind of yin-and-yang way, but others were not really capable of being reconciled. There was no easy reconciliation between the world views represented by Fritz Perls and Michael Murphy: a profoundly bleak world view and an irrepressibly bright one, a deep pessimism and a great optimism. Esalen, Murphy insisted, stood for hope.

Yet there was a deeper polarization, within Murphy himself, about the very image of buoyancy that he projected forth into the world. Of all the criticisms that came to be leveled at Esalen, the one that troubled Murphy the most was the charge that its content was lightweight and overly optimistic, lacking in a recognition of reality. This was the criticism that Rollo May made on several occasions, and it touched a theme about which Murphy was exquisitely sensitive. It implied that he, personally, was what Fritz would call a joy boy. Curiously, the sunniness that seemed to come so easily to him, and that people found so winning, was one of his greatest personal problems. At Stanford, he sometimes had experienced a sense of real pain in his face, an inner resistance to the physical act of smiling. At one of the first encounter groups at Esalen, the group at one point turned on Murphy. They said he smiled too much, and it troubled him that people might think of him as facile.

But the gift of joy was real, and the smile and the optimism did come easily. They influenced his style of leadership. Instead of intimidating the people who worked with him, he praised them and encouraged them. He was forever congratulating people. The natural corollary of the let's-do-it spirit was to celebrate things done, and such celebrations were often premature, victories proclaimed before the battle had barely been joined. In the early days of the San Francisco operation a young red-haired woman named Sara Unobskey ran a workshop using some encounter-group techniques, but also giving people rewards, in the manner of behaviorist psychology, when they behaved authentically. Murphy promptly declared this a breakthrough, a reconciliation of the humanist and the behaviorist realms that to many seemed irreconcilably split. "We always knew they could be brought together," he told her, giving her a hug and a congratulatory kiss, "and you did it, Sukie. You did it!"

It was a genuine contribution, perhaps, but certainly not the collapse of the wall between the behaviorists and the humanists. A few months later, Murphy announced to a gathering of representatives from other growth centers that Esalen was going to marry the design revolution to the consciousness revolution. Esalen did not do that either, although a few promising steps had been taken in that direction, including a program at Grace Cathedral that featured a panel called "Designing Environments for Expanding Awareness" and a lecture by Buckminster Fuller.

It took only a spark of enthusiasm to set a new activity in motion, add another discipline to Esalen's lore, bring aboard a new seminar leader. Some of the new projects thus conceived perished of neglect in dusty corners; others successfully moved out into the world.

One of the early results of Murphy's foundation-hustling expeditions was a grant from the Ford Foundation for a project to explore new directions in education. George Brown, a professor of education at the University of California at Santa Barbara, had become an Esalen regular, chiefly as a student of Fritz's, and out of his experiences he began to form some new ideas about education. The essence of his approach was that learning had to do with both thinking and feeling; he spoke of "confluent education" and called for an integration of the "cognitive domain" and the "affective domain."

Brown, looking at the activity at Big Sur with an educator's eye, had seen something that escaped people who worried about whether it was psychotherapy or not. It was clearly adult "compensatory" education. People made up for what they had failed to learn (or had been forced to unlearn) in grammar school, high school, and college. At Esalen they learned to feel, trust, and express their feelings; to get in touch with their senses; to rediscover the unity of body and emotions. Brown thought it might be possible to develop approaches to education that would integrate the schooling of the mind, the body, and the senses all the way along, and thereby eliminate the need for people to come to Big Sur in their adulthood to try to discover the lost parts of themselves all at once in some weekend orgy of tears and back rubs.

He assembled a staff of teachers, and they went to work taking stock of all the human potential technologies and looking at ways to use these in the service of confluent education. The stock-taking process was itself a mix of the cognitive and the affective, of thought and

190

action. Nobody got by just reading books about humanistic psychology. The teachers came to monthly meetings at Big Sur, where they not only talked about theory and compared classroom techniques, but were put through all kinds of sensory-awakening and creativity-stimulating experiences. They had long and emotionally intense gestalt sessions with Fritz, and during breaks they gathered in the hot tubs to discuss their experiences. The first group of teachers became a training cadre that went on to hold workshops and longer programs for other educators. The funding was small—the Ford Foundation barely could have noticed it—but it was an important step in Esalen's outreach efforts, and it provided some substantiation for Murphy's insistence that Esalen was not just another growth center, a place that put on encounter groups and the like, but a unique institution of education and inquiry.

Further support for this claim was provided by another program, co-sponsored by the National Council of Churches and entitled "Theological Reflections on the Human Potential." Like the confluent education project, it aspired to carry the human potential movement beyond the therapy and encounter-group territory in which it was rapidly making itself at home. The idea was that a group of prominent theologians, from different churches and different parts of the country, would come together to participate in experiential sessions involving encounter, gestalt, and sensory awakening, and then would look at the process in the light of such theological concepts as liberation, redemption, and the good life. This was a project that closely resembled Bishop Pike's notion of a theological think tank, and Pike, who that spring announced that he was leaving the church, came from Santa Barbara to join in.

Starting in the late 1960s, Esalen also got into publishing. A cooperative venture was worked out with a New York publisher (first McGraw-Hill, then Viking) for a series of Esalen Books. Among the first comissioned were two products of the confluent education program. *Anger in the Rocking Chair,* by Janet Lederman (one of the members of the first group of teachers), was a powerful account of the use of affective techniques with children in a ghetto school in Los Angeles. *Human Teaching for Human Learning,* by George Brown, was the basic text on confluent education, a plea for a new approach, informed by gestalt and humanistic psychology, to the ancient aspiration of education for the whole person. Other Esalen Books were *Secrets of the Trade,* Joe K. Adams' reflections on psychosis and psychotherapy, and *Hot Springs,*

Stuart Miller's memoir of his adventures in the second residential program.

Miller was general editor of the Esalen Books series, and, with the title of director of development, a major mover in these years when Esalen's thrust was increasingly outward.

Miller had the right kind of background for this. He was an honors graduate of Oberlin, a former Fulbright scholar at the University of Florence, a Ph.D. in comparative literature from Yale. He had moved promisingly through teaching and administrative positions in various universities, and knew his way around the foundation world that Esalen had been trying, so far with only modest success, to interest in supporting the human potential movement. He had been dispatched to Big Sur in 1967 at the expense of the State University of New York, Old Westbury, to immerse himself in human potential lore so that he could apply it to the design of an experimental college program.

Even within the collection of diverse and vivid personalities that made up the second residential program, Miller was different. He had come charging down Highway 1 in a silver Corvette, wearing Brooks Brothers clothes, intent on making as many conquests as he possibly could in this place he called "the very honey pot of eroticism." Although he had been an avid spokesman for encounter at Old Westbury, he found the program under Schutz's leadership too hard-driven, too unrelenting in its quest for the limits of emotional experience. Within the group, Miller distinguished himself for his sexual pursuits and for his attire; he is very likely the only person who ever wore a necktie on a hiking trip into the Ventana wilderness. But he did not really take to Big Sur or to the residential program. He became a nonattender at the daily encounter sessions and went up to San Francisco to try to get Murphy to intervene by firing Schutz or forcing him to ease up. He went through a period of religious conversion, during which he studied the Bible, and when a financial crisis hit and the residents turned to helping run the Big Sur operation, he dedicated himself to serving others as wine steward in the dining room.

Although Murphy had disappointed Miller by failing to intervene in the residential program, Miller admired him. When the program was over, Miller again went to the San Francisco office and told Murphy that he would like to work with him.

Miller's impressive academic credentials were important. No less important was that he and Murphy had fun together. The creative atmosphere in which Murphy thrived was one of playfulness, and the people he liked to work with were those who could enter with him into that ambience of fast-flying ideas and laughter. He had fun with Dick Price. He did not have fun with Fritz Perls. He had fun with Will Schutz and with George Leonard. And he had fun with Miller. The first time he met Miller (wrote Miller in *Hot Springs*), they had "simply giggled with each other for five minutes."[1]

That Miller had failed to make himself at home at Big Sur and then did so well at San Francisco illustrates the difference between the two centers. Although Esalen was still one organization with a common cadre of program leaders, it was, in subtle ways, evolving into two distinct societies, each with its own style and its own value system. At Big Sur the style was rural, the value system egalitarian. All the staff members lived in cabins, and the houses occupied by such eminent citizens as Fritz and Schutz were of modest dimensions. Salaries were low. Most people took their meals in the main dining room. Everybody dressed informally. Cars collected dust in the parking lot. There was little opportunity for conspicuous consumption, and to live at Big Sur was to live simply.

In San Francisco the city dominated. Working for Esalen in San Francisco was different in many ways from other jobs, but it was still a job, nine to five with a lunch break, and when the day was over people went home. Salaries in San Francisco, though modest, were higher than those at Big Sur. They had to be so, but this became a touchy issue. Big Sur employees inevitably compared the salaries of San Francisco employees with their own. San Francisco employees compared their own salaries with those of other people working in other educational or psychological organizations. Stuart Miller said that people who worked in the San Francisco office ought to live like grownups; that is, have decent professional salaries and life styles to match.

Big Sur itself, the fragrant and magical site that Esalen occupied, was in itself one cause of this cleavage. People who took up residence there for any length of time—and, for that matter, many who only visited occasionally—came to see the place as in itself a source of growth and wisdom, no less life-giving than the therapies and psychologies and religions and philosophies that had pitched their tents there in the 1960s.

From the perspective of those at Big Sur, one could not help taking that green piece of land, the cliffs and the hot springs, to be the true

Esalen; the place captured its own flag, and one could move gently to the conclusion that it was a worthy purpose, even a religious calling, to cherish and tend it.

In 1969, at the same time that Stuart Miller was getting into motion as director of development in San Francisco, his former classmate of the residential program, Ben Weaver, was part of the management at Big Sur. Writing in an Esalen newsletter, Weaver gave an approving nod to the aspirations for social change held by the San Francisco annex, adding:

> For my part, and I think I speak for most of the Big Sur staff here, I believe that it is good and sufficient that we do our thing here, on the land, according to our own lights, and bear witness to the world that there may be a better way of living . . .
>
> As our roots go deeper in the Big Sur soil, people here are sharing their religious feeling more freely. Let me share some of mine with you. The other morning at the baths I fell to meditating on the beauty of this place and its people and suddenly I was weeping joyous tears and saying, "Thank you, God, thank you for all this beauty." Then I fell into a reverie and had a vision of our place shining from the earth, and our work being to make it shine, shine ever more brightly as we realize God in us and in everything about us, and to give it back to Him and say, "Here, God, here is what we have done with what You gave us. Isn't it a beauty?"

Such was the effect of the place. Out of this grew the idea of putting on programs at Big Sur that would feature merely being there for a week, with improvised exposures to Tai Chi, massage, Rolfing, perhaps some work in the garden: "Experience of Esalen," these programs were called.

As seen from San Francisco, the Big Sur property was a marvelous resource, but at times a bit of a drag; it seemed to cast a spell on people. They would go down there and get into meditating and practicing some art or craft or discipline, and forget about the rest of the world. The place had some of the properties of the land of the lotus eaters. Furthermore, it was a scene stealer. A journalist dispatched from the East Coast to get the truth about Esalen would head straight for Big Sur, eyes peeled for nude bodies, touchy-feely groups, and bearded therapists. The more this image became fixed in the public mind, the harder it was for Murphy and Miller to convince foundation executives that Esalen was a serious institution of research in human potentialities.

As seen from Big Sur, the San Francisco office was a shaky edifice built upon the foundation of the real Esalen, a worthwhile project, perhaps, a channel for restlessness and excess energies, but still an unproven quantity. It was an experiment at best, and at worst a waste of scarce resources. Esalen was more or less continuously in the red, and maintaining the San Francisco office, a financial loser from the beginning, could easily be regarded as an unnecessary indulgence.

There was little blame or debate or arm-wrestling on the issue. As much as possible, it was treated as a complementarity, not a conflict. But the difference was real and profound, and it became a factor in many other controversies.

By the late 1960s, the interracial encounter group was a tight team of people, black and white, proud of the fact that they worked well together and were friends together. On a Sunday in April 1968, a week after Martin Luther King was assassinated—a shattering time for anybody who cared about relations between the races, a time when the prospects of reconciliation looked bleak—some of them got together and went to a park out in the country for a picnic. Nothing special happened that Sunday, but it was a memorable day for those who were there. By merely socializing, they were declaring that it was still possible for people of different races to be friends and to do ordinary things together. Yet one year after that day in the park, the Esalen interracial encounter program collapsed in an angry misunderstanding.

The conflict that ultimately destroyed the program started out as a minor and not particularly unusual dispute between two people. It rapidly expanded into a complex and multidimensional argument that had racial overtones and also involved the shadowy complexities of Esalen's internal factions, including the latent rivalry between the Big Sur and San Francisco wings. It started one day when Ron Brown, one of the black graduate students who helped run the group, called the San Francisco office and raised the subject of money. At the time, each encounter marathon was led by a team of leaders, one white, one black, and the pay for each was a flat fee of $125. Brown, an overweight and usually easygoing young man, thought the work of running one of these sessions—most of them well attended, all of them emotionally explosive—was worth more. He got about three sentences

195

into his argument when Bill Smith, an administrator in the San Francisco office, said, "Fuck you," and hung up. Brown got into his car, drove over to the Esalen office, and confronted Smith. There was much anger and shouting, and Smith threatened to call the cops. This was where the matter became serious, because for Brown it was inconceivable that somebody would have threatened to call the police on a white man in a similar situation.

"Shit, I was just doing some confrontation," Brown told his friends. Confrontation was the big thing around Esalen, he said. People were shouting at people all the time. Will Schutz was always shouting at somebody. But nobody ever said, "I'll call the police."

Cobbs, when he heard of the police-calling threat, also perceived it as a racial slur. There ensued a series of excited telephone calls and angry demands. Brown wanted an apology; Smith refused. There was talk of demanding that Smith be fired. Cobbs and Leonard got together for lunch and agreed that there was only one way to resolve the problem: have an encounter group. They set a time for the meeting and agreed that it would be at Cobbs's office. Leonard called Murphy, who was in New York on a fund-raising trip with Sukie Unobskey and Stuart Miller. It is evidence of how seriously Leonard took this incident that he asked Murphy to get on a plane and come back immediately to attend this meeting; it is evidence of how seriously Murphy took Leonard that he did just that.

Murphy was not, it should be noted, one of the world's great encounterers. True, encounter was once on his list of New American Yogas, but he had never taken strongly to it. He had a quality of openness that was harmonious with the encounter ethic, but he did not like people to get angry at him, and he did not easily show anger toward others. In groups, he hung around the edges. Once, in one of the interracial groups in San Francisco, Leonard suddenly grabbed him by the ankles and dragged him from his comfortable place on the outskirts into the center of the group. Murphy sat there for a minute and then began to scuttle sideways like a crab until he was back on the fringes. Nevertheless, he came back to San Francisco and joined the group that crowded into the small conference room at Cobbs's office and sat around on the floor to encounter their way through this issue.

Among the participants in this session were David Barr, formerly Bishop Pike's chaplain and at the time the manager of the Esalen San Francisco office, Bill Smith, George Leonard, Price Cobbs, Ben Weaver, Will Schutz, Ron Brown, and two other co-leaders of the interracial groups. The presence of Weaver and Schutz, Big Sur residents, angered the interracial group leaders, who felt that their program was not supported at Big Sur and was possibly even resented. Ron Brown always referred to Big Sur as "the South." There were six whites and three blacks in the group. Seven were San Francisco people, two from "the South." There were no women. (One woman, who had driven up from Big Sur with Weaver, invited herself into the meeting, but they threw her out. Racism was the issue they were concerned with. Sexism would come later.)

Smith, the central figure in this event, was also the one least enthusiastic about participating in it. Before the meeting he had had an emotional conversation with Murphy, during which he wept and protested that he was not a racist and talked of having worked as a lobbyist on behalf of civil rights legislation. When he went into the meeting, he promptly ran into the anticipated blast of black rage. People yelled and got angry. David Barr cried. Murphy lost his temper and tried to tell them about what Smith had done on behalf of civil rights. The blacks didn't want to listen to that. That was the old stuff that always came up in the encounter groups: whites protesting that they were free of racism. The blacks wanted some concession from Smith that he was *not* free of racism, that there had been racist overtones to his treatment of Brown. Smith wouldn't give in. It had been, he insisted, just a conflict between two people. After an hour, perhaps less, Smith excused himself, saying he had to go to the bathroom, and did not return. Since that closed off the option of getting Smith to do or say anything that would resolve the problem, the remainder of the meeting, another hour or more, was focused on getting Esalen to do something about Smith. The blacks weren't demanding that he be fired, but that *something* be done. The solution that finally emerged and won a confused consensus from the group was that Smith would be sent down to Big Sur for a period of rehabilitation. The idea, not impressive in retrospect, seems to have been that he would become a deeper person. It is difficult to believe that anyone really thought that going to Big Sur would cure a case of unacknowledged racism, and surely a sojourn at one of the most beautiful spots on the Pacific Coast is not what you could call punishment. Moreover, the sentence was inconsistent with the perception that Big Sur was not focused on interracial issues, as San Francisco was. No details about the banishment were discussed. Smith did not participate in the decision, and Murphy's assent was several miles short of a firm commitment. Nevertheless, the encounterers felt good about this outcome and repaired to a nearby bar to celebrate.

"I had a kind of feeling," Leonard admitted, "that this wasn't quite right. But anyway we all went over to the Red Roof. We drank toasts to this great meeting, to the future. Those were corny days."

Even while the toasts were being raised, the agreement was unraveling. Smith had called Dick Price as soon as he left the meeting and had reported to him what was going on. Price didn't like it at all. From where he stood, it looked like another power issue, another test of Esalen's independence, another round of capture the flag. The interracial group was trying to tell them what to do. Price called Murphy and warned him against getting pushed around. The next day Murphy called Leonard to tell him of the furor that had blown up over this affair. He wanted to think about the possibility of just having breakfast with Smith every day; he would keep talking to him about this problem and see to it that there were no further incidents.

To Leonard's ears this was a betrayal, a backing-away from what had been agreed on in the group. Leonard felt a strong urge to break off with Esalen and say to hell with the whole thing. And, after asking Murphy to hold the line while he went off and discussed the matter with his daughter, that is what he did. He told Murphy they would still be friends, but he was resigning as vice-president of Esalen.

At that precise moment, the interracial encounter program perished.

Cobbs and his associates soon severed their connections with Esalen. They did some other programs of a similar nature, working on interracial conflicts in organizations, but they did no further work through Esalen. Smith went on down to Big Sur anyway, saying he didn't mind, if that was what people wanted. He sat around down there for a while, presumably reflecting on the affair. Murphy fired him a few months later—he had been intending to anyway, but hadn't wanted to do it in response to pressure. Esalen did not organize any more interracial encounter groups.

In the aftermath, Cobbs and Ron Brown would always say that Mike Murphy was a great guy and they could go to the 49ers games with him every year, but they were convinced that he just never understood the racial part of it. Murphy searched long and hard within himself, but could never find the secret prejudice that was supposed to lurk there.

The Murphy-Leonard friendship survived, although it was strained and distant for a while. Relations between the races remained about the way they had been, although few people can have passed through one of those weekends and come out the other side without some small enhancement of wisdom or compassion about that infinitely difficult dimension of American life.

What really changed, about the time of the interracial group's demise, was Michael Murphy. He would still actively carry the Esalen message to the world for a few years yet, but some of the evangelical energy began to diminish. Murphy kept Esalen moving forward, but he would say later that when he thought about the events of the late 1960s he was reminded of something Lyndon Johnson had said. The president had compared progress to whiskey: a little of it is a good thing; too much, and it starts to come up on you.

The residential program had been the first bearer of Murphy's hopes for carrying Esalen into the world, and it is significant that after the 1967–1968 residential term the program was scaled down to shorter sessions of about four months. Not only were they not as extensive; there was far less rhetoric about their being at the vanguard of human progress.

There are many reasons why the residential program was displaced from the center of Esalen's aspirations: Murphy's increasing involvement with new projects in San Francisco, the insistence of Stuart Miller (who became vice-president of Esalen after George Leonard resigned) that they were dangerously overreliant on intensive encounter, the repercussions of the Schutz-Fritz feud, and Price's feeling that they had been a premature project to begin with. In addition, however, to all of these causes, there was a much larger and overwhelming one: death.

The first to die had been Lois Delattre. She had been at Esalen in the first program; she had worked in the San Francisco office. And what happened to her was unsettling to anyone who believed, as virtually everyone connected with Esalen did at the time, that psychedelics were part of the answer. The way she died was not directly connected to Esalen, but nobody could quite put it aside as a meaningless accident.

As the second residential term drew to a close, there was another death: that of Marcia Price, who committed suicide. Her lover had a Volkswagen camper that he parked on the Esalen grounds and in which he kept a rifle. Marcia was found in the camper. She had held the rifle to her head and pulled the trigger.

Marcia had attached herself to Esalen and occupied various roles there: workshop participant, office employee, patient of Fritz's, mistress of Fritz's. Fritz had rejected her as patient and mistress but she stayed on as a student in the residential program. She was a physically robust woman—somebody who saw her one day, breasts bare, swinging an axe to break rocks for a wall that was being built, thought she looked like an Amazon—but she was not so hardy emotionally, and some of the graduates of the residential program remember her as a touching, even fragile, presence. John Heider recalled:

> She was a clearly crazy, beautiful, gifted, ungrounded woman of spirit, and it was hard not to love her. I think everyone loved her. She was not so crazy that she couldn't have reintegrated if we had had a grounded concept of programing. But you have to remember that the whole place was crazy. She withdrew from the program. She'd been working in the office . . . [and] she fell in love with a very beautiful young man on the staff. He was busted; he was put in jail for a month. It's hard to know what happened. They were fairly withdrawn from the program. She and her husband, who lived up in Palo Alto with their kids, had bought some land south of Big Sur. She and the lover were going to make a home there. They were starting, and I don't know, I don't think anyone will ever know, why she shot herself.

The news that Marcia had shot herself went like an electric shock through Esalen. It was especially devastating to the other members of the residential program, who had never thought that personal disasters of such magnitude could occur amid this feast of therapeutic growth. They spent a lot of time in the group dealing with Marcia's death, and Schutz believed that the incident's impact on the residents was, on the whole, a positive one. It sobered them, banked some of the wildness. They would have been more sobered yet if they had known that Art Rogers, the humorless, pipe-smoking psychologist from San Jose who had left the program, would later, after a divorce, also take his life.

Then early in 1969, a woman named Judith Gold drowned herself in the baths, right there where the life-giving waters issued from the hills. She was not one of the residents, but her death was the towering event in the course of a four-month residential program that was then underway.

One of the residents, Jacqueline Doyle, was in the baths the morning it happened.

> In the middle of my training program there [she recalled], a woman came to be in one of Fritz's five-day groups. She was a psychologist, about my age, with a couple of kids at home, who evidently had suicidal—had threatened suicide several times before. Like with many people, this wasn't the first time she had ever breathed the word "suicide." But what happened is, she came into Fritz's group and was told to take the hot chair the second or third person. She didn't do anything useful for herself with it, and was degraded aloud and mocked by Fritz. Which was not an unusual thing for him to do. He could be quite verbally malicious. She left the group that night very distraught. Later, I believe, she called her husband, talked to him, expressed to her roommates her betrayed feeling—and went down the next morning and drowned herself in the baths. It was a deliberate act on her part.
>
> I happened to be one of the people that tried to resuscitate her, that came upon the scene shortly after . . . within minutes of her death. There were three or four people there trying to resuscitate her, including an M.D. who had been gotten down from the dining room. I was part of this team that, with her body still warm from the baths, arbitrarily decided to let her go. It was clear that her pupils were fixed and that she was brain-damaged beyond recall. We couldn't tell if she was still there or not. It was the closest I had ever been to death.
>
> I had a lot of identification with this person that I had never met before, and I felt a great anger at Fritz about his irresponsible handling of clients. This was not the first time I had seen or heard of an interchange which I thought was irresponsible. I went up into my own group and had a long, very intense experience of working with my anger and despair about this kind of thing happening. Everyone there was totally frightened and spooked by this, and there was a lot of confusion of feelings toward Fritz. Fritz was being very offhand and callous, no grief being expressed. Just: "Ach, people who play games—" You know, his way.

Another member of that residential group was the Reverend Robert Cromey, one of Bishop Pike's former lieutenants, who was also on his way out of the ministry. Cromey officiated at a ceremony in the baths. Members of the residential group, Esalen employees, seminarians, and miscellaneous hangers-on, all crowded in among the tubs and the massage tables, and took part in the simple makeshift ceremony, part funeral and part exorcism, that Cromey led in an attempt to soothe the community and send the dead woman's spirit to rest.

Actually, the two women's suicides had less to do with the carefree nature of the residential program than with Fritz and the way he dealt with the dangerous game of a potential suicide. Ever on guard against maneuvers to get him to live up to somebody's expectations, he refused to be sucked in, would give no sympathy. Threaten to kill yourself, and he would tell you to go right ahead. There is a film of a gestalt therapy session with Marcia Price that Fritz allowed to be released after her death. In it, he taunts her with her suicide threats. And if there had been any talk of suicide in the brief gestalt session he ran with Judith Gold, the woman who drowned in the baths, Fritz would have insisted that it didn't make any difference. He believed that people who talked of suicide should be treated like anybody else.

After the deaths, Fritz's reaction was almost nonchalant. He went about saying it didn't matter, and the residents worked out their rage at him in group meetings, under Will Schutz's supervision. Fritz did not attend the ceremony in the baths.

Despite Fritz's involvment, and the resulting bitterness toward him, in time the residential program came to be blamed more than Fritz's brand of gestalt therapy, perhaps because there had been such optimism about the program, whereas Fritz had never promised anything. The spirit of the program was broken; it could not be reconciled with Marcia Price in a camper in the parking lot, half her head blown away. A few people were saying already that the whole idea of a residential program was too dangerous and intense. More people would join them later, because there were more suicides to come.

Fritz had started acting strangely at the 1968 AAHP convention. He had stomped about the hotel restlessly, wandering in and out of the sessions. One afternoon he had walked up to Murphy, who was talking to Virginia Satir and some others, and said, with no prologue, "Mike, I have decided that you are one of the phonies. You hang around with the phonies." Murphy asked Fritz what phonies he was talking about, but Fritz didn't elaborate. He stood there for a minute and then walked away.

Murphy didn't realize that Fritz was profoundly disturbed by what was going on in the country. What he saw was fearfully familiar: riots in the streets, police beating up civilians. He thought America was ripe for fascism. He had begun to suspect things were headed that way as early as 1966, when Ronald Reagan was elected governor of California. In 1968 he became more and more concerned as he watched the resurgence of Richard Nixon, whom he associated with the witch hunts of the 1950s, and the third-party right-wing candidacies of George Wallace and General Curtis LeMay.

Few people at Esalen understood Fritz's fears, because they believed in an entirely different vision of history. For Murphy, Leonard, Schutz, and others, it was all part of a marvelous movement toward a new dawning of the human potential. For Fritz, who had survived Hitler and Mussolini, history was a bloody struggle in which victory for the good guys was by no means assured. He said: "I think there is a race going on between humanism and fascism, and I am much in doubt as to the outcome of that race. The humanist tends to live for self-actualization and to be alive. The fascist lives for exerting control and for making things out of people. I'm afraid the fascists are progressing more rapidly."

People told Fritz he was being paranoid. He told them he had been accused of being paranoid once before, in Germany in the 1930s, and that many people who had ignored the Nazis had ended up in concentration camps. He had gotten out of Germany ahead of the Nazis, and out of South Africa ahead of the racists who took over after Smuts, and now he proposed to get out of America. He returned to Esalen and announced he was planning to leave the country. At first no one believed him, but soon after the deaths of Marcia Price and Judith Gold, he left the country for Canada, which would be his last home.

Fritz had students in British Columbia, and he thought it would be a likely place to establish himself and a gestalt therapy institute. Although he was seventy-five years old, he was still full of plans for the future. His scheme was to buy a small resort hotel or motel that would serve as a training institution for gestalt therapies. There were several institutes already around the United States, and he thought his could serve as the major center for the others, an advanced resource for the professional training of psychologists and psychiatrists. Eventually it might even develop into something grander, perhaps a university.

He went up to British Columbia and purchased a motel on Lake

Cowichan on Vancouver Island, a few hours away by ferry and bus from the city of Vancouver. The motel was for sale for about $40,000, and Fritz had enough cash available to make a down payment of more than a quarter of the total cost. It wasn't much, this little motel on a rainy island across the water from Vancouver, but it was all his. There would be no wives—at least not of his own—no collaborators, no kids, no dogs, no joy boys, no turner-onners, no rivals.

The first group of students arrived in the summer of 1969, and the Gestalt Institute of British Columbia was off to a good start. Fritz was pleased to get this operation in motion and gratified to discover that he was becoming a local personage. Vancouver paid attention to his arrival and to the establishment of the institute. He was interviewed on the local TV and radio shows, and people recognized him when he came to Vancouver, as he often did, to attend concerts. Some of the local businessmen around Lake Cowichan had misgivings about the influx of gestalt therapy students, most of whom, to the unschooled eye, were undistinguishable from hippies. Fritz made remarkable efforts to allay their fears and establish friendly relations with his neighbors. He even went so far as to join the local chamber of commerce, and appeared as a guest speaker at one of their meetings to tell them about gestalt therapy.

Fritz knew, when he moved to Canada, that he had only a short time left to live—maybe a year, perhaps five if he was lucky. He wanted to leave something behind. For most of his life he had been a one-man band. In his last few years, he had begun to realize—and had struggled against the realization, because he was not much of an organizer—that gestalt therapy might die with him unless he worked for its perpetuation. Although continuity seemed to be assured—there were gestalt therapy institutes in several cities, gestalt therapists everywhere— much needed to be done. Another series of training workshops was to begin at Lake Cowichan in 1970, and he also had lined up before him a demanding schedule of workshops and lectures on the road.

In the winter of 1969–1970, he took a last trip to Europe, alone. He visited some of the old capitals, went to plays and concerts, sent postcards to his friends in America. He did not tell them much, and one can only guess at how it felt to be seventy-six and sick, wandering in winter through the streets of Vienna.

He was seriously ill, although he did not know what the illness was.

He went to physicians in Europe who talked vaguely of arthritis and gallstones. When he came back to the United States in February of 1970, he spent a couple of days in New York with Frank and Ilana Rubenfeld; Frank was a gestalt therapist, Ilana a practitioner of the Alexander technique of body work. They thought Fritz had some kind of flu, something he would get over. Fritz led his last gestalt therapy session in Rubenfeld's Greenwich Village office and sent Rubenfeld in his place to lead one that he had been scheduled to do in Washington, D.C. Then he went on to Chicago, where he was to give a public lecture through the University of Illinois Extension and lead a workshop for the Chicago growth center, Oasis. But he couldn't manage either of those. He was too weak and in too much pain. He saw a doctor in Chicago and agreed to enter a hospital.

Fritz called his wife in those last days—she was in California then, giving a workshop for the Gestalt Institute of San Francisco—saying he was very ill and was going into the hospital. She asked him if he wanted her to come to Chicago. He said she didn't have to come, but she knew he wanted her to be with him. She flew to Chicago, and they had a few more days together before Fritz died—days that were, by all accounts, like most of their marriage: Laura kept taking over, and Fritz resented it.

The doctors operated on him to find out if he had cancer—he did—and he never recovered from the operation. He remained in bed, under sedation, being fed intravenously, until he died. Official cause of death was a heart attack, the outcome he had feared was imminent when he came to Esalen years before, and which he had, he believed, staved off with generous doses of Ida Rolf, hot tubs, and admiration.

There is a story that, in his last minutes, Fritz tried to get out of bed—an act that would have disconnected the complex apparatus of tubes that were connected to him to keep him alive—and was told by a nurse to lie down. "Don't tell me what to do," he supposedly replied to her before he died. But one of Fritz's biographers, Jack Gaines, interviewed the nurses who had attended him in his last minutes and could find no one who had heard him say that.[2] Whether or not it is literally true, it's a meaningful tale. People are often known largely by the legends that grow up around them, as well as by the things they actually say and do. This final legend admirably encapsulates the Perls sermon to the world and, for that matter, a good portion of what might be called the gestalt ethic: Take responsibility for yourself; do not revel in being either the helper or the helped.

Seldom has the death of such a disagreeable man brought forth such an outpouring of emotion. The word traveled out through countless telephone calls, through the national network of gestalt therapists, former students, former patients, former friends and lovers. There were memorial meetings at Lake Cowichan and at Esalen; Fritz's official funeral was in New York. Paul Goodman was the eulogist and, never one to sacrifice hard truth to sentimentality, offered a terse and unforgiving little speech in which he gave a nod to Fritz's contributions but also reminded the mourners that Fritz had many shortcomings and was not much of an intellectual. Laura thought the eulogy was quite satisfactory, but some of the others found it insulting, and the old conflict between the Fritz gestaltists and the Laura gestaltists flared up again, mitigated not at all by the somber occasion.

In death as in life, Fritz fared better on the West Coast. The members of the Gestalt Therapy Institute of San Francisco rented a hall and put on a memorial service that was attended by over five hundred people. Fritz had said he wanted Anna Halprin, who had led dance workshops at Esalen, to dance at his funeral. She danced to a recording of one of the Mahler symphonies that Fritz had liked and got people out of the audience to dance with her and then pass through the auditorium with lighted candles. People stood up before the group and delivered their own little eulogies. Abe Levitsky, a psychologist who had been one of Fritz's closest friends and associates, delivered the official eulogy. It ended: "How you thirsted for your place, your chapter in history. You have it now. We, gathered here tonight, appreciate that you were with us, that we met and touched each other. And we say to you: Farewell, Fritz, and thank you for being."

11

By the early 1970s Esalen was an institution with a nationwide reputation and a secure place on the crest of what was now taken, by both its friends and its enemies, to be a national movement: the human potential movement.

According to listings that were occasionally cited by Esalen and by the Association for Humanistic Psychology, there were a hundred or more growth centers, modeled on Esalen, around the country and the world. This was an inflated number, since it included humanistically oriented private therapy firms, gestalt training centers, programs within colleges, and several institutions that were, in reality, nothing more than a printed letterhead and a hatful of hope. Nevertheless, there were at least thirty or forty real centers that regularly held workshops, and many of these could afford to pay for some of the chief figures from Esalen, such as Alan Watts, Bernie Gunther, and Will Schutz.

By this time there were really three Esalens. There was a gestalt-Esalen, living in the memory of Fritz, populated by top-tier former students of Fritz; it was linked to Cowichan, to the other gestalt therapy institutes, and to the national network of therapists who considered themselves to be practicing in the gestalt tradition. Some of these were now leading gestalt workshops at Esalen; far more gestalt programs were listed in the brochures in the 1970s than there had been when Fritz was alive. There was an encounter-Esalen, populated by Will Schutz and his students, mostly graduates of the second residential program. Some of these, like Betty Fuller, Steve Stroud, and John Heider, became well-known encounter leaders, and some of them became leaders of the shortened second generation of residential programs. For a while there was a team, made up of Schutz and a half-dozen of his students, who called themselves the Flying Circus and went about the country running large-scale groups. And there was the

San Francisco Esalen, centered on Murphy. This last was a multidimensional entity all by itself, but it had certain distinguishing features, among them an openness to new projects, an emphasis on religious issues, an interest in informing the world that Esalen was not entirely gestalt and encounter, and, increasingly, a goal of creating a slightly different *persona* to carry into the new decade.

The three Esalens were not distinct cliques or factions: there was much cooperation and some blurring at the edges. Still, they represented different agendas, and sometimes there were mild conflicts. Murphy and Price repeatedly asked Schutz to try to refrain from giving the impression, which, in his enthusiasm, he often did, that encounter and the Flying Circus were more or less the same thing as Esalen.

As the Esalen leaders found a wider audience for their personal appearances, there was a corresponding proliferation of Esalen ideas through the publication of books. George Leonard sometimes said that the human potential movement was really a literary movement, and in the final analysis that may be the best definition of it. The Esalen Books program was only a fraction of the literary output during those years that the Esalen ideas spread outward through the culture. Fritz's rambling and raunchy autobiography, *In and Out the Garbage Pail,* was published in 1969, and after that came a flood of books by his students and followers. Schutz published *Here Comes Everybody,* a book about the various body-work disciplines. Gia-fu Feng wrote a book on Tai Chi and the I Ching. Bernie Gunther, revealing a literary touch that would have surprised anyone who thought of him simply as the masseur from Los Angeles, produced several successful books on his own methods, books with such engaging titles as *Sense Relaxation: Below Your Mind* and *What to Do Till the Messiah Comes.* George Leonard had written a book on education, *Education and Ecstasy,* and was working on *The Transformation,* a book about the coming evolutionary leap. Alan Watts was still producing a new book every couple of years. There may not have been a hundred growth centers, but there were easily, by the early 1970s, more than a hundred books from and about Esalen and its related disciplines.

Esalen seemed to have the ability to move various disciplines from obscurity into something like national prominence. This was the generally accepted belief, and the source of some of its internal power struggles. It may or may not be true; perhaps Esalen did not so much confer fame as ride to fame itself on the cumulative energy of its various offerings. These things did have a momentum of their own, strong enough to pull Esalen away from its early evolutionary musings and put it into the business of serving up experiential methods, some of which Murphy and Price didn't even particularly like.

Yet it is hard to believe that any other place would have served so well as a showcase, or that any other organization would have been so resolutely eclectic. That was Esalen's clearest policy and contribution: it put together pieces that had not been put together before and introduced them to a new and growing public. In so doing, it created a subculture. This was not precisely Theodore Roszak's counterculture, although it was close. It was more therapeutic, less political. Paul Goodman, one of the props of Roszak's counterculture, was only distantly related to Esalen, and Herbert Marcuse's philosophical connections to what went on at Big Sur were more tenuous still. The Esalen mixture was much closer to Aldous Huxley's original vision of a blend of human potentialities methods, except that it was now not a proposal, but a reality experienced by many people.

By the time Esalen had been in existence for a decade, there was a fairly sizable group of people who made Esalen teachings part of their lives.

If you were of this subculture, you had participated in some encounter groups, had had some gestalt therapy, and had acquired from them some new ways of handling your interpersonal affairs. You were a little more free with your emotions and a little more comfortable with the truth about yourself. When other people expressed their feelings, you said, "I hear you," and sometimes you really heard. You thought about taking care of your body and understood it to be connected to your emotions. You knew how to give a massage. You meditated, at least occasionally. You knew something about Zen and were generally more open toward things mystical than you used to be. You had tried LSD and other psychedelic drugs and, whether or not you were a regular user of them, you no longer believed that the first puff of marijuana was the first step down the road to addiction. You thought of yourself as a person who had changed; metanoia was the true badge of membership. Your change might have taken outward manifestations—a change of partners, a change in hair or clothing styles—or it might not. But you knew that you saw things differently from the way you once had, not so long before, and you talked about your old self with a certain distant amusement.

Like other subcultures, this one was amorphous, its edges not clearly defined. There were those who were clearly of it and those who only passed through briefly or absorbed a portion of the lore. It had its changes and variations, its fads, its right wing and its left. You could see it in its purest form at Esalen itself. Its presence was so heady there that for some people the conversations in the baths and the lodge were more overwhelming experiences than the seminars. The air was full of personal revelations and transformations, analyses of relationships, shoptalk about therapies and therapists, news of ascendant gurus, and frequent use of words like "energy." If there was something you wanted to do, you would say you had energy for it, and if there was somebody you were attracted to, you would say, "I like your energy."

Out of such large and small things—ideas and words and ways of being—are subcultures made. The Esalen subculture diffused through the society, touched a person here and there, merged with all the other new sounds that were struggling for a place in the American consciousness.

Esalen itself—as a formal institution, as a business—had not expanded in proportion to its fame or influence. Esalen did not, to its eternal credit, embark on the kind of expansion program that would have seemed logic itself to the average American businessman. It did not set forth to create a chain operation, a network of therapeutic Holiday Inns with centers in every major American city and resort area. It did not even set up a franchise operation, licensing other growth centers to call themselves Esalen Institutes—another likely expansionist strategy. It traded only discreetly on its name. No certificates were given for completion of its programs; graduates of its residential programs were explicitly forbidden to advertise themselves as certified group leaders. It remained a nonprofit institution, not too well managed, paying modest salaries to its staff, turning a considerable portion of its income into the endless building program at Big Sur that was slowly and organically transforming the old resort.

The difference between the 1960s and the 1970s has been in some ways overstated by our fast-food approach to history, which strives to stamp a clear personality on every decade. But there was a transition. Within a span of one year, 1969–1970, Esalen lost three men who had each contributed something to the revolutionary spirit of the 1960s: James Pike, Fritz Perls, and Abe Maslow. Their deaths signified real change. So did the fact that 1970 was the year Murphy and Price each turned forty.

A few months before Fritz's death the media had carried the story of James A. Pike's final adventure. Then fifty-six, Pike, who had become one of the country's most famous clergymen, certainly its most controversial, was writing a book about the historical Jesus ("a revolutionary study of Christian origins," he called it in his biographical entry in the announcement of an Esalen program entitled "Theological Reflections on the Human Potential") and was going to the Holy Land to do research. He had raised some eyebrows the previous year with publication of *The Other Side*, the account of his efforts to contact the spirit of his deceased son, and then again, in early 1969, when he announced that he was taking his third wife, who was then thirty-one, and was leaving the church to direct the Foundation for Religious Transition, an organization to help other people who were also leaving the church. (The church, he said, suffered from a credibility gap, a relevance gap, and a performance gap.) Pike and his wife were driving in the desert, not far from the Dead Sea, when their rented car became stuck in the ruts of a dry creek bed. They left the car and, in temperatures well over a hundred degrees, tried to find help. Pike could walk for only a few hours in the heat. His wife left him and, after a heroic trek, notified authorities. They tried to rescue Pike, but finally found his body two days later.

In late 1970, about six months after Fritz died, his old adversary Abe Maslow died also. The news of his death radiated out through a different network. Maslow had founded no school, had no corps of patients and disciples, and had not pursued such an eventful sex life, but he had many students, followers, and friends, and had colleagues all over the world with whom he had exchanged papers.

Despite their differences, Fritz and Maslow had had common threads of ancestry, in their Jewishness and their connection to the existentialist-humanistic philosophical tradition. Both had belonged to the school of psychology that Maslow called the Third Force, and they had found their ways into a mutually unsatisfactory alliance in the Esalen camp: Maslow as Esalen's long-suffering intellectual conscience, forever making the case for more reading, more research, a stronger philosophical base; Fritz as the polar opposite, the man who jeered at head trips and sang of the here and now.

Each of the three men had in his own way been a mentor and father figure to Esalen. Maslow was Esalen's chief spokesman among the psychologists and was Murphy's East Coast host. Pike was a contact among theological dissidents everywhere, and a sponsor of Esalen's move to San Francisco. Fritz was the first of Esalen's resident attractions, and a teacher and therapist to Price. Murphy and Price both lost their real fathers during the same period. Richard Price's father died soon after a visit to Esalen in 1969. John Murphy died about a month after Maslow. John Murphy had, like Dennis, always professed that he didn't quite understand what Esalen was supposed to be about, but he had been a friend to it in his own way. He had drawn up the papers when they incorporated as Big Sur Hot Springs, Inc., and again when they formed the Esalen Institute as a nonprofit educational institution. He and Marie had built the South Coast Motel, a mile or so up the road from Esalen, and had lived there for a while in 1965 and 1966, occasionally coming down to have a look at their son's curious enterprise. John Murphy's only complaint about Esalen was the failure to enforce the separation between the men's side and the women's side at the baths. All those naked men and women, strangers, splashing about in what he would always think of as the family baths, made him uncomfortable.

The deaths of those various mentors had the effect of sealing off the previous decade into the irrecoverable past, not only for Murphy and Price, but for the ever-shifting Esalen clientele. There would be no more crowded and emotion-laden gestalt therapy sessions with Fritz, no more philosophizing with Maslow. People who had taken part in those events spoke of them with a nostalgia that made it seem as though they had happened long ago, in a Golden Age of Old Esalen.

Special projects and attempts to set the human potential movement marching through this or that segment of society were not, on the whole, Richard Price's thing. His mission was to keep Esalen moving along with some degree of stability from day to day, and to shop around among its changing wares for things of value to his own mind, body, and spirit. But he had always hoped that somehow Esalen might be able to do something for people who had been through ordeals like his—psychotic episodes and rough treatment in psychiatric wards.

Many years after his own hospitalization, Price had obtained his medical records and learned that at the same time that he was being given massive insulin injections, he was also given heavy shots of Thorazine, a depressant. None of this had been done with his consent; he always believed afterward that the treatment had been harmful,

212

and that he would have recovered much more effectively if he had been left alone.

There was rumbling into existence then an alternative—even revolutionary—view of madness and the treatment of madness. Among the spokesmen for it were Thomas Szasz, the psychiatrist who challenged the medical view of schizophrenia as a definable and treatable disease; Erving Goffman, the sociologist who had documented the mistreatment of patients in mental asylums; and Joe K. Adams, the psychologist who had written of his own experiences as a mental patient.

Some members of the mental health establishment were beginning to share this view, and there was a movement among mental patients for a stronger definition of their rights. Because this new movement called for paying heed to the individual's rights, talked about states of consciousness, and revived the ancient belief that there was divine purpose in madness, it became a part of the stream of countercultural thought. It was closely linked to the psychedelic movement; if there could be value in drug-induced expeditions into different states of consciousness, might there not be value—perhaps even greater value —in alterations of consciousness that arose out of the deep processes of the human organism itself? Timothy Leary thought this was so. Alan Watts did also, and often spoke of such matters in his Esalen seminars.

Of all the sources cited in this alternative view, none was more eminent than Esalen's sometime seminar leader Gregory Bateson. Bateson's "double bind" theory of the origins of schizophrenia was widely quoted, and so was his belief, based on anthropological research, that the Western approaches, such as hospitalization, drugs, and shock treatment, were not the most enlightened way to deal with such happenings. He wrote:

> It would appear that once precipitated into psychosis the patient has a course to run. He is, as it were, embarked upon a voyage of discovery which is only completed by his return to the normal world, to which he comes back with insights different from those of the inhabitants who never embarked on such a voyage. Once begun, a schizophrenic episode would appear to have as definite a course as an initiation ceremony—a death and rebirth—into which the novice may have been precipitated by his family life or

213

by adventitious circumstances, but which in its course is largely steered by endogenous processes.

In terms of this picture, spontaneous remission is no problem. This is only the final and natural outcome of the total process. What needs to be explained is the failure of many who embark upon this voyage to return from it. Do these encounter circumstances either in family life or in institutional care so grossly maladaptive that even the richest and best organized hallucinatory experience cannot save them?[1]

Among the spokesmen for this point of view, none was more brilliant or charismatic than the Scottish-born R. D. Laing, who in the late 1960s rapidly emerged as conventional psychiatry's most eloquent adversary. Laing talked about his work at Kingsley Hall in London, where patients were given space, time, comfort, and support—but no drugs, no shock treatments. They were allowed to move through psychosis at their own pace. His was a radical philosophy that was profoundly suspicious of psychiatric authority, doubting any presumption that the doctors were so much healthier than the patients that they were entitled to impose painful treatments in the name of therapy.

Murphy and Price were both great admirers of Laing—Ronny Laing, they called him—and brought him to Big Sur for a weekend seminar in 1967. In the description of his Esalen seminar he wrote: "Humanity is estranged from its authentic possibilities. This limited vision prevents any unequivocal view of the sanity of commonsense, of the madness of the so-called madman."

Price wanted more on this subject than one seminar. He hoped to expose more people to Laing's ideas, and he was beginning to think about starting, perhaps as an annex of Esalen, a treatment center modeled on Kingsley Hall. A project along these lines did develop. Its organizer and driving force was a young clinical psychologist named Julian Silverman. Silverman, who worked in the National Institute of Mental Health center in Bethesda, Maryland, first wandered into Big Sur early in 1967 during the last months of the first residential program, only a few weeks after Laing had been there. Silverman had come out to the West Coast to do some consulting work at the Langley-Porter Neuropsychiatric Clinic in San Francisco, and one day he ran into Ed Maupin, whom he knew from graduate school. Maupin had brought some of the residents to Langley-Porter to meet Joe Kamiya, a psychologist and friend of Esalen who was doing research on the effects of meditation on brain waves. While the residents were taking turns meditating on the electroencephalograph, Maupin invited Silverman to come have a look at Big Sur. This was a momentous occurrence for Silverman, who ended up staying a long time.

Silverman, a lean, animated, fast-talking New Yorker, had seen a lot of campuses, clinics, and federal offices, but he had never seen anything like Esalen. It was like entering another world. "It was the most exciting, heavy—it was awe-ful, in the hyphenated sense of the word," he said. "I felt like I was about two thousand years in the past. I was in this place, and here were these girls in long skirts serving meals at these tables. The atmosphere was very bawdy, and the scene was extraordinarily sensual. The place was lit by candlelight. I walked into the lodge, and the next thing I knew I was sitting here talking to this dark-haired, magical, sparkling-eyed guy who was going 'wow' and 'golly' and 'whee' to whatever I was saying."

The dark-haired guy was Murphy, who had not yet moved on to San Francisco, and what he was being enthusiastic about were Silverman's accomplishments in research. Silverman was, at the time, head of the section on perceptual and cognitive studies in the Adult Psychiatry Branch at the National Institute of Mental Health. He was especially interested in schizophrenia and had done laboratory experiments with a group of schizophrenics in which he correlated visual stimuli with brain wave responses and established that they could somehow turn down the volume of sensory input from the outside world. He had studied the literature of psychedelia, and had personally experimented with LSD. He had researched the attitudes of other primitive cultures in regard to altered states of consciousness, and had had an article about shamanism and schizophrenia published in *The American Anthropologist*. And he, too, was a fan of Ronny Laing's.

Murphy told Silverman there was somebody he had to meet— meaning Price, who was away that weekend—and signed him up to come back to Big Sur and lead a seminar. It was entitled "Shamanism, Psychedelics, and the Schizophrenias" and was held in the summer of 1967. Price attended the seminar, and he and Silverman became good friends. Price was delighted to make an ally of a hotshot young psychologist who shared some of his views and had good connections to the psychiatric-scientific establishment; Silverman was delighted to have an excuse to spend time at Big Sur.

Together, they began planning a more ambitious project, a series of seminars, workshops, and symposia under the overall title "The Value of Psychotic Experience." Silverman was to be the coordinator of the series, which would be held mainly in Big Sur, with a couple of special events in San Francisco, and Laing was to be the visiting expert. It became a major Esalen event in the summer of 1968. Among the participants were some of the best local authorities—Joe Adams, Alan Watts, the Jungian analyst John Perry—as well as the Polish psychiatrist Kazimierz Dabroski, who had developed theoretical work on the concept of "positive disintegration," and the Czech psychiatrist Stanislav Grof, one of the leading European practitioners of psychotherapy with LSD. Fritz Perls did gestalt dream work with the people who came to the five-day program at Big Sur, and Allen Ginsberg joined in a symposium on "The Poetry of Madness" up in San Francisco. It was, on the whole, a successful event. Its only serious setback was when Laing, after having agreed to come, decided at the last minute that the United States of America in 1968 was not a place he felt safe in visiting. He thought there was about to be some kind of a civil war, and he didn't want to be around when it started. Silverman and Price had long telephone conversations with him, and even got Watts to talk to him and try to get him to change his mind, but Laing refused to set foot on American territory.

Although Laing was not present in person, which caused some embarrassment, since his name was on the printed program, his presence was felt. The conference churned up a lot of enthusiasm among the panelists for some further effort, perhaps even a new institution based on the Kingsley Hall model.

While the new project was being discussed, early in 1969, Price had another psychotic episode. It may have been caused by some of the stresses and excitements of running Esalen, but it had a more obvious link to a visit from his father, Herman Price, in late 1968.

The elder Price used to come out once in a while for a duty visit; he would stay, uncomfortably, for a day or two. Esalen was not quite the place for a retired corporate officer in his mid-seventies. This last visit—and it was the last visit before his death—he and his son had an unusual exchange, a genuine conversation, in which the father talked about himself. He fell into a kind of reverie and reminisced about his boyhood in Lithuania. This monologue was seasoned with recollections of violent events: he talked about coming into a room in which a young man lay dying, shot by Zionists for having informed to the police; he talked about another time, when he saw a group of

Zionists, in chains, being herded through the streets by czarist soldiers. He had never before shared such things with his son—stories about his youth and about his Jewish background. Richard got more of a picture of his father's life that one day than he had in his entire previous thirty-eight years. The images lingered in his memory after his father had left, became more vivid the more he thought about them, and began to take on a powerful hallucinatory reality. Price knew he was slipping into psychosis.

When he felt the psychosis coming on, Price took care to ensure that he would not be sent away to an institution and that his parents would not find out. He wanted to be able to go through with it, whatever it was, without insulin and electroshock therapy. His friends made arrangements for him to stay back in the hills with an accommodating Big Sur Heavy who had a remote marijuana farm. When he did not come out of the psychosis as quickly as they had hoped, they moved him to another house, nearer Esalen. They were finding out something they had not, perhaps, fully understood about the Laing approach to dealing with psychosis: caring for someone in a psychotic state is an incredible amount of work, a gargantuan consumer of patience and hours. There was nobody available with the skill or the time to stay with Price through an episode whose duration no one could predict. Finally Jack Downing, a psychiatrist, took responsibility for having Price committed to the state mental hospital at Agnews, near San Jose. After a week or so there, he was ready to go home again.

It had been a trying time, but Price would always laugh when he told people about the conclusion of it, because the irony was too good: Agnews was the hospital that had agreed to work with Esalen on a model program for alternative approaches to treating psychosis. It had not yet begun when Price was there, but it did start not long after he was released. The building he was in stood just across a courtyard from the one that would be used for this project. Price could lounge at the window there, like Moses on the hills above the promised land, and look out over what would be, for a while, California's outpost of Kingsley Hall.

It was called the Agnews Project and was a joint enterprise of the state, the National Institute of Mental Health, and Esalen. Silverman left his job at Bethesda and came on as a full-time staff psychologist at Agnews. They had hoped to get Laing to become a part of the project, but he still refused to set foot in the United States. The project proceeded without him. It was a three-year research program, its main

217

purpose to test the ability of patients to recover and integrate their personalities without the use of the standard psychiatric treatments (that is, medication), and its secondary purpose to develop a humane environment within which people undergoing severe mental disturbances could be cared for.

A ward was allocated to the project, and a special staff was selected and trained. The project involved psychological testing not only of the patients, but of the staff members to find out who had the personal qualities that meshed most effectively with the challenges. Some of the staff members visited Esalen for workshops and seminars, and some of the Esalen people came to Agnews as trainers and consultants. They had encounter groups and gestalt training sessions for staff members, in which they were encouraged to get in touch with their own feelings about madness. It was a lively place, what with encounter groups, gestalt therapy, massage and touchy-feely sessions, and patients passing through the sometimes tumultuous phases of madness. "Ding-dong city," Silverman irreverently called it.

Yet the morale among both staff and patients was considerably higher than in the usual psychiatric ward, and at the core of the project was a rigorous research study. The subjects were young patients, male, who had been admitted to the institution as schizophrenics. They were divided into two groups: half were given the medication (chlorpromazine) that was then standard for people undergoing such psychotic breaks, half were given placebos. At first, during the period that the patients were in the hospital, those who were receiving the medication appeared to be making better progress. But follow-up research (conducted by "blind" researchers who did not know which patients had had the medication) reported that those who had been allowed to recover without medication showed more long-term clinical improvement, lower rates of rehospitalization, and "better overall functioning in the community between one and three years after discharge." The results of the study were written up with a properly scientific title ("Schizophrenics for Whom Phenothiazines May Be Contraindicated or Unnecessary") and eventually published in a scientific journal. It was hardly a final word in the debate about the care of psychosis, but it was a solid contribution and provided some support for Murphy's insistence that Esalen was not just a growth center.

After Price came out of Agnews, in the summer of 1969, he and Silverman traveled together to British Columbia and took part in Fritz's first gestalt training session at Lake Cowichan. Price worked on

218

the things that had sent him into the psychotic episode, and Fritz pronounced him to be recovered and ready to start leading groups. It had been four years since Price had first started working with Fritz; Fritz said the internship was now over.

Price returned to Esalen and set up a training program, in cooperation with Fritz, but Fritz died in March, one month before he was supposed to return to Big Sur. Price was leading groups by this time, and continued in his role as general manager at Big Sur. When the Agnews project was completed, Julian Silverman joined Price as a group leader; he never went back to Bethesda.

Privately, Murphy may have been tiring of big ideas and new projects, but the idea of changing the world was so much a part of Esalen that it seemed to generate its own momentum. There were many proposals for what the institution might become, but not much interest in maintaining the status quo. Esalen was always conceived only as something in motion.

Stuart Miller had married Sukie Unobskey (the woman who had experimented with the use of behavior-reinforcement techniques in encounter groups), and together with Murphy—the Three Bears, they called themselves—they kept up a steady flow of new projects for carrying Esalen forth into the world. Among them was an Esalen benefit in New York City and a trip to Europe.

The benefit was held over a weekend in April of 1970 at the Hotel Diplomat in midtown Manhattan. It cost $75 a person for the entire weekend, and over a thousand people came, crowded into the hotel's ballrooms and meeting rooms to see the movement's celebrities—Alan Watts, Bernie Gunther, Will Schutz, Ida Rolf, and a dozen or so others —and to see and hear and feel what Esalen's offerings were like. There were lectures, panel discussions on psychological research, sensory-awakening sessions, encounter groups, gestalt, bioenergetics. The New York newspapers covered the event, and *The New Yorker* sent a reporter to write it up for the "Talk of the Town" section. The usually flawless *New Yorker* was guilty of one of its rare errors when the reporter wrote that many of the sessions were "experimental." Apparently the word "experiential," so basic to human potential jargon, and used several times on the printed program to describe specific sessions, had not gained admission to *The New Yorker*'s vocabulary.

The trip to Europe was, like the New York show, primarily a missionary expedition, to bring Esalen firsthand to the growing numbers of people in England who were interested in such things, to spread the word. That was the intent of its main financial backer, Helen Stephens, and its organizer, Jacqueline Doyle, both graduates of a four-month residential program that Will Schutz had led in 1969. But there were other reasons for the trip, not the least of which was that it would be a hell of a lot of fun—which it was.

Among those who went to England with Murphy were Stuart and Sukie Miller, Alan Watts, Will Schutz, Pamela Portugal, Betty Fuller, George Leonard, Jacqueline Doyle, and Helen Stephens.

For over a month, they held court in London, where they attended gala parties put on for them by English friends of Esalen. They met with all manner of people: Buddhists and theosophists and members of Parliament, tarot card readers and mind readers; swamis and professors of philosophy; cosmologists and Asia scholars; therapists and theologians. Alan Watts, whose works were popular in England, was the biggest star in the Esalen delegation and also the most at home in these circles. They held all-day sessions at a West End hotel, smaller versions of the events that had been put on in New York but, if anything, weighted less with the intellectual Esalen fare—the sober discussions of meditation and brain wave research and the like—and more with the experiential: Watts in his black Zen kimono with gongs and chanting, Schutz getting people to jump up and down and yell or get down on the floor and arm-wrestle. Schutz and Betty Fuller ran an encounter group that met regularly during the month they were in London. They visited R. D. Laing's treatment center for schizophrenics, Kingsley Hall, and some of them spent a strange evening at Laing's house, when Laing and his associates played their famous game of "get the guest," which consisted of talking about their visitors as if they were not present and periodically breaking into hilarious laughter. The practice was said to be for the purpose of improving social cohesion within the Laing group, but it had the effect of destroying any number of parties, including this one. They were interviewed by the BBC and written up in the yellow journals (STRANGE CULT VISITS ENGLAND), had a grand time, and left behind them a number of people who considered themselves to be more or less a part of the human potential movement.

From London, Murphy and the Millers proceeded to Florence, where they were to see Dr. Roberto Assagioli, the founder of the philosophical-therapeutic system called psychosynthesis. Assagioli had built a coherent philosophy around a theory of how the human personality can become integrated, its divergent energies harnessed to the purposes of the individual's highest and best self. His system had deep philosophical roots, an interest in such things as parapsychology, creativity, and spiritual growth, and an eclectic approach to therapy that was open to the use of any number of techniques, from music to marathons (Assagioli kept up on all the new developments) when they seemed applicable to the needs of the patient. Psychosynthesis was already a minor theme of Esalen. Robert Gerard, Assagioli's leading American student, practiced in Los Angeles and had led programs at Big Sur; Schutz had spent some time with the Psychosynthesis Institute in New York City during his self-training phase and had adopted some of the methods into his own encounters, notably those involving the use of guided daydreams or meditations.

Murphy had not originally intended to go see Assagioli; the idea germinated while they were in England, partly as a result of a meeting there with Piero Ferruchi, an associate of Assagioli's (and a nephew of Laura Huxley's), partly as a result of Stuart Miller's desire to revisit Florence, where he had spent a happy year as a Fulbright scholar. It was, then, merely an interesting side trip, but it turned out to have an effect on Esalen's future development and a profound impact on the lives of many people connected with Esalen, particularly Stuart Miller.

They spent several days in Florence, going every day to the spacious apartment where the old man lived. Assagioli was in his mid-eighties then, a tall, slightly stooped man with a white goatee. In conversations with him, Murphy began to believe that psychosynthesis could and would become a larger part of the Esalen package. The experience was more than that for Stuart Miller; for him it was a genuine religious conversion.

At first, when Assagioli talked about his idea of developing a person's ability to act from the highest self, Miller balked. This sounded too preachy and seemed to contradict what Miller had learned about being real from gestalt and encounter. Truth, at Esalen, had often seemed to be a matter of being true to one's neuroses, flaunting one's shortcomings. Assagioli insisted that, although the gestalt and encounter methods were perfectly compatible with psychosynthesis, it was necessary to keep a steady eye on what was most real—the higher self—and on the purpose of the therapy. Miller was profoundly impressed by the old man's cogency and persistence on this subject, and also by the fact that he made his case without deprecating other therapists.

I had heard so many irritated teachers denounce the work of other teachers [Miller wrote in an Esalen newsletter]. And that had been hard, because I had seen value in all of them. Assagioli excluded no plausible technique, but he did seem to know of a place from which one could judge when and where and for whom a technique might be valuable. His openness toward the myriad of Esalen approaches seemed predicated on some steady vision of the nature of human development. I began to think that his approach could provide a framework for the *synthesis* of Esalen's techniques.

As a result of this meeting with its venerable founder, psychosynthesis became a much more important component of Esalen programming.

Psychosynthesis owed its new prominence at Esalen partly to Stuart Miller and partly to Murphy, who liked its comprehensiveness and its religious dimension, and who was not averse to the idea that it might shove gestalt and encounter aside and become identified with Esalen in the public eye.

The first 1971 catalogue led off with a write-up on "Psychosynthesis: A Comprehensive Approach to Personal Growth." A panel discussion on psychosynthesis was held at the San Francisco First Unitarian Church—Murphy and Miller were among the panelists—and some weekend workshops on psychosynthesis were offered. The next catalogue had a whole section of psychosynthesis workshops, as well as several programs that combined psychosynthesis with gestalt, and psychosynthesis with encounter. A couple who had studied with Assagioli, James and Susan Vargiu, started the Psychosynthesis Institute in Palo Alto. Arrangements were made to publish a paperback edition of Assagioli's *Psychosynthesis* as an Esalen Book.

Psychosynthesis also became the philosophical core of yet another special project, the Esalen Program in Humanistic Medicine. This was roughly modeled on the education project and started from the observation that medicine in America was even more emotionally backward than education. Doctors were estranged from their patients, and patients from their feelings. Disease and healing were treated as antagonists that fought for custody of the patient's body while the patient looked on as a passive spectator. There was very little "I and Thou" in modern medicine, and much assembly-line, move-them-through-the-office treatment. The authoritarianism of the healers, and subdued resentment of the patients, made it a promising field for humanization.

Stuart and Sukie Miller conceived the idea of putting a group of health professionals through a training program in encounter, gestalt, sensory awakening, meditation, and body work. They got funding for it, recruited some doctors and nurses and health administrators, and launched Esalen's contribution to what later became known as the holistic health movement.

The body of esoteric practices that became known as the Arica training was the other major new discipline that joined Esalen in the 1970s. Arica, a teaching said to be handed down from the Sufis, the holy men of Islam, came into the human potential movement as a by-product of the adventures of a Chilean, Claudio Naranjo, who was for several years, in the late 1960s and early 1970s, a prominent leader of Esalen programs.

Naranjo was a psychiatrist, a multitalented young man who had also been a composer and concert pianist. He made his first visit to the United States in the early 1960s to take his mother, who had a rare eye ailment, to a specialist in Massachusetts. During that trip he took some time to visit Harvard and look up a few American psychologists. One of the people he met was Frank Barron, then making a reputation as a researcher in the psychology of creativity, who was on a one-year visiting professorship at Harvard. The next time Naranjo visited the United States he made a special trip to visit Barron at his home base, the Institute of Personality Assessment and Research (IPAR for short) at Berkeley. And the time after that he returned for a year, on a Guggenheim grant, as a visiting research fellow at IPAR.

There were not then, nor are there now, many scholars on the Berkeley campus with ties to Esalen, but, as it happened, Naranjo got to know two of them. One was Barron; the other was the anthropologist Michael Harner. Naranjo had wandered into the anthropology department on his first visit to Berkeley, looking for somebody who knew about the Jivaro Indians of the Amazon, a special interest of his, and had found Harner, who was a student of shamanism, of the Jivaro, and their psychedelic *jage* plant. Not long after Naranjo returned to Berkeley and began his fellowship at IPAR, Harner invited him to drop around the corner and meet a young man who was doing some work Naranjo might like to hear about. So Naranjo was introduced to Carlos Castaneda, then a graduate student in anthropology at UCLA. Castaneda was going to assist Harner in giving a seminar on shamanism at Esalen, and Harner invited Naranjo to join in. Naranjo ended up going to Big Sur with Castaneda, and on the drive down the coast Castaneda talked about his anthropological field work, which he was doing with a Yaqui medicine man, Don Juan.

When the weekend seminar began, Naranjo was delighted to learn that one of the participants would be Fritz Perls, who had just taken up residence at Esalen. He had read *Gestalt Therapy,* and finding its author here in the Big House, sitting in on a weekend seminar on shamanism, added to his growing amazement at how much was going on in America, especially in California.

This was the weekend that some people would remember as the time of a confrontation between Fritz and Castaneda. It happened after the seminar was over. A San Francisco TV station had sent some people down to cover the event, and they set up a group interview with Harner, Castaneda, Naranjo, Murphy, and Perls, out on the open deck by the main lodge. In the course of the interview Castaneda expounded his theory of consensual reality—the gist of which is that reality is not an absolute, but a social product; everything we believe we *know* is learned from others. "How do I know that I exist?" Castaneda asked rhetorically. Quick as a Zen master, Fritz slapped him in the face.

Naranjo's recollection of the incident differs from that of Murphy, who was also present. Naranjo insists that the act was not an expression of hostility, and that Fritz was not particularly threatened by Castaneda's charm or the favorable impression he made on the other participants. Castaneda put up with a lot from Don Juan; no doubt he could accept a gestalt slap from Fritz Perls.

Over the next few years, Naranjo became a close friend of Castaneda's. Castaneda was restless and erratic, no less mysterious in his comings and goings than Don Juan himself. He would turn up in Berkeley unannounced, stay for a while, and then leave unexpectedly. Sometimes he brought messages from Don Juan. Don Juan said he knew Naranjo. He had "smoked" him; that is, had seen him in a vision while smoking marijuana. Once, Castaneda proposed that they go to see Don Juan immediately. They could get in Castaneda's car and drive straight down to Mexico, nine hours or so on the road. Naranjo was tempted but was uncertain that his visa would enable him to get back into the United States, so the trip did not come off.

During the late 1960s, Naranjo was also in an apprenticeship of sorts, studying gestalt therapy. He went to Fritz's weekend and five-day workshops and to the special training workshops. By 1969 he was one of the second-generation gestaltists leading gestalt seminars at Esalen. His gestalt workshops were a highly individualistic mixture of elements: he combined gestalt, meditation, and encounter. He did one workshop in collaboration with Ann Armstrong, a clairvoyante, which combined psychic readings with gestalt therapy; he did others with Karen Bolander, an astrologer, combining gestalt dream work with horoscopes. These explorations earned him the reputation of being somewhat far-out, a definite asset in that time and place, and he quickly built up a following of his own.

When Naranjo returned for a period of over a year to Chile, he took giant strides away from the conventional Freudian therapy he had practiced there in the past. With the support of the University of Santiago, he established a program of LSD therapy. In his private practice, he instituted a group approach that was primarily gestalt, with touches of encounter, sensory awareness, meditation, and occasional use of psychedelics.

Back in the United States, he soon had a falling-out with Fritz, one that was almost a re-enactment of the celebrated breaks between Freud and some of his disciples. Naranjo, for all his eclecticism, *had* been a disciple; *Gestalt Therapy* had profoundly influenced him when he read it in Chile. And the first time he saw Fritz, coming out of the Big House in a shaggy white sweater, it was love at first sight. Fritz became not only his teacher but also his therapist, and the main reason he returned to the United States was to get some help from Fritz in finding his way through a difficult relationship with a woman—whom he later married. During that trip, however, Naranjo made the mistake of telling Fritz about a book he was then writing, about gestalt as an approach to therapy with psychedelics. It was to be entitled *Gestalt Therapy Revisited.*

Naranjo had supposed that Fritz would be pleased and would see him as carrying on the torch. Instead, Fritz thought Naranjo was trying to one-up him, and said so. Naranjo, trying to smooth the matter over, quoted something that had reportedly been said by Wilhelm Steckel, a psychiatrist of the Viennese school.[2] Naranjo reminded Fritz that when people had asked Steckel how he could presume to see more than Freud, Steckel had replied that a dwarf who stands on the head of a giant can see more than the giant. Fritz replied with a topper that Naranjo had never heard before. He said that Freud's response to this was "A louse on my head doesn't see any more than I do." The rest of that weekend Fritz was hostile toward Naranjo, and at one point ordered him out of a meeting of a group of trainees. It was not until a long time afterward, shortly before Fritz died, that the two of them came anywhere near recovering the warmth of their former relationship.

At the same time, Naranjo's own disciples, the group that had come together under his guidance in Chile, were proceeding uncertainly in his absence. Some people thought the group needed a new leader. One had done some work with Oscar Ichazo. Ichazo came from Arica, the seaport city where he lived, to Santiago and met some of the other members of the group. One of them wrote to Naranjo at Esalen and told him that a teacher, a man with great gifts, had turned up in Santiago. Later Naranjo got a letter from another member of the Chilean group, even more enthusiastic: "The fairy tale is true," the letter said. "The machine [he meant the human organism] can be made to work; there are people who *know*." The letter also alluded, somewhat mysteriously, to a "School," which, said the writer, had been a major force in human history for centuries, although its existence was virtually unknown. Eventually Naranjo responded to that letter and was invited to meet Ichazo in Santiago and then to spend several months studying with him in Arica.

When the two met, Oscar Ichazo was delivering a series of lectures to members of the Chilean Psychological Association in Santiago. The content of his lectures ran closely parallel to the ideas of Gurdjieff: he talked about mentations, the factors of cognition, the Gurdjieffian mind-map of nine basic personality types. But Claudio, who had studied Gurdjieff extensively and had also been studying Sufi lore under the tutelage of the Sufi master Idries Shah, discerned numerous occasions when Oscar raised subjects that were not in Gurdjieff's work. That was encouraging: it hinted that the man from Arica was indeed the possessor of teachings that were not available elsewhere.

In private conversations with Oscar—a medium-sized, balding, bespectacled, and altogether ordinary-looking man in his late thirties, who had a way of talking as if everything he said were indisputably correct—Claudio probed for information about the source of his teaching. He was also on the trail of information regarding a question that had intrigued many scholars of esoterica: the source of Gurdjieff's teaching. Oscar confirmed that they were the same. He, like Gurdjieff, was connected with the legendary Sufi order known as the Sarmouni or the Bees. Oscar referred to it only as the School. He told of having been contacted several times during his life by emissaries of the School and of having traveled to Afghanistan, where he was blindfolded and guided to its headquarters in the mountains. Claudio was favorably impressed by Oscar's credentials and by his wide knowledge of Sufic and Gurdjieffian concepts. He was not so favorably impressed by Oscar himself; he got a powerful impression that the man was dishonest and manipulative. This would be a serious obstacle if he were to go off to Arica with Oscar, as had been suggested, for a six-month period of intensive study. In the best Esalen manner, Claudio brought the issue out into the open. "How," he asked, "can I possibly work with you if I distrust you so much?"

"Honor your distrust," Oscar replied. "It is understandable that you *feel* this way. But you don't *know.* You can only know by the fruit. I recommend that you go through the experience. If you work and let me work, that's all that's needed."

Claudio decided to go ahead, and returned first to California with the intention of going to Arica. He spent about six months in California, part of the time at Esalen, before he returned to Chile. During those months, the number of people who were to return with him expanded steadily. At first he was to go alone, then with a group of friends, perhaps five at the most. The contingent kept growing. Timothy Leary's old collaborator in the Harvard psychedelic experiments, the former Richard Alpert, was then around Esalen, recently returned from an identity-changing trip to India, where he had become a student of a mountain yogi and had taken on the name Baba Ram Dass. For a time Ram Dass was planning to go to Arica. Later, he changed his mind and decided to go back to India. But Jack Downing, the psychiatrist and a student of Fritz's, did go to Arica. So did Steve Stroud and John Lilly, the famed dolphin scientist, who had been in an Esalen four-month residential program. Finally, more than thirty other assorted Esalen leaders and Esalen followers joined Claudio. "Arica," Dick Price said, "cleared our bench."

Arica, a busy little port on the site of an old oasis where the Chilean desert abuts the Pacific, had no building ready to receive this influx of seekers, who spread out and found lodgings in pensions and apartment houses around the town. The group's sessions were held in various borrowed spaces, including an old factory. Claudio, in collaboration with a couple of wealthy members of the group, set in motion a plan to build a structure that would serve as a permanent meeting place and residence: the first South American growth center.

227

Claudio occupied a special position within the group. He was the chief agent in its coming together, since most of the students were Americans whom he knew through Esalen. He was treated by Oscar as almost (but not quite) an equal, certainly as the first among the students. There was an understanding that after the first training was over, Claudio would remain at Arica and be the teacher for future groups. Claudio, alone among the others, was permitted to undergo the supreme training experience, an ordeal of forty days and nights alone in the desert. (This, Oscar had explained, was a teaching that the School had given him special permission to impart. It was not normally used, because it was regarded as a forcing of destiny—like twisting God's wrists—and was only for special persons in special circumstances.) Claudio spent the time performing meditation exercises that Oscar had prescribed for him, and returned convinced that he had been through the most momentous event of his adult life. He regarded the desert ordeal as a productive one, and it enhanced his respect for Oscar as a teacher, but there were other ordeals that made him think his original misgivings about Oscar—that he was dishonest and manipulative—had been right. There were lies, rumors, palace intrigues, and reports from Oscar on the "deficiencies" of various students. Strangest of all, Oscar kept it a secret that he had directed Claudio's stay in the desert, and permitted the group to form the belief that it was some kind of megalomaniacal Jesus trip, done on Claudio's own volition. Finally, after much prodding from Oscar, the group voted Claudio out, and he agreed to sell his share of the house and training center.

Claudio left Arica in a daze, and for years wondered what had happened to him. Sometimes he believed he had been put through a complex exercise designed to set him free of Oscar and the School and send him forth to do his work in the world with no further ties; sometimes he thought it had been a piece of sleazy trickery to eliminate a potential rival for leadership, perhaps to punish him for not originally signing over his share in the building to Oscar (as had been suggested once). "You have not been generous to me," Oscar had said one day toward the end. Claudio, always a seeker of the mysteries, often wondered about this.

After Claudio left Arica, Oscar changed his mind and abandoned his plan to set up a permanent training center there. He came up with a much larger project: he would transplant the whole operation to New York City. He chose New York because it was the very center of the

American establishment, the place where the greatest number of people of wealth and power were to be found. The plan was to attract such people as trainees, and proceed from there with the transformation of American society. Oscar went to New York, and most of his trainees from Arica went with him to become the cadre of the new Arica School. When the school was ready to begin, it announced itself in a full-page advertisement in the *Wall Street Journal.* At about the same time, other Arica graduates were beginning to incorporate some of the meditations and exercises of the School into their offerings at Esalen and other growth centers. And so one more system of personal development, with an assist from Esalen, had found its way into American culture.

12

Esalen would inhabit a different cultural environment in the 1970s. The hippie phenomenon, wild-eyed younger cousin of the human potential movement, had declined swiftly from its media-hyped climax in 1967 to its nadir in 1969, the year when Charles Manson's followers—young people whose appearance and style were indistinguishable from that of the flower children who rollicked in the Haight-Ashbury and the Big Sur hills—murdered actress Sharon Tate and four other people one bloody night in Los Angeles.

But although the hippie movement was, to say the least, faltering, its essential message—that youth would save America—lived on. Its true believers stepped gingerly around such disappointments as the Manson case and stated their creed in new ways. Charles Reich's *The Greening of America* was published in 1970, became a best-seller, and came out in paperback in the summer of 1971. It declared that a revolution was on the way, and that it would produce a beautiful and humane metamorphosis of every aspect of American society:

> This is the revolution of the new generation. Their protest and rebellion, their culture, clothes, music, drugs, ways of thought, and liberated life-style are not a passing fad or a form of dissent and refusal, nor are they in any sense irrational. The whole emerging pattern, from ideals to campus demonstrations to beads and bell bottoms to the Woodstock Festival, makes sense and is part of a consistent philosophy. It is both necessary and inevitable, and in time it will include not only youth, but all people in America.[1]

Reich invented a new term, Consciousness III, to distinguish the bearers of the revolution from the custodians of the old order. His thesis was that there were three different types of consciousness operating simultaneously in American society: Consciousness I, a relic of

231

the nineteenth century, was the ethic of rugged individualism, the mind-set of the small farmer and the small businessman. Consciousness II, forged in the first half of this century, was the outlook of the organization man. Consciousness III, just emerging and embodied in beaded and bell-bottomed youth, was the consciousness of people no longer driven by socially determined needs to achieve and conform. "The foundation of Consciousness III," said Reich, "is liberation. It comes into being the moment the individual frees himself from automatic acceptance of the imperatives of society and the false consciousness which society imposes."[2]

All this talk about consciousness and revolution was strongly reminiscent of Roszak's *The Making of a Counter Culture*. Roszak had said that consciousness, not class, was now the generating principle of revolution. But there are great differences between the late 1960s book and the early 1970s one. *Counter Culture* had been critical of some aspects of the youth movement, especially its enthusiasm for psychedelic revelation, and had predicted that it had a long, rocky path ahead, picking its way through the "socio-political obstacle course," a task that Roszak thought "may take the better part of a generation."[3] Reich could spare no time for such qualifications and misgivings; although heavy in his criticism of the weaknesses of adults of all persuasions, he saw nothing but wisdom and strength of purpose in the young. "His razor," one reviewer drily noted, "is not exactly double-edged."[4]

Some people took *The Greening of America* to be the last incense-scented gasp of the 1960s, but it was really an outline of an emerging *Weltanschauung* that was much more at home in the 1970s. "The meaning of liberation," Reich explained, "is that the individual is free to build his own philosophy and values, his own life-style, and his own culture from a new beginning."[5] If you thought about it, this was a lot easier than participating in some *social* transition, in which you had to work with others, take into account their visions of the future, and build it a brick or two at a time. Reich made it sound like something you could do all by yourself and all at once. The revolution was a trick of the mind that you could bring off without either cooperation or conflict. "There is nobody whatever on the other side. Nobody wants war except the machine. And even businessmen, once liberated, would like to roll in the grass and lie in the sun. There is no need to fight any group of people in America . . . There is no reason to fight the machine."[6]

232

Not surprisingly, any number of politically oriented reviewers jumped on Reich about this. One of the most scathing criticisms was the one in the *New York Times Book Review,* by Peter Marin, a California therapist and educator who had led workshops at Esalen. Marin pointed out several varieties of political *un*consciousness in Reich's perception of consciousness. "The fact that 'liberated' persons are part of a monied class still living off stolen land, labor and time . . . The inability of those with new consciousness to find any viable way to express it in politics . . . The existence of a growing, revolutionary and almost traditional violence among those with Consciousness III . . . The simultaneously unliberated condition of every minority group."[7]

This criticism of Reich did not directly bear on Esalen or the human potential movement. Yet clearly there was a close fit between Reich's vision and Murphy's consciousness revolution—the new paradigm, the upstart spring—which had been foretold in countless Esalen seminars and proclaimed in Esalen literature. Marin detected this, and a few years later, in a *Harper's* article entitled "The Narcissism of the Human Potential Movement," he was accusing growth-center customers and humanistic psychologists of precisely the same political shortcomings. It soon became a commonplace assumption that the youth movement à la Reich, the human potential movement à la Esalen, and the humanistic psychology movement were all of a piece— euphoric, naïve, and depoliticized visions of a hastening upper-middle-class millennium.

This assumption required Esalen to do what it had not had to do in the first years, when it was a happy testing ground for new ideas and techniques. It became more and more necessary not only to welcome new friends but to counter opposition, to tell the world not only what it was for, but what it was against. This was not easily done, because Esalen's policy had always been one of no policy, so the matter of shaping its new 1970s' stance in the world happened here and there, in what seemed to be unrelated incidents.

A kind of drawing-in had begun. More attention was being paid to business management. There was less of the big-bang spirit, not quite so much openness to new schools of therapy and spiritual growth; Esalen had clearer boundaries. Murphy and Price were, in different ways, both withdrawing slightly from Esalen. And the most ambitious of all of Esalen's endeavors, the residential program, was coming to an end.

The first one had been planned in 1965, when Murphy and Leonard were supporting one another in the conviction that Esalen would soon fire a shot heard round the world. It had turned out to be something of a misfire, but the second had commenced with all the original enthusiasm intact. It stands out as the archetype of the whole project, the one with the most of everything: the most talented members, the most sustained energy, the most excitement, the most wildness and excess and ungrounded expectation. It was led by Will Schutz at a time when his own abilities and energies were at their peak, and it lived out its brief life amid the florid climax of the hippie scene. After that there were no more nine-month programs. Instead, there were the shorter sessions. Schutz led one of them; the others were led by various combinations of graduates—Ed Maupin, Steve Stroud, John Heider, Seymour Carter, who was a former member of the Flying Circus. The groups were both shorter in duration and humbler in presentation. The operation took on more of a professional tone; people who joined these later groups spoke of "being in the training program." Esalen pointedly gave no certificates, but it was obvious to one and all that several people from the first groups had gone on to become Esalen group leaders. Others naturally aspired to do the same thing, or to use their experience in some kind of therapeutic work. This was considerably more down to earth than viewing the program, as the first residents had been encouraged to do, as preparation for ushering in the millennium. The last of the four-month sessions ended in January 1971. Later, Betty Fuller led one three-month session and, later still, Janet Lederman led a gestalt training program, but there was no longer a series of residential programs as a regular part of Esalen's operation. From its conception to its demise, the residential project lasted about six years. Many reasons were given for ending it, but the overwhelming reason seemed to be that altogether too many of the people in it ended up committing suicide.

Early in 1970 a young man who called himself Sunshine had turned up around Esalen. He was handsome and crazy and vulnerable, and he had a lot of money. He bought a house near Esalen, hoping to find something like a home there. He entered the residential program that Steve Stroud was co-leading in the spring of 1970 and became a patient and disciple of Stroud's. Then Stroud went off to Arica. Sunshine stayed around and attached himself to the next residential program and to John Heider. At the conclusion of that program, some of the residents formed a group—the Big Sur Family, they called it—that was going to live together and lead groups at Esalen. Sunshine was accepted as a member of the commune; he had a sort of mascot status, not having been an official member of that particular residential program. They rented a house at Pfeiffer Beach and had no sooner moved in than the place burned down. For the others this was a setback; for Sunshine it was a disaster. He was passionately committed to the plan that they would live together, be a family. They had a meeting and talked about what to do. Sunshine was in favor of keeping the group together. He thought they should put up a big tent, anything, and look for another house. But the cohesion was not strong enough to survive the house-burning and keep the Big Sur Family going. Some people were already thinking about doing other things. One of them wanted to go study with Ida Rolf. They didn't have energy for it.

Sunshine's time of distress coincided with a party that was going on at the Big House. Bunny, Michael's grandmother, had died in 1966 and had left parcels of her property to various Murphys. Dennis, who inherited the Big House, leased it to a wealthy young man from Southern California, another princeling of the drug culture. From the time he moved in, the Big House became a very special local attraction. The occupant entertained frequently and took pride in the variety and quality of delights he had available to offer his guests: many kinds of marijuana, a hashish that was said to be the type favored by the shah of Iran, and a fruit punch laced with psilocybin and perhaps a few other things. This weekend the fruit punch was being served, and several people got stoned out of their minds. Somebody collapsed in the vegetable garden, thinking he was dying, and had to be resuscitated. Sunshine drank some of the punch, went off to a nearby building— an old barn that had a loft studio where a friend of his lived—found a gun there, and shot himself.

Seymour Carter, who had been one of Sunshine's closest friends, heard the news and went to the barn. He found Sunshine, still alive, with a bullet in his head. Carter was like Sunshine in some ways; he was another outlaw who had come to Esalen to try to turn his life around. He had had better luck at it. After working in the kitchen, he became a member of the second residential program and the Flying Circus, and then manager of the residential programs. He was a survivor, but he had had his own near-suicidal moments, and he remembered those as he watched Sunshine thrash about in the little loft. The others had called the sheriff's office, told them to send an ambulance, but those things take a while along the Big Sur coast. Carter waited there about an hour.

"His body really wanted to live," Carter recalled. "The power of it was extraordinary. Immense surges, attempts to continue breathing." Finally the breathing stopped, and the ambulance arrived to take him away.

There were others. Nick Gagarin had first heard of Esalen while an undergraduate at Harvard. He and his father, Andy Gagarin, a Russian émigré who had married well and made a fortune in manufacturing, came to the Esalen New York soirée in 1970 and were favorably impressed. Nick wrote some articles about Esalen for the *Harvard Crimson* and, with his father's approval, went out to Big Sur for a four-month residency. He had a good experience in the residential program, according to others who were in it with him, but later he developed delusions, believing himself to possess extraordinary powers, and was hospitalized for a while in New York. Finally, on Thanksgiving Day, he shot himself in his father's house.

Another former member of the same residential program, a woman named Jeannie Butler, apparently also committed suicide. A man she had been living with, somebody she had known from the Arica training (which she had gone into after the residential program), dropped her off at Esalen. They found her clothes on the edge of the cliff behind the Big House. Her body was never found.

Sunshine's parents believed that Esalen was directly responsible for his death. Nick Gagarin's father, on the other hand, remained a close friend and supporter of Esalen. He loaned it money and donated his considerable managerial efforts to making it financially stable.

Recollections of the deaths by people close to Esalen—Murphy and Price and others—summon up explanations: reminders that people commit suicide in mental hospitals, colleges, luxury hotels, and summer camps, and that most of the suicides were lost and damaged people who had been close to suicide for years. All such statements are attempts to say that Esalen was not to blame for these tragic events. Yet the sense of blame, or responsibility, or guilt, remains. It comes with the territory. Whenever you offer to people something in the nature of therapy, you have assumed for yourself some part of the responsibility for its outcome, no matter how much you may promulgate an ideology that claims all responsibility remains with the individual. If you are willing to accept any credit for the successes—the peak experiences, the moments of joy, the flashes of personal insight, the discoveries of new and nourishing directions—then you are also part owner of the failures, including the suicides.

Stuart Miller argued that the suicides, in particular, were a consequence of the intensity of the residential programs, of Schutz's penchant for intense encounter work, of encounter itself. Murphy would say wryly that they demonstrated the failure of the idea that extending the length of Esalen work would eliminate the letdowns that so often followed the euphoria after a Big Sur weekend. It turned out only that the letdown came later and went deeper.

Esalen had always been reasonably restrained in the claims that it made—and that its group leaders were permitted to make—about the therapeutic results of its programs. But despite the modest descriptions in the brochures, there grew up a towering edifice of expectations that were nurtured in more subtle ways. Among others was the genuine and contagious belief of some of Esalen's leading figures that Big Sur held magical keys to human development. People came there with hope—in the lodge the air was thick with it—and in some people that hope was not distinguishable from desperation.

Yet the explanations and defenses offered are not to be dismissed entirely. If Esalen is to be blamed, the blame must be generously distributed. Most of the suicides had been, or were being, treated by conventional psychotherapists. Two of them, Art Rogers and Judith Gold, were themselves clinical psychologists, products of graduate schools and certified by state licensing boards. Nick Gagarin, at the time he committed suicide, recently had been treated and released from one of the best mental hospitals in New York City. For most of the suicides, in short, Esalen was not all of life—only a chapter, another attempt, and another failure.

Michael Murphy, while still involved in all of Esalen's happenings, was trying hard to establish some identity of his own.

When Esalen had been in its first San Francisco headquarters, Murphy had lived in a room upstairs. When the offices were moved to a new space on Union Street, he found an apartment on Telegraph Hill. So, for the first time since Esalen had started, he had a residence of his own that was completely separate from it. This move was a significant personal transition, a time of maturing and turning inward. He was living like a grownup. All his adult years had been passed in rented rooms and in odd spaces here and there on the Big Sur property. The new place was a real apartment, and a secluded one at that, not easily reached from the street and conducive to privacy and quiet.

In the summer of 1970, soon after he returned from his trip to England and the Continent, he began writing a book. He found it a wonderfully liberating experience to be working alone, dealing with ideas of his own and not merely acting as a broker and promoter for the other people's ideas, some of which he was not always sure he fully understood or agreed with.

The book that he was working on was very much his own. It had been in gestation for a good fifteen years, since his first journey abroad, when he had gone to the Aurobindo ashram and had, on the way, visited Scotland and played on the St. Andrews links, golf's Garden of Eden. The book was about that, but it was not simply a memoir. It is a book that is hard to categorize. In some ways, it resembles the works of Carlos Castaneda: it appears to be autobiography, but verges over—who can say precisely when?—into fantasy. It is also about a mystical teacher. In this case the teacher is Shivas Irons, a singular Scotsman whose discipline—his yoga, you might say—is golf, which becomes a source of wisdom about the world and the self, a key to mighty experiences and cosmic truths. *Golf in the Kingdom* was published in 1972 and had a generally favorable acceptance in both spiritual and sporting circles, although there must have been golfers out there in middle America who didn't know what to make of the book when they got it home and tried to read it. Murphy's mother was pleased to have still another writer in the family. There was Dennis, whose novel *The Sergeant* had been made into a movie and who was in Southern California writing screenplays, and now there was Michael, who had turned out to be something like what his brother had once called him, a golfing yogi.

Murphy became less accessible and more selective about how he spent his time. He sometimes referred to Esalen as though it were a being with a life of its own, a demanding creature that would reach out and scream for its needs to be met when he had other things he would rather do. This was especially true when some of the chores it thrust upon him were unpleasant, as when he had to drive to Salinas to testify at a lawsuit that resulted from Judith Gold's death in the baths.

Even while he struggled to get some distance from Esalen, he remained deeply concerned about threats to its reputation. One of the most odious was the attempt to link Esalen with Charles Manson.

There were certain tenuous connecting threads between Esalen and Manson. Once, just before the Tate murders, Manson had driven up Highway 1 in search of new followers and had picked up a girl, Stephanie Schram, south of Big Sur. They spent the night at a camp along the coast, and Manson bought some gasoline at Lucia (the place that had a sign in the window banning "hippies and beatnicks"). He paid for the gas with a stolen credit card. The pair drove into Esalen the next evening, and, while the girl slept in the van, Manson went into the lodge and put on an impromptu concert. There were two seven-day workshops going on—a humanistic education seminar with George Brown and a gestalt training workshop led by James Simkin and Jack Downing—and a few people were hanging around the dining room that night. According to *Helter Skelter,* the definitive history of Manson's adventures, the concert was not much of a success. Manson told a friend: "Some people pretended that they were asleep, and other people were saying, 'This is too heavy for me,' and 'I'm not ready for that,' and others were saying, 'Well, I don't understand it,' and some just got up and walked out."[8] After a while, Manson gave up and left, and three days later orchestrated the decade's most publicized mass murder.

There was also a connection between Esalen and the victims. The coffee heiress Abigail Folger, one of those slain in the Tate mansion, had been to seminars at Esalen, and so had several of her friends. When the police went over the record of telephone calls from the Tate house, they found that somebody had called Esalen about a week before the night Manson went there: a brief station call to the main number. It may have been somebody inquiring about a program; it may have been someone trying to reach a friend who was staying at Esalen. Nobody ever found out. A lot of people were at Esalen that week. There were several programs going on at the same time, including a More Joy workshop led by Schutz's Flying Circus.

The links between the Manson case and Esalen do not amount to much, except, perhaps, in the sense that the bloody crime committed by Manson's followers in the hills of Los Angeles in late 1969 represented a sort of convergence of two vastly different wings of the Esalen culture: the hip and wealthy young people who repaired to Big Sur often for relaxation and adventure and psychotherapy; and the other young people, the hill dwellers and migrant hippies who drifted through the place and occasionally stayed on for a month or two as kitchen hands or chambermaids.

Manson, with his long hair and blazing eyes, looked almost exactly the archetypal hippie or the campus demonstrator who appeared in the newspaper cartoons. In the national conflict between the forces of the establishment and the forces of dissent, the establishment side was most willing to give Manson to the dissenters, and the dissenters were most eager not to take him. In 1970, when the Manson case was at its apex, a major Southern California newspaper began making inquiries for a news story about Manson's connection to Esalen. There was a report circulating that Manson had been a student at Esalen; the source of this was the Springer News Service, an agency that was actually a "dirty tricks" operation under the management of White House aide Charles Colson. The newspaper assigned one of its reporters to check out this interesting angle on the Manson case—the press had a huge appetite for new angles—and the reporter telephoned Esalen.

This news quickly reached Murphy, who was terribly upset about it. He could envision lurid headlines, millions of readers forming the impression that Esalen was a training camp for homicidal hippie cult leaders. There was much excited long-distance telephoning; Esalen's lawyer wheeled into operation and threatened lawsuits. In the end, the Manson-at-Esalen article was not published—there was not much to justify one, anyway—and later the story of this little adventure was told with much gusto. There was something gratifying, after all, about being important enough to have operatives of the president of the United States trying to ruin your reputation. It became folklore, but Murphy was profoundly disturbed about it at the time. He had a really hard time with these dark happenings that kept crawling out from the underside of life. He would deal with such emergencies, but they only made him want all the more to concentrate on other things: his own life, his own work.

About this time Murphy met a woman who became a major part of his life. George Leonard and his wife, Lillie, brought it about. Lillie had known her first. Her name was Dulce Cottle, she was recently divorced, attractive, about the right age, and she meditated. The Leonards arranged a gathering to bring the two together. Dulce came but—such was the reputation of Esalen—had last-minute doubts about whether she was ready to be presented to its founder, who would no doubt be long of hair and fearsomely liberated. There was a ladder standing alongside the house, and Dulce made use of it to peek through a window and look at Murphy. Having determined that he was clean-cut, youthful-looking, and handsome enough for anybody, she went in and was introduced, and they hit it off immediately.

Dulce had an urge to dedicate herself to something, and she rapidly dedicated herself to Murphy's work. She became his typist and editor, and then began helping out on things having to do with Esalen—writing letters, making appointments. Murphy had been trying to get some distance from Esalen, and Dulce quietly and efficiently made that infinitely more possible by serving as a buffer between him and Esalen. It was much different from his life a few years earlier at Big Sur, when anyone with a complaint or an idea could accost him on the premises or come wandering, unannounced, into his room at the Big House.

Richard Price also tried to get some distance from Esalen. Early in 1971 he handed responsibility for the Big Sur operation over to a surprised Julian Silverman and went off to New York to take the Arica training. This was in part a declaration of independence, in part a long-overdue vacation, and in part a search for some mortar to hold together the odd assortment of therapies and practices that he had made a part of his life. He always said that one of his chief hopes about Esalen was that he would find something there for himself. He had found a lot of things, but to be where he was, so near the center of the human potential movement, was to be continually hearing of new and better systems of self-improvement. None had more allure than Arica, with its heritage of ancient mystical schools, with all those Esalen eminents sailing off to Chile and returning with tales of their adventures, and with that enormous repertoire of exercises and meditations. He was drawn to the Arica training—and he needed to get Esalen off his back.

Arica One, it was called: the first formal presentation to an audience in the United States of the lore of the Sarmouni. However one gained admittance to the monastery of the Bees in Afghanistan, in New York it was done the American Way: you read the ad in the newspaper and sent in your check. There were about seventy trainees and some forty trainers, the group from Chile having relocated en masse to New York with Oscar. In calling this month-long session Arica One, they were declaring that it was the beginning of something; the school was rich with anastrophic expectations.

241

Price found he didn't much care for the Arica training in some ways, but he enjoyed the strenuous regimen of meditation and physical exercises, the structured time. "It was fun following someone else's orders—at least for a while," he recalls. "The day was set up like high school; you'd go to this fifty-minute class and the bell would ring and you'd go to the next one. Oscar was at something of a remove. You could sign up and get an individual twenty-minute appointment, if you wanted to. He would come in and out, maybe four times a week."

In the second six weeks of the program, the entire group, trainees and trainers alike, was separated into nine subgroups, corresponding to the nine basic personality types. It is a fundamental part of the Arica system (as it is of the Gurdjieffian) that all people fall into one of these nine categories, each marked by a single overriding tendency or passion—anger, fear, indolence, withdrawal—which is, in fact, that person's ego, his or her technique for maintaining a false self that is alien to the true or awakened consciousness. The object of any spiritual or psychological work is to disarm the ego and awaken to the true self. This is a profound doctrine and worthy of much consideration; it is also, as Price soon saw, one that humiliates the student.

"There is something about this type of thing," he has said, "that goes like this: 'If you haven't had our training, then you're not really a person. You're unconscious. And I can do anything I want with you. You exist to be manipulated for your own good.' I had a very hard time with this."

There were specific things that Price had trouble with during the Arica training. One was the recruitment, the pressure to make a more lasting commitment to the school. It was simply announced one day that everyone had been accepted for an additional three months' training period. This came as a considerable surprise to Price, since he had never *applied* for an additional three months' training. He had come to New York with a clear understanding that he was going to take part in an educational process that would last three months, no longer, and that was going to send him back to his work and his life with improved abilities.

One day there was a meeting of the entire membership of the school. They sat on the floor in two concentric circles: the seventy neophytes were the outer circle; the other forty, including Oscar, were the inner circle. They did group chanting, and they did a *mudra. Mudras,* gestures with the hands or sometimes with the entire body, are an integral part of nearly all spiritual traditions; this particular one was a complete extension of the right hand and arm, precisely like the Nazi salute.

Price looked around and saw that many of the people sitting there and extending their arms toward Oscar were Jews. He protested this, contending that it was, if nothing else, in poor taste, and several members of the training group told him he was out of line and had no business challenging the practices. The fact that he was a big shot from Esalen only made it all the more apparent that this was his ego acting up.

Price dropped out of the Arica training eight days before it was over. He had learned some practices, but the real outcome was a reinforcement of his philosophy about how Esalen's own teachings were to be offered. He put it this way: "We present, and make no claims, no promises. There is no proselytizing, especially. The idea is one hundred percent availability and zero percent coercion."

This philosophy had been there, perhaps not always clearly understood or clearly expressed even by Murphy and Price themselves. Murphy, of the two, was the more explicit about it, because he was the one who had had firsthand experience with the smiling tyranny that manifests itself in such schools, even when they are, as the ashram at Pondicherry was, founded by searchers after synthesis and openness of thought. Price had understood this and approved of it in principle, but had not had any experience to make it a deeply felt conviction. The Arica training gave him that, and thereby made its greatest contribution to Esalen, by helping it define its identity in a decade that became well acquainted with the word "cult."

The period of Price's sojourn among the Aricans was the first time that Esalen Big Sur was not under the direct supervision of Murphy or Price, particularly Price, who had taken responsibility for Esalen's daily business. Others had held the job of general manager at Big Sur, but there was a big difference between being the manager with Price present and being the manager with him away in New York.

Silverman's taking charge was one part of a long and traumatic and ultimately successful effort to put Esalen on a solid business foundation. The real driving force behind this effort was Andy Gagarin, who retired in 1971 and took on Esalen as a kind of hobby. He was just beginning to take a role in the management when Silverman took over at Big Sur. Neither Murphy nor Price had ever pretended to be a businessman, and the influence of Gagarin, a hard-nosed industrialist, made a tremendous difference in the way things were run, a difference that not everybody found appealing. Gagarin was around Big Sur most of the time, but he had his own house and was rarely seen in the lodge. Silverman was right there every day, working in the office and taking his meals in the dining room. He was, as far as the staff was concerned, the boss.

Although Silverman had avant-garde ideas about psychotherapy, his philosophy of management was strictly conventional, formed by a couple of undergraduate business courses, a hitch in the military police, and a long period of employment in the federal scientific bureaucracy. Taking his new job seriously, he bought some books on management and tried to apply their teachings to the task of running Esalen, but that did not work out too well.

Will Schutz, who was also around, had his own ideas about management. He thought that a place like Esalen, which aspired to offer to the world a new vision of human potentialities, had an obligation to get away from the old hierarchical way of doing things. At mealtime he would join Silverman in the dining room and give him suggestions about how this could be done. Try a little more democracy, he would say. Let the employees get together in groups and decide things among themselves: their work shifts, their responsibilities, their salaries.

Schutz knew—as Silverman, whose background was in experimental psychology, apparently did not—that a new school of management psychology was emerging, influenced by humanistic psychology and the group therapies. Many of Schutz's friends, at such places as NTL in Bethel and WBSI in La Jolla, were involved in this. Abe Maslow had written a book about what he called eupsychian management. There was a growing body of literature that made the case for fundamentally different ways of running organizations. The classic statement, the one most often quoted, was Douglas McGregor's.[9] McGregor said there were two approaches to management. Theory X, the traditional approach, proceeded from the assumption that neither managers nor workers have it within themselves to do anything at all, unless they are goaded in the proper direction through the application of rewards and punishments. The alternative, Theory Y, humanistically presumed that people had inherent motivations to produce and were capable of setting and reaching their own goals. The administrator, in this latter view, had the fine Rogerian role of facilitator. His or her job was not to push and terrorize employees, but to remove obstacles and create opportunities for them to grow and change and to realize their potentialities on the job.

Schutz's colleagues were busily carrying this message into the corporate halls, using sensitivity training as their vehicle. Schutz believed that his own approach to group work, the open encounter, had even greater potential. In his most recent book, *Here Comes Everybody,* he had written:

> If open encounter is used routinely in a business setting, transcendent rewards follow, like seeing work as a meditation. Bitching about your job gives way to seeing the here-and-now pleasure in work and feeling the joy of realizing your human potential. These feelings are within reach if the sham, venality, and hypocrisy of business, labor, and industry are overcome and people come together in the joint effort of accomplishing a civilization's work together.[10]

Schutz saw Esalen as a logical place to put to the test his vision of encounter management. He has said:

> The issue was: Shall we run Esalen the way we talk about in the workshops? It's always been a high value for me to live the way I talk, and I thought, if any place should be able to do that, it should be Esalen. I looked around at it, with the background of the organizational development work I'd done for many years, and it looked like a 1932 Ford plant. Run in the worst possible way: very authoritarian, very arbitrary, very crappy. When Julian took over, I thought, Here is an opportunity to really start something.

From Silverman's point of view, the trouble with leaping into some new and more democratic style of management lay in the transience of things at Big Sur. The place was the living embodiment of the ancient Buddhist maxim that everything changes. The faculty came and went, the students came and went, and the employees—among whom Schutz proposed to implement Theory Y—also did a lot of coming and going. They were a marvelously mixed bag of people. Some came looking for a quiet place to live simply, in the old Big Sur tradition; some aspired to sit at the feet of Esalen's teachers and perhaps to find careers for themselves as group leaders or Rolfers; some were deeply troubled and in quest of therapy; some were rootless wanderers interested mainly in bed and board; and quite a few were barely a jump ahead of the narcotics officers. A few stayed for years, truly making Esalen their home and life's work, but most moved on. The average employee was there for about six months, perhaps less. Silverman did not believe this was the raw material out of which was to be molded a living demonstration of the principles of eupsychian management. Responsibility for Esalen had been given to him, not to a ragtag band of gardeners and kitchen hands, and he did not propose to share it.

The conflict widened. First it consisted of dialogues between Schutz and Silverman in the dining room. Then Schutz began having little meetings with a few people at his house, where they would discuss the possibility of running things a different way. Members of the staff—a fairly rebellious group, on the whole—joyously joined the conflict and were soon calling meetings on their own. Some of them came to Silverman with an ultimatum, demanding that they be given full participation in the making of management decisions.

Silverman gave in to the extent of allowing an experiment: only the kitchen would become self-governing. To initiate this program, Silverman had to edge out the incumbent kitchen manager, a lady of authoritarian personality and strong vegetarian beliefs. (Some people think the kitchen was selected for this venture partly as a maneuver to change the diet, which ran heavily to chard in those days.) For several months, the kitchen crew made their own work schedules, decided among themselves who would hold what positions, parceled out the money. At first it was a smashing success. The kitchen was spotlessly clean and humming with activity. Schutz insists to this day that it remained a success and that Silverman was so threatened by it that he arbitrarily ended it. Silverman says that the honeymoon ended, there were turnovers and personnel problems, and he finally had to put a kitchen manager in charge. In any case, the experiment was finished, and the kitchen reverted to Theory X.

Regardless of the precise nature of the events leading up to it, Silverman's decision to declare the experiment over was a power move, pure and simple. Silverman often made such moves; he liked to go around shaking things up, issuing orders, making sudden changes. This way of doing things kept people off guard, and nobody got complacent. It was good, old-fashioned management.

Some time after the end of the kitchen experiment, the board of directors had a meeting at Big Sur. The board, which was the apex of

Esalen's official nonprofit corporate structure, consisted at the time of Murphy, Price (still away in New York), Silverman, John Clancy, a lawyer who had lived at Slate's Hot Springs in the early 1960s, Andy Gagarin, and George Calmenson, then the manager of the San Francisco branch. Will Schutz asked for time to address the meeting, and then presented a document he had written. It was part manifesto, part ultimatum. It outlined the principles of humanistic management, argued that Esalen had an obligation to practice those principles, and laid out some proposals for how to proceed. There had been times in the past when this would have been potent stuff and might have turned Esalen completely around. This was not such a time. Gagarin's own management reforms were beginning to take hold. The directors were behind Gagarin, and Gagarin was behind Silverman. The prospect of getting Esalen into the black was highly attractive, and the prospect of initiating an endless round of encounter groups in every department was not. The directors heard Schutz out and then asked him to refrain from involving himself in the management.

Schutz insisted that he wanted no personal power in the managerial structure. Silverman had, in exasperation, offered more than once to let him take over the place, run it his own way, and Schutz had said he didn't want that. There was no reason he should: he had a rewarding and enjoyable position as a superstar on the encounter-group circuit and hardly needed a job. But that was not the same as having no opinions about how the job should be done. For Schutz, encounter was not just an approach to running groups; it was a philosophy and something of an obsession. It was his agenda for social change, his vision of the greening of America. In *Here Comes Everybody*, his manifesto, he had written of an encounter culture that he saw spreading through the country, affecting psychotherapy, business, religion, education, the arts, daily life, and ultimately transforming the entire civilization. Many of the staff at Big Sur had read Schutz's book; all of them knew, or thought they knew, what his ideas were.

Although Schutz had been ordered to remove himself from campus politics at Big Sur, the little revolution simmered along. Meetings were held, new strategies discussed. Silverman was certain that Schutz was the driving force behind this, and that without Schutz's active encouragement the whole thing would blow away—that, in fact, Schutz was violating the board of directors' edict. So Silverman proceeded to institute the largest of his many managerial shake-ups. He telephoned

Schutz (who lived on the other side of Hot Springs Creek, on the northern edge of the property) and told him that he was henceforth forbidden to enter the lodge, lead groups at Big Sur, or even show his face on the premises. Schutz apparently took this with good grace. "One thing that Will always appreciated," recalled Silverman, "was clarity."

Although Schutz took the news well, the directors, when they heard what Silverman had done, did not. They thought Silverman had gone far beyond his authority in arbitrarily ostracizing a man who had done much to put Esalen on the map. The ban was rescinded, and Schutz again could venture with impunity across Hot Springs Creek.

This marked, for Schutz, the final conclusion of his part in capture the flag. He gave up attempts to influence the managerial style at Big Sur and revised sharply downward any hopes he may once have had that Esalen would become the home base of the encounter culture. Encounter was, if anything, on the decline there. It had been soundly rejected as a tool of management, and, with the end of the residential program, it was no longer a very strong force at Big Sur. Those clusters of residents were no longer adventuring about the premises, and the daily news of their encounter doings no longer surged through the dining room. Encounter programs were still offered, by Schutz and others, but they were only part of the programming, not the center of it.

After a while Schutz decided to leave Big Sur. He had been thinking about it anyway, and his final decision was precipitated by Andy Gagarin's announcement that the rent on his house was to be raised from $250 a month to $750 a month. This had more than just financial significance. The arrangement of low rent on a house and free meals in the lodge had been Esalen's way of declaring that Schutz was somebody special, a person to be honored for his contributions. Raising the rent $500 a month took a lot of the heart out of that declaration. Schutz thought all these things over and decided it would be nice to live near a city again. In 1973 he moved to the San Francisco area.

Silverman stayed on as manager and ran things according to his own philosophy, best summarized in a statement he made one day to some employees. They were arguing with him about how something ought to be done, and he said: "You may have ideas about what to do around here, but remember this: I got all the marbles." They never let him forget that line, and later somebody made up a T-shirt for him with the inscription:

ESALEN'S MANAGING DIRECTOR
I. G. A. T. M.

With Silverman firmly in charge of daily operations at Big Sur, with Andy Gagarin masterminding Esalen's march toward financial solidarity, Price was free to pay attention to those aspects of Esalen which interested him most, especially improving the buildings and grounds.

He did this through the work of a man named Selig Morgenrath, who was simultaneously one of the most influential persons in the history of Esalen and one of the least known. If you had been around Big Sur in the early 1970s, you might at any time have had the privilege of resting your gaze on some of the most celebrated figures in Esalen's history. While you were looking at them, the odds were that your vision would slide without pause over Selig, a graying, weathered, steady-eyed man who was a living bridge between the old Big Sur of Henry Miller and the new human potential academy. He can truly be described as the man who built Esalen.

The physical aspect kept changing, mostly for the better, and the changes had an organic quality. The place seemed to grow as a child grows, so that each time you saw it, it was recognizably the same yet different in subtle ways from what it had been. Buildings were expanded, but the new always harmonized with the old. A rutted pathway up the hill from the lodge was in time replaced by stairs of stone pieces marvelously fitted together without mortar. The landscaped areas were gorgeous expanses of flowers and lawns that seemed to be at once works of art and natural outgrowths of the terrain. Selig was the mind behind Esalen's physical development.

He was yet another ambassador to Big Sur from old Europe. He was born in one of those much fought over parts of Poland, where people of German language and culture lived. Brought to the United States as a child, he grew up in Brooklyn and became an artist in New York. According to the testimony of old-timers who knew him, he showed great promise at painting, but abandoned the Big Apple art world entirely, having found it corrupt. After a period in a conscientious objectors' camp during World War II, he married and came west, and found his way to the Big Sur country, where he spent the rest of his life. He became renowned there both as an accomplished painter and sculptor, and as a man who had a knack for practical things, building and fixing. He was not the only man in the Big Sur who knew how to swing a hammer, but there was a certain mystique about him; he had a spiritual attitude toward his work and was given to long discourses about it. Henry Miller, in *Big Sur and the Oranges of Hieronymous Bosch,* reminisced about Selig—they called him Jack Morgenrath then —as a consummate artist and question-answerer, wise beyond his years:

> If he thinks and moves like eternity itself, it's because he's *living* in a state of eternity. Thus, whether he's asked to build a fence, lay a sewer, prune an orchard, dig a ditch, repair a busted chair, or lay bricks, Jack goes about it with that somnambulistic clairvoyance which drives "active" people crazy. But when Jack is finished with a task, it's done. It stays done. And if you ask him a question it's answered full and straight, answered for good, so to speak.[11]

Fritz Perls, decades later, was similarly impressed by Selig, by his quiet seriousness and reverence for life, and in his own memoirs referred to Selig as one of his personal gurus:

> Here is truly a *Mensch,* a human being of complete unpretentiousness, humility, wisdom, and know-how. As a city-dweller, I had not much contact with nature. To watch him and his involvement and understanding with humans, animals, and plants, to compare his unobtrusiveness and confidence with my excitability and primadonna-ishness, to feel at last the presence of a man to whom I feel inferior, and finally the feeling of mutual respect and friendship that came about—all of this has helped me to overcome most of my pompousness and phoniness.[12]

A man of power and presence, then, possessed of a certain kind of charisma. Selig lived a short distance to the south of Esalen, on another old property, called Livermore Ledge. Inevitably, he was called on to perform chores at Esalen. Paul Herbert, who is now Esalen's oldest staff member—both in terms of age and of on-the-job seniority—is another Big Sur artist-handyman who often worked with Selig. He recalls that they were often employed by Bunny Murphy, and later by the woman who managed Slate's Hot Springs. When Mike Murphy and Dick Price took over, Selig was already a part of the local environment.

The first job they hired him for—one not really commensurate with the Morgenrath legend—was fixing up the baths so that Clare Boothe

Luce could use them without being seen. Mrs. Luce was then one of the most famous women in America—playwright, politician, wife of *Time-Life* publisher Henry Luce. She was planning to visit an old friend, a lady who lived up on Partington Ridge, and the lady wanted to bring Mrs. Luce to the baths, provided some way could be devised to give them privacy. Selig obligingly constructed a cumbersome rolling screen to conceal one of the tubs. Mrs. Luce changed her plans; it was never used and was later dismantled.

Selig was hired for other jobs, one thing and another, and as they recognized the dimensions of his skill and dedication, he eventually became the master planner. He was responsible for guiding the gradual expansion and conversion of the old resort.

Like Silverman, Selig was not one of your humanistic managers. He had a strong respect for authentic relations between people, but he also had strong ideas about the possibilities of that jewel-like piece of real estate. He had walked over every inch of it, looked at it with an artist's eye from many perspectives. He was familiar with its plants and animals and the shape of its terrain, knew the strengths and weaknesses of its miscellaneous buildings. He formed his own concept of how to work with that material, what should be the overall shape and feel of the site as it developed. That concept, once formed, lived in Selig's mind as a question answered full and straight. It was not subject to amendment according to the whims of other people who had not taken the trouble to think it through. He might listen to suggestions or objections, but his usual response would be to explain with rocklike certitude why he was right. Once, some staff members pointed out to him that it was awkward to get from the northern end of the lodge, where the office was, to the southern end, which led to the baths. People had to walk through the lodge, or go down across the lawn between the lodge and the cliffs, or take a detour past the cabins above the lodge. It wasn't convenient, and they thought it would be nice to have a walkway on the ocean side of the lodge in front of the big windows. Selig told them he was no freeway-builder. He wanted that view from the lodge windows to remain uncluttered by human traffic. He wanted to invite people to take their time along the way, perhaps be drawn into conversations in the lodge or silent contemplations of the view.

You can see the evidence of his vision manifested in the present shape of Esalen. There is no walkway on the ocean side of the lodge, and there are no buildings between the lodge and the cliffs. From the windows you look out across an uncluttered expanse of grass, a swimming pool, flowers, and cacti. Where there are fences, they are light and airy structures of welded iron that do the job of discouraging you from sliding over the cliffs but do not block the view of the ocean. The rooms, up behind the lodge, are simple quarters with walls of bare wood. Parking areas are long and narrow, bordered by evergreen trees Selig planted years ago that are big enough now to screen and soften the visual presence of the dozens of cars likely to be crowded into that small space on a busy weekend.

They say that Selig became a central figure in Esalen's loose community, especially in the 1970s after Fritz was gone. A community requires a resident elder, a wise man, a moral authority, and Selig filled that role admirably. By putting his stamp on the physical environment, he extended his influence into every group and seminar and to the personal experience of every visitor. The psychological and philosophical activities at Esalen were always essentially searches for truth, but in such quests people are tempted to settle for flashy and specious half-truths. The peacefully honest surroundings weigh in on the side of the whole truth. When matters are in the balance, as they often are, the walls give good counsel.

13

In the early 1970s, Esalen, seen from the outside, appeared to be still on the march, still expanding. There was building and development at Big Sur, and the San Francisco office moved twice, each time to larger quarters: first from the makeshift rooms in Murphy's cousin's house to a flat upstairs from a boutique on Union Street, then across the street into a much larger space that contained offices, a reception room–bookstore, and sizable meeting rooms that obviated the need to hold all the programs in rented spaces around town.

Union Street was a place that had undergone a miracle of gentrification. Once a staid neighborhood where Italian families lived upstairs from plumbing-supply stores, it was now a garden of youth, style, and affluence. Flowers blossomed in window boxes, and paint gleamed on restored Victorian houses; along the street were clothing shops and art galleries, antique stores and singles bars. Union Street was also the human potential business district.

The flat that Esalen vacated was taken over by Betty Fuller and Dub Leigh, both graduates of Esalen residential programs. Together they opened the Health Farm Chapel and New Age Body Shop, a hard-to-classify business—somebody called it a mom-and-pop growth center —that offered lessons from Betty in the Feldenkreis method of body work which had recently become popular, and Rolfings from Dub, an amiable, middle-aged man originally from Utah. Other people—an acupuncturist, miscellaneous encounter-group leaders—rented space for their various activities and added more to the human potential activity on the block.

Also on the 1700 block of Union Street was the Gestalt Institute of San Francisco. By this time gestalt had become the sixth most common affiliation of American psychotherapists, having passed the Jungians and other heirs of the old European intellectual aristocracy that had cowed the young Fritz Perls. The institute was a thriving concern, running dozens of prospective therapists and counselors through its quarterly training sessions.

Then an organization called est opened up offices in a building across the street from the Gestalt Therapy Institute. It was in more ways than one the new kid on the block, having commenced its trainings only in late 1971. However, there was nothing diffident about either est (Erhard Seminars Training) or its founder, Werner Erhard, and from the time they made their appearance, the human potential movement was never quite the same again.

Erhard *Americanized* the human potential movement in a way that Esalen had never done or tried to do. At Esalen the content was always openly identified as a mélange of many traditions, and even if you had no particular interest in their histories, you knew you were in the presence of imports from other times and places. This message was communicated by Zen books, incense, and yoga teachers, by Fritz's German accent and the invocations of the memories of Freud, Jung, and Reich. Eastern and European influences went into the est training, too, but they were totally submerged by the all-American sales-seminar atmosphere of it: the ambience of the hotel ballrooms where the trainings were held, the bright-eyed and shoe-shined neatness of the trainers and their assistants.

Erhard earned immortality in the annals of the human potential movement by grafting it onto the ancient body of American literature and thought having to do with self-help, positive thinking, and personal success. Dale Carnegie is high among the invisible gurus of est, standing up there with Alan Watts, Fritz Perls, Abe Maslow, and the founder of Scientology, L. Ron Hubbard. Psychology, too, makes strange bedfellows.

It had never occurred to Murphy or Price to mine the positive-thinking vein, for the simple reason that it had never been a part of their own formative years. For Erhard, it had been. He came from a different background. He had not gone to college, and had earned his living, from the time he was a couple of years out of high school, as a salesman: first a car salesman, later a traveling salesman for a correspondence school, later still a Great Books salesman. Apparently he was one hell of a salesman and, as he matured, one hell of a trainer of salesmen. He was an avid reader of self-help literature. Among the books that moved him the most, his biographer tells us, were

Napoleon Hill's *Think and Grow Rich* and Maxwell Maltz's *Psycho-Cybernetics.*[1]

When Erhard's prospering sales career brought him to the San Francisco Bay Area, he began to take an interest in the ideas that were circulating there. An employee introduced him to the works of Maslow and Rogers. He read about gestalt therapy, went to Esalen a couple of times, met Fritz, did an encounter workshop with Schutz and a gestalt workshop with Julian Silverman. He read Alan Watts's works and started going to seminars at Watts's houseboat in Sausalito. This was one of the major formative influences on him. Erhard was much taken with Zen. He liked Watts's irreverent approach to Zen, which implied that you could get the message without buying the Oriental medium. Perhaps most of all, he liked Watts himself, his humor, dynamism, and gift of gab. Erhard's own speaking style showed a distinct Watts influence. He did not quite match Watts's erudition and lucidity, but he did master a little chuckle, a staccato *heh-heh-heh* that would come out once in a while, as he mused on the follies of unenlightened humanity, and that friends of Watts recognized as an eerily perfect imitation.

Erhard gobbled up Zen, took a Dale Carnegie course, plunged into other Oriental disciplines, including martial arts, did more encounter and gestalt, experienced sensory awakening with Selver and Brooks, and went deeply into Scientology. He became, for a time, an instructor of Mind Dynamics, a form of self-improvement training that had been developed by an Englishman, Alexander Everett, whose own spiritual progress had taken him through theosophy, Rosicrucianism, the Edgar Cayce psychics, and Silva Mind Control. So by the time he hung out his own shingle, Erhard had done his homework. He had chewed his way through a large piece of what, though we rarely recognize it as such, is as much our cultural heritage as Shakespeare or calculus: the sometimes respectable, sometimes not, ideas and practices having to do with mobilizing the human psyche toward personal success in the world of business.

The Erhard Seminars Training took off like a skyrocket, and in a very short time Werner Erhard moved from total obscurity to a place of striking prominence. Like all such arrivistes, from Napoleon to Henry Ford, Erhard was controversial, seemingly invulnerable to criticism, and possessed of a mountain of *chutzpah*. He operated est for a while in a suite of offices on Broadway, in a garish neighborhood of bars and strip joints, and then opened an office across the street from the Gestalt Therapy Institute, just down from Esalen, as if to remind them both that est was not to be ignored.

   This concentration of human potential activity on Union Street was still only a minuscule portion of the total activity of that nature in the Bay Area. The region had a large and rapidly growing army of encounter leaders and gestalt therapists, masseurs and Rolfers, teachers of yoga and meditation. Some of these were established professionals with their own offices and/or meeting rooms; others were newcomers just struggling for a meager following. You saw their announcements tacked up on telephone poles and bulletin boards and in the classified sections of little newspapers. If you were on the right mailing lists, you received daily announcements of new opportunities to enlighten yourself, improve your sexual performance, work on your relationships, and in sundry other ways become a better being.

   All of this activity was symbolic of Esalen's success as cultural midwife, yet at the same time it created problems. Esalen's position in San Francisco was not entirely secure. It had a special prestige, and its widely distributed brochures brought in a steady stream of newcomers and out-of-town visitors; but, lacking the magic of the Big Sur setting, it did not really have that much with which to compete locally amid this proliferation of personal-development organizations and independent practitioners.

   And, in truth, Esalen did not really try to compete. With its sizable overhead, it was in no position to offer lower prices, but there were other things a more hardhearted business might have done that were not even considered. No attempt was made, for example, to place any strictures on the many workshop leaders who worked with competing organizations, or to prevent them from organizing their own programs, as many did upon discovering that they could thereby make more money and charge their customers less by short-circuiting the Esalen overhead. Nor did Esalen, in its public statements, ever proclaim its special position within the movement or suggest that it was superior. Its prose was occasionally smarmy, true, but always in a diffuse way and never with any kind of implication that it had an exclusive product to sell. Mike Murphy, in private, might have something critical to say about some of the local gurus when he was laughing it up with his friends, but he never played the destroy-the-competition game that was popular at the time among the various schools of human development. The forward progress of the movement remained his first concern, despite the precarious status of the San Francisco office, which was, at the time, his closest connection to it.

Instead of competing in the ordinary commercial sense, Murphy did things to make Esalen more distinctive, more innovative, and more a reflection of his particular interests. He had always thought of Esalen as a kind of college, and for a while, in the 1970s, the Esalen College Program was offered. It started out as an arrangement whereby students at local colleges could get credit for attending Esalen workshops and seminars, and then it expanded into a more elaborate offering, with "master seminars," like "Philosophy and the Evolution of Consciousness" led by Murphy and Leonard. Here, too, however, there was competition. Local colleges had courses, even degree programs, in humanistic psychology. The University of California Extension, in its local adult education programs, was heavily into humanistic psychology, encounter groups and seminars on consciousness. Down at Santa Barbara, there was the confluent education program that had been inspired by George Brown's work at Esalen.

Another specialized subgroup was the Women's Studies Program, an outgrowth of the new feminist movement that had done so much to merge personal growth with political activism. The Women's Studies Program attempted to take this synthesis a few steps farther. It offered a curious mixture of workshops that combined feminist radicalism with every conceivable adaptation of the routine Esalen material: legal rights, natural childbirth, feminine archetypes, sexuality, gay consciousness, wilderness survival, overcoming sex-role socialization, revolutionary movements, massage for women, Tai Chi for women, Aikido for women. There were evening lecture programs, with such speakers as Anaïs Nin, the diarist, and Phyllis Chesler, the author of *Women and Madness*. This was a new departure for Esalen, but there was competition here also: feminist activism with a human potential flavor was strong in the San Francisco area. There was even a women's growth center. It was called Alyssum and had its offices on Union Street, in the same building as the Gestalt Therapy Institute.

The one truly *different* department that emerged during this time was the Sports Center. This was a favorite project of Murphy's, his own strategy for disseminating the human potential movement into the mainstream of American culture.

Changes are coming. Sports represent a key joint in any society.

> To turn this society toward peaceful, humane change, we can begin with reform of sports. Some intellectuals have ignored this aspect of our life, believing somehow that sports are beyond serious consideration. They are quite mistaken. There is nothing trivial about the flight of a ball, for it traces for us the course of the planet. Through the movement of the human body, we can come to know what the philosopher Pythagoras called *kosmos,* a word containing the idea of both perfect order and intense beauty. Sports are too beautiful and profound for simplistic slogans. How we play the game may turn out to be more important than we imagine, for it signifies nothing less than our way of being in the world.

So proclaimed George Leonard in the brochure for one of the Sports Center's first offerings, a public conference. The center organized several of these symposia to popularize new concepts and practices of athletic endeavor: new approaches to physical education, more respect for the connection between physical and mental well-being, and perhaps even—Murphy's most cherished dream—a wider acceptance of the possible link between sports and psychic experience.

The Sports Center brought together its own little constellation of program leaders, and it had a separate staff within the San Francisco office. They were somewhat different from the usual run of Esalen people, who still tended to come primarily from psychotherapy, academia, and other above-the-neck fields of endeavor. Bob Kriegel, who was director of the Sports Center, had been a skiing and swimming instructor and a basketball coach. The associate director was David Meggyesy, a former linebacker for the St. Louis Cardinals. Also very active were the Spinos, Mike and Dyveke. Mike, a wiry little dark-haired man, was a nationally ranked marathon runner. His wife, Dyveke, was an exuberant and heroically proportioned Danish woman who had, among various athletic and artistic accomplishments, high standing as a tennis pro and a ski instructor. Tim Gallwey, another of the Sports Center regulars, was a professional tennis teacher.

They were all graduates of the basic curriculum of Esalen experiences—body awareness, yoga and meditation, fantasies and visualizations, massage, and sensory-awakening exercises—and they were all working on ways to integrate that into sports. The aim was yet another kind of synthesis, a new cultural mixture of East and West, body and mind. At the symposia you saw coaches, physical education teachers, football players, dancers, Tai Chi and Aikido masters, hypnotists, and encounter leaders, all throwing their diverse skills and perspectives into the new blend. The Esalen catalogues carried a special section of sports programs—evening lectures ("Western Sport as Yoga," Mike Murphy); weekend workshops ("Inner Game of Tennis," Tim Gallwey); ongoing training programs ("Jogging, Conditioning, and Creativity," Mike Spino). There were also more of the kind of outdoor programs that had been offered years earlier: hiking, cross-country skiing, river rafting, and skin diving.

The pieces were not new in themselves, but the combinations were new, and many of them worked. There is a real difference between the usual American approach to a sport like tennis—all gritting teeth and inner conflict—and the supple, meditative styles that people learned in the Esalen programs. The Sports Center's influence also spread in another direction, out through the ranks of the faithful who had already done gestalt and encounter and the rest of the Esalen basics. The word seeped through that subculture that sports were part of the answer, and that if you were seriously working on your growth, you should be doing something athletic. The martial arts, especially Aikido, were high on the approved list, with yoga and running close behind. And as the word spread, a new genre of sports books appeared. The best known of these was Tim Gallwey's *The Inner Game of Tennis.* Gallwey also wrote *The Inner Game of Golf* and later collaborated with Bob Kriegel on *Inner Skiing.* Mike Spino wrote *Beyond Jogging: The Innerspaces of Running.*

All of these works were influenced by Eugen Herrigel's classic, *Zen in the Art of Archery,* which had so lucidly shown how the calmed and meditative mind manifests itself in the performance of a physical action, and how the ego can get in the way of such performance. You could also catch strong echoes of yoga—Gallwey dedicated his tennis book to the teen-age guru Maharaj Ji—and of gestalt therapy. The tennis student's path was described in terms of a relationship between a "conscious teller" and an "unconscious doer," which sounded very much like Fritz's famous top dog and underdog. Spino had also been influenced by psychosynthesis, with its repertoire of visualizations, and his book told of visualizations for long-distance runners.

This was, in a way, a logical outgrowth of the work in psychotherapy that had been pioneered at Esalen—the body awareness in gestalt, the physical side of encounter, the neo-Reichian therapies and massage techniques. Nobody but Murphy, though, would have thought to make sports itself, that citadel of commercialized middle-American secular machismo, a vehicle of spirituality and self-discovery. The Sports Center was the product of his personal vision of sports and love for it, a consequence of the fact that his sudden discovery of Oriental religion back at Stanford had not erased a boyhood of playing baseball and golf and cheering at football games.

He was still a sports fan, a faithful follower of the San Francisco 49ers and a dedicated golfer. For a while he tried Aikido, and although he did not stay with that, he did become a serious runner. He clocked some impressive times on the mile run and did his first marathon when he was forty-three. He and Spino went running almost every day, eight miles or so along the Marina Green at the northern edge of San Francisco.

The running was in part a campaign against aging. "I just don't believe in that stuff about getting old," he would say. He was serious about it. He proposed to fight off the calendar, and training like a college athlete was one way of doing it.

But there was much more to sports for Murphy than merely keeping in shape. You could see that in *Golf in the Kingdom.* It was truly a vision; he saw something in athletic endeavor that was not what other people saw. Other people who went to a 49ers game saw a bunch of jocks bumping into each other; Murphy saw a transcendent dance of body and mind, a game played with the wind and the forces of gravity, an afternoon's journey into an altered state of consciousness. Some of his friends developed similarly expanded perspectives on sport, and some of them out-Murphyed Murphy. George Leonard once said, in describing a game in which the quarterback had completed a spectacular long pass in the final seconds of play, that "it spoke for all connectedness."

At about the time the Sports Center was getting started, Murphy became acquainted with John Brodie, the great 49ers quarterback. The meeting was arranged by a friend, who asked Murphy to come down to his house and give somebody a golf lesson. It seemed a strange request, but Murphy obligingly drove down to Palo Alto and was suitably stunned when the prospective student turned out to be Brodie.

Brodie had read *Golf in the Kingdom* and was a student of Scientology; he was interested in Murphy's ideas about extraordinary experiences in sports and told about some of his own. There were moments, he said, when his sense of time changed, so that, even when he stood behind the line with the football in his hands, with the opposing linemen charging toward him and his receivers racing down the field, he felt as though it were all happening in slow motion. There were occasions, he said, when he threw a pass more out of intuitive hunch than out of a clear knowledge of where the receiver was. And there had been one time, in a game against the Washington Redskins, when a long pass that he had thrown was almost intercepted. But then the ball seemed to rise higher in the air, and it sailed over the defending player and went safely into the receiver's hands for a touchdown.

It was almost too much. Murphy had been a fan of Brodie's ever since the 1950s, when Brodie had been quarterback at Stanford, and now here was Brodie in person, talking about extraordinary sports experiences and professing his admiration of *Golf in the Kingdom.* Brodie even suggested that he and Murphy might write a book together.

The two became good friends. Brodie spoke at one of the Esalen sports symposia. Murphy went down to Santa Barbara to visit Brodie at the 49ers training camp and interviewed him for a magazine article about the mystical side of sports. He agreed to collaborate with Brodie on a book. For a while, he even took up Scientology. Brodie believed in it deeply and thought that if they were to work together, Murphy should become a "clear." That was a tough request to make of a man who had spent the better part of his adult life opposing authoritarianism in religion and therapy—the Scientologists were widely known to be spiritual storm troopers without equal—but Murphy actually went into the program. Probably nobody but a 49ers quarterback could have gotten him to do such a thing, but even Brodie's influence was not enough to keep Murphy happy among the Scientologists. He dropped out after a few months.

The book project collapsed, too, after Brodie read the first draft of Murphy's manuscript. Murphy had worked on the book for nine months and completed a first draft of what was nominally a book about football. It was, like *Golf in the Kingdom,* a work of the imagination. But where *Golf in the Kingdom* had veered ever so slightly into the occult, this one plunged in head first. It told a bizarre adventure story involving the Irish Republican Army, the Roman Catholic Church, and the San Francisco 49ers. The climactic scene took the reader into a secret underground war room beneath the Vatican, where data were processed from all the confessionals in all the churches, thus yielding a picture of how the Devil was moving through the world. "I really let go on that one," Murphy recalled. "It was probably the weirdest science fiction novel anybody ever wrote." Brodie read it, shook his head, and said it wasn't what he had in mind.

The book project, like the Sports Center, came out of Murphy's newfound determination to pursue his own interests and not act merely as an impresario for other people's ideas. So did the 1973 conference that Esalen sponsored, "Spiritual and Therapeutic Tyranny: The Willingness to Submit."

The conference title, which was Murphy's, expressed his concern about the direction things were taking. Esalen had been founded, after all, to bring more knowledge of Eastern religion into American life, but to bring it in such a way that Americans would be able to absorb some of that wisdom without falling prey to the authoritarianism such schools were given to, and of which Murphy had had a strong sample at the Aurobindo ashram. But as the Western interest in spiritualism proliferated, those ancient evils were asserting themselves in new ways. There was, for example, the Arica School, which Dick Price had found a couple of years earlier to be faintly fascistic. Arica now had a thriving branch in San Francisco, largely as a result of the assist it had been given by Esalen, and it was behaving strangely. The word had recently come down from Oscar Ichazo that some momentous national upheaval—he called it a Wave—was going to take place in the very near future. Members of the Arica School, he said, should stand ready to assume positions of leadership in the society when this happened.

Then there was est, whose special brand of tyranny was a sinuous double-talking salesmanship that managed to convince its "graduates" that any failure on their part to discover great truths in its teachings was their own shortcoming, but all breakthroughs and achievements were to be ascribed to the training. Graduates were informed that if they had gotten "it" (the message of the training), they were now in full control of their lives—indeed, were godlike creators of their universe. At the same time, they were assiduously hustled to sign up for more seminars and still more, until they had purchased the whole, almost endless, encyclopedia. Erhard's Americanized gleaning of ancient disciplines had its Americanized version of the ancient and tyranny-breeding certainty that righteousness consisted in staying within the fold. And there was Scientology. It was not precisely in the human potential orbit, but Murphy, having recently been exposed to it, was acutely aware of its flaws.

The conference would, it was hoped, air all the issues and make people more aware of the dangers inherent in schools of personal and/or spiritual development, and perhaps inspire some self-examination among the emerging crop of spiritual/psychological teachers. And, no less important, it would demonstrate to the world that the human potential movement was capable of cleaning its own house, dealing with the very issues and problems that were raised by its critics. It would demonstrate, furthermore, that Esalen was the movement's conscience, not merely its fountainhead and entrepreneur. So the word went out, the printed brochures went out, and several hundred people gathered in San Francisco on a Friday night in December of 1973.

Those who came looking for contention and conflict were well served. The first thing they encountered as they arrived at the auditorium was a group of women from the Esalen Women's Studies Program, who were handing out leaflets and picketing the conference. The women's case was a cogent one. The roster of conference speakers had been artfully put together, with some well-known teachers—Werner Erhard, the Tibetan lama Chogyam Trungpa; some strong critics of authoritarian tendencies, spiritual and therapeutic—Esalen's old friend Joe K. Adams, the dissident psychiatrist Thomas Szasz; and some radical activists—Berkeley Free Speech Movement leader Michael Rossman, Jerry Rubin (sometime radical leader, now est student, George Leonard's future son-in-law); and miscellaneous other notables, including the editor of the *Realist,* Paul Krassner; Claudio Naranjo; Will Schutz; and John Vasconcellos, a California assemblyman. Apparently it had not occurred to anybody, during the weeks of planning this cutting-edge event, to invite any women to be among the twenty-six panelists. There were no blacks or Orientals either (Chogyam Trungpa didn't show up), but that was not the issue of the movement. Women were among the major consumers of the wares of gurus and therapists, and there were specifically feminist issues—such as the exploitation by stud group leaders—that a conference on spiritual and therapeutic tyranny should have explored.

While the women leafleted outside the auditorium, Sam Keen, a theologian and writer, gave a keynote address that was distinctly iconoclastic and clearly intended to generate heated discussion. Keen had interviewed most of the prominent gurus on the American scene for *Psychology Today.* He did not seem to have been deeply impressed. He announced that the title of his talk was "The Tyranny Game, or, How to Play Follow the Leader," and proceeded to outline the basic

263

rules of the game: (1) It takes two to play; there can be no tyranny without somebody ready to be tyrannized. (2) It begins with the presumption that something is wrong with the patient/client/disciple. (3) In order to play the game, the patient/client/disciple must be taught the rules according to the therapist/guru and must accept the rightness of that specific set of rules. (4) The goal has to be set so high that nobody can ever get there, since getting there would render the therapist/guru obsolete. (5) The payoff is the illusion of power—that we can control life.

Although the auditorium was full of patients, clients, disciples, therapists, and gurus, Keen's talk appeared to be warmly received. He got appreciative chuckles along the way when he pointed out that the leading lights of the human potential movement had their own short-comings—Will Schutz was not always joyful, Ida Rolf needed Rolfing —and there was long, long applause at the conclusion. But only a few minutes later, when the first panel convened, Stanley Keleman, a bioenergetic therapist, led it off by accusing Keen of having tyrannized the whole conference. When that was said, the audience gave *Keleman* a long round of applause. There was much of that sort of applause throughout that evening and the full day of conferencing that followed. The people who had come to it seemed prepared to cheer anybody who attacked anybody else.

It was a remarkably angry meeting. The panelists attacked one another, speakers from the audience attacked the panelists, occasionally the panelists attacked the audience. Peter Marin, speaking on a panel on Saturday morning, expressed his disgust with the whole gathering. He said he had been able to take about ten minutes of the previous night's meeting and had then repaired to a pool hall. The people at the conference, he said, did not seem to be the kind of people who loved the world. People who loved the world, he said, had a different appearance. With that brief sermon on the power of love, Marin succeeded in attacking everybody present. He was, at the time, a visiting fellow at the Center for the Study of Democratic Institutions at Santa Barbara, and he said that the discussions at Santa Barbara were more intelligent. George Leonard, who was moderating the panel, said he had been to some of the meetings at the center and had found them pompous and dull. Marin retorted that if Leonard wouldn't hold him responsible for the center, he wouldn't hold Leonard responsible for *Look* magazine.

Not all of the conference was angry, to be sure. Some of it was confusing, as when Werner Erhard launched into solos of misty est prose ("I neither agreed with you or disagreed with you," he said to Sam Keen), which had the effect of enabling him to avoid dealing with any direct criticism of est. Some of it was distracting: Paul Krassner, who was on the panel with Leonard and Marin, disregarded its designated subject matter ("The Appeal of the Esoteric") and rambled off into a long exposition of his theory that Charles Manson had been an agent of the CIA, engaged in a conspiracy to discredit the counterculture. And much of it was moderate and intelligent and to the point.

The conference did, in fact, admirably explore the issues it had been meant to explore. Yet it left a trail of dissatisfaction in its wake, and no visible change. The Aricans were still ready to take over the world; est still assured its graduates that they were now fully in control of their lives while simultaneously pressuring them into more seminars; the Scientologists still maintained their science fiction military hierarchy. If anything, things got worse. The Psychosynthesis Institute, another Esalen offspring, which had started out reflecting the high-minded spiritual philosophy of its founder, became more and more authoritarian, more and more strident in its conviction that psychosynthesis was the One Truth. By the late 1970s students were being relentlessly indoctrinated, and those who tried to drop out were threatened with the assurance—a staple of spiritual tyranny—that to abandon that specific path was to abandon all hope of improving one's life.

Nor was the conference's public relations payoff particularly rewarding. The most influential piece of media coverage that resulted from it was Peter Marin's article, "The New Narcissism," in *Harper's*. Marin was not positive about the conference itself ("beneath the ruffled but still reasonable surface of the crowd lay a hysteria that would in other settings take on any one of several forms, none of them particularly pretty"); he was deadly on est; and he did not see that est's shortcomings were noticeably different from those of the human potential movement in general. Indeed, he found est to be "in many ways the logical extension of the whole human potential movement of the past decade. The refusal to consider moral complexities, the denial of history and a larger community, the disappearance of the Other, the exaggerations of the will . . ."[2] He found in the movement only a sterile rejection of society, a preoccupation with the needs of the self, self-love, narcissism. It was a powerful charge, and later critics of the movement seized upon it happily and stated it in new ways. The

Spiritual Tyranny conference thus brought into being the strongest indictment of the movement as a whole; it was like a mythic allegory in which the hero forges the weapon that is later used against him.

Conceivably, the conference might have had an entirely different outcome. Esalen might somehow have found a way to mobilize the energy and anger that had been stirred up there, carry out a long-range program to keep those issues before the public. There was some talk, before the conference, of further events of that nature, but none came to pass. Murphy remained concerned about the issue and organized some small-scale group meetings around it, but it was no longer an important piece of Esalen business. Murphy had resigned as president of Esalen by this time, and Esalen was too preoccupied with the upheavals resulting from that change to embark on a sustained adventure as moral arbiter of the human potential movement.

In resigning, Murphy made official what he had been trying to do for years—get himself disentangled from Esalen and find more space and time in which to follow his own interests. He hoped that new leadership would set Esalen onto a new stage of expansion and development, and it was evident from the kind of successor he chose that he wanted that course to be in the direction of greater substance and respectability. The whole movement was getting a lot of criticism now, and Murphy wanted to make sure that Esalen was not numbered among the cults and the narcissists.

Richard Farson, who became president of Esalen just before the Spiritual Tyranny conference, was a top-drawer humanistic psychologist, a professional and a scholar. He had been closely associated with Carl Rogers for over twenty years, since the time he went to the University of Chicago as a graduate student. He had taught at Harvard and had been a member of the Western Training Laboratories staff in the mid-1950s, when the California sensitivity-training explosion was just beginning. He had founded and for many years managed the Western Behavioral Sciences Institute at La Jolla. WBSI was a unique institution, part think tank and part growth center, that was deeply involved in researching, teaching, and using group process. He and Murphy had been friends for a decade, and the two organizations, Esalen and WBSI, had enjoyed a parallel association. Murphy characterized it as Huck Finn and Tom Sawyer, in that order; one the renegade, the other a more cautious explorer.

Esalen had any number of wings, subgroups, cliques, and depart-ments; there were many different people who could have been recruit-ed for its presidency. Many different *kinds* of people—a gestalt therapist, say, or one of Schutz's encounter trainees; an ex-clergyman, perhaps; an educator; a Rolfer; a health professional; a student of the occult; an athlete; a woman. Each would have brought a certain style, certain strengths and weaknesses. Farson came from that brigade of eminents whose names had appeared in the Esalen brochures in the 1960s as advisers. He was a tall and handsome man—a writer once called him the Cary Grant of psychology—he was articulate, well dressed, and on good terms with big-time psychologists, university presidents, and foundation officials.

Farson's thinking had a radical streak—he had recently written a book advocating the rights of children—and at WBSI, under Carl Rogers' influence, he had gone farther than Esalen ever did in the direction of management by group process. But those aspects of him never managed to shine through the image that formed as soon as he walked into the San Francisco office in his tweed jacket: that he was square and authoritarian; that he had been hired to trim Esalen's wilder fringes, improve its public image, and get grants. There was just enough truth to that image, just enough abrasiveness in Farson's way of dealing with people, to keep his radical and Rogerian side from showing itself. Small things blew up into major issues, and Farson repeatedly found himself playing the heavy.

The feminist issue, for example. The leaflets for the Spiritual Tyran-ny conference had already been printed when Farson first came to work in the San Francisco offices, and he was aghast when he looked over the list of participants and found it to contain not a single female. His first official act was to appear as master of ceremonies at the conference. In his opening remarks there, just before introducing Sam Keen as keynoter, he directly confronted the problem—acknowledg-ing the feminist picketers, acknowledging the rightness of their cause, and refraining from saying that he had not personally taken part in the planning of the conference. (In fact, the conference had been organized by a committee consisting mainly of women—not the same women who were picketing outside, but card-carrying females nonetheless.) Farson took it on the chin, saying Esalen had made a mistake and would not make the same one another time.

Farson considered himself one of the good guys. He was one of the first males who had recognized the validity of the feminist cause and enrolled in its service. He had worked with Gloria Steinem and other leaders of that movement, had written an article called "The Rage of Women" for *Look* magazine—an unwaveringly profeminist article that pictured the new women's movement as a positive and long-overdue force likely to deliver great benefits to the society as a whole. When Farson came to San Francisco and surveyed the department store arrangement that had evolved there, he saw the Women's Studies Program as the best existing example of what Esalen should be doing. He wanted Esalen to be more involved in the community, more of a service organization, more political. Yet almost from the moment he arrived, he was in trouble with women.

First there was the business of picketing the conference. After it was over, he told the women that he sympathized with their cause but did not think it was proper for people who were on Esalen's payroll to be actively trying to sabotage one of its events. The women did not take to a reprimand from the new president, even though he was supposed to be on their side. Then there was the business of internal organization. The women wanted the Women's Studies Program to be a collective, a totally separate entity within the San Francisco office. It would receive a certain amount of money for salaries, and the women would determine how to use it. Farson said that wouldn't work; they would continue to be paid their individual salaries, and the women's workshops would continue to be administered as integral parts of the San Francisco operation. The women then launched a boycott of Esalen itself. They pulled out of the office, stopped giving workshops, and asked the other women who had been associated with the program to stop giving workshops. They systematically began calling *all* Esalen leaders in the Bay Area, asking them to stop working for Esalen. Esalen survived, but the Women's Studies Program did not. And Farson's aspirations of taking Esalen into other sorts of community service and political consciousness-raising were soon snowed under by other conflicts, having largely to do with Farson's position on the hip-square spectrum.

Farson did not, for example, care much for the ambience of the San Francisco office as he found it when he went there. It was a handsome suite of rooms in a beautifully restored old San Francisco building, but if you walked into its reception room, which was also the bookstore, you were likely to see somebody standing there, wrapped in a towel, reading *The Tibetan Book of the Dead*. Rolfers used the meeting rooms in the daytime, and prospective Rolfees frequently waited in the reception room. Farson thought a reception room should not have people wandering around wrapped in towels, and he dealt with the problem by getting rid of the Rolfers. It was no big deal, but it was duly noted that Farson considered Rolfing a dispensable part of the San Francisco center's activities, and—more critical—that he didn't want to offend strangers who might visit the office. This was different: it was part of the unspoken Esalen value system that a little mind-blowing was a good thing.

Then there was the Timothy Leary business. Leary was then in prison in Southern California, and Farson and Murphy thought it might be a good idea to write to him and offer him some kind of position at Esalen, such as senior fellow at Big Sur. They both knew and liked Leary, and thought it might help him to get paroled if he had a position awaiting him. Now, offering Tim Leary a job was a fairly radical thing to do, but, ironically, it served only to harden Farson's straight image. Some of the people at Big Sur were not pleased with the prospect of having Leary on the premises, because it revived the old fear of the big narcotics bust. Leary attracted narks as a light attracts moths. Farson said he didn't understand: Wasn't it Esalen's policy that no drugs were to be used at Big Sur? Murphy had assured him it was. If there was any doping going on, said Farson, they could just clean it up.

In reality, Esalen's official policy about drugs had about as much relevance to what went on at Big Sur as the Nineteenth Amendment had to do with American drinking habits in the 1920s. Things were not as wild as they had been, but the use of marijuana, LSD, and other psychedelics was commonplace, and that was the way everybody wanted to keep it. Leary never responded to Murphy and Farson's job offer, and Farson did not start an antidope crusade at Big Sur. But the incident helped crystallize Farson's reputation as an outsider.

Farson also irritated Dick Price, but not necessarily because of his personality. From Price's point of view, Esalen was Big Sur. The San Francisco branch was a plaything of Murphy's, and it had started out with the understanding between the two founders that it was to be an inexpensive plaything: a modest office, a small staff, events held in the churches and auditoriums. But the staff had grown, the offices had moved twice, and soon the payroll included not only administrators and secretaries but radical feminists and ex-linebackers. Then Murphy had brought in Farson at a salary that was modest for a man of his qualifications, but outrageously high by Esalen standards: $30,000 a year, twice what Murphy had received as president. Murphy was still on the payroll also, as chairman of the board. George Leonard had just been paid $18,000 for a six-month writing project, a report entitled "The Esalen Survey on Work-In-Progress in Perception, Consciousness and Being," which, despite its impressive title, was never published, except for a one-and-a-half-page excerpt that appeared in the front of the January 1974 brochure. Big Sur was finally becoming a profit-making concern, but San Francisco was losing large amounts of money. Price might have had good reason to become angry with Murphy about this, but he was not in the habit of becoming angry with Murphy. Doing so would have violated the unspoken rules of their partnership. He had, however, no comparable reservations about becoming angry with Farson.

A blowup was bound to come sooner or later. When it did, it concerned money and power. Andy Gagarin had made Esalen a large interest-free loan, and he now proposed to change the agreement and be paid interest. This was a mere technicality and would cost Esalen nothing, he said, since he would agree to make donations each year that would equal the amount of the interest. Although Farson and Gagarin generally got on well, they were not in accord on this issue. As Farson saw it, the interest-free loan was a major asset of the organization; it had been negotiated in good faith, and Esalen's only legal obligation was to repay the principal. Paying interest on the loan would take about all the cash Esalen had available for discretionary use. It would mean that the president and the executive committee would have that much less real authority and would have to go to Gagarin throughout the year for handouts.

Dick Price wasn't worried about this, and neither was Julian Silverman. The issue was argued at a meeting on the lawn in front of the Big House on one of those soft and lovely California afternoons. Murphy, who might have given Farson some support, did not attend that meeting. Farson counted one ally among those present: Leigh Rhett, the man he had brought in as director of the San Francisco office, and who was, like himself, overqualified for the job and out of place at Big Sur. (Rhett had a law degree and a Ph.D. in economics; his last job had been as dean of the school of business at a Southern California university.) The others were willing to go along with Gagarin's request. Farson kept arguing against it, and he could see that Price was becoming angry as he talked. After he finished his statement, Price responded, "Fuck you, Mr. President."

They took a vote, and Farson lost. He felt shut out from Big Sur, only nominally in control of San Francisco, not much like a president, and not at all sure that he could make anything of Esalen. The next time he saw Murphy, he said, "They've got me on the run." Not long after, he resigned.

Farson had been expected to function as both an administrator and a fund raiser. His tenure in office was the last moment of life for the idea—once high on Murphy's list—that Esalen might become a vigorous receiver and disburser of grants, a beehive of research programs, special conferences, and new explorations of human potential. When Farson resigned, it was most unlikely that there would be a sustained campaign to overcome the Big Sur image and turn the San Francisco branch into a center of research and social-outreach projects. The center of George Brown's confluent education program had already shifted from Esalen to the Santa Barbara campus, a move born of the regretful recognition that major funding would be more easily obtained for a project connected with the University of California than for one connected with an institution nationally known as the home of nude bathing and touchy-feely encounter groups. Later, Stuart and Sukie Miller moved their humanistic medicine program out of Esalen for similar reasons.

In November 1973, Esalen lost another of its patriarchs: Alan Watts, who had given the very first seminar at Big Sur Hot Springs, well before Esalen was Esalen, and had remained one of its featured attractions ever since. He loved Big Sur and was often seen there, feasting in the dining room (although not critical about many things, he paid close attention to the quality of the cuisine) or standing at the baths— as he sometimes did late at night—looking out to the sea and chanting mantras, stark naked, with a slight pot belly, like that of a Zen patriarch. He had never become much involved in Esalen's administration or in its politics; he had no particular cause, founded no school, accepted no formal students, and would have thrown a beer bottle (taking care to empty it first) at anybody who claimed to be his disciple. His comment on Gurdjieff reflected his feelings about being a guru: "Some people came and listened to him and understood, and left. Others came and listened and did not understand, and stayed." Watts had always been rather supercilious toward the growth-and-therapy side of Esalen, although he might have benefited from it. Beneath his frisky façade he was not feeling well, and once or twice, among old friends, he admitted as much. They tried to get him to take

271

better care of himself, especially to cut down on his drinking, but he wouldn't do it. "Alan could always play Alan, drunk or sober," Dick Price said. So he kept doing his thing, and died one night of a heart attack, fifty-eight years old.

In the fall of 1973 Esalen was reorganized again. Dulce, who had been working in the San Francisco office, became its manager (after 1974 no one would be listed in the brochure as Esalen's president). Murphy became more actively involved for a short time, but he soon went back to writing and staying away from the office.

The San Francisco branch, although closer to its demise than anyone suspected, was still busy, offering sports seminars and occasional special events, such as a conference on Wilhelm Reich in 1974, gestalt programs, encounter groups, and a rich series of neo-Reichian bioenergetics workshops under the leadership of Stanley Keleman. The Sports Center, with Mike Spino as director (he had succeeded Kriegel), continued, but the Esalen College Program was dropped.

Murphy and Dulce got married; he gave up the Telegraph Hill apartment, and they moved to Dulce's house in Mill Valley. Although Esalen made few demands on his time, he was not entirely detached from it. He remained closely involved with the course of the human potential movement and, watching its new developments, brooded over its welfare.

He was especially concerned about est, observing its rise to prominence with a fretful and ambivalent good will that must have been very much like the way Abe Maslow had watched the rise of Esalen. It was impossible to avoid taking a stand toward est. It was so energetically and overbearingly *there,* and had so quickly shouldered its way into the center of the circle, that indifference was out of the question.

Murphy and Erhard genuinely liked one another, and although their friendship was a tempestuous one, it did not erupt into battles, as it might have. There were great differences between the Jewish ex-auto salesman from Philadelphia and the golfing yogi from Salinas and Stanford, but they also had much in common. They were handsome men who looked younger than they were; each of them had energy, charisma, intelligence, and a raunchy sense of humor. They had good times together, arguing and telling stories and debating philosophy. Erhard, who was something of a student of philosophy, as Murphy was, had a library at Franklin House, his mansion on Franklin Street.

He was pleased to be able to display, when Murphy came to visit, a shelf with the complete works of Sri Aurobindo.

But the differences in style are worth noting here. Murphy and Dulce lived in a modest home. Murphy was a generous host, with many friends and connections to prominent people, but there was nothing glamorous about his daily routine. He spent his time meditating, running, writing, and meeting his friends for lunch or a cup of coffee. Erhard, in contrast, moved through the world like a Hollywood producer. Even before est made him famous, he always went about with an entourage; if he showed up at a party, he strode in with a half-dozen people trailing him. He held a series of dinner parties at Franklin House for Murphy and his friends. The servants were formally dressed est graduates, who gladly volunteered for such duty in order to be in the presence of their teacher. Erhard poured excellent wines, and the conversation ran heavily to discussions of psychology and philosophy.

Erhard was eager to win the support of the Esalen contingent, and, officially, he had. Whenever reporters came to interview him and asked questions about how est was regarded by the better-established schools of personal development, Erhard would tell them to go talk to Murphy, and Murphy would say he thought est was a valuable contribution to the movement.

Yet Murphy and his friends had serious misgivings about est, and these were endlessly aired and deliberated among them when they were not in Erhard's company. The subject of est had a tendency to take over their conversations; they would start to talk about something else, then somehow est would be mentioned and they would find that they had spent another evening agonizing about it. They were particularly bothered by the personality cult around Erhard, the deceptive hard-sell, the lack of any acknowledgment of the sources of the training itself, the lack of social consciousness and compassion (not to mention common sense) in the est tenet that every person is the total creator of his or her own life, responsible for everything that happens.

Murphy was not afraid to share his doubts with Erhard. They often got to yelling at one another over dinner at Franklin House—thereby providing great entertainment for the unpaid servants—and once, when Erhard came down to visit Big Sur, they had something that looked very much like a fight. They were in a room at the Big House and got into one of their arguments. Murphy playfully aimed a kick

273

at Erhard and missed; they started pushing one another; and then, while a roomful of guests looked on in astonishment, the two got into a wrestling match, rolling about on the floor like an unhappy couple in a Will Schutz encounter group. It ended with Werner holding Murphy down and shouting at him. A few minutes later they were dusting themselves off and laughing. It was all taken as a joke—Erhard and Murphy were great kidders—but there had been real rage in it.

In the late 1970s the Murphys stopped going to Erhard's dinner parties. They gave this and that reason; the truth was that Murphy was fed up. In private, he even wrote down a list of things about est that he couldn't take. After a while one of Erhard's lieutenants came to visit Murphy. "Werner senses that you are angry with him," he said. Murphy agreed that he was. Werner, the lieutenant said, wanted to hear the things Murphy was angry about, and Murphy accepted the invitation to meet with Erhard.

"You chickenshit bastard," Erhard yelled at Murphy when they got together—high volume was part of his style in these situations—"if you care about somebody, you come tell them what's the matter, you don't go slinking off."

So Murphy talked of his complaints. They were all things that he had argued about with Erhard before, at one time or another. Several of them had to do with Erhard's charismatic-authoritarian style. All of est was built around Erhard, and one's grasp of its wisdom tended to be measured in terms of how much one managed to look and act like Erhard. Erhard encouraged this. When he first promoted some of his employees to the status of trainer (meaning that they were to begin leading the huge est sessions that he had, at first, done himself), they were informed that they were now to become duplicates of him. Murphy thought this was an outrageous perversion of personal growth; instead of people finding their own feelings and their own thoughts, they merely learned to ape their leader. Erhard insisted there was nothing wrong in this. He was a person worthy of emulation. So was Murphy, he said; so were a lot of other people. He named several of Murphy's friends, all of whom, he thought, would be justified in similarly cloning themselves.

Erhard's auto-racing hobby was another issue. Erhard had taken up competitive racing, announcing that it was a quest for a greater comprehension of the principles of life. Murphy could go along with this, up to a point; he was, after all, a connoisseur of transcendence through sports competition. Auto racing was a form of athletic endeavor, loosely defined. It had to do with coordination, concentration, and physical strength. However, it was also a form of team sport. The team existed to support the driver—and of course Erhard was the driver. His supporters included not only the members of his racing crew, but est graduates who provided the money for what Erhard called "Break-through Racing, A Research Group." Erhard regarded all of this, including the giving of nondeductible contributions to buy racing cars, a part of the transcendent experience. "One of the highest qualities," he had said to a meeting of contributors, "is to be big enough to be able to be supported by people. Every time someone makes a contribution to Breakthrough Racing, the team has to expand to include that someone actually did that."[3] This, Murphy said, was baloney.

Murphy was also concerned about the profits from the ever-expanding training operation. There were rumors that Erhard was amassing an enormous personal fortune, which was being squirreled away in shadowy investments and foreign bank accounts. Confronted with this, Erhard got Murphy to meet with his lawyers, who convinced him that, while the est corporate structure was indeed heavy with cash and circuitously invested, Erhard himself was living on a reasonable salary and not building a Rockefeller-size estate from the thousands of people who turned to est for help.

Erhard invited Murphy to get a group of people together and draw up a formal list of criticisms of est, promising he would give it his full attention. Murphy had a couple of meetings at his house for this purpose. Among those present were Donald Michael, a professor of social psychology on sabbatical from the University of Michigan who had recently taken the est training and had some strong feelings about it; George Leonard; Murphy; and a couple of Werner Erhard's assistants. Out of the meetings came a list of major defects in the est operation.

The list of criticisms and suggestions for change was formally presented to Erhard by George Leonard, and this guaranteed that it would be presented as diplomatically as possible. Leonard had a personal friendship with Erhard and with the est organization; his brother-in-law, John Poppy, formerly of *Look,* was editor of the est magazine. Leonard was a student of Aikido, and he had often said that the way to deal with Erhard was not to confront him directly but to keep him on your side. He would demonstrate how this was done. If you stood in front of a man and put up your fists, he would say, you were inviting a frontal attack; but if you stood next to him and put your hand on his shoulder, you had him neutralized. In this spirit, Leonard presented the material to Erhard. Erhard thanked him, and that was it. No attempt was made to follow through and see that anything was done.

The criticisms reveal some of the weaknesses of est, and the way they were handled reveals some of the weaknesses of Esalen. Esalen was never really able to take an active role as the conscience of the human potential movement. Murphy and Leonard were concerned about the issues involved, but not concerned enough to take a public stand about them. There was no way for the general public—the many people who admired Murphy and Leonard and who might have been influenced by their opinions on the matter—to know that they privately considered est to be guilty of many violations of ethics and good taste. In their public statements, they maintained a united front in defense of the movement in general and its obstreperous newcomer in particular.

Leonard believes that the exchange did have some effect on est, even though it did not bring about any major overhaul of either the organization or its leader. He points out that at least matters did not become any worse; est did not go berserk in the way some personal-growth empires had—everybody knows plenty of examples—and he believes Esalen's influence was a steadying one. A more objective observer, Sam Keen, believes that Erhard was somewhat in awe of Murphy and Esalen. The est organization was booming, true, but a *Newsweek* article had called Esalen "the Harvard of the Human Potential Movement," and Murphy had recently been the subject of a profile in *The New Yorker.* Erhard had plenty of sycophants who would applaud anything he said, as well as a growing number of enemies who found est detestable and were unwilling to concede that it had any value whatsoever. Murphy was a friendly, influential critic. And Erhard, to his credit, encouraged Murphy to say what he thought. Murphy did more encountering in his dealings with Erhard than he had ever done at Esalen.

Murphy always said that he admired Erhard and denied any envy of Erhard's supreme self-confidence and wealth. The latter statement would probably not survive a gestalt therapy workshop: Murphy could not fail to see that Erhard reaped vast financial rewards from est. The money it generated enabled the organization to do things that Esalen could not. Out of its prosperity it established a foundation that financed various projects for research into the frontiers of consciousness, including some of Murphy's own most cherished subjects. Among the beneficiaries of grants from the est foundation were SAGAS (Self Awareness Through Games and Sports), a project of Bob Kriegel's, the former director of the Esalen Sports Center; and a grant for a study called "Evolutionary Transformations in the Human Body," the recipients being Murphy and his associate James Hickman.

14

The first 1977 Esalen brochure carried an announcement that began: "In January Esalen's office in the Bay Area is being moved from San Francisco to Mill Valley. With this change in location we are simplifying our programming. We will focus on those programs which are unique to Esalen rather than duplicating the programs offered by other centers." What this really meant was that Esalen San Francisco was going out of business. The Mill Valley office was, in reality, Murphy's home. There were a few programs, such as Sports Center activities, going on in the region, enough to justify the claim that a northern annex of Big Sur still existed. But the truth was that they had given up on the San Francisco branch.

So Esalen as an institution disappeared from the San Francisco Bay Area, but its progeny were everywhere. Esalen's impact on the culture of the Bay Area—on the things that people did and talked about, the books they read, the way the region was perceived by outsiders—was enormous. Marin County, where Murphy lived, was developing an entirely new image. Once, it had just been another piece of San Francisco suburbia, a stretch of hills, redwood forest, and cozy little towns like Mill Valley. Now it was gaining a reputation as the locus of an affluent and self-indulgent subculture, the milieu of people who entertained themselves with the pursuit of personal growth, human potential style. Murphy, living a quiet and hard-working life in a house that didn't even have a hot tub, hardly knew what to make of all this. He had done more than any other person to create this subculture, yet clearly it was a long way from what he had conceived when he was first inspired by visions of the human potentiality. He lived amid it in benign perplexity, like a man with a large family that hasn't turned out quite the way he had expected.

*　*　*

It was about a decade since the national press first took notice of Esalen, and the development of its public image had gone mostly in an unfavorable direction. Reports on the human potential movement, groups, Esalen, and the personal-growth subculture tended more and more to criticize them—or, what was worse, to ridicule them.

The first waves of national publicity had been largely favorable. Although some writers seemed a bit confused by Esalen and uncertain about how to label it, they usually described it as pleasant and interesting and possibly even important. Those who took the trouble to come to Big Sur and find out what Esalen was really like generally wrote about their personal experience openly and honestly, with a sense of discovery. Jane Howard's 1967 article in *Life* told of her own emotional outbursts in an encounter group and described her exploration, via guided fantasy, into her inner self. She ended up taking a leave of absence from *Life* to write a book, *Please Touch*. Rasa Gustaitis, a free-lance writer, had been assigned by *New York* magazine to report on one of Schutz's New York encounter groups early in 1967. She found it both bizarre and, in unexpected ways, rewarding:

> The weekend turned out to be a mind-bender. I got so involved with that group of strangers (all normal neurotics like me), I felt so strongly about them by Sunday, that it seemed we had been shut up together not two days but two years.
>
> The people I met were mostly professionals—businessmen, teachers, social workers, psychologists. Yet all of us behaved in a most uncivilized manner. One woman broke two toes attacking another; a successful financier cowered on the floor and begged people to touch him; I cried, got into a rage, was extremely affectionate, totally lonely, and for the first time in my life physically fought another woman.
>
> For several days after that house party I was shaky. But I also discovered that I was seeing differently. On Monday I went to talk with an editor who wanted to discuss an idea for a book. As he sat behind his desk telling me what he had in mind, I observed that he wasn't talking with me at all—he was talking at me. He was performing with words. It was almost as if he were making faces at himself in a mirror—a one-way mirror that had a little hole through which he could pellet words in my direction. Many other scenes, people, and relationships also now had a new clarity.[1]

In fact, she was so taken by the experience that she went to Esalen, sampled its offerings, and wrote a book called *Turning On.* Another writer, Richard Atcheson, from *Holiday* magazine, took a trip to Big Sur and came back to announce "I got in touch with my body this winter—I made contact with my Self—and it was the best trip I've ever had."[2]

Murphy, Price, and others at Esalen were appropriately gratified by such responses, but also took it for granted that people would be favorably impressed by what Esalen had to offer. They assumed that when people experienced its message, they would become allies. Murphy was not naïve when it came to enticing benefactors, but there was a certain innocence to his expectations about how Esalen would be perceived by others. He simply wanted it to be liked and assumed that it would be. There is something engaging about this, compared to the heavy-handed evangelism of such competing philosophies as fundamentalist Christianity, Marxism, and psychoanalysis, and it is easy to see why some people became captivated by Esalen's more casual attitude. Yet some of those who were close to the leadership of the human potential movement in these early years later came to believe that it would have been more successful if it had had a healthier respect for the vastness and difficulty of its task.

Murphy, who had emerged suddenly into public life in the giddiest years of the 1960s, leaping into his entrepreneurial role from a background of reading and meditation, really didn't appreciate how fortunate he was that so many friendly journalists discovered Esalen. He expected more of the same and was not prepared for the inevitable backlash. It began to become apparent early on that some people were not susceptible to Esalen's charm. East Coast liberal intellectuals in particular found it left much to be desired. In a review of Schutz's *Joy* that appeared in the *Nation* in 1968, Robert Claiborne blasted Schutz's writing and its presumed source, Esalen:

> You can diagnose a sick society by its placebos. The spa was invented for the aristocracy and *haute bourgeoisie* of the latter 19th century whose surfeit of *Sachertorte* and *Goldwasser, chemin de fer* and sex could be temporarily dissipated by a course of the waters at Vichy, Saratoga or Marienbad. The educated American middle class of the latter 20th century, however, is plagued with spiritual starvation. And to dull its hunger pangs we now have the neo-spa, devoted to "expanding human awareness" and "developing human potential."
>
> Most fashionable of these Pepsi-generation Marienbads is Esa-

len Institute, at Big Sur, California, whose scenic acreage, once the site of an unsuccessful old-time spa, has been converted by the brilliant promoter Mike Murphy into a haven for the middle-to-upper-bracket deprived.[3]

Claiborne criticized Esalen as superficial, slick, and, most important, nonpolitical. He thought it *psychologized* human problems, made them merely intrapersonal or interpersonal in nature rather than recognizing them as embedded in the power structure of institutions. What causes most of us to feel controlled, said Claiborne, "is far less our peers than our institutional superiors in the bureaucracies of government, industry, education and labor." And a workable recipe for change, he said, must include a strong measure of hardheaded political conflict. To live joyfully [he concluded],

> we must indeed learn to relate to our fellows in freedom and honesty. But to suppose we can do this without tangling with the institutions that deal daily in fear and dishonesty is to offer a cataplasm for a social cancer. The kingdom of God may well be within us—but to truly know it, we must also contend against the kingdom of Satan that surrounds us.[4]

The reviewer's charge in the *Nation* that the human potential movement was either apolitical or covertly conservative became a recurrent theme sounded in journals of the intellectual left. Coincidentally, that same year the *Nation* published a much different interpretation, coining a new term: counterculture. In a four-part series of articles that appeared in March and April of 1968, Theodore Roszak, a historian, theorized that a second American culture, in many ways antithetical to the values and beliefs of the prevailing, established, "official" one, was emerging. The articles were later expanded into his book, *The Making of a Counter Culture.* In this analysis Roszak was not talking about the human potential movement—a phrase that had not yet come into general use—or about Esalen. Esalen was mentioned in the book only once, in a footnote, as a "hip spa." Roszak was primarily analyzing the young people, the hippies in the hills and the activists on the campuses, and the ideas that held them together. His search led him to investigate the works of writer-gurus of the rebellious young: the Freudian radicalism of Herbert Marcuse and Norman O. Brown, the Eastern mysticism of Allen Ginsberg and Alan Watts, the psychedelic preachings of Aldous Huxley, Timothy Leary, and Watts, the social criticism (and gestalt therapy) of Paul Goodman. He characterized those seven as leading theorists of the counterculture.

Esalen was closely associated with all seven men in many ways. Marcuse and Brown owed much to Wilhelm Reich, as did Esalen's gestalt and body therapies. Brown, Ginsberg, Leary, and Watts had all been personally involved with Esalen from its beginnings and had led programs there at one time or another. Goodman was Fritz's estranged student and former collaborator on *Gestalt Therapy*. The closeness of fit between the counterculture and Esalen was noted by many people. More than any other institution in the country, Esalen appeared to be the fountainhead of this curious revolution.

Roszak insisted that the counterculture *was* revolutionary in nature, and that it represented a new and different sort of revolution. Its subversive doctrines were not about class, power, and industrial productivity, but about psychotherapies, psychedelic drugs, and the mind-liberating themes of Eastern religion. "Sociology has yielded to psychology as the generative principle of revolution," Roszak said. "Consciousness, not class, is now taken to be the root of social reality . . ."[5]

Roszak was critical of some elements of the new politics of consciousness (especially the psychedelic, which he discussed in a chapter headed "The Counterfeit Infinity"), but he was overwhelmingly more kind toward the counterculture than toward the deadening technocratic culture it opposed. Unknowingly, however, he provided its enemies with an instrument they had badly needed: a term, widely used and recognized, that bunched together political and psychological movements and branded them revolutionary. Never mind that there were, as Roszak had pointed out, many revolutionary political activists in America who wanted no part of Zen, gestalt, or psychedelia. From the vantage point of the far right such distinctions became invisible, and all the upheavals of the decade could be blamed on this composite of the new consciousness. The John Birch Society and other right-wing groups were already charging that sensitivity training and encounter were newfangled methods of communist brainwashing, and it soon became a common belief, even among conservatives of a more moderate cast, that the human potential movement was inherently antiestablishment. A psychiatrist, expressing this point of view, wrote an article denouncing encounter groups generally and Esalen specifically as instruments of the "quest of the counterculture" aimed at "an exorcism of the superego" and a massive assault on "many of the sanctions which modern society has deemed essential to a civilized community."[6]

So Esalen became a subject for argument and discussion in the national media, attacked from both right and left. The attacks from the right were no problem. Some of that was to be expected. Nobody at Esalen was disturbed about the opposition of Birchers and conservative psychiatrists, and some found it downright gratifying. But it hurt to be dismissed, as they were by many serious critics on the left, as dispensers of opiates to the middle class.

Peter Marin's article, the one tangible result of the 1973 Spiritual Tyranny conference, set the tone for most of what was written for the rest of the decade. His word, "narcissism," put the movement's diverse and sometimes conflicting thoughts and actions into a single neat cubbyhole. Tom Wolfe wrote an article about est, Esalen, and related matters for *New York* magazine in 1976, and followed the narcissism line. The 1970s, he announced, were the "Me" decade, and the Esalen methods were the decade's prototypical tools for tinkering with a self that became for each person the supreme possession and the absolute boundary of what mattered. "The old alchemical dream," Wolfe reported, "was changing base metals into gold. The new alchemical dream is: changing one's personality—remaking, remodeling, elevating, and polishing one's very *self* . . . and observing, studying, and doting on it. (Me!)"[7]

Christopher Lasch, a historian at the University of Rochester, gave the narcissism theme new intellectual respectability in articles for publications like the *New York Review of Books* and *Partisan Review* and in his book *The Culture of Narcissism.* Quoting Marin and Wolfe, he attacked the "awareness movement" as the purest expression of a widespread American malaise in which all sense of society and history is lost, replaced by a preoccupation with the self and the appeasing of its hungers. "To liberate humanity from . . . outmoded ideas of love and duty has become the mission of the post-Freudian therapies and particularly of their converts and popularizers, for whom mental health means the overthrow of inhibitions and the immediate gratification of every impulse."[8]

As the narcissism indictment gained momentum, it was taken up in other media. A California woman, Cyra McFadden, wrote a book called *The Serial,* which satirized the empty lives of the self-indulgent

Marin County subculture. It was later made into a movie, *Serial*, in which Tuesday Weld, alumna of the famous Fritz Perls gestalt demonstration in Jennifer Jones's patio, played a therapy-addicted housewife. *Serial* was the second movie takeoff on the human potential movement; some years before there had been *Bob and Carol and Ted and Alice*, starring another of Fritz's dissatisfied clients, Natalie Wood. *Serial*'s impact was small compared with that of a TV special called "I Want It All Now," which had been inspired by the same book. The NBC camera crews went out looking for evidence that Marin County really *was* populated by narcissistic consumers of therapy and pseudospiritualism, and found all they needed. The documentary's most memorable scene was of a woman being stroked, at the end of a luxurious massage, with a peacock feather. That was indeed a picture worth a thousand words; the peacock feather symbolized all that was airy and negligible in the human potential movement.

People who already didn't much care for Esalen and related matters greeted these messages from the media with something like a sigh of relief. If this stuff was indeed silly, selfish, even antisocial, then they did not have to harbor any secret thoughts that perhaps they needed some of it themselves. They were further convinced by the repeated implication that none of it really worked. Wolfe jeered at the hapless couples who tried encountering: "So they communicate with great candor! and break up! and keep on communicating! and they find the relationship hopelessly doomed."[9] Similarly, reading *The Serial*, you could not avoid concluding that none of those characters so busily attending to their personal growth ever really changed, had an insight, clarified a value, performed an act of courage or compassion, or chipped away the smallest crumb from the corner of a neurosis.

Those who did care for Esalen were bewildered by this battery of attacks and looked around for explanations. There had to be reasons for so many people setting out to discredit the entire movement.

Not surprisingly, the reasons they found tended to be psychological ones. Some heavy fantasizing had to be involved. How else could you explain Lasch's claim that the human potential movement's idea of mental health was "the overthrow of inhibition and the immediate gratification of every impulse"? Clearly such statements told you something about the person who made them. Dick Price said Esalen ought to be called the Ink Blot Institute. Murphy spoke in terms of the theory of projection: whatever was going on inside your own psyche that you could not accept or let yourself become aware of, you projected onto others. It became generally accepted in Esalen circles that the East Coast critics, daydreaming in their chilly offices, were projecting their own desires and fears by creating a California of hedonistic liberty—and simultaneously disapproving of their own creation.

George Leonard's personal experience with *Look* affirmed this. He had been the magazine's hero when he was championing the civil rights movement, but when he became a spokesman for the human potential movement, some of his colleagues in New York began to treat him as though he had gone round the bend. The reason, as he saw it, was that they were afraid—uptight liberals, out of touch with themselves, faced by something they did not comprehend.

Something larger than personal psychology was involved. The consensus among the human potential leadership was that a battle of paradigms was taking place, a conflict between an emerging world view and a beleaguered old one. The intellectuals of the East Coast were clinging to the old rules, whereby you could only think of social change in terms of Marx and talk of psychology in the jargon of Freud. Thomas Kuhn's book *The Structure of Scientific Revolutions* was often offered in support of this analysis. Kuhn had written of how a paradigm, a prevailing view of reality, periodically takes shape in a field of science and reigns despotically until overthrown. It is overthrown because there has been an accumulation of anomalies, things the old paradigm could not explain and chose to disregard. Then some new form-giver came along and put the pieces together in a new way.

Kuhn's view of scientific history was, in itself, a new paradigm, because it successfully challenged the old belief that science is an objective and peaceful accumulation of knowledge, one fact being added to another. It was a much more psychological view of scientific progress than the conventional one; it rested its case on the human mind's capacity to undergo metanoia and arrive at entirely new ways of seeing things.

Within the human potential movement it was unanimously believed that Kuhn's thesis applied outside the realm of science (an extrapolation that Kuhn himself did not think was valid) and could be used to explain large-scale social transitions. At humanistic psychology meetings and at the various New Age conferences that began to become a part of the cultural scene in the 1970s, the air was thick with references to Kuhn and talk of paradigms. Often speakers would refer simply to "the new paradigm," and their audiences always seemed to know what they were talking about. Actually, it was a phrase that changed meaning at every turn. Sometimes it meant an emerging alternative world view that challenged every aspect of Western rational thinking; sometimes it meant new ideas in specific fields such as psychology and physics; sometimes it meant a new and different way of interacting. Traditional codes of behavior, like Roberts' Rules, stood in danger of being branded part of the old paradigm and hence unacceptable. The term was used so promiscuously that it became useless as a conveyor of meaning, but it was dependable as a badge of membership. Using it signified that you were on the winning side, that you had been over into the future and knew that it worked.

New paradigms seemed to live in California. The perception of critics and defenders of the human potential movement as Easterners versus Westerners, a huge and persuasive half-truth, settled down early around the debate and shows no sign of rising. The movie *Serial* and NBC's "I Want It All Now" did their part to fix this image in the public mind by telling the world that in California in general, and in Marin County in particular, self-indulgent therapies and Oriental religions were the cultural mainstream. And Murphy and Leonard, who certainly knew better, often spoke as though Esalen's enemies were all New York intellectuals. This geographical explanation made distinctions and definitions easier for all concerned—especially for the mass media, where people do not get rich on nuances—yet it abused reality. It permitted the Esalen forces to pay less heed to the legions of West Coast journalists, intellectuals, and political activists who didn't like the human potential movement any more than their Eastern counterparts did. It permitted Easterners to overlook the considerable flowering of human potential activities in their own region. Theodore Roszak, living in Berkeley and often consulted by the press on matters countercultural, once got a long-distance call from a New York journalist who was about to leave for California to research a story on the proliferation of exotic spirituality. He wanted leads to gurus and cults around the Bay Area. Roszak pointed out that all of those existed in plenty in New York, and most of them could readily be located by looking through a copy of the *Village Voice.* The reporter was not impressed. He didn't just want people studying yoga and Zen; he wanted California people, *hot tub* people, indulging themselves vainly and glamorously in strange religions.

It *is* true that there are genuine cultural differences between the East Coast and the West Coast, and it is also true that the human potential movement emerged in California and has its strongest foothold there

—but the Continental Divide is not the boundary line this oversimplified version of the controversy pictures it to be. A criticism of Esalen had begun to surface in the humanistic psychology movement as early as 1968, at that memorable convention in San Francisco. Rollo May, one of the founders of humanistic psychology and an early Esalen mentor (and currently a resident of Marin County), now finds Big Sur somewhat cut adrift from reality, and thinks Esalen's philosophy is dangerously lightweight, unwilling to deal with what he speaks of as the dark side of human experience. Richard Farson (in La Jolla) has similar reservations about the organization over which he once presided. He insists that there is a clear distinction to be made between humanistic psychology and the human potential movement, and says this in a way that leaves no doubt as to which he considers more valuable. But these are not the things from which TV specials are made.

The deteriorating quality of the debate, as more and more of the reporters got their information and insights from earlier reports and not from any contact with the therapies on which they were passing judgment, made it easy for the Esalen faithful to do what they most wanted to do—shrug off the whole indictment. If you read Tom Wolfe's description of Fritz's therapy, you would recognize immediately that Wolfe knew nothing about gestalt and was simply handing out a garbled replay of what he had heard or imagined. "His [Fritz's] sessions," Wolfe informed the public, "were a variety of the 'marathon encounter.' He put the various candidates for personality change in groups, and they stayed together in close quarters day after day. They were encouraged to bare their souls and to strip away one another's defensive façade."[10] But Fritz did not do marathons, nor was he interested in whether or not his patients stayed together in close quarters. Gestalt therapy had some common philosophical ancestry with encounter, but was not a variety of it. Fritz discouraged interactions between members of his groups. They worked with him, not with each other, in sessions that often ran less than an hour.

And if you looked closely at Wolfe's account of the dismal results of confrontations between couples, you would see that he was not reporting on the basis of any personal experience with couples in groups; he was talking about two couples he knew who had tried some encountering after having been to see Ingmar Bergman's *Scenes from a Marriage.*

Wolfe's report may have formed opinions among some people, but

it did not change any among people who had some firsthand knowledge of the things he was talking about; he did not put forth anything
that would inspire an agonizing reappraisal. Nor did Wolfe himself,
with his white suits and look-at-me prose, cut much of a figure as a
preacher against self-indulgence. As seen from Esalen, he appeared to
be nothing but a glib hit man for the old order.

Yet, although the average exposé of the human potential movement
was careless with facts and about as original as Werner Erhard's
chuckle, there was a good deal of rough truth in the criticism and the
public image that formed around it. Despite their protests, most of
those on the receiving end knew this. They had, however unwillingly,
recognized most of the problems themselves and made frequent efforts
to do something about them, even as they reassured one another that
the whole thing was merely a poorly disguised regional vendetta, an
attempt by a fading and insecure East Coast intellectual-literary establishment to discredit and ridicule an upstart culture that threatened its
own.

As much as the narcissism charge rankled, it was obviously true that
a focusing on the self, one's own mind and body, was a central part
of what went on in most varieties of group work. Through all the
residential programs there had been a frequently expressed sense of
incompleteness, a general belief among the residents that they were
getting too much of something and not enough of something else.
They talked of the need for "grounding." In search of it, they tried
yoga and meditation. In some residential programs they worked on the
buildings and in the garden—psychologists and graduate students
wrestling with rocks, clearing weeds, planting trees, literally digging
into the ground in search of that missing something outside themselves. The more conventional things that people used as foundations
for their personal lives—families, jobs, communities, organized religions—were often the very things the residents had abandoned when
they set out for Esalen along the path of self-development.

In the shorter programs, the regular weekend and week-long workshops, there was a similar preoccupation with the enhancement of the
individual self and a tendency to view society as an organized conspiracy against the human potential. In Fritz's gestalt therapy the goal
was the development of self-awareness, the integration into the personality of thoughts and feelings stifled by parental disapproval or
social conformity. Fritz used to tell people that the goal of therapy was
self-actualization, not self-image actualization; you became who you

were, not who you thought you ought to be. Schutz extolled personal honesty and responsibility, and his games and exercises were meant to surprise you into actions that would reveal and express your true feelings.

Self-awareness, self-discovery, self-actualization, self-expression: these are the lifeblood of personal growth, qualities essential to the make-up of the healthy individual—and also clearly the stuff of which narcissists are made. You could easily catch a good case of narcissism around the growth centers; it was their iatrogenic disease.

A *little* narcissism is a good thing; a period of deliberate self-absorption is often a necessary prelude to true maturity. For many people, coming out of years of walking death in stultifying relationships and meaningless jobs, a time of turning inward—helped along by a few visits to Esalen or places that offered similar experiences—was exhilarating and nourishing. They drew some strength from it and put together new lives, of greater value to themselves and to others. But others never quite made the transition, got stuck in the phase of self-absorption, and remained more or less permanently on the therapy circuit, connoisseurs of its wares. Whether you made the transition was pretty much up to you; it was one of the things your gestalt therapist or encounter group leader would not take responsibility for. The dynamics of such transitions had been amply explored in the literature of humanistic psychology, but they never quite made it into the main body of human potential experiences.

The narcissism problem overlaps with that of Esalen's lack of a clear political focus or purpose—another favorite complaint of its critics, and another subject of much internal agonizing. Joan Baez was advocating a more political stance when Murphy and Price were just starting to put together their first programs, and the same urging came many times from others in the decades that followed.

It was not that Esalen was quite the apolitical Shangri-la some pictured it to be. There had often been political themes and ideas of social change in its subject matter, especially in the early futuristic visions of such seminar leaders as Gerald Heard and Willis Harman. There were the interracial groups, the Women's Studies Program, the Spiritual Tyranny conference. There was the conference, in San Francisco in the 1970s, on that most revolutionary and political of therapists, Wilhelm Reich. Richard Price and Joe Adams were both active on behalf of efforts to protect the civil rights of mental patients, especially their right to refuse electroshock and other traumatizing forms of treatment. There were major actors on the American political scene, such as Daniel Ellsberg and Andrew Young, who had attended Esalen workshops and found something of value to take back into their public lives. In the early 1970s, Assemblyman John Vasconcellos, a well-known friend of Esalen, had organized a venture in humanizing government by getting several of his colleagues from the California legislature to join him in encounter weekends that were held at Big Sur with Will Schutz as their group leader. You could point to many such efforts to move beyond the realm of personal growth, but somehow they did not seem to add up to any coherent program of political action or education—certainly not one that would give the human potential movement any position on the vanguard of social change. The person-al-growth therapies flourished, the political activists went their own way, learning to speak with disdain of "growth trips," and the press began to talk of narcissism and the Me decade—putting Esalen at the leadership of what was taken to be the 1970s' retreat from political commitment into sterile self-love.

Perhaps, countered some of those who believed most deeply in the essential decency of the human potential movement, there *is* something political within the technologies of personal growth. Perhaps it was consciousness that needed to change, not only institutions, and perhaps the humane society the civil rights activists and peace protesters sought was to be reached by a long march through the psyche, through countless acts of personal transformation. A group experience could be a dramatic consciousness-raiser; it could alter your view of the world, make you think in new ways about such things as conformity, authority, responsibility. And that self-searching—could it not be, in some sense, a force for social change?

In *Person/Planet,* a book that sought to make some sense out of the confusing social currents of the 1970s—as *The Making of a Counter Culture* had done for the 1960s—Theodore Roszak spoke of a vital and powerful new awakening in the world, a movement uniting the apparently disparate struggles of oppressed peoples—racial minorities, women, gays, the aged, the handicapped—with the much-battered legions of the human potential movement. He called it the quest for personhood and declared it to be as revolutionary as the quest for the "rights of man" had been for the oppressed of centuries past. The quest, as he described it, is essentially the urge toward affirmation of one's own value. It is selfish only insofar as it treads on the official verities of what an individual life is permitted to be. Carried far enough, it goes well beyond the self, because the needs and rights of the person are congruent with the needs and rights of the planet.

Roszak, like others who rallied to the defense of the human potential movement in the narcissism debate, chided the critics for being ill informed about the subject and not always in a good position to throw stones. He pointed out that Peter Marin's article, blasting the new therapies for their lack of concern for the impoverished, appeared in *Harper's* opposite an ad for the new Cadillac Eldorado; that R. D. Rosen, author of a book called *Psychobabble,* had been, before he took up arms against therapeutic self-indulgence, a restaurant reviewer for *Boston* magazine. Roszak accused the critics of being quite respectful toward personal soul-searching when it was done by members of the appropriate artistic or cultural elites, and hostile toward it only when it was taken up by the general population:

> Let "ordinary" people once get wind of the importance of self-knowledge and personal autonomy [he wrote], and they are all too likely to think that idea has something to do with taking themselves very seriously, brooding over their tastes and motivations, delving into their experience, rebelliously asserting their peculiarities—in short, becoming, in one degree or another, what others will then denounce as "egocentric," "narcissistic," "self-absorbed."[11]

Roszak's defense of the human potential movement gave it a political dimension worthy of respect, made the journey into self a struggle for freedom, and not merely the sterile pastime of an irresponsible elite. It is an eloquent statement, but it is hard to find convincing evidence at Esalen or its progeny that the work of personal growth is truly grounded in a process of such global dimensions. If you listen to the lullaby of lunchtime conversations at Esalen—the shoptalk of new remedies, the travel talk of trips to meditate in the Orient or commune with the gardens at Findhorn—you find little sense of a person/planet connection made a working reality, of concrete actions taken out into the pained and polluted world.

Esalen, in the late 1970s and early 1980s, made earnest efforts to hold programs on social and political subjects. More often than not, they were canceled for lack of attendance. The image had, in a way, created its own reality. People thought of Esalen as a place to come to for rest and therapy, not for seminars on political activism. If they had political commitments, they left them at home. Some had abandoned then entirely, and regarded any tendency to fret about the world's problems as evidence of an insufficiently developed inner radiance. Michael Murphy was one of the very few who really worried about Esalen's apolitical image; he kept trying to do something about it, and is trying still.

A third persistent line of criticism, closely connected to the matter of Esalen's place along the self-indulgence–political commitment spectrum, was the charge that it was anti-intellectual and/or trivial in its content. Murphy was particularly disturbed by this, because he had, after all, spent a large portion of his life studying philosophy and had always seen Esalen as a place that would be congenial to thinkers.

Certainly the place was intellectual enough in its very early years, but there is no getting around the fact that the transition to experiential programming that began to take place in the early 1960s—and that soon gained an uncontrollable momentum—turned into a revolution against the oppressive intellect. "Lose your mind and come to your senses," Fritz proclaimed, and the seminarians rushed to follow his advice. So did a good portion of the country; it may have been the best-heard message that ever emanated from Esalen.

For many educated middle-class Americans, life in general and psychotherapy in particular had become strapped into a straitjacket of conceptualization, and a restoration of some balance between the head and the heart, the mind and the body, seemed an excellent idea. There was surely a good case to be made for less intellectualism in therapy. Everybody knew someone who had spent ten or fifteen years in some kind of analysis and had little to show for it except an exquisite understanding of the causes of his or her misery. Anybody who participated in a group could see that one of the ways people ran headlong from reality was to rationalize or explain it. A little anti-intellectualism, along with a little narcissism, was a healthy antidote to that.

But moderation was not in the air along the Big Sur coast in the 1960s, and the pendulum, once it started swinging, swung rapidly to an anti-intellectual extreme, well beyond the wise midpoint at which both mind and body are given equal value. In the groups, people were regularly assailed for being too much "in their heads," but there was no corresponding criticism for being too emotional or too physical. Joe Adams was one of the first to charge that there was a form of tyranny in this; Abe Maslow was one of the first to fear that Esalen was in danger of pulling loose from its philosophical moorings and needed to teach people to think as well as feel.

Some people saw the problem as not exactly anti-intellectualism but overoptimism; it was not that Esalen lacked a philosophy, but that its philosophy represented a dangerously superficial vision of human progress. Rollo May expressed this in his concern about the unwillingness to look at the dark side of human nature. Others, both critics and friends of Esalen, argued for a stronger sense of history. They pointed out that there had been, down through the centuries, other disciplines of personal development, other visions of coming millennia, other awakenings—and that they had all been steps along a long road, not complete and perfect transformations.

There floated around Esalen, around the movement of which it was a part, a tendency to believe that there was nothing to worry about, that if you just performed the right trick of the mind and got your act together, all would be well everywhere. This was that psychologization of issues that the *Nation*'s reviewer had worried about, and it also worried a lot of Esalen's friends, who saw that a sojourn there could be not only nourishment but escape. It is one thing to take a breather from the world, if you are lucky enough or smart enough or rich enough to get to Big Sur, but it is something else entirely to drift toward the belief that if only everyone would absorb a few New Age ideas, he or she would become as happy as the lovely people who massaged one another in the California sunlight and ate organically grown vegetables in the lodge.

The personal-responsibility ethic, which had started out as a forthright way of talking about the risks and benefits involved in going to an Esalen workshop, a rough-and-ready response to the classic neurotic blaming game, rapidly took leave of its senses and became a crackpot theology that viewed everything in the cosmos as subject to human volition. The est training contributed greatly to this by hoisting the folksy American ideology of positive thinking to new and dizzying heights. The message came through clearly that if you "got" est, you realized that you were the all-powerful creator of your universe.

Will Schutz, one of several Esalen leaders who was strongly influenced by est, became convinced that there were absolutely no limits to what could be accomplished through the ethic of personal responsibility. "Each of us is running her or his own life," Schutz wrote in his book *Profound Simplicity*. "The laws of nature only function if we want

294

them to . . . As my awareness increases, my control over my own being increases . . . When I become aware that I am choosing everything, I may take over my life and live it any way I choose." Schutz insisted that there were no involuntary victims of circumstance, only people who choose to be victimized. It is an ethic that does not encourage one to become seriously concerned about circumstances that victimize people or pay much attention to life-threatening catastrophes. Schutz claimed:

> All around us people are defying natural laws. Biofeedback subjects alter their blood pressure, cancer patients stop the growth of their disease, psychics bend keys and move objects with their minds, and people respond to jealousy situations without becoming jealous. We are not required to follow any laws. We are running this show.[12]

It is a philosophy that lays down a veritable taboo against being overly impressed by the huge and evil forces that stalk the world. Fearing for the future, suggesting that anything may be out of control or heading toward ruin, is taken as evidence that you need to do a bit of work on yourself. Carried to an extreme but logical conclusion, it is a philosophy that suggests starving children are responsible for their lack of food, and Hiroshima victims are accountable for having an atomic bomb dropped on them.

This is not the official Esalen philosophy. Murphy does not accept it, at least as baldly as Schutz states it, but it is highly influential. It has close links to the things that have shaped Esalen, from Huxley's human potentialities notions through Murphy's athletic and psychic enthusiasms, and is widely accepted among paradigm-watchers as an important element in the new world view. If there is an official Esalen philosophy, a real central guiding principle, it is the idea of the Great Evolutionary Leap. From the day Gerald Heard gave Murphy and Price his cosmic pep talk in Santa Monica, Esalen was wedded to the notion that a major transition—a basic shift in how people experienced themselves and the world—was imminent. Huxley had alluded to such a leap in his Human Potentialities lectures and had described some aspects of a human potential utopia in his novel *Island.* He seemed to think the leap was a possibility. Heard, his more volatile sidekick, believed it was inevitable.

Inevitability was what Heard preached with fervor in his early seminars at Big Sur Hot Springs, and variations on that theme were the central subject matter of many programs that followed. The speakers talked of new visions, emergent paradigms, the upstart spring that signaled an end to the frozen misery of centuries. They would usually acknowledge some of the great evils present in the world and others that might yet come, but that was chiefly a matter of getting unpleasant preliminaries out of the way in order to concentrate on the Leap. It was the subject the speakers wanted to talk about and the listeners came to hear about. If you wanted to dwell on population explosion, the nuclear threat, the ecological crisis, you would go somewhere else. Esalen's business was proclaiming the breakthrough.

Surely the world needs messages of hope, perhaps even overstated ones; it was the inevitability that worried some people, and that began to inspire new charges that Esalen's content was a walk on the light side. If the transformation was inevitable, then no personal effort was called for. All you had to do was lean back in the hot tub and wait for it to arrive. Quite a few people pointed this out, and the disparaging phrase "instant transformation" was sometimes used. This became a very sore point with Murphy and Leonard, especially with Leonard, who over the years had become one of the Leap's most ardent spokesmen. Leonard began to say, in the late 1970s, that the transformation would be very difficult to achieve. This was in itself a sign of changing times. In his 1965 introduction to the Esalen brochure, he had written, "Such a change is inevitable . . . indeed, it is imminent." His 1972 book *The Transformation* had been subtitled *A Guide to the Inevitable Changes in Humankind.*

Such were the issues that troubled Esalen and its leadership. They were the subject of countless arguments at Big Sur and the growth centers, discussions in Esalen board meetings, debates at conferences of the Association for Humanistic Psychology. They were also the things that found their way, sometimes accurately and sometimes not, into the media and into the public perception of the human potential movement.

Curiously, the subject that might have been expected to generate the most controversy—sex—was not in itself really much of an issue. This is not to say that there wasn't plenty of it around.

If you come driving into Esalen on a sunny afternoon, you may pass a section of lawn where people—staff employees, usually—are playing volleyball in the nude. You may well have come prepared for nude sunbathing and massage and hot-tub soaking, but all those jiggling appendages and tanned bodies, before you even get to the registration desk, serve notice that you have come to quite a liberated place. Liberated and sensuous. The body is well taken care of at Esalen: soaked in the hot waters, relaxed in the sun, massaged, exercised, deliciously fed. Esalen's brand of sensuousness is healthy and simple, but it is still sensuousness. Combine that with the social dynamics of many people passing through for a weekend or so, meeting in groups where frankness is encouraged and friendships formed quickly, and the inevitable result is a fair amount of mating.

Esalen was the model for Sandstone, the notorious Southern California sex spa that Gay Talese described in *Thy Neighbor's Wife*, where the group orgy was the basic medium of communication, but Esalen itself is not the sexual fun house it is often imagined to be. It carved out for itself a relatively modest role in the sexual revolution. There were periods of excess—notably in a couple of the residential programs—yet overall Esalen managed to avoid being as wildly naked and free as some of its leaders, notably Fritz, thought it should be. It offered nude bathing, massage, and a variety of disciplines of body work, but its programming never ran heavily to sex therapy or the advocacy of sexual freedom. Paul Bindrim, the founder of nude therapy, complained publicly that his offer to lead programs at Esalen was rebuffed, an indication of where Murphy and Price drew their limits.

Perhaps the shadiest sexual undercurrent—one that had a lot to do with Esalen's failure to win the wholehearted sympathies of the feminist movement—was the behavior of some of its male luminaries toward women. There were many occasions when women who came to Big Sur with serious personal issues to resolve found themselves, in times of confusion and vulnerability, having to cope with ardent advances from their charismatic group leaders.

Over the years there has grown up a respect for individual wishes, a certain maturity; you can stay away from the baths, you will not be required to describe your sexual fantasies to the members of your gestalt group, and once you get past the volleyball game you can probably manage to have a quite unerotic time, if that is what you came for. Indeed, if Esalen's brand of sexuality turns out to be the new paradigm, the country can count itself fortunate.

"Mother Esalen gives permission," Ed Maupin used to say. And indeed it did give out plenty, but even then there were limits, and they are very much present now, part of the place's complex etiquette. Once in a while a new guest, giddy with the sense of freedom, ventures naked into the lodge at mealtime and is asked to dress for dinner —in anything at all, as long as it is clothing. Such withdrawal of permission is done as gently as possible, and the giving of permission is done unobtrusively too, ideally without being noticed at all.

Once, in the mid-1960s, while he was still living at Esalen, Mike Murphy went down to the baths late at night, remained sitting quietly in the tub after his friends had left, and discerned in the semidarkness a couple who believed themselves to be alone, making love on one of the massage tables—not merely making love, but going at it in a leisurely and artful manner, with many changes of position. Murphy, too considerate even to clear his throat, sat there and steeped politely in the dark corner until they left.

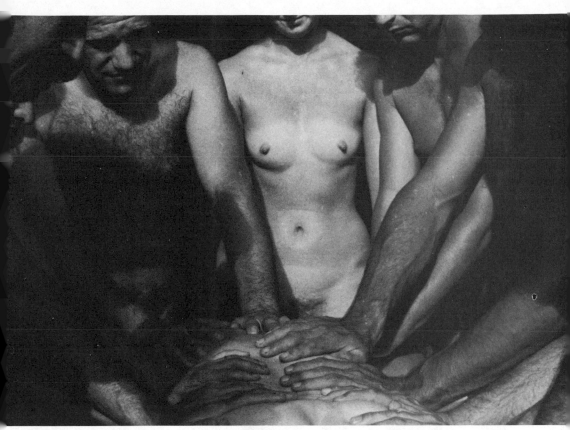

Residential fellows massage class, 1966. (PAUL HERBERT)

Joan Baez at the Big Sur Folk Festival, June 1967. The festivals, coordinated by Joan Baez, although not a part of Esalen programming, were an annual event for several years and featured major artists including Simon and Garfunkel, Judy Collins, and Bob Dylan. (PAUL HERBERT)

Bernard Gunther teaching massage
awareness class, 1966. (PAUL
HERBERT)

Fritz Perls at Lake Cowichan, 1969. (REAL
PEOPLE PRESS)

Stuart Miller, 1966. (MORT KAYE STUDIOS)

George Leonard and Annie Styron Leonard demonstrating "energy awareness" exercise, 1982. (KATHY THORMOD)

Paul Horn and Chungliang Al Huang and workshop participants, 1981. (KATHY THORMOD)

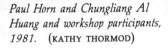

Joyce Rogers and Christine Price in gestalt workshop, 1981. (STEVE BECK)

Michael and Dulce Murphy, Cambridge, 1983. (COURTESY DULCE MURPHY)

Richard and Christine Price, 1980. (JOYCE ROGERS)

George Leonard demonstrating the Japanese martial art of Aikido, 1982. (KATHY THORMOD)

Children in the Gazebo, Esalen's school. (JOYCE ROGERS)

The new outdoor hot tubs, completed in 1982. (KATHY THORMOD)

Esalen's youngest and oldest residents in May 1978: Karina Rogers-Lyke, three days, and Gregory Bateson, seventy-four years. (BENJ LANGDON)

Richard Price and Michael Murphy, 1982. (KATHY THORMOD)

15

By the mid-1970s, many people had come to regard Richard Price as a spiritual and psychological leader of stature and maturity, well beyond the stage of seeking new gurus. He regularly gave workshops in gestalt therapy and had a unique status as a founder of Esalen and a close friend of Fritz's. He did not appear to be in need of any helping hands. He was happily married to a beautiful young woman, the former Christine Stewart, who led gestalt groups with him. They had a lovely child, Jennifer, and they lived in the Little House, a charming cottage near Hot Springs Creek with a vast expanse of deep green lawn in front.

But life was not as easy for Price as those outward things would have led you to believe. He still carried the memory of his time in the sanitarium, the lingering physical pain and the feeling of betrayal, and although he handled those things well, it was hard work. He never just moved from day to day, but applied himself vigorously to the practice of yoga, to therapy and massage. He took long and strenuous hikes into the hills. He sampled therapies, sampled psychedelic drugs, was Rolfed more times than you would think a human body can bear—and still his eye scanned the horizon.

Baghwan Shree Rajneesh was looming large on the horizon then. You saw his disciples frequently, and you recognized them when you saw them, because they dressed all in orange, wore necklaces with a picture of Rajneesh, and had new names, given them by Rajneesh. He was a pioneer, the first Eastern spiritual leader who openly incorporated Western methods and ideas into his teaching. True, Western culture had looped through India in many ways before—Gandhi had been influenced by the theosophists in London, Aurobindo had studied Western philosophy and psychology—but nobody before Rajneesh had been so eclectic. In his talks he was likely to tell a Sufi parable and then start rambling on about Wilhelm Reich. The daily regimen at his school in Poona was not only meditation and lectures; it also included gestalt therapy and encounter groups. The place wasn't just an ashram; it was an Indian growth center.

Price read some of Rajneesh's books and listened to tapes of Rajneesh's discourses, and found much in them. Rajneesh came equipped, as had Oscar Ichazo, with a large repertoire of practices. There were whirling meditations like the dances of the Dervishes, and others that involved sitting cross-legged and moving the hands in harmony with music. The standard Rajneesh meditation involved jumping up and down, chanting, dancing, sometimes freezing in position, and finally enjoying a period of deep rest on the floor. To see a roomful of people doing these meditations would confirm your worst preconceptions about loony spiritualism, but those who tried them found them oddly moving—and a good workout. Price thought the basic Rajneesh idea of linking meditation with emotional catharsis and physical exercise made a good deal of sense.

In 1977 Price announced to his surprised friends that he and Christine and Jennifer had all become *sannyasins.* He made it sound like kind of a prank. There were two ways to be admitted formally to the ranks of *sannyasins.* One was to go to Poona and take your vows directly from Rajneesh; the other was to write to him. You would get your *mala* (the necklace) and your new name by return mail. Price had done this and had received the name Geet Govind. But he was not using that name, nor were he and his family dressed in orange. People concluded that he was not taking it too seriously, but then he went off to spend some time studying at Poona. A significant piece of news: if Price was truly becoming Rajneesh's disciple, it would be a major transition for Esalen and an important development in the larger cross-fertilization of Eastern and Western disciplines, of which Esalen had been a shaping influence. It would probably clear the bench again. There would be more Esalen people swearing allegiance to Rajneesh, and a corresponding increase in the influence of Rajneesh's thinking and his practices in American therapy and encounter.

The symbolic structure around the teaching—the orange clothes, the names—made it that much more formidable. To become a Rajneesh *sannyasin* meant taking a decisive step that would profoundly affect your inner and outer life. It altered your very definition of yourself—as it was meant to do—announced to the world that you were a convert, and helped you remain one. Once you had appeared

300

in your new clothes and told your friends you had a new name, you were unlikely to announce a week later that you had changed your mind. It signified also that the Rajneesh teachings had primacy. One could be, as Price was, a student of Alan Watts, Fritz Perls, and Ida Rolf, and the heir of a hundred other teachings as well, but to wear orange and call himself Geet Govind would state that the first teacher, the Master, was Baghwan Shree Rajneesh. Such a statement would not be lost on others; there were always a fair number of people standing ready to gallop over whatever appeared to be the next spiritual hill.

So Price's pilgrimage to Poona was widely followed. *Time* took note of Rajneesh in January of 1978. The article dismissed his teaching as "mostly pop-Hinduism and anything-goes homilies," but noted with some awe that over fifty thousand seekers had made their way to Poona to get some of it, and that among them had been well-known entertainment figures and even the marquis of Bath. "Now," the article announced, "the guru is instructing his best-connected disciple yet: Richard Price, co-founder and director of the Esalen Institute, the very fount of the encounter craze. Price will return to the Big Sur, Calif. center in mid-January to apply the teachings of his new master."[1]

The *Time* article referred to Poona as "Esalen East," but the obvious implication of the story was that Big Sur was about to become Poona West. That did not happen. Price became profoundly disillusioned with the work at the ashram during his month-long stay there.

The first two weeks or so, he stayed in the ashram's "meditation camp," doing the Rajneesh exercises, and all went well. Then he graduated into the encounter group. Its leader was a man named Teertha, who had been, in his pre-Rajneesh existence, an English psychotherapist, much involved with the London branch of the human potential movement, and founder of a London growth center, Quaesitor. Teertha had participated in the encounter groups that Will Schutz had led in London. His own approach went well beyond Schutz's. There was more explicit sexuality and there was more violence. In the encounter group that Price was attending, a woman got into a fight and ended up with a broken arm. In another group, a few days later, another woman had her leg broken. Price had never been much of an admirer of violent encounter. He found the Poona approach immature and repugnant, and he left the ashram.

Thus, the Rajneesh adventure ended in almost the same way as the Arica one had. The issue was different, but the outcome was the same: disillusionment and a break with the school. Price wrote a letter to

Time, correcting the impression that an Esalen-Poona collaboration was in the making:

> Rajneesh is well worth reading . . . He can speak brilliantly of the transformative possibility of human life. His "meditations" I find worth practicing. However, the ashram "encounter" group is an abomination—authoritarian, intimidating, violent—used to enforce conformity to an emerging orange new order rather than to facilitate growth. Broken bones are common, bruises and abrasions beyond counting. As such it owes more to the S.S. than to Esalen. Until the compassion Rajneesh speaks about with such eloquence is reflected in his groups, I am content to be known as "Richard Price" rather than as "Geet Govind."[2]

As Price turned away from Rajneesh, so did several other Esalen people who had been following him in that direction. There are still *sannyasins* on the staff at Big Sur, and Rajneesh's discourses are still on sale in the Esalen Bookstore, but that is the extent of the connection. For a while the only major Esalen figure still in orange was Bernie Gunther, who had been at various times yoga teacher and masseur, patient and promoter of gestalt therapy, practitioner of sensory awakening and general turner-onner, student of psychosynthesis. He lived for a time in India and was known as Amrit Prem. Later, he went back to being Bernie Gunther. Baghwan Shree Rajneesh, having failed to turn Esalen into Poona West, eventually came to the United States and founded a center in Oregon.

After the Rajneesh episode, Price became involved in another adventure along the psychological-spiritual front, one that did not make it into the pages of *Time* but that caused a considerably greater disturbance at Big Sur.

Esalen was at one of its stagnant phases. Old disagreements simmered along from week to week, flaring up, impeding the effectiveness of everyone's work. Some people thought Esalen was no longer moving in any discernible direction. Julian Silverman was perhaps the most restless. He had spent the better part of the decade at Big Sur, and although he had seriously thought about moving on, he had never managed to do so. Now he thought that the place was foundering and that something big needed to be done.

At that time, a young Englishwoman named Jenny O'Connor was more or less a permanent fixture at Esalen. Betty Fuller, a tireless seeker after new truths, had discovered her. Jenny was a psychic.

People in the know spoke not of Jenny, but of the Nine, since Jenny purported to be a medium for nine beings, nonhuman entities based on the star Sirius. She delivered their messages by means of automatic writing. She would sit down in a room, make herself comfortable, take off her shoes, drink canned cola, and smoke cigarettes while people asked questions of the Nine. Jenny would begin writing with amazing rapidity on a legal-sized notepad, ripping off the pages and handing them to somebody else to read the answers.

Price had begun incorporating the Nine into his gestalt work. Each group participant would be invited to take a turn with the Nine, and whatever came up might then become the basis of a therapy session. It was experimental, he said; it didn't matter whether the material came from Sirius or from Jenny's unconscious. The value was in what the patient chose to do with the experience. Nevertheless, the growing reliance on the Nine made some people at Esalen nervous.

When Silverman approached Price with his concerns about the general malaise affecting Esalen, Price suggested that the senior directors of Big Sur (Price, Silverman, and Janet Lederman) have a meeting with the Nine. Lederman was a quiet, dark-haired woman who had once been a teacher in one of the tougher sections of Los Angeles. Her book, *Anger and the Rocking Chair,* a distillation of her experiences, had been published under the Esalen Books program. She went on to become a gestalt therapist and a major figure in the confluent education program. In the 1970s she had become co-director, with Silverman, of Esalen Big Sur. She was unenthusiastic about the suggestion, but agreed to go along with it.

So they gathered in the Little House for this pioneering, if somewhat strange, venture in management consulting. When Price asked Jenny some questions about Esalen, the Nine responded by saying that Esalen was in a very bad state and perhaps would soon face its demise unless major changes were made. This prompted a heated discussion of what the problems at Esalen were. The meeting went on for some time, with extensive questioning of Jenny, discussion of her responses, and angry arguments between Silverman and Lederman.

Some of the staff members had known this meeting was to take place, and there had been much gossip about it. Imagine, then, the shock waves that traveled through the small community when Silverman emerged from the meeting and fired two key manager-level staff people. He then announced that he and Janet Lederman would also leave their management jobs. She would be involved only with the newly formed Esalen elementary school; he was moving on to new things.

It was the most sudden organizational upheaval Esalen had ever undergone. Some saw Jenny O'Connor as a female Rasputin, wielding extraordinary power over the Esalen management. Silverman and Lederman, both former students of Fritz, insisted that Jenny had only been a catalyst and that they were not duly awed by psychic phenomena. "It could have been anybody," Janet said. "It could have been the Wizard of Oz."

Word of Jenny's exploits reached the San Francisco muckraking magazine *Mother Jones,* which sent a reporter, Jeffrey Klein, to Big Sur. His article, "Esalen Slides Off the Cliff," declared that Esalen had descended into utter silliness. He dismissed the place as a playground for upper-middle-class escapists, noted a general penchant for social irrelevance (". . . in the name of spontaneity, Esalenites have collectively tried to suppress all impulses toward social self-criticism"), and zeroed in on Jenny. Klein was unimpressed by her gifts and unimpressed by Esalen for having taken her in—or having been taken in by her. His article was illustrated by a photograph of Jenny sitting in a hot tub, and concluded with the statement: "How ironic, and perhaps inevitable, that the birthplace of encountering needed such a dummy to ventriloquize through."[3]

Jenny and the Nine continued to be a part of Esalen, listed among the program leaders in the back of the catalogue. The Nine are the only nonhumans to have achieved this distinction. In their biographical entry they were described as "giant reflectors of your selves, gestalt practitioners, marriage counselors—pure energy of emergence quality available to all." They were also listed, elsewhere in the catalogue, as members of the Esalen Gestalt Staff. Had Fritz not died already, surely that would have killed him.

Jenny O'Connor's role at Big Sur seemed entirely bizarre to *Mother Jones* readers and to others not familiar with Esalen folkways; seen closer up, it was not so surprising. The general population at Big Sur was precariously open-minded toward all manner of psychic, spiritual, and supernatural phenomena not normally acceptable to Western scientific/rational thinking. That kind of thinking, in fact, is taken to be more or less the same thing as the old paradigm. That was why Fritz's various sallies against the mystics had caused such excitement; to stand up at Esalen and denounce a world-famous psychic, as Fritz did, was equivalent to standing up in church and saying there is no

God. Belief systems varied, of course, but among the staff the level of credulity was very high. Most of the employees were prepared to believe not only that Jenny read minds but, as Janet Lederman put it, that she read the universe's mind as well. The other thing that made it less surprising was that a certain capriciousness at the higher management levels was generally accepted. Esalen was democratic in many ways, but its authority structure was essentially feudal. If Price wanted to use a psychic as a management consultant, nobody could stop him—nobody except Murphy, and Murphy and Price never crowded one another.

So Price never felt particularly pressured to justify his interest in Jenny O'Connor or to explain precisely what he thought of her. He described it as a research project in paranormal intelligence and said he inclined toward the hypothesis that she had extraordinary powers of insight—perhaps even psychic abilities—and somehow found it necessary to express them with the help of the story of the Nine. He was just testing that, in various experiments.

Many of Jenny's messages were evasive maunderings that could be taken for either wisdom or foolishness, but once in a while she did make some remarkably acute observations about people and even predictions of things to come. In January of 1983, Price asked her to predict the winner of the Super Bowl. She said the Washington Redskins would take it, by a score of 27 to 21. Price told his friends about this, and many people followed that game with a special curiosity to see how Jenny's forecast would hold up. She was wrong—the Redskins won 27 to 17—but she was closer than most of the pundits of the sporting world, who had predicted a low-scoring game and had favored the Miami Dolphins by three points.

So Price followed his interests, and Murphy followed his. Murphy's were more and more concentrated on what Price called his three R's—running, writing, and Russians.

His explorations of sports and extraordinary human abilities took him and Esalen in new directions that might, he hoped, offer some refutation to the charges of its social irrelevance. He discovered something very like a human potential movement emerging in Russia, something that he came to believe was comparable to the one he had done so much to create and shape in the 1970s. To nourish this movement and connect it up with its American counterpart is now, in the 1980s, Murphy's new quest.

Murphy's Russian connection began in 1971, the year he made his first visit to that country. This was the second of the Esalen expeditions to Europe, a year after the big London encounter-group event. He traveled again to Florence, paid a last visit to Roberto Assagioli, stopped over in Czechoslovakia, and went on to Moscow. Officially, the purpose of this visit was to seek out and evaluate some of the research that had been reported in the popular 1970 book, *Psychic Discoveries Behind the Iron Curtain.* Actually, it was a lark. Sukie Miller had thought it up, and then Stuart Miller and Murphy got caught up in her excitement, and off they went.

They spent two weeks in Moscow, meeting some of the psychics and scientists who had been mentioned in the book. It was an exciting time, with the adventure of learning about research on the frontiers of science flavored by hints of mystery and intrigue: speculation that the Russians were interested in psychic phenomena because they hoped to find military uses, or because they feared that Americans had already found them.

Murphy and his friends did find impressive evidence of Russian interest in psychic research. They met Vladimir Raikov, a psychiatrist who was studying reincarnation, and Genady Sergeyev, a mathematician who was studying the relationship between brain waves and telepathy. In a hotel suite in Moscow, overlooking Red Square, they saw a demonstration of room-to-room telepathy between Russia's most famous team of psychics.

The "receiver" in this demonstration, Karl Nikolaiev, agreed to work with Murphy on an experiment in long-distance telepathy. After he returned to California, Murphy got Dr. Charles Tart, a psychologist at the University of California at Davis, to design it. It called for the two participants—Murphy as sender, Nikolaiev as receiver—to set aside a certain time, three days a week, during which they would attempt to communicate. On each occasion, Murphy was to be given an object that he had not seen before; he was to hold it and concentrate on it while Nikolaiev, half a world away, wrote down whatever images came to him at that precise moment. The first attempt was startling. The object Murphy held was a toy wooden elephant. Nikolaiev reported feeling a wooden grainy texture, a round end, and from the other end something protruding—something, he wrote, that felt like a wooden nose dropper. After that tantalizing beginning, however, not much happened. The experiment produced no conclusive scientific proof that telepathic communication had taken place, and all Murphy finally had to show for it was a fascinating anecdote.

For some years after that he was concerned chiefly with writing a series of books that set forth his unique vision of body, mind, and spirit. First there was *Golf in the Kingdom,* which he described as a "metaphysical sports fantasy." Then came a second novel, *Jacob Atabet,* which was another kind of metaphysical fantasy. Its narrator is named Darwin Fall; he is a student of psychic phenomena and very much resembles Michael Murphy. Jacob Atabet is a young San Francisco artist, a mystic, a voyager into strange psychic and physical terrain (the book describes him as a *dehasiddha,* a master of bodily transformation), and he too resembles Murphy. He is of Basque descent; the name Atabet is a family name from Murphy's mother's side. The book ends with Fall and Atabet, the scholar and the mystic, agreeing to work together to bring greater knowledge and understanding of such matters into public consciousness. Murphy's next book was *The Psychic Side of Sports,* written in collaboration with a parapsychologist, Rhea A. White. It was a compendium of accounts of extraordinary performances and mystical sensations experienced by athletes, and it argued for Murphy's belief that psychic-physical phenomena were everywhere, needing only to be recognized and accepted into our belief system.

By the time *Jacob Atabet* was published, with its characters dedicating themselves to the study of bodily transformation, Murphy himself was already doing that in his own life. He and a young man named James Hickman had started the Esalen Institute Transformation Project. Their main purpose was to build an archive that would enable a researcher to submit a query about what material exists on a given subject, and to get a readout of available literature. It is a conventional library with the usual computerized paraphernalia, but most unusual in its subject matter—articles about extraordinary performances of the human body and mind, everything from psychic healing to outstanding marathon race times. As of this writing, the archive has some twelve thousand articles stored in its files, and it is probably the only place in the world where you can locate all the available scientific research on a subject like stigmata. The purpose is consistent with Thomas Kuhn's account of what causes scientific revolutions. Anomalies, or data that cannot be explained within the old paradigm, collect, so a new paradigm must arise to explain what was previously unexplainable. Murphy, who has always believed that life is rich with happenings that contradict our conventional beliefs about human nature, suggests we manage to ignore them because we never have to confront them in their totality. He hopes to amass sufficient evidence to make that impossible. He is collecting anomalies.

Hickman, who is now the research director of the Transformation Project, got Murphy interested in Russia again. Hickman had worked as a research assistant to Dr. Stanley Krippner, one of the leading American parapsychologists. Krippner had visited Russia and had made a documentary film of some of the Russian experiments with such powers as psychokinesis, the ability to move objects without touching them. In 1972 Hickman had participated in a scientific conference in New York on the Russian-developed technique called Kirilian photography, which takes pictures of the electromagnetic field around the human body. Later that year he went to Russia for a scientific conference on bioenergy and met people who were interested in such things as accelerated learning, self-healing, and accelerated sports performance.

In 1979 Hickman went to Russia again and met more frontier-probing scientists. In Siberia, he met Dr. V. P. Kaznacheyev, president of the Siberian Academy of Medical Sciences, who had done research on the mysterious communication that sometimes seems to take place between separate cell structures. In Moscow Hickman met Dr. V. V. Kuznetsov, another prominent scientist in the Soviet hierarchy and founder of a field of research called "anthropomaximology," the study of maximum mental and physical abilities. He met educators and psychic healers. He met a high-powered man of barrel-like stature named Joseph Goldin, who had launched something named the Commission for the Complex Study of Man, devoted to a subject area that he called "hidden human reserves." This concept, hidden human reserves, is what Murphy began to see as the Russian version of human potentialities.

Hickman's 1979 visit was the real beginning of the Esalen-Russia cooperation. In 1980 the first secretary of the Soviet embassy in Washington, Valentin Berezhkov, came out to Esalen to discuss the outlines of an official Soviet-American exchange program. That summer, Murphy and Hickman went to Russia together as invited speakers at a conference, "Sports in Modern Society." It was a full-scale international scientific congress, with some fifteen hundred participants—physicians, psychologists, social scientists, philosophers, historians, biochemists, and psychologists—all exploring various aspects of sports and physical culture. Murphy and Hickman presented papers drawn from the research of the Transformation Project. Joseph Goldin was there, talking about the possibility of transferring the methods of Olympic-level athletic training to other kinds of endeavor. This was the first time Murphy met Goldin, and, as Hickman had predicted, the two hit it off. Murphy later made Goldin a member of Esalen's board of trustees.

Everywhere Murphy went, he found signs of an awakening that seemed to him strikingly similar to the human potential movement. In Georgia, he met a group of young people, mostly artists, who met regularly for meditation and who had developed a group discussion style that was very much like encounter. In Moscow he learned that the social psychology department at Moscow State University had gone in for encounter groups, and he was astounded when a young woman stood up at one meeting and gave a well-informed summary of the difference between the T-group and Esalen varieties of encounter. He found that a circle of people in Moscow, to whom Hickman had earlier given some books about marathon encounters, were holding five-day marathon group sessions. He found many people who were interested in, and knowledgeable about, the basic works of humanistic psychology, and who read Abe Maslow on self-actualization, Fritz Perls on awareness, and various writers on encounter.

And everywhere he found Russians involved in some kind of spiritual pursuit: followers of Gurdjieff and Ouspensky, healers, psychics, spiritualists, scientists studying psychic phenomena and self-healing, people interested in sport and in maximizing human performance.

Murphy saw in this a deep and thwarted mysticism that is now finding a socially legitimate outlet in science. "It's the old Holy Russian passion for the mysteries," he would say, "coming up through the floorboards." The idea of an "aura" is in the realm of spiritualism, but the concept of a "biofield"—really the same thing—is science. At Kazakh State University, in Alma-Ata, Murphy and Hickman were permitted to visit a large and well-financed laboratory dedicated entirely to biofield research.

For a while in the early 1980s the most visible forum and rallying point for people interested in such things was provided by the events that Joseph Goldin periodically staged in an auditorium in a Moscow park. Goldin, who in a capitalist society would surely be an entrepreneur, produced a series of weekend extravaganzas that he called "expeditions to the hidden human reserves." They were attended by an impressive cross-section of Russian society—athletes, artists, young people, scholars, and scientists. At one gathering, a Russian cosmonaut spoke of the need for further development of human capacities, a group of children demonstrated their athletic skills on a huge contraption of ropes, Jim Hickman presented a slide show on Esalen, and a Russian psychologist led the audience in relaxation exercises.

Whether all this adds up to some version of the American human potential movement is something else again. The Russian interest in psychic phenomena and extraordinary human performance is well documented, but the social context is vastly different, and so are the times. There is no equivalent of the vast surge of social forces that shuffled along in a roughly similar direction through the American 1960s and 1970s—the changing values, the increasing personal openness, the sexual revolution, the protest groups, the youth movement, the psychedelic explorations, the self-help and liberation movements. The Russian movement, if there is one, lacks a place like Esalen to serve as its crucible. It also (although this may not be to its disadvantage) lacks the mass media to carry its message to the public. And it is hard to believe that the Russian government would tolerate something that, even in America, shocked the establishment and unleashed massive social and political counterforces. Nevertheless, Murphy determined to make a link between the Russian and American movements a major thrust of his—and of Esalen's—activities.

Hickman's and Murphy's various trips to Russia were at first exploratory; they were for making contacts, learning about what was happening there, letting the Russians know more about Esalen in general and about its Transformation Project in particular. Then the interaction began to generate plans and activities, such as a project to set up working groups of Soviet and American experts in subjects related to sports and health. In these areas authorities are not so nervous about possible military or intelligence uses of the research, and there is consequently a better opportunity for open communication. Several small groups of scientists from both countries, working in such fields as regenerative biology, mental training in sports, voluntary control of physiology, and exceptional human functioning, will meet once or twice a year and, it is hoped, work productively as friends and colleagues. The objective is a long-term, ten-to-fifteen-year, collaboration.

Other projects were generated; new allies emerged. In some ways it began to resemble the giddy days of the 1960s. Among the new allies were several top-level Russian diplomats and scholars. Among the projects was a series of astronaut-cosmonaut meetings, with former astronaut Rusty Schweickart as general coordinator. Murphy was again on the move, but instead of hanging out at psychology conferences, he was taking annual trips with Dulce to Moscow, and instead of wooing therapists and educators to the Esalen cause, he was recruiting scientists, diplomats, and Sovietologists.

Murphy and Hickman speak sensibly about this, acknowledging that it is a modest cluster of projects, many of which will take years to bear any fruit. Yet such is the predilection toward euphoria in human potential circles, so strong is the accumulated resentment from years of browbeating on the "social relevance" issue, that some of Esalen's champions cannot refrain from pumping a bit of helium into it. Listen to George Leonard warm to the subject before a New Age audience, and you will come away convinced that the Russian human potential movement is on the march.

It is a chapter yet unwritten, although in the long run it may prove Esalen's most significant. It is a change of the reality of what Esalen is about, and there are signs that the image may be changing also, that Murphy's efforts may have produced a slight blurring of the 1960s' picture of Esalen. *Newsweek,* in January 1983, reported favorably on Esalen's "hot tub diplomacy," calling it an important informal channel of international communication and noting, with some awe, the sight of a Russian economist (a guest of Murphy's) jogging in the tree-lined streets of Mill Valley and taking an energy-awareness course. The economist (Georgi Skorov, of Russia's Institute of United States and Canada Studies) was quoted as saying: "The word 'Esalen' is magic to me. It is a symbol of people who, like myself, understand the value of things other than material wealth."[4]

16

As the 1970s gave way to the 1980s, as the newness wore off the things that Esalen was known by, as Murphy and Price passed their fiftieth birthdays, as the media grew less exercised about the promise (or threat) of the human potential movement, it seemed to many of Esalen's friends—especially to old hands who had been present during that frisky first decade—that its work was done. The enterprise was judged to have been partly a success, in that so many of its techniques had found their way into conventional therapy and counseling, and partly a failure, in that the millennium had not arrived on schedule. The salient fact for most was simply that the years had moved along and Big Sur was no longer, at least for them, the fount of discoveries. In San Francisco and Los Angeles, among people who had suggested or led or attended early seminars, talk of Esalen was inevitably laced with nostalgia and sometimes even with a certain wonder that the institute was still doing business at the old stand.

Esalen was so closely linked with new things that some believed its only salvation would be to find more new things. They likened it to an unused launch pad, waiting only for an appropriate missile to fire into the skies. Others suggested to Murphy and Price, half-seriously, that they ought to shut the place down. There were legends of Sufi schools that had come into being for a limited period of time, to communicate certain teachings to certain people within a certain moment of history, and had then declared their work done, folded their tents, simply disappeared. Maybe that was the best model.

Such notions, however persuasive, overlooked the reality of a quiet, organic process of development that had been going on. Esalen had matured as a business. After all those years of red ink and recurrent crises, the institute was making money. And it was maturing as a place. It had a more stable sense of community, and at the same time it functioned well as a resort, as a seminar, as a retreat—a secular monastery, somebody called it. The physical site, with money and work continually poured back into it, had developed into an ever-lovelier and more smoothly operating facility.

Selig Morgenrath could not be the overseer of this development—he had died in 1977—but his influence carried on. The austere style of design he had imposed upon his browbeaten employers became the Esalen motif and merged with the new consciousness of energy and environment. Selig's apprentices and successors built a contraption to heat the swimming pool with water from the hot springs, constructed a laundry with a green-growing sod roof and solar collectors, and then drew up a master plan for energy independence. It envisioned heating the rooms with hot water circulated from the springs, and perhaps building a small hydraulic turbine on Hot Springs Creek to generate electricity. On a few acres of land on the northern fringe of the property, they cleared land for a vastly expanded food-growing operation: more vegetables, about a hundred fruit trees, beehives, greenhouses, vats for breeding fish. In this, Esalen was following the lead of another kind of growth center that had begun to appear here and there around the country, places like the New Alchemy Institute in Massachusetts, Windstar in Colorado, the Farallones Institute in Northern California: working temples of solar energy and organic gardening, wind power and aquaculture.

Each of the new additions became, in its own way, part of the curriculum. The environment had always been one of Esalen's great assets. People came to listen to Alan Watts *and* to go for a walk up Hot Springs Creek while thinking about Zen, to work with Fritz Perls *and* to get in touch with their senses while sitting in a hot tub amid naked bodies and incense and the sound of surf. Over the years, as the managers comprehended this more deeply, they worked out ways to integrate the experience of being at Big Sur into the more formal programming. The work scholar program is the most successful of these integrations. There had always been people who wanted to stay around Esalen for some longer period of time, to rest or study or grow or repair their lives, but arrangements for this had been haphazard. Some had had money and simply worked out long-term room and board arrangements. Some managed to get jobs. Some lived on the edge, sleeping on the floor in some meeting room and paying for workshops or, if they could figure out a way to do it, attending for nothing.

The work scholar program, formalized in the 1970s, imposed order on this, and in the process eroded the boundary lines that had separated the staff from the members of the residential program, and both of those from the ordinary customers. People start out in the program by signing up for a period of one to three months, during which time they put in thirty-two hours a week of work—in the kitchen, in the cabins, on the grounds—and also attend group meetings and workshops. They begin by paying Esalen for this privilege, but the amount they pay goes down each month, and after a while *they* get paid a small stipend and are regarded as members of the staff.

All this tends to make the internal social structure much more homogeneous than it was in the late 1960s. Now the tribal distinctions are no longer so clear, more people stay for longer periods, and everybody works. Even the weekend customers are asked to put in a little time, clearing dishes or helping out in the kitchen. The brochure calls this karma yoga.

And as Esalen matured as a community, it found a place for children. For a long time, children were not welcome there. There were always a few around anyway, sociable, suntanned, and frequently naked little urchins wandering through the lodge. Any children you saw were likely to be the offspring of some more or less permanent staff member; guests were discouraged from bringing children and had to make their own arrangements for child care or take their chances on losing their progeny over the side of the cliff. The few children of school age caught the yellow bus to an indifferent country schoolhouse about twenty miles away. That changed in the 1970s, with the opening of Esalen's own school, the Gazebo.

The Gazebo's founder was Janet Lederman, who, over her years with Esalen, had observed the activities there with a teacher's eye. She noted that children were excluded from most of what went on at Esalen and had only the most indirect and accidental exposure to its personal-growth lore. She saw something very special about the children who had grown up there, a remarkable physical vitality and grace—and saw in them also a lack of cognitive vitality. They did not talk much, nor did they seem to think with any agility comparable with that they displayed walking on rocks and climbing trees. She also noted something about the adults—which was that they indulged in

315

a good deal of childlike behavior without any reference point of real children.

Finally, with Esalen prospering, she persuaded the board to let her start the Gazebo—in effect, to admit children to membership in the community. The grounds crew built a real gazebo, out of redwood, and later the school's facilities were expanded to include other buildings, a couple of horses, a shifting population of dogs, goats, and chickens, and a stationary school bus full of computer equipment. It is a relaxed place but not, its teachers insist, a "free school." The philosophy is confluent education, which does indeed take the emotions and the body more seriously than traditional schooling does, but also pays attention to the development of the intellect. The environment, the buildings, and the general ambience of the Esalen grounds are all regarded as integral parts of the learning process. Lederman speaks heatedly about the close architectural similarity between ordinary schools and minimum-security prisons. The children often leave Big Sur for adventures and field trips in other areas—sometimes, for example, they go up to Marine World near San Francisco and swim with John Lilly's dolphins—but Esalen is their school and their home.

Overall, the community consists of about forty permanent staff members, twenty people in the paid work scholar category, and forty people in the paying work scholar group—about a hundred in all, plus some mates and children. This accounts for about half the population of Esalen at any given time, since there is space for about one hundred transient guests at the main site and at its annex, the South Coast Center, about a mile up the road, which was once John and Marie Murphy's motel and was acquired by Esalen in 1973. That is all the people it will hold.

Although Esalen has grown in acreage, the number of buildings, and the size of its permanent population, newcomers are frequently surprised when they discover how small it is. Its community is still shifting. Some of its members are old timers who have been around as long as Esalen has, or longer, and some are work scholars who come and go with the changing months. Yet it retains an awareness of itself and a certain solidarity. There are community meetings, community social events, and talk of a new building that will serve as a community center.

In appearance, the present population is not too different from its earlier counterpart. It remains a mixture of young and old, although perhaps there are fewer people under the age of twenty than there once were. The population is overwhelmingly white, middle class, and well educated. The clothing styles still have a bit of the flavor of the hippie era. The colorful and loose-flowing clothes are most favored among the masseurs and Rolfers—the body people, who do not believe in encasing themselves in buttons, belts, and zippers. Sandals are much in evidence. Traces of 1967 linger in the sea air, and in some ways, Big Sur seems like a last outpost of the hippie movement. One could easily imagine that, in decades to come, when the hippie scene has long since been embalmed in the history books, the last flower child will be found wandering, stoned, in the hills above Esalen, like a counterculture Rip Van Winkle.

The most telling change is one that you are more likely to hear than see. Many of the people at Esalen are speaking accented English, or another language altogether—Spanish, German, French. Once a California place, then an American one, Esalen is now an international place. Murphy's Russian project has added a new dimension to this. As more and more government officials and scientists are brought to Big Sur, there is always a chance that the gentleman soaking next to you in a hot tub is a biologist from Moscow or a high-level dignitary from the Soviet embassy in Washington. The Russian association has required the addition to the staff of Anya Kucharev, as research assistant, translator of documents, and interpreter for visiting dignitaries. She lives in the Big House in a wing that, except for some remodeling, is approximately the same as the one occupied twenty years earlier by Hunter Thompson. As befits such an occupant, she has an M.A. in Russian history and is a polarity therapist and masseuse.

Despite such transitions, which cumulatively have made Esalen vastly different from what it once was, the weekend and five-day workshops that are its staple have not changed much. If you glance through a current brochure, you will not be likely to notice anything strikingly different from what you might have found a decade or so before. The content is still largely gestalt, awareness work, group experiences, celebrations of the body, and Eastern and Western (mostly Eastern) religions. This consistency is itself a change. There are no more sudden shifts from the cognitive to the experiential, no more discoveries of the newest American yoga, no more meteoric appearances of new therapists and their therapies. The material has become standardized.

Most of the workshop leaders are now second or third generation. They studied with Fritz or with a student of Fritz's or are graduates of one of the residential programs. Most are eclectics who have been around Esalen a lot, have taken in a variety of methods and ideas, and incorporated them, according to one recipe or another, into their own work.

Although gestalt is a regular part of the workshops offered to the public, and a commonplace word in the Esalen vocabulary, you don't hear much about encounter anymore. Encounter groups, identified as such, are absent from the regular program listings. Some of the staff members have meetings to discuss interpersonal issues, but these are pointedly called "process groups."

In the 1976 *New Yorker* Profile of Michael Murphy, Calvin Tomkins reported that Murphy had "serious reservations about the ultimate value of the encounter process."[1] When Will Schutz read the article, he was pained to see that the thing Murphy most wanted to tell the world was that he didn't care much for encounter. Schutz was even more hurt when, a few years later, Price changed the name of the FIRO meeting room to Rolf. Schutz began to feel as though he and encounter were being written out of Esalen history. He was not far wrong. The heritage of T-groups, sensitivity training, and encounter is present, but only insofar as individual leaders have absorbed it into their work.

The de-encounterization of Esalen, which both Murphy and Price favored, was a deliberate effort to modify Esalen's image, reflecting a move away from the tell-it-like-it-is ethic of the 1960s and a reaction against the press's urge to equate Esalen with encounter. It was also part of an effort to get away from the most intense forms of group experience. Today's second- and third-generation gestalt leaders at Esalen are considerably gentler than Fritz, and most of the current experiential programs are more in the tradition of Bernie Gunther; they run heavily to massage, body movement, and personal energy exercises. They are safe. Perhaps people still experience some fluttering stomachs en route to Big Sur, but the trip is no longer quite the dance of anticipation and risk it once was, when what lay ahead was a Perls gestalt workshop or a Schutz encounter group.

It is debatable that Esalen was ever quite the Vatican City of encounter that some people took it to be. Certainly it is not that now. There are organizations all over the country, from churches to factories, that are more committed to encounter work and that do it better. The most revealing aspect of the explosive staff meeting with Jenny

O'Connor is that a psychic and nine invisible beings from outer space were the best resource Esalen could muster when it needed a group facilitator to help work through some personnel conflicts. On the subject of Esalen's unimpressive record in using the methods it helped popularize for its own problems, Richard Price wryly cites what he calls Esalen's Law. The law, he says, is that you always teach others what you most need to learn yourself. Its corollary is that you are your own worst student.

Although Will Schutz still returns to Esalen occasionally to lead seminars, his move to the San Francisco area in 1973 ended the age of the titans at Big Sur. Since then, Esalen has carefully avoided becoming a host to resident leaders who represent any rising school of therapy. There are still occasional long-term residents, but they are people like the late Gregory Bateson, who lived for two years in Fritz's house and who aspired to capture no flag.

Bateson had a long history with Esalen. He had been a professor of Price's at Stanford and one of the very first seminar leaders in the early 1960s. His best-known work was a collection of epistemological treatises, *Steps to an Ecology of Mind.* It was an uncompromisingly difficult work, and Bateson was as surprised as anybody else when he became, in the mid-1970s, quite famous, a kind of New Age hero. People rarely understood what he was talking about but thought that it was good stuff, nonetheless. Stewart Brand, publisher of the Whole Earth Catalog, introduced him to California's governor Jerry Brown, who invited him to speak at the annual prayer breakfast (an honor usually bestowed on clergy) and then appointed him to the board of regents of the University of California. Bateson, who was an enormously tall, stoop-shouldered, brilliant, and quixotic old man, seemed to enjoy being a regent. His main interest, a losing cause, was trying to get the university out of nuclear weapons research.

Early in 1978 Bateson, who had been a heavy smoker for fifty years, was diagnosed as having lung cancer. He was rushed to a hospital in San Francisco, where he was subjected to various tests and exploratory surgery, and very nearly died. The doctors told his wife he would be gone by morning. But he did not die; he summoned a Filipino faith healer named Rosita Rodrigues, who thumped his chest, sniffed at him, and told him the cancer was dead. He went back home and, with the help of his daughter (by a previous marriage, to Margaret Mead), finished his last book, *Mind in Nature.* He then accepted an invitation to come to Esalen as a scholar-in-residence.

The duties were light. He gave an occasional seminar, worked on another book, went to body-movement workshops (where he was a striking figure, pirouetting across the carpeted floor of the Huxley room), and held forth in the lodge at mealtimes. There was always somebody who wanted to talk with him, and he would spend long hours sitting in the sunshine on the deck outside the lodge, taking in this endless stream of human contact. He would reminisce about Aldous Huxley and Gerald Heard; about taking LSD with Joe Adams; about Fritz Perls and Abe Maslow. He liked to tell the story of Rosita Rodrigues marching into the hospital, past stunned doctors and nurses. He would talk about Esalen: he thought it was lacking in rigor, needed a bit more iron in its veins, was a touch too *sweet.* But as institutions go, he noted, the choice seemed to be between sweet and sour. Given that, he would take the sweet.

A true community needs a wise elder or two, and Bateson filled that role, as Fritz and Selig had done before him. He gave the place a certain stature and vitality, a sense of important things going on. Once in a while the governor would pass through and spend the day philosophizing with him at Fritz's old house. Bateson's health seemed to be improving, but he lived life with the clarity that comes with knowing it is in limited supply.

He died on July 4, 1980, during a visit to the Green Gulch Zen Center near San Francisco. He had been a student of Zen for many years and sometimes used Zen concepts in his discussions of epistemology. They had a funeral ceremony for him at Green Gulch. Michael and Dulce Murphy attended it, and Richard Baker, an old friend of Michael's who had become a Zen *roshi,* officiated. Governor Brown read the Twenty-third Psalm.

Murphy and Price, as much as it might surprise them, are themselves regarded as wise elders by many of the employees and guests at Esalen—seen as full of years, rich in knowledge and experience. They have indeed seen a lot in the twenty-some years since they came to Big Sur, and they both wear their age well. Each is happily married, and each has found his own path of work and learning.

Price is graying and wiry; he has the tan and weathered look of a man who spends much of his time out of doors. His impact has been on the physical site, and also on the nature of the work practiced there—something that is, in the final analysis, inseparable from the place itself. The Esalen Indians, so legend has it, believed the hot springs area to be a place of healing, and the sense of its restfulness, its recuperative function, underlies much of what happens there—the healthful foods, the baths and massages, the group experiences that invite the participant to go at his or her own pace. This is an approach that also happens to harmonize with Price's strong personal feelings, born of experiences he will never forget, about coercion in psychotherapy. So when he talks of the future, he talks of projects for improving the buildings and grounds and of modest, incremental improvements in the programming.

This, he explains, is where his interests have always lain. He speaks of Murphy's conviction that Esalen was to serve as midwife to a new age, a millennium, and says: "I was never as sold as some people on that idea. My focus was more on the question of how you operate the type of counseling and psychological work that goes on here. That's more interesting to me than bringing in the millennium. If the millennium happens in the process, that's fine too."

Murphy looks younger than Price and retains a certain boyishness. He has young assistants who regard him as their guide and mentor, but he seems to be more at ease with white-haired Russian diplomats, with whom he can play the part of respectful junior. He is much involved with Russians, with his research on bodily transformation, with projects that seek to demonstrate Esalen's political relevance and intellectual vigor. Esalen now plays host several times a year to special invitational conferences. The prototype for these was a conference, held in the mid-1970s, of physicists interested in Bell's theorem—a mind-boggling piece of theory that has to do with connected simultaneous events happening in different places. That became an annual event, and now there is a group of psychologists interested in interpersonal bonding, a group of political theorists interested in new forms of governance, and several other groups. Their meetings, in the Big House, last for five days. Once in a while the participants take time out from their deliberations for a soak in the baths, and they eat their meals in the main lodge, where they get into heavy debates strikingly different from the usual run of Esalen table talk, which tends toward interpersonal raps of the kind known in the local jargon as D & M (deep and meaningful).

Judging from the success of such programs, one could easily imagine that, had Esalen gone down a different fork of the road in the 1960s, it might have evolved into a feverishly intellectual sort of place. It has some of the qualities of a slightly damp Athens, and the scholars who gather there find it as congenial to their pursuits as do those who once came in search of other kinds of stimulation. It is difficult, in fact, to imagine any pursuit for which that enchanting piece of land would not be an asset.

Murphy comes down to Big Sur often. He still entertains fantasies of a career somehow apart from Esalen, but his life and the existence of the piece of property his grandfather acquired are inextricably connected. For better and for worse. It is hard to imagine that his Russian activities would have progressed as they have without that institutional base. Esalen supports his various enthusiasms, and it also reaches out to him, as it has always done, and demands his attention. In 1983, when a season of unusually heavy rains and mudslides forced Esalen to shut down temporarily and threatened to bring the cliffs crashing down around the hot tubs, Murphy dutifully drove to Big Sur as one might hurry to the bedside of an ailing friend. With Price and a geologist, he looked over the terrain and began to make plans for an ambitious new construction project to keep the cliffs where they are.

On the subject of Esalen itself, he remains fervently ambivalent. He grows quite critical of some aspects of it, loves to tell stories about its more ludicrous moments, but grows quickly defensive when it is criticized by others. He speaks of the prospects for change with enthusiasm, but uses words that indicate a more modest set of expectations. He talks of revised timetables, of backlash, of making a difference in small ways. Yet behind that talk, the old vision shines as brightly as ever. He still looks for the Great Evolutionary Leap, a breakthrough that will be a falling-away of old paradigms, an awakening to new realities, a Renaissance and Enlightenment and new Copernican revolution put together. To help this come into being is now, as it has always been, his work. That is what his research project is about, as are the Russian activities and the special invitational conferences at Esalen. Bell's theorem excites him not merely because it is an interesting piece of theoretical physics, but because it is a paradigm-shatterer that suggests an essential unity of the cosmos, patterns of connection that defy time and space.

Murphy has always had a certain weakness for signs and portents, indications that the breakthrough is about to happen. In the past he saw it in such things as the rise of the psychedelics, with all manner of once-straight people voyaging into new realms of consciousness, and in the hippie movement, with what seemed at the time to be a whole generation breaking away permanently from the American mainstream. Although grown older and wiser, he still tends to find such indications wherever he looks. He finds them in Russia among the people interested in such things as hidden human reserves, and among the population in general, which he believes is passing through a major cultural transition. He finds them in America, but professes to have no formed beliefs about when the big awakening will come or what specific form it will take when it arrives. "I still believe the essential ideas are right," he says, "but it all seems to get more complex all the time." Then he smiles swiftly and adds, "It gets more interesting."

In the 1960s it was fashionable to quote Stokely Carmichael's pronouncement that whatever was not a part of the solution was a part of the problem. The statement's simplistic morality seemed to bring some order out of a vastly confusing era of social upheaval, and was so widely accepted that it became in itself a part of the problem.

Esalen's legions of left-leaning critics took Esalen and the human potential movement to be clearly problem: at best, an irrelevant parade of self-indulgences; at worst, the counterrevolution itself, a massive choice of concern for self over concern for society. Esalen's defenders, notably Murphy and Leonard, never conceded, at least in public dialogue, that the institute's activities might in some ways be a part of the problem, a reflection of some of the less lovable aspects of American culture, a captive of an old paradigm or two. They saw it always as a force for progress and sometimes, in more expansive moments, still slip into speaking of Esalen as if it were the solution itself—the meeting place of all the ideas and techniques out of which the new age will be created.

But of course there are many movements of thought and action sweeping through the world that are scarcely noticed within the context of Esalen's activities, and there is much that Esalen's cluster of philosophies and practices have to offer to the world.

Rather than debate about whether Esalen's proper home is in the problem or the solution column, it makes a good deal more sense to recognize that it is definitely a part of the dialogue. Because, although we are not accustomed to thinking of the decades through which

Esalen has lived as a time of dialogue, that is surely what they have been. All the events that have flashed through the public consciousness in those years—rock bands, psychedelics, teach-ins and peace marches, Watergate, Ronald Reagan, the liberation movements and their opposition forces, and definitely the human potential movement —are parts of what may well be the most far-reaching give-and-take about basic issues of human existence that any society has ever engaged in. It is hard to find in the record of history any other time or place when so many values and beliefs have been dragged out into full view to be questioned, defended, overhauled, and revised.

The process is not yet ended—indeed, it may only have begun—and none of us knows what manner of new ages it will ultimately bring forth. Esalen's contributions—its therapies, its explorations of frontline thinking in several fields, and its role as America's premier secular monastery—stand an excellent chance of becoming significant parts of the culture of the future. The current drift appears to be toward a society that is at once more physical and more spiritual, and it would be surprising if a paradigmatic change or two does not come along to force us all to look in new ways at the cosmos. Esalen may end up looking, at least in some ways, surprisingly like mainstream America.

Esalen's very quirkiness is one of its great assets. Murphy was right in his claim that it was not to be numbered among the growth centers that proliferated for a while in the late 1960s and 1970s. None of those establishments explored so many byways, put together any comparable package of thought and experience—and very few of them survived. And, although the tendency of Esalen's two founders to follow their own interests and whims has often dismayed its employees, certainly no other center produced anything comparable to Murphy's research project in bodily transformation. It is another part of the dialogue, a subject well worth exploring.

Esalen has touched the lives of many people, mostly for the better, and has made its imprint on the times. It has served as a temporary home for souls in need of repair and for ideas and techniques that needed some place to rest and find their followings. It has produced much joy, much peace, much healing, some despair, a lot of excitement, a good measure of foolishness, and no small amount of hubris. It is a mixed blessing, but a blessing nonetheless.

Notes

Preface: Looking In, Looking Out

1. The first person to point out this connection was Joe K. Adams, who, in a talk at the 1969 meeting of the American Association for Humanistic Psychology, likened encounter groups to the Antinomialist sects of the colonial era. Tom Wolfe also took up the similarity in his essay on the "Me Decade." (See reference, Chapter 14.)
2. David Orr Hatch, *The Sacred Cause of Liberty* (New Haven: Yale University Press, 1977), p. 149.

Chapter 1

1. "Human Potentialities," lecture delivered at the University of California, San Francisco Medical Center, 1960.

Chapter 2

1. Henry Miller, *Big Sur and the Oranges of Hieronymous Bosch* (New York: New Directions, 1957), p. 36.
2. Elaine Steinbeck and Robert Wallsten, eds., *Steinbeck: A Life in Letters* (New York: Viking, 1975), pp. 549–550.
3. *Time,* July 21, 1958, p. 49.
4. Stephen Mahoney, "The Prevalence of Zen," *Nation,* November 1, 1958, p. 311.

Chapter 3

1. Hunter Thompson, "Big Sur: The Tropic of Henry Miller," *Rogue,* July 1961, pp. 34–50.
2. Alan Watts, *In My Own Way* (New York: Pantheon, 1972), pp. 115–116.
3. Alan Watts, *This Is It and Other Essays on Zen and Spiritual Existence* (New York: Collier Books, 1967), p. 2.
4. Ibid., p. 13.

Chapter 4

1. Abraham Maslow, *Motivation and Personality* (New York: Harper & Row, 1954), p. 180.
2. Abraham Maslow, *Toward a Psychology of Being* (New York: Van Nostrand, 1962), p. 4.
3. Franz E. Winkler, *Man: The Bridge Between Two Worlds* (New York: Harper & Brothers, 1960), p. 251.
4. Watts, *This Is It,* pp. 24–25.
5. Aldous Huxley, *The Doors of Perception* (New York: Harper & Brothers, 1954), p. 19.
6. Grover Smith, ed., *Letters of Aldous Huxley* (Harper & Row, 1969), p. 945.
7. Timothy Leary and Richard Alpert, "The Politics of Consciousness Expansion," *Harvard Review,* Summer 1963.

Chapter 5

1. J. L. Moreno, *Who Shall Survive?* (Beacon, NY: Beacon House, 1953), p. xix.
2. John O. Stevens, ed., *Gestalt Therapy Verbatim* (Lafayette, CA: Real People Press, 1969), p. 171.
3. "Workshop vs. Individual Therapy," paper delivered at the American Psychological Association Convention, New York City, September 1966.
4. Transcript from Claudio Naranjo, *The Techniques of Gestalt Therapy* (Berkeley, CA: SAT Press, 1973), p. 49.

Chapter 6

1. George Leonard, "The Explosive Generation," *Look,* January 3, 1961, p. 17.

Chapter 7

1. Christopher Fry, *A Sleep of Prisoners* (New York: Oxford University Press, 1951), pp. 47–48.
2. Fritz Perls, *In and Out of the Garbage Pail* (Lafayette, CA: Real People Press, 1969), pages unnumbered.
3. George B. Leonard, "Where the California Game Is Taking Us," *Look,* June 28, 1966, pp. 108–116.

Chapter 8

1. William Schutz, *FIRO: A Three-Dimensional Theory of Interpersonal Behavior* (New York: Holt, Rinehart & Winston, 1960).
2. William Schutz, *Joy: Expanding Human Awareness* (New York: Grove Press, 1967), p. 15.
3. Stuart Miller, *Hot Springs: The True Adventures of the First New York Jewish Literary Intellectual in the Human Potential Movement* (New York: Viking, 1971).
4. George Leonard, "A Southerner's Appeal," in *The Man & Woman Thing* (New York: Delta), 1970, p. 23.

Chapter 9

1. Perls, *In and Out of the Garbage Pail.*

Chapter 10

1. Miller, *Hot Springs,* p. 87.
2. Jack Gaines, *Fritz Perls Here and Now* (Millbrae, CA: Celestial Arts, 1979). See also Martin Shepard, *Fritz* (New York: Saturday Review Press, 1973).

Chapter 11

1. Gregory Bateson, Introduction to John Perceval, *Perceval's Narrative: A Patient's Account of His Psychosis, 1830–1832* (Stanford, CA: Stanford University Press, 1961), pp. xiii–xiv.
2. Steckel had once been a leading Freudian, co-editor with Freud of the *Zentralblatt für Psychoanalyse,* a distinguished professional journal whose international board of editors included C. G. Jung in Zürich and Roberto Assagioli in Florence. Then some of the Freudians went their own ways:

first Alfred Adler, then Jung, then Steckel, who began publishing non-Freudian papers in the *Zentralblatt*. All this was common lore to Naranjo and Perls, both trained as psychoanalysts.

Chapter 12

1. Charles Reich, *The Greening of America* (New York: Random House, 1970), p. 2.
2. Ibid., p. 241.
3. Theodore Roszak, *The Making of a Counter Culture* (New York: Doubleday, 1969), p. 72.
4. *Book World*, November 22, 1970, p. 1.
5. Reich, *The Greening of America*, p. 241.
6. Ibid., p. 378.
7. *New York Times Book Review*, November 8, 1970, p. 3.
8. Vincent Bugliosi with Curt Gentry, *Helter Skelter* (New York: W. W. Norton, 1974), p. 275.
9. D. M. McGregor, "The Human Side of Enterprise," in *The Planning of Change*, edited by W. G. Bennis, K. D. Benne, and R. Chin (New York: Holt, Rinehart & Winston, 1961).
10. William Schutz, *Here Comes Everybody* (New York: Harper & Row, 1971), p. 276.
11. Miller, *Big Sur*.
12. Perls, *In and Out of the Garbage Pail*.

Chapter 13

1. W. W. Bartley III, *Werner Erhard* (New York: Clarkson Potter, 1978).
2. Peter Marin, "The New Narcissism," *Harper's*, October 1975, pp. 45–46.
3. "Financial Support," *The Graduate Review*, July 1979, p. 7.

Chapter 14

1. Rasa Gustaitis, *Turning On* (London: Weidenfeld & Nicolson, 1969), p. xvii.
2. Richard Atcheson, "Big Sur: Coming to My Senses," *Holiday*, March 1968, p. 18.
3. Richard Claiborne, "This Year at Marienbad," *Nation*, June 24, 1968, pp. 831–832.
4. Ibid., p. 832.

5. Theodore Roszak, "Counter Culture IV: The Future as Community," *Nation,* April 15, 1968. Other references are to Roszak, *The Making of a Counter Culture.*

6. Gary Allen, "Hate Therapy," *American Opinion,* January 1968. Also Ed Dieckmann, Jr., "Communism in Our Midst: They Call It Sensitivity Training," American Freedom Center, Glendale, CA. These and other articles are cited in Thomas C. Greening, "Sensitivity Training: Critical Statements and Articles," *Psychological Service Associates,* Los Angeles, California, 1968.

7. Tom Wolfe, "The 'Me' Decade and the Third Great Awakening," *New York,* August 23, 1976. Reprinted in *Mauve Gloves & Madmen, Clutter and Vine* (New York: Farrar, Straus & Giroux, 1976), p. 143.

8. Christopher Lasch, *The Culture of Narcissism* (New York: W. W. Norton, 1978), p. 13.

9. Wolfe, "The 'Me' Decade," p. 158.

10. Ibid., p. 146.

11. Theodore Roszak, *Person/Planet* (New York: Doubleday, 1978), pp. xxvi–xxvii.

12. William Schutz, *Profound Simplicity* (New York: Bantam, 1979), p. 4.

Chapter 15

1. " 'God Sir' at Esalen East," *Time,* January 16, 1978, p. 59.

2. Letter from Richard Price to *Time,* January 21, 1978 (unpublished).

3. Jeffrey Klein, "Esalen Slides Off the Cliff," *Mother Jones,* December 1979, p. 33.

4. *Newsweek,* January 10, 1983, p. 32.

Chapter 16

1. Calvin Tomkins, "New Paradigms," *The New Yorker,* January 5, 1976.

Index